HAVANA

CHRISTOPHER P. BAKER

Contents

HAVANA

HAVANA

Havana (pop. 2.2 million), political, cultural, and industrial heart of the nation, lies 150 kilometers (93 miles) due south of Florida on Cuba's northwest coast. It is built on the west side of a sweeping bay with a narrow funnel entrance—Bahía de la Habana—and extends west 12 kilometers to the Río Jaimanitas and south for an equal distance.

Countless writers have commented on the exhilarating sensation that engulfs visitors to this most beautiful and beguiling of Caribbean cities. The city's ethereal mood, little changed through the centuries, is so pronounced that it finds its way into novels. "I wake up feeling different, like something inside me is changing, something chemical and irreversible. There's a magic here working its way through my veins," says Pilar, a Cuban-American character from New York who returns to Havana in Cristina García's novel *Dreaming in Cuban*. Set foot one time in Havana and you can only succumb to its enigmatic allure. It is impossible to resist the city's mysteries and contradictions.

Havana has a flavor all its own; a strange amalgam of colonialism, capitalism, and Communism merged into one. One of the great historical cities of the New World, Havana is a far cry from the Caribbean backwaters that call themselves capitals elsewhere in the Antilles. Havana is a city, notes architect Jorge Rigau, "upholstered in columns, cushioned by colonnaded arcades." The buildings come in a spectacular amalgam of styles—from the academic classicism of aristocratic homes, rococo residential exteriors, Moorish interiors, and art deco and

HIGHLIGHTS

◖ Museo Nacional de Bellas Artes: Divided into national and international sections, this art gallery competes with the world's finest (pages 24, 28).

◖ Capitolio Nacional: Cuba's former congressional building is an architectural glory reminiscent of Washington's own Capitol (page 24).

◖ Museo de la Revolución: The former presidential palace now tells the tale of the Revolution in gory detail (page 28).

◖ Plaza de la Catedral: This small, atmospheric plaza is hemmed in by colonial mansions and a baroque cathedral (page 31).

◖ Plaza de Armas: The restored cobbled plaza at the heart of Old Havana features a castle, museums, and heaps of charm (page 33).

◖ Plaza Vieja: Still undergoing restoration, this antique plaza offers offbeat museums, Havana's only brewpub, flashy boutiques, and heaps of ambience (page 42).

◖ Hotel Nacional: A splendid landmark with magnificent architecture and oodles of history, this hotel is a great place to relax with a *mojito* and cigar while soaking in the heady atmosphere of the past (page 64).

◖ Necrópolis Cristóbal Colón: This is one of the New World's great cemeteries, with dramatic tombstones that comprise a who's who of Cuban history (page 68).

◖ Parque Histórico Militar Morro-Cabaña: An imposing castle complex contains the restored Castillo de los Tres Reyes del Morro and massive Fortaleza de San Carlos de la Cabaña, with cannons in situ, soldiers in period costume, and various museums (page 89).

◖ Tropicana: Havana at its most sensual, the Tropicana is home to a spectacular cabaret with more than 200 performers and dancers in fantastical costumes (page 102).

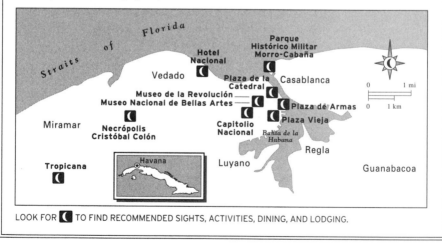

LOOK FOR ◖ TO FIND RECOMMENDED SIGHTS, ACTIVITIES, DINING, AND LODGING.

art nouveau to stunning exemplars of 1950s moderne.

At the heart of the city is enchanting Habana Vieja (Old Havana), a living museum inhabited by 60,000 people and containing perhaps the finest collection of Spanish-colonial buildings in all the Americas. Baroque churches, convents, and castles that could have been transposed from Madrid or Cádiz still reign majestically over squares embraced by the former palaces of Cuba's ruling gentry and cobbled streets still haunted by Ernest Hemingway's ghost.

Hemingway's house, Finca Vigía, is one of dozens of museums dedicated to the memory of great men and women. And although most of the older monuments—those of politically incorrect heroes—were pulled down, at least they were replaced by dozens of grandiose monuments to those on the correct side of history.

Balmy city streets with walls in faded tropical pastels still smolder gold in the waxing sun. Sunlight still filters through stained-glass *mediopuntos* to dance on the cool marble floors. And time cannot erase the sound of the "jalousies above the colonnades creaking in the small wind from the sea," in the words of Graham Greene.

The heart of Habana Vieja has been in the midst of an impressive restoration for over a decade, and most of the historically important structures have been given facelifts, or better. Some have even metamorphosed into boutique hotels. Nor is there a shortage of 1950s-era modernist hotels steeped in Mafia associations. And hundreds of *casas particulares* provide an opportunity to live life alongside the *habaneros* themselves. There's something for every budget, although most hotels are overpriced, some outrageously so. As for food, Havana is the only place in Cuba where you can dine well every night of the week (for a price).

Then there's the arts scene, perhaps unrivaled in Latin America. The city offers some first-rate museums and galleries. Not only formal galleries, but informal ones where contemporary artists produce unique works of amazing profundity and appeal. There are some tremendous crafts markets, and boutique stores selling hand-made Cuban perfumes. Afro-Caribbean music is everywhere, quite literally on the streets. Lovers of sizzling *salsa* have dozens of venues from which to choose. Havana even has a hot jazz scene. Classical music and ballet is world class, with numerous venues to choose from. And neither Las Vegas, Paris, or Rio de Janeiro can compare with Havana for sensational and sexy cabarets, with top billing now, as back in the day, being the Tropicana.

Planning Your Time

The vast majority of visitors to Cuba spend at least some time in Havana, a city so large and the sights to be seen so many, that one week is the bare minimum needed.

Metropolitan Havana sprawls over 740 square kilometers (286 square miles) and incorporates 15 *municipios* (municipalities). Like all fine cities, Havana is a collection of neighborhoods, each with its own distinct character that owes much to the century that each developed. Since the city is so spread out, it is best to explore Havana in sections, concentrating your time on the three main districts of touristic interest—Habana Vieja, Vedado, and Miramar—in that order.

If you have only one or two days in Havana, then I recommend a get-your-bearings trip by Habanabustour, or an organized city tour offered by Havanatur or a similar agency. This will provide an overview of all the major sites. Concentrate the balance of your time around Parque Central, **Plaza de la Catedral,** and **Plaza de Armas.** Your checklist of must-sees should include the **Capitolio Nacional,** Gran Teatro, Partagás cigar factory, **Museo de la Revolución, Museo Nacional de Bellas**

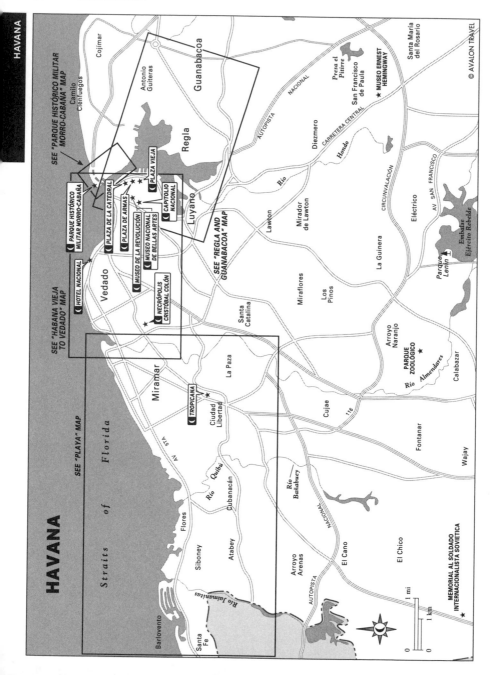

HAVANA

Straits   of   Florida

Barlovento

Santa Fe

SEE "PLAYA" MAP

SEE "HABANA VIEJA TO VEDADO" MAP

SEE "PARQUE HISTÓRICO MILITAR MORRO-CABAÑA" MAP

Cojimar

Camilo Cienfuegos

Antonio Guiteras

Guanabacoa

Regla

Luyanó

Vedado

Miramar

Ciudad Libertad

La Paza

Santa Catalina

Flores

Siboney

Atabey

Arroyo Arenas

El Cano

Río Quibú

Río Cubanacán

Río Bañabuey

Cujae

El Chico

Fontanar

Wajay

Calabazar

AV 5TA

AV

NACIONAL

AUTOPISTA

NACIONAL

Lawton

Miraflores

Los Pinos

La Guinera

Arroyo Naranjo

Mirador de Lawton

CIRCUNVALACION

AV   SAN   FRANCISCO

Eléctrico

Río Almendares

116

PARQUE ZOOLOGICO ★

Parque Lenín ⚓

Embalse Ejército Rebelde

San Francisco de Paula

Diezmero

Hondo

Río

CARRETERA CENTRAL

AUTOPISTA   NACIONAL

Presa el Pitirre

Santa María del Rosario

★ **MUSEO ERNEST HEMINGWAY**

SEE "REGLA AND GUANABACOA" MAP

◗ **PARQUE HISTÓRICO MILITAR MORRO-CABAÑA**
◗ **PLAZA DE LA CATEDRAL**
◗ **PLAZA DE ARMAS**
◗ **PLAZA VIEJA**
◗ **CAPITOLIO NACIONAL**
◗ **MUSEO DE LA REVOLUCIÓN**
◗ **MUSEO NACIONAL DE BELLAS ARTES**
◗ **HOTEL NACIONAL**
◗ **NECRÓPOLIS CRISTÓBAL COLÓN**
◗ **TROPICANA**

MEMORIAL AL SOLDADO INTERNACIONALISTA SOVIETICA

0   1 mi
0   1 km

© AVALON TRAVEL

Artes, the Catedral de la Habana, and the Museo de la Ciudad de la Habana (in the Palacio de los Capitanes Generales). For visitors who intend to linger in the city, Habana Vieja (Old Havana), the original colonial city within the 17th-century city walls (now demolished), deserves a minimum of three days. You might base yourself here in one of the charming historic hotel conversions close to the main sights of interest. Be sure to journey across the harbor to visit **Parque Histórico Militar Morro-Cabaña,** featuring two restored castles attended by soldiers in period costume.

Centro Habana has many *casas particulares* but few sites of interest and its rubble-strewn, dimly lit streets aren't the safest. Skip Centro for Vedado, the modern heart of the city that evolved in the early 20th century, with many ornate mansions in Beaux-Arts and art nouveau style. Its leafy streets make for great walking. Many of the city's best *casas particulares* are here, as are a majority of businesses, *paladares,* hotels, and nightclubs. The **Hotel Nacional,** Universidad de la Habana, Cementerio Colón, and Plaza de la Revolución are among the prime sights not to miss.

If you're interested in Beaux-Arts, art deco, or even 1950s moderne architecture, then once-glamorous Miramar, Cubanacán, and Siboney regions, west of Vedado, are worth exploring. Miramar also has several excellent restaurants, deluxe hotels, and fine beaches, plus some of my favorite nightspots.

Most other sections of Havana are run-down residential districts of little interest to tourists. A few exceptions lie on the east side of Havana harbor. Regla and neighboring Guanabacoa are together a center of *santería* and Afro-Cuban music. The 18th-century fishing village of Cojímar has Hemingway

the Capitolio Nacional, from the roof of the Hotel Saratoga

associations, and the nearby community of San Miguel de Padrón is where the great author lived for twenty years. A visit to his home, Finca Vigía, today the Museo Ernest Hemingway, is de rigueur. About 15 kilometers east of the city, a series of long, white-sand beaches—the Playas del Este—prove tempting on hot summer days.

Despite Havana's great size, most sights of interest are highly concentrated, and most exploring is best done on foot. Ideally you'll want wheels for touring beyond Habana Vieja. The taxi system is efficient and fairly priced, as is the bus system, although the latter is crowded and petty theft is an issue.

All touristed areas are patrolled by police, but don't let your guard down for a second.

History

The city was founded in July 1515 as San Cristóbal de la Habana, and was located on the south coast, where Batabanó stands today. The site was a disaster. On November 25, 1519, the settlers moved to the shore of the flask-shaped Bahía de la Habana. Its location was so advantageous that in July 1553 the city replaced Santiago de Cuba as the capital of the island.

Every spring and summer, Spanish treasure ships returning from the Americas crowded into Havana's sheltered harbor before setting off for Spain in an armed convoy—*la flota*. By the turn of the 18th century, Havana was the third-largest city in the New World after Mexico City and Lima. The 17th and 18th centuries saw a surge of ecclesiastical construction. The wealth of the Americas helped fill the churches and convents with gold and silver.

In 1762, the English captured Havana but ceded it back to Spain the following year. The Spanish lost no time in building the largest fortress in the Americas—San Carlos de la Cabaña. Under the supervision of the new Spanish governor, the Marqués de la Torre, the city attained a new focus and rigorous architectural harmony. The first public gas lighting arrived in 1768, along with a workable system of aqueducts. Most of the streets were cobbled. Along them, wealthy merchants and plantation owners erected beautiful mansions fitted inside with every luxury in European style.

By the mid-19th century, Havana was bursting its seams. In 1863, the city walls came tumbling down, less than a century after they were completed. New districts went up, and graceful boulevards pushed into the surrounding countryside, lined with a parade of *quintas* (summer homes) fronted by classical columns. By the mid-1800s, Havana had achieved a level of modernity that surpassed that of Madrid.

Following the Spanish-Cuban-American War, Havana entered a new era of prosperity. The city spread out, its perimeter enlarged by parks, boulevards, civic spaces, and dwellings in eclectic, neoclassical, and revivalist styles, while older residential areas settled into an era of decay.

By the 1950s Havana was a wealthy and thoroughly modern city with a large and prospering middle class, and had acquired skyscrapers such as the Focsa building and the Hilton (now the Habana Libre). Ministries were being moved to a new center of construction, the Plaza de la República (today the Plaza de la Revolución), inland from Vedado. Gambling found a new lease on life, and casinos flourished.

Following the Revolution, a mass exodus of the wealthy and the middle class began, inexorably changing the face of Havana. Tourists also got the message, dooming Havana's hotels, restaurants, and other businesses to bankruptcy.

Festering slums and shanty towns marred the suburbs. The government ordered them razed. Concrete high-rise apartment blocks were erected on the outskirts, especially in Habana del Este. That accomplished, the Revolution turned its back on the city. Havana's aged housing and infrastructure, much of it already decayed, have ever since suffered benign neglect. Even the mayor of Havana has admitted that "the Revolution has been hard on the city."

Meanwhile, tens of thousands of poor peasant migrants poured into Havana from Oriente, shipped in by the Castro government to bolster Fidel's natural base of support. The settlers changed the city's demographic profile, as most of the immigrants were black (as many as 400,000 *"palestinos,"* immigrants from Santiago and the eastern provinces, live in Havana, their presence resented by a large segment of *habaneros*).

Finally in the 1980s, the revolutionary government established a preservation program for Habana Vieja and the Centro Nacional de Conservación, Restauración, y Museología was

THE MOB IN HAVANA

For three decades, the Mafia had dealings in Cuba, and prerevolutionary Havana will forever be remembered for its presence. During U.S. Prohibition (1920-33), mobsters such as Al Capone had contracted with Cuban refineries to supply molasses for their illicit rum factories. When Prohibition ended, the Mob turned to gambling. The Mafia's interests were represented by Meyer Lansky, the Jewish mobster from Miami who arrived in 1939 and struck a deal with Fulgencio Batista, Cuba's strongman president – "the best thing that ever happened to us," Lansky told national crime syndicate boss Salvatore "Lucky" Luciano. Lansky, acting as lieutenant for Luciano, took over the Oriental Park racetrack and the casino at Havana's Casino Nacional, where he ran a straight game that attracted high rollers.

World War II effectively put an end to the Mob's business, which was relatively small scale at the time. Lansky returned to Florida; Batista followed him in 1944 when he lost to Ramón Grau in the national election. Lansky's aboveboard operation soon withered in the Mob's absence, replaced by rigged casinos, and Havana's gambling scene developed a bad reputation.

Following the war, the United States deported Luciano to Italy. In 1946, he moved to Cuba, where he intended to establish a gambling and narcotics operation and regain his status as head of the U.S. Mob. He called a summit in Havana's Hotel Nacional. The meeting was immortalized in *The Godfather*, and the official cover, records Alan Ryan, "was that it was meant to honor a nice Italian boy from Hoboken called Frank Sinatra," who went down to Havana to say thanks. The United States, however, pressured Grau to deport Luciano back to Italy. Before leaving, Luciano named Lansky head of operations in Cuba.

The Mob's Cuba presence was given a boost when Florida's casinos were closed down, followed by a federal campaign to suppress the Mob. Mobsters decided Cuba was the place to be. A new summit was called at Batista's house in Daytona Beach, attended by Cuban politicians and military brass. A deal was struck: Batista would return to Cuba, regain power, and open the doors to large-scale gambling. In return, he and his crooked pals would receive a piece of the take. A gift of US$250,000 personally delivered by Lansky helped convince President Grau to step aside, and on March 10, 1952, Batista again occupied the presidential palace. New laws were quickly enacted to attract investment in hotels and casinos, and banks were set up as fronts to channel money into the hands of Cuban politicos.

The "family" headed by Cuban-Italian Amleto Batistti controlled the heroin and cocaine routes to the United States and an emporium of illegal gambling from Batistti's base at the Hotel Sevilla. Tampa's Mafia boss, Santo Trafficante Jr., operated the Sans Souci casino-nightclub, plus the casinos in the Capri, Comodoro, Deauville, and Sevilla-Biltmore Hotels. Watching over everyone was Lansky, who ran the Montmartre Club and the Internacional Club of the Hotel Nacional. Anything was permissible: gambling, pornography, drugs. Nonetheless, no frivolities were allowed. Games were regulated, and cardsharps and cheats were sent packing, although cocaine and prostitutes were supplied to high rollers. (In 1957, Mob boss Santo Trafficante claims to have set John F. Kennedy up with a private party, supplying three prostitutes in a special suite in the Hotel Comodoro.)

The tourists flocked. Lansky's last act was to build the ritziest hotel and casino in Cuba – the US$14 million Hotel Riviera and Gold Leaf Casino, which opened on December 10, 1958. Once Castro took power, the casinos were closed down and in June 1959, Lansky, Trafficante, and other "undesirable aliens" were kicked out of Cuba. Said Lansky: "I crapped out."

created to inventory Havana's historic sites and implement a restoration program that would return much of the ancient city to pristine splendor. Much of the original city core now gleams afresh with confections in stones, while the rest of the city is left to crumble.

Sights — Habana Vieja

Habana Vieja (4.5 square km) is defined by the limits of the early colonial settlement that lay within fortified walls. The legal boundary of Habana Vieja includes the Paseo de Martí (colloquially called the Prado) and everything east of it.

Habana Vieja is roughly shaped like a diamond, with the Castillo de la Punta its northerly point. The Prado runs south at a gradual gradient from the Castillo de la Punta to Parque Central and, beyond, Parque de la Fraternidad, from where Avenida de la Bélgica runs southeast, tracing the old city wall to the harborfront at the west end of Desamparados. East of Castillo de la Punta, Avenida Carlos Manuel de Céspedes (Avenida del Puerto) runs along the harbor channel and curls south to Desamparados.

The original settlement extended roughly north–south from Castillo de la Real Fuerza to Plaza Vieja. Here are the major sites of interest, centered on the Plaza de Armas and the smaller but more imposing Plaza de la Catedral. Each square has its own flavor. The plazas and surrounding streets shine after a complete restoration, their structures newly painted, like confections in stone.

The restoration now extends to the area east of Avenida de Bélgica and southwest of Plaza Vieja, between Calles Brasil and Merced. This was the great ecclesiastical center of colonial Havana and is replete with churches and convents.

In the 20th century, many grandiose structures went up around Parque Central. Today, the park is the social hub of Habana Vieja, and forms a nexus for sightseeing in the region.

Habana Vieja is a living museum—as many as 60,000 people live within the confines of the old city wall—and suffers from inevitable ruination brought on by the tropical climate, hastened since the Revolution by years of neglect. The grime of centuries has been soldered by tropical heat into the chipped cement and faded pastels. Beyond the restored areas, Habana Vieja is a quarter of sagging, mildewed walls and half-collapsed balconies. You'll frequently find humble and haughty side by side. The much-deteriorated (mostly residential) southern half of Habana Vieja has relatively few sights.

PASEO DE MARTÍ (PRADO)

Paseo de Martí, colloquially known as the Prado, is a kilometer-long tree-lined boulevard that slopes southward, uphill, from the harbor mouth to Parque Central.

The beautiful boulevard was initiated by the Marquis de la Torre in 1772 and completed in 1852, when it had the name Alameda de Isabella II. It lay *extramura* (outside the old walled city) and was Havana's most notable thoroughfare. Mansions of aristocratic families rose on each side and it was a sign of distinction to live here. The *paseo*—the daily carriage ride—along the boulevard was an important social ritual, with bands positioned at regular intervals to play to the colorful parade of *volantas* (carriages).

French landscape artist Forestier remodeled the Prado to its present form in 1929. It is guarded by eight bronze lions, and its central median is an elevated walkway bordered by an ornate wall with alcoves inset into each side containing marble benches carved with scroll motifs. At night it is lit by brass gas lamps with globes atop wrought-iron lampposts in the shape of griffins. Schoolchildren sit beneath shade trees, listening attentively to lessons presented alfresco. An art fair is held on Sundays.

HAVANA

© CHRISTOPHER P. BAKER

bronze lion at the base of the Prado

Castillo de San Salvador de la Punta

This small, recently restored fortress (Av. Carlos M. de Céspedes, esq. Prado y Malecón, tel. 07/860-3196; Tues.–Sat. 9:30 A.M.–5 P.M., Sun. 9 A.M.–12:30 P.M.; entrance free) guards the entrance to Havana's harbor channel at the base of the Prado. The fortress was initiated in 1589 directly across from the Morro castle so that the two fortresses might catch invaders in a crossfire. A great chain was slung between them each night to secure Havana harbor. It has a few cannon.

Gazing over the plaza on the west side of the castle is a life-size statue of Venezuelan General Francisco de Miranda Rodríguez (1750–1816), while 100 meters east of the castle is a statue of Pierre D'Iberville (1661–1793), a Canadian explorer who died in Havana.

Parque de Mártires and Parque de los Enamorados

The park immediately south of the castle, on the south side of Avenida Carlos Manuel de Céspedes, at the base (and east) of the Prado, is divided in two by Avenida de los Estudiantes.

Parque de los Enamorados (Park of the Lovers), on the north side of Avenida de los Estudiantes, features a statue of an Indian couple, plus the **Monumento de Estudiantes de Medicina,** a small Grecian-style temple shading the remains of a wall used by Spanish-colonial firing squads. Here on November 27, 1871, eight medical students met their deaths after being falsely accused of desecrating the tomb of a prominent loyalist, Gonzalo Castañón. A trial found them innocent, but enraged loyalist troops—the Spanish Volunteers—held their own trial and shot the students. The students are commemorated with a national holiday each November 27.

Parque de Mártires (Martyr's Park), on the south side of Avenida de los Estudiantes, occupies the ground of the former Tacón prison, built in 1838. Nationalist hero José Martí was imprisoned here in 1869–70. The prison was demolished in 1939. Preserved for posterity are two of the punishment cells and the chapel

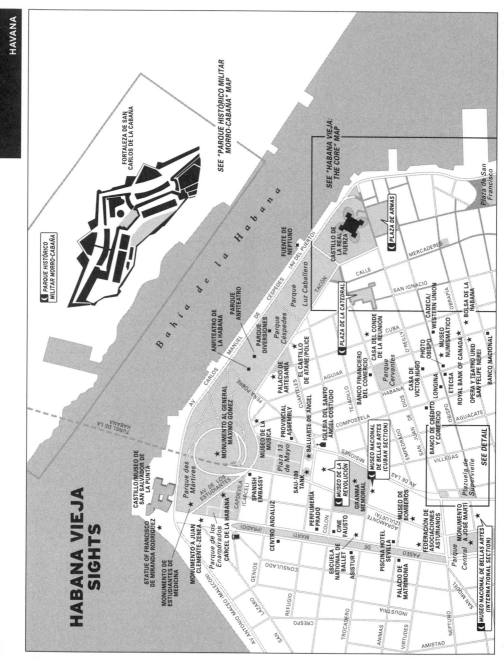

HABANA VIEJA SIGHTS

Bahía de la Habana

FORTALEZA DE SAN CARLOS DE LA CABAÑA

PARQUE HISTÓRICO MILITAR MORRO-CABAÑA

SEE "PARQUE HISTÓRICO MILITAR MORRO-CABAÑA" MAP

SEE "HABANA VIEJA: THE CORE" MAP

Plaza de San Francisco

PLAZA DE ARMAS

CASTILLO DE LA REAL FUERZA

FUENTE DE NEPTUNO

MERCADERES

CALLE

SAN IGNACIO

OBRAPIA

PLAZA DE LA CATEDRAL

CUBA

BOLSA DE LA HABANA

CASA DEL CONDE DE LA REUNIÓN

CADECA/ WESTERN UNION

O'REILLY

PHOTO OBISPO

MUSEO NUMISMÁTICO

BANCO FINANCIERO DEL COMERCIO

Parque Cervantes

CASA DE VICTOR HUGO

LONGINA

ROYAL BANK OF CANADA

PALACIO DE ARTESANÍA

EL CASTILLO DE ATANE/POLICE

ETECSA

OPERA Y TEATRO URID SAN FELIPE NERI

BANCO NACIONAL

CUARTELES

AGUIAR

TEJADILLO

HABANA

DE

OBISPO

BANCO DE CRÉDITO Y COMERCIO

SAN JUAN

AGUACATE

MONUMENTO AL GENERAL MÁXIMO GÓMEZ

PROVINCIAL ASSEMBLY

IGLESIA DEL SANTO ANGEL CUSTODIO

COMPOSTELA

EMPEDRADO

VILLEGAS

SEE DETAIL

MUSEO DE LA MÚSICA

BALUARTE DE ÁNGEL

MUSEO NACIONAL DE BELLAS ARTES (CUBAN SECTION)

Plazuela de Supervielle

Plaza 13 de Mayo

MUSEO DE LA REVOLUCIÓN

GRANMA MEMORIAL

MUSEO DE BOMBEROS

FEDERACIÓN DE ASOCIACIONES ASTURIANOS

SAU-100 TANK

PERFUMERÍA PRADO

CINE FAUSTO

AGRAMONTE (ZULUETA)

MONUMENTO A JOSÉ MARTÍ

SPANISH EMBASSY

COLON

Parque Central

MUSEO NACIONAL DE BELLAS ARTES (INTERNATIONAL SECTION)

CENTRO ANDALUZ

MARTI (PRADO)

DE

PASEO

SAN MIGUEL

ESCUELA NACIONAL DE BALLET ASISTUR

PISCINA HOTEL SEVILLA

PALACIO DE MATRIMONIA

NEPTUNO

CÁRCEL DE LA HABANA

CAPDEVILA

AV. DE LOS ESTUDIANTES

Parque de los Enamorados

MONUMENTO A JUAN CLEMENTE ZENEA

GENIOS

CONSULADO

INDUSTRIA

AMISTAD

VIRTUDES

ANIMAS

TROCADERO

REFUGIO

CRESPO

SAN LAZARO

AV ANTONIO MACEO (MALECON)

STATUE OF FRANCISCO DE MIRANDA RODRÍGUEZ

MONUMENTO DE ESTUDIANTES DE MEDICINA

CASTILLO/MUSEO DE SAN SALVADOR DE LA PUNTA

Parque des Mártires

TÚNEL DE LA HABANA

ANFITEATRO DE LA HABANA

PARQUE ANFITEATRO

PARQUE DIVERSIONES

Parque Céspedes

CÉSPEDES

Parque Luz Caballero

TACON

AV DEL PUERTO

MANUEL

DE

CARLOS

AV

PEÑA POBRE

LAZARO

SAN

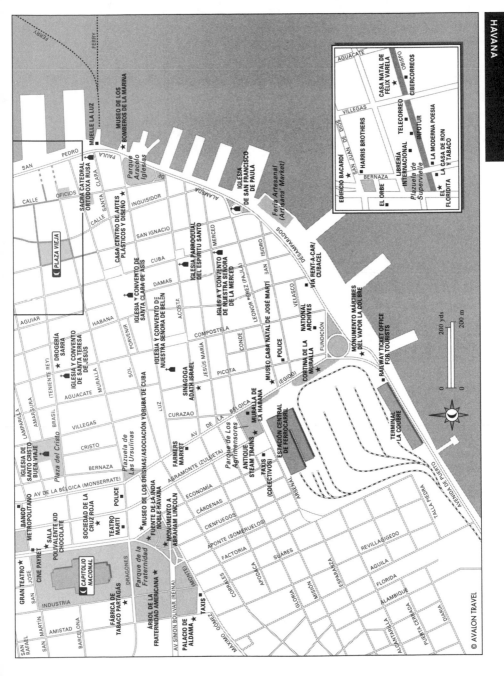

© AVALON TRAVEL

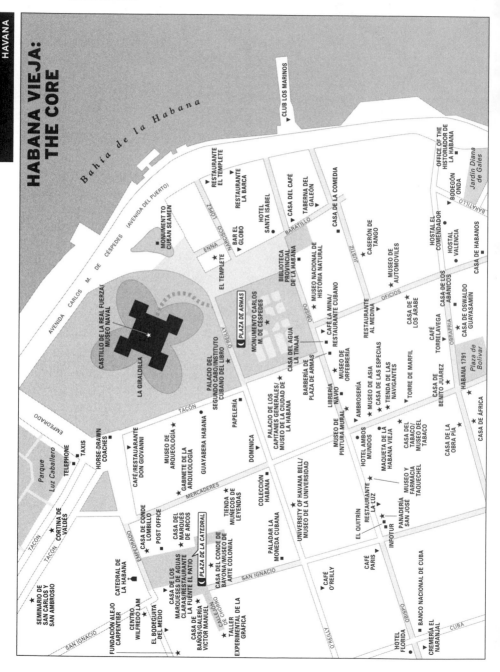

HABANA VIEJA: THE CORE

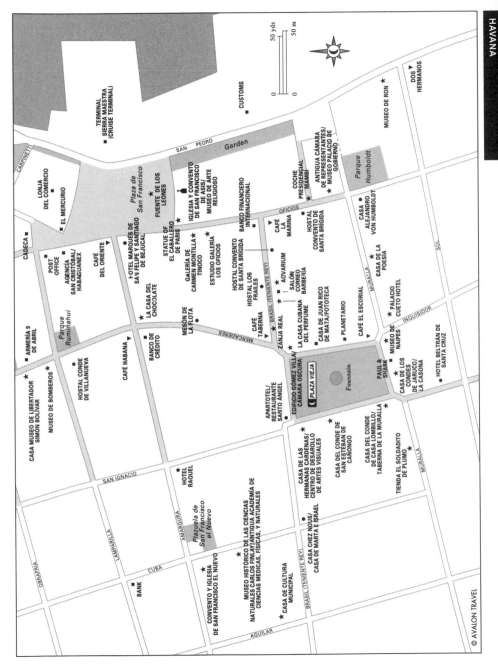

50 yds

50 m

TERMINAL SIERRA MAESTRA (CRUISE TERMINAL)

CUSTOMS

SAN PEDRO   Garden

CARPINETTI

LONJA DEL COMERCIO

EL MERCURIO

CADECA

POST OFFICE

AGENCIA SAN CRISTÓBAL/ HABAGUANEX

CAFÉ DEL ORIENTE

Plaza de San Francisco

FUENTE DE LOS LEONES

IGLESIA Y CONVENTO DE SAN FRANCISCO DE ASÍS/ MUSEO DE ARTE RELIGIOSO

ANTIGUA CÁMARA DE REPRESENTANTES/ MUSEO PALACIO DE GOBIERNO

COCHE PRESIDENCIAL MAMBÍ

Parque Humboldt

MUSEO DE RON

DOS HERMANOS

HOTEL MARQUÉS DE SAN FELIPE Y SANTIAGO DE BEJUCAL

STATUE OF EL CABALLERO DE PARÍS

BANCO FINANCIERO INTERNACIONAL

OFICIOS

CAFÉ LA MARINA

HOSTAL CONVENTO DE SANTA BRÍGIDA

CASA ALEJANDRO VON HUMBOLDT

ARMERÍA 9 DE ABRIL

Parque Rumiñahui

GALERÍA DE CARMEN MONTILLA TINOCO

ESTUDIO GALERÍA LOS OFICIOS

HOSTAL CONVENTO DE SANTA BRÍGIDA

CASA DE LA POESÍA

MURALLA

SOL

CASA MUSEO DE LIBERTADOR SIMÓN BOLÍVAR

MUSEO DE BOMBEROS

LA CASA DEL CHOCOLATE

BANCO DE CRÉDITO

MESÓN DE LA FLOTA

HOSTAL LOS FRAILES

ACVARIUM

SALÓN CORREO BARBERÍA

BRASIL (TENIENTE REY)

PLANETARIO

CAFÉ EL ESCORIAL

PALACIO CUETO HOTEL

INQUISIDOR

HOSTAL CONDE DE VILLANUEVA

CAFÉ HABANA

CAFÉ TABERNA

ZANJA REAL

LA CASA CUBANA DEL PERFUME

CASA DE JUAN RICO DE MATA/FOTOTECA

MERCADERES

APARTOTEL/ RESTAURANTE SANTO ÁNGEL

EDIFICIO GÓMEZ VILLA/ CÁMARA OSCURA

PLAZA VIEJA

Fountain

PAUL & SHARK

MUSEO DE NAIPES

CASA DE LOS CONDES DE JARUCO/ LA CASONA

HOTEL BELTRÁN DE SANTA CRUZ

SAN IGNACIO

HOTEL RAQUEL

CASA DE LAS HERMANAS CÁRDENAS/ CENTRO DE DESARROLLO DE ARTES VISUALES

CASA DEL CONDE DE SAN ESTEBAN DE CAÑONGO

CASA DEL CONDE DE CASA LOMBILLO/ TABERNA DE LA MURALLA

TIENDA EL SOLDADITO DE PLOMO

MURALLA

AMARGURA

LAMPARILLA

Plazuela de San Francisco el Nuevo

MUSEO HISTÓRICO DE LAS CIENCIAS NATURALES CARLOS FINLAY/ANTIGUA ACADEMIA DE CIENCIAS MÉDICAS, FÍSICAS, Y NATURALES

CASA CHEZ NOUS/ CASA DE MARTA E ISRAEL

CUBA

BANK

OBRAPÍA

CONVENTO Y IGLESIA DE SAN FRANCISCO EL NUEVO

CASA DE CULTURA MUNICIPAL

BRASIL (TENIENTE REY)

AGUILAR

© AVALON TRAVEL

used by condemned prisoners before being marched to the firing wall.

PARQUE CENTRAL

Spacious Parque Central is the social epicenter of Habana Vieja. The park—bounded by the Prado, Neptuno, Zulueta, and San Martín—is presided over by stately royal palms and almond trees shading a marble **statue of José Martí.** Erected on the 10th anniversary of the national hero's death, it was sculpted by José Vilalta de Saavedra and inaugurated in 1905. Baseball fanatics gather near the Martí statue at a point called *esquina caliente* ("hot corner") to discuss and argue the intricacies of *pelota* (baseball).

The park is surrounded by historic hotels, including the triangular **Hotel Plaza** (Zulueta #267), built in 1909, on the northeast face of the square. Babe Ruth stayed in room 216 in 1920; the room is preserved as a museum, with his signed bat and ball in a glass case.

Hotel Inglaterra

Much of the social action happens in front of the Hotel Inglaterra (Paseo de Martí #416), which opened in 1856 and is today the oldest Cuban hotel still extant. The Café Louvre, in front of the hotel, was known in colonial days as the Acera del Louvre and was a focal point for rebellion against Spanish rule. A plaque outside the hotel entrance honors the "lads of the Louvre sidewalk" who died for Cuban independence.

Inside, the hotel boasts elaborate wrought-ironwork and exquisite Mudejar-style detailing, including arabesque archways and *azulejos* (patterned tile). A highlight is the sensuous life-size bronze statue of a Spanish dancer—*La Sevillana*—in the main bar.

Gran Teatro

Immediately south of the Inglaterra, the Gran Teatro (Paseo de Martí #452, e/ San Rafael y Neptuno, tel. 07/861-3077; daily 9 A.M.–5 P.M.; CUC2 with guided tour) originated in 1837 as the Teatro Tacón, drawing operatic luminaries such as Enrico Caruso and Sarah Bernhardt. The current neo-baroque structure dates from 1915, when a social club—the Centro Gallego—was built around the old Teatro Tacón for the Galician community.

Its exorbitantly baroque facade drips with caryatids and has four towers, each tipped by a white marble angel reaching gracefully for heaven. The entire edifice is crumbling dangerously, however, though it still functions as a theater for the National Ballet and Opera. The main auditorium—the exquisitely decorated 2,000-seat Teatro García Lorca—features a painted dome and huge chandelier. Smaller performances are hosted in the 500-seat Sala Alejo Carpentier and the 120-seat Sala Artaud.

Museo Nacional de Bellas Artes (International Section)

The international section of the National Fine Arts Museum (San Rafael, e/ Zulueta y Monserrate, tel. 07/863-9484 or 862-0140, www.museonacional.cult.cu; Tues.–Sat. 10 A.M.–6 P.M., Sun. 10 A.M.–2 P.M.; entrance CUC5, or CUC8 for both sections; guided tour CUC2) occupies the Centro Asturiano, on the southeast side of the square. The building, lavishly decorated with neoclassical motifs, was erected in 1885 but rebuilt in Renaissance style in 1927 following a fire and until recently housed the postrevolutionary People's Supreme Court. A highlight is the stained-glass window above the main staircase showing Columbus's three caravels.

The art collection is displayed on five floors covering 4,800 square meters. The works are separated by nationality and span the United States, Latin America, Asia, and European masters—including Gainsborough, Goya, Murillo, Rubens, and Velásquez, and various Impressionists. The museum also boasts Latin America's richest trove of Roman, Greek, and Egyptian antiquities.

A 248-seat theater hosts cultural activities.

Capitolio Nacional

This statuesque building (Paseo de Martí, e/ San Martín y Dragones, tel. 07/861-5519; daily

A WALK DOWN THE PRADO

Begin your walk of the Prado at Parque Central and Neptuno. Heading downhill, the first building of interest, the **Palacio de Matrimonio** (Prado #306, esq. Ánimas, tel. 07/862-5781; Tues.-Fri. 8 A.M.-4 P.M.), on the west side, at the corner of Ánimas, is where many of Havana's wedding ceremonies are performed. The palace boasts a magnificent neo-baroque facade and an ornate stuccoed interior in desperate disrepair.

Up and down the Prado you'll see tiled mosaics reflecting the Moorish style that influenced Havana's colonial architecture. The most stunning example is the lobby of the **Hotel Sevilla** (Trocadero #55), which is like entering a Moroccan medina. It was inspired by the Patio of the Lions at the Alhambra in Granada, Spain. The hotel opened in 1908 and became a place of repose for fashionable society. The gallery walls are festooned with black-and-white photos of famous figures who have stayed here, from singer Josephine Baker and boxer Joe Louis to Al Capone, who took the entire sixth floor (Capone occupied Room 615). The top-story restaurant is a magnificent exemplar of neoclassical decor –

perfect for sampling a Mary Pickford (rum, pineapple juice, and grenadine), invented here. The Sevilla was the setting for the comical intrigues of Wormold in Graham Greene's *Our Man in Havana*.

At Trocadero, budding dancers train for potential ballet careers in the **Escuela Nacional de Ballet** (National School of Ballet, Prado #207, e/ Colón y Trocadero, tel. 07/862-7053; call 07/803-0817 for permission to visit). Across the street, on the west side, the **Casa de los Científicos** (Prado #212, esq. Trocadero, tel. 07/862-1607), the former home of President José Miguel Gómez, first president of the Republic; pop in to admire the fabulous stained-glass work and chapel where locals come to make offerings.

At Prado and Colón, note the **Cine Fausto,** a modernist building with an ornamental band on its upper facade harking back to art deco; and, two blocks north, the mosaic mural of a Nubian beauty on the upper wall of the **Centro Cultural de Árabe** (between Refugio and Trocadero).

The bronze **statue of Juan Clemente-Zenea** (1832-71), at the base of the Prado, honors a nationalist poet shot for treason in 1871.

---

9 A.M.–7 P.M.; entrance CUC3, guided tours CUC1, cameras CUC2), one block south of Parque Central, dominates Havana's skyline. It was built between 1926 and 1929 as Cuba's Chamber of Representatives and Senate and was obsequiously designed after Washington's own Congress building. The 692-foot-long edifice is supported by flanking colonnades of Doric columns, with semicircular pavilions at each end of the building. The lofty stone cupola rises 61.75 meters, topped by a replica of 16th-century Florentine sculptor Giambologna's famous bronze Mercury in the Palazzo de Bargello.

A massive stairway—flanked by neoclassical figures in bronze by Italian sculptor Angelo Zanelli and representing Labor and Virtue—leads steeply up to an entrance portico with three tall bronze doors sculpted with 30 bas-

reliefs that depict important events of Cuban history.

Inside, facing the door is the **Estatua de la República** (Statue of the Republic), a massive bronze sculpture (also by Zanelli) of Cuba's voluptuous Indian maiden. At 17.54 meters (56 feet) tall, she is the world's third-largest indoor statue (the other two are the Buddha in Nara, Japan, and the Lincoln Memorial in Washington DC). In the center of the floor is a 24-carat diamond replica that marks Kilometer 0—the point from which all distances on the island are calculated (rumor has it that the original is kept in Fidel's office). Above your head is the dome with its gilt-covered, barrel-vaulted ceiling carved in refulgent relief.

The 394-foot-long **Salón de los Pasos Perdidos** (Great Hall of the Lost Steps), so named because of its acoustics, is inlaid with patterned marble motifs and features bronze bas-reliefs, green marble pilasters, and massive lamps on tall carved pedestals of glittering copper. Renaissance-style candelabras dangle from the arched frescoed ceiling. The semicircular Senate chamber and Chamber of Representatives are at each end; former congressional offices line the hallway; and there's a mahogany-paneled former congressional library.

The Capitolio is the headquarters of the **Academía de Ciencias** (Academy of Sciences); the library—the **Biblioteca Nacional de Ciencias y Naturales**—is on the Capitolio's south side (Mon.–Sat. 8 A.M.–5 P.M.).

PARQUE DE LA FRATERNIDAD AND VICINITY

Paseo de Martí (Prado) runs south from Parque Central three blocks, where it ends at the junction with Avenida Máximo Gómez (Monte). Here rises the **Fuente de la India Noble Habana,** in the middle of the Prado. Erected in 1837, the fountain is surmounted by a Carrara-marble statue of the legendary Indian queen after whom the province is named. In one hand she bears a cornucopia, in the other a shield with the arms of Havana. Four fishes lie at her feet and occasionally spout water.

The **Asociación Cultural Yoruba de Cuba** (Prado #615, e/ Dragones y Monte, tel. 07/863-5953; daily 9 A.M.–5 P.M.) has an upstairs **Museo de los Orishas** (CUC10, students CUC3) dedicated to the various *orishas* of *santería.*

The Constitution for the Republic was signed in 1901 in the **Teatro Martí** (Dragones, esq. Zulueta), one block west of the Prado. It was being restored in June 2009. Around the corner, the **Sociedad de la Cruz Roja** (Red Cross Society, Zulueta, e/ Muralla y Brasil) is housed in an exquisite classical building.

Parque de la Fraternidad

This park was laid out in 1892 on an old military drill square, the Campo de Marte, to commemorate the fourth centennial of Columbus's discovery of America. By the mid-1850s, it was the site of the city's train station, terminating the railway that ran along today's Zanja and Dragones. The current layout by Forestier dates from 1928, with a redesign to celebrate the sixth Pan-American Conference, held in Havana that year.

The **Árbol de la Fraternidad Americana** (the Friendship Tree) was planted at its center on February 24, 1928, to cement goodwill between the nations of the Americas. Busts and statues of oustanding American leaders such as Simón Bolívar and Abraham Lincoln watch over the comings and goings.

Palacio de Aldama

The Palacio de Aldama, on the park's far southwest corner, is a grandiose mansion built in neoclassical style in 1844 for a wealthy Basque, Don Domingo Aldama y Arrechaga. Its facade is lined by Ionic columns; its interior features murals of scenes from Pompeii; the garden courtyard features ornamental fountains. When the owner's nationalist feelings became known it was ransacked and the interior defaced in 1868 by the Spanish Volunteers militia. Today, duly restored, it houses the **Instituto de la História del Movimiento Comunista y de la Revolución Socialista de Cuba** (Institute of the History of the Communist Movement and the Socialist Revolution of Cuba, Amistad #510, e/ Reina y Estrella, tel. 07/862-2076), but is not open to the public.

Fábrica de Tabaco Partagás

A highlight of any stay in Havana is a visit to the Partagás cigar factory (Industria #520, e/ Dragones y Barcelona, tel. 07/863-5766; Mon.–Fri. 9–11 A.M. and noon–3 P.M.; guided tour CUC10), on the west side of the Capitolio. The classical Spanish-style facade of this four-story structure is capped by a roofline of baroque curves topped by lions. Here you can see Cuba's premium cigars being hand-rolled for export. The factory specializes in full-bodied cigars such as the Montecristo and, of course, the Partagás, one of the oldest of the Havana brands, started

VISITING HAVANA'S CIGAR FACTORIES

You'll forever remember the pungent aroma of a cigar factory, a visit to which is de rigueur. The factories, housed in fine old colonial buildings, remain much as they were in the mid-19th century. Though now officially known by ideologically sound names, they're still commonly referred to by their prerevolutionary names, which are displayed on old signs outside. Each specializes in a number of cigar brands of a particular flavor – the government assigns to certain factories the job of producing particular brands.

The six major factories welcome visitors. Unfortunately, the tours are not well organized and often crowded with tour groups. Explanations of tobacco processes and manufacturing procedures are also sparse. Tours usually bypass the tobacco preparations and instead begin in the *galeras* (rolling rooms), then pass to the quality-control methods. Visitors therefore miss out on seeing the stripping, selecting, and dozens of other steps that contribute to producing a handmade cigar. Duties vary by floor, with leaf handling on the ground floor, and stemming, sorting, rolling, box decorating, and ringing on the upper two floors.

No cameras are permitted.

FACTORIES WITH ORGANIZED TOURS

Fábrica Partagás (Calle Industria #502, e/ Dragones y Barcelona, Habana Vieja, tel. 07/862-0086 or 878-4368; 9-11 A.M. and noon-3 P.M.) offers 45-minute guided group tours (CUC10).

Fábrica Corona (20 de Mayo #520, e/ Marta Abreu y Línea, Cerro, tel. 07/873-0131; Mon.-Fri. 9-11 A.M. and 1-3 P.M.; CUC10 with guide) has guided group tours.

Tickets must be purchased from the Hotel Saratoga or Hotel Habana Libre Tryp.

FACTORIES REQUIRING PERMISSION TO VISIT

Requests to visit the following factories should be made through **Tacuba** (Virtudes #609, e/ Escobar y Gervasio, Centro Habana, tel. 07/877-6861), which is in charge of the industry.

Fábrica H. Upmann (Calle 23, e/ 14 y 16 , tel. 07/835-1371) makes the famous H. Upmann brand of cigars, plus cigarettes. Note that this is *not* the original H. Upmann factory (Amistad #407, e/ Barcelona y Dragones), which no longer manufactures cigars.

Fábrica El Laguito (Av. 146 #2302, e/ 21 y 21A, Cubanacán, tel. 07/208-2486) makes Cohibas. Since Cohibas are made from only the finest leaves, El Laguito is given first choice from the harvest – "the best selection of the best selection," says factory head Emilia Tamayo. El Laguito also makes the best cigar in the world – the Trinidad, a 7.5-inch-long cigar made exclusively for Castro to present to diplomats and dignitaries.

Fábrica Héroes del Moncada (Av. 57 #13403, e/ 134 y 136, Marianao, tel. 07/260-6723) makes most major brands of export cigars, including Cohibas.

Formerly permitting visits, **Fábrica Romeo y Julieta** (Padre Varela, e/ Desague y Peñal Verno, Centro Habana, tel. 07/878-1059 or 879-3927) is now a cigar-rollers' school.

in 1843 by Catalan immigrant Don Jaime Partagás Ravelo. Partagás was murdered in 1868—some say by a rival who discovered that Partagás was having an affair with his wife—and his ghost is said to haunt the factory.

Guided tours (45 minutes) are offered every 15 minutes. You must buy your ticket in advance at either the Hotel Saratoga or Hotel Habana Libre Tryp.

CALLE AGRAMONTE (ZULUETA)

Calle Agramonte, more commonly referred to by its colonial name of Zulueta, parallels the Prado and slopes gently upward from Avenida de los Estudiantes to the northeast side of Parque Central. Traffic runs one-way uphill.

On the north side of Avenida de los Estudiantes (Cárcel) is the **Monumento al General Máximo Gómez.** This massive monument of white marble by sculptor Aldo Gamba was erected in 1935 to honor the Dominican-born hero of the Cuban Wars of Independence who led the Liberation Army as commander-in-chief. Generalissimo Gómez (1836–1905) is cast in bronze, reining in his horse. Its base features three bas-reliefs.

◖ Museo de la Revolución

The ornate building facing north over Plaza 13 de Mayo was initiated in 1913 to house the provincial government. Before it could be finished (in 1920), it was earmarked as the Palacio Presidencial (Presidential Palace), and Tiffany's of New York was entrusted with its interior decoration. It was designed by Belgian Paul Belau and Cuban Carlos Maruri in an eclectic style, with a lofty dome. It was from here that a string of corrupt presidents spun their webs of dissolution.

Following the Revolution, the three-story palace (now much deteriorated) was converted into the dour Museum of the Revolution (Refugio #1, e/ Zulueta y Monserrate, tel. 07/862-4091; daily 10 A.M.–5 P.M.; CUC5, cameras CUC2, guide CUC2).

The marble staircase leads upstairs to the Salón de los Espejos (the Mirror Room), a replica of that in Versailles (replete with paintings by Armando Menocal and other notable Cuban painters); and Salón Dorado (the Gold Room), decorated with yellow marble and gold leaf and highlighted by its magnificently decorated dome.

Rooms are divided chronologically, from the colonial period to the modern day. Maps describe the progress of the revolutionary war. Guns and rifles are displayed alongside grisly photos of dead and tortured heroes. One section is dedicated to the revolutionaries who died in an assault on the palace on March 13, 1957, when Batista escaped through a secret door. Don't miss the Rincón de los Cretinos ("Corner of Cretins"), which pokes fun at Batista, Ronald Reagan, and George Bush.

A room to the right of the entrance celebrates the ill-fated efforts of Che to inspire a revolution in Bolivia.

At the rear, in the former palace gardens, is the **Granma Memorial,** preserving the vessel that brought Castro, Guevara, and other revolutionaries from Mexico to Cuba in 1956. The *Granma* is encased in a massive glass structure. It's surrounded by vehicles used in the revolutionary war: armored vehicles, the bullet-riddled "Fast Delivery" truck used in the student commandos' assault on the Presidential Palace in 1957, and Castro's Toyota Jeep from the Sierra Maestra. There's also a turbine from the U-2 spy plane downed during the missile crisis in 1962, plus a naval Sea Fury and a T-34 tank.

◖ Museo Nacional de Bellas Artes (Cuban Section)

The Cuban section of the National Fine Arts Museum is housed in the soberly classical Palacio de Bellas Artes (Trocadero, e/ Zulueta y Monserrate; tel. 07/863-9484 or 862-0140, www.museonacional.cult.cu; Tues.–Sat. 10 A.M.–6 P.M., Sun. 10 A.M.–2 P.M.; entrance CUC5, or CUC8 for both sections; guided tour CUC2). The museum features an atrium garden from which ramps lead up to two floors exhibiting more than 1,200 works of art; a complete spectrum of Cuban paintings, engravings, sketches, and sculptures laid out according to eight themes in 24 *salas*. Works representing the vision of early 16th- and 17th-century travelers merge into colonial-era pieces, early 20th-century Cuban interpretations of Impressionism, Surrealism, and works spawned by the Revolution.

AVENIDA DE LOS MISIONES (MONSERRATE)

Avenida de los Misiones, or Monserrate as everyone knows it, parallels Zulueta one block to the east (traffic is one-way, downhill) and follows the space left by the ancient city walls after they were demolished last century.

Iglesia del Santo Ángel Custodio

This Gothic church (Monserrate y Cuarteles, tel. 07/861-8873), immediately east of the Palacio Presidencial, sits atop a rock known as Angel Hill. It was founded in 1687 by builder-

A WALK DOWN ZULUETA AND MONSERRATE

A stroll down Zulueta from Parque Central, returning via Monserrate, reveals several sites of interest, in addition to the "must-sees."

One block north of Parque Central, at the corner of Zulueta and Ánimas, a mosaic on the paving announces your arrival at **Sloppy Joe's,** commemorated as Freddy's Bar in Hemingway's *To Have and Have Not.* At last visit, the near-derelict building remained shuttered, its interior a dusty shambles, awaiting the restoration now sweeping Habana Vieja. Across the way is the old Cuartel de Bomberos fire station, housing the tiny **Museo de Bomberos** (Museum of Firemen, Zulueta #257, e/ Neptuno y Ánimas)

As you cross Refugio, on your right is an **SAU-100 Stalin tank** fronting the Museo de la Revolución; it was used in the Bay of Pigs. Immediately beyond is **Plaza 13 de Mayo,** a grassy park named to commemorate the ill-fated attack of the presidential palace by student martyrs on March 13, 1957. It was laid out by French landscaper Forestier. At the base of Zulueta, at the junction with Cárcel, note the flamboyant art nouveau building housing the **Spanish Embassy.**

Turn right and cross Plaza 13 de Mayo to reach Monserrate.

At the base of Monserrate, at its junction with Calle Tacón, is the **Museo y Archivo de la Música** (Capdevila #1, tel. 07/861-9846 and 863-0052; closed for restoration at last visit), housed in the sober Casa de Pérez de la Riva, built in Italian Renaissance style in 1905. The museum traces the evolution of Cuban music since early colonial days; its collection of antique instruments includes venerable pianos and drums. In a separate room, you can listen to old scores drawn from the record library.

Following Monserrate uphill, southward, you'll pass the Iglesia del Santo Ángel Custodio (see the main text). Opposite, a semi-derelict watchtower – **Baluarte de Ángel** – erected in 1680 stands in front of Museo de la Revolución. Monserrate continues south three blocks to Edifico Bacardí and **Plazuela de Supervielle,** commemorating Dr. Manuel Fernández Supervielle, mayor of Havana during the 1940s.

One block south brings you to **Plazuela de Albear,** with a bust of Francisco de Albear, who last century engineered the Malecón and Havana's first water-drainage system. On its south side, adjoining El Floridita, is the **Casa del Ron,** where free rum samples are given.

---

bishop Diego de Compostela. The tower dates from 1846, when a hurricane toppled the original, while the facade was reworked in neo-Gothic style in the mid-19th century. It's immaculate yet simple within: gray marble floor, modest wooden Gothic altar, statues of saints all around, pristine stained-glass windows. Cuba's national hero, José Martí, was baptized here on February 12, 1853.

The church was the setting for both the opening scene and tragic marriage scene that ends in the violent denouement on the steps of the church in the 19th-century novel *Cecilia Valdés* by Cirilo Villaverde. A bust of the author stands in the *plazuela* outside the main entrance, to the rear of the church, on the corner of Calles Compostela and Cuarteles.

Edificio Bacardí

The Bacardí Building (Monserrate #261, esq. San Juan de Díos), former headquarters of the Bacardi rum empire, is a stunning exemplar of art deco design. Designed by Cuban architect Esteban Rodríguez and finished in December 1929, it is clad in Swedish granite and local limestone. Terra-cotta of varying hues accents the design, with motifs showing Grecian nymphs and floral patterns. It is crowned by a Lego-like pyramidal bell tower topped by a brass-winged bat—the famous Bacardi motif.

The building now houses various offices. Access is restricted to the Café Barrita bar (daily 9 A.M.–6 P.M.)—a true gem of art deco design—to the right of the lobby, up the stairs.

El Floridita

This famous restaurant and bar (corner of Monserrate and Calle Obispo, tel. 07/867-9299; 11:30 A.M.–midnight) has been serving food since 1819, when it was called Pina de Plata. It is haunted by Ernest Hemingway's ghost. You expect a spotlight to come on and Desi Arnaz to appear conducting a dance band, and Hemingway to stroll in as he would every morning when he lived in Havana and drank with Honest Lil, the Worst Politician, and other real-life characters from his novels.

A bronze bust watches over things from above the dark mahogany bar where Constante Ribailagua once served frozen daiquiris to the great writer (Hemingway immortalized both the drink and the venue in his novel *Islands in the Stream*) and such illustrious guests as Gary Cooper, Tennessee Williams, Marlene Dietrich, and Jean-Paul Sartre. There's even a life-size bronze statue of Hemingway, by sculptor José Villa, leaning with its elbow upon the bar.

El Floridita has been spruced up for tourist consumption with a 1930s art deco polish. They've overpriced the place for the package-tourist crowd, but sipping a (watery) daiquiri at El Floridita is a must.

THE HARBOR CHANNEL

Throughout most of the colonial era, sea waves washed up on a beach that lined the southern shore of the harbor channel and bordered what is today Calle Cuba and, eastward, Calle Tacón, which runs along the site of the old city walls forming the original waterfront. In the early 19th century, the area was extended with landfill, and a broad boulevard—**Avenida Carlos Manuel de Céspedes** (Avenida del Puerto)—was laid out along the new harborfront. **Parque Luz Caballero,** between the Avenida and Calle Tacón, is pinned by a statue of José de la Luz Caballero (1800–62), a philosopher and nationalist.

Overlooking the harborfront at the foot of Empedrado is the **Fuente de Neptuno** (Neptune Fountain), erected in 1838.

Calles Cuba and Tacón

Calle Cuba extends east from the foot of Monserrate. At the foot of Calle Cuarteles is the Palacio de Mateo Pedroso y Florencia. Today known as the **Palacio de Artesanía** (Cuba #64, e/ Tacón y Peña Pobre; Mon.–Sat. 8 A.M.–8 P.M., Sun. 9 A.M.–2 P.M; free), this magnificent mansion was built in Moorish style for nobleman Don Mateo Pedroso (a slave trader and former mayor) around 1780. Pedroso's home displays the typical architectural layout of period houses, with stores on the ground floor, slave quarters on the mezzanine, and the owner's dwellings above. Today it houses craft shops and boutiques and has folkloric music in the patio.

Immediately east is **Plazuela de la Maestranza,** where a remnant of the old city wall is preserved. On its east side, in the triangle formed by the junction of Cuba, Tacón, and Chacón, is a medieval-style fortress, **El Castillo de Atane,** a police headquarters built in 1941 as a pseudo-colonial confection.

The **Seminario de San Carlos y San Ambrosio** (e/ Chacón y Empedrado, tel. 07/862-8790; Mon.–Sat. 9 A.M.–5 P.M.; free), a massive seminary running the length of Tacón east of El Castillo de Atane, was established by the Jesuits in 1721 and is still a center for young men studying for an ecclesiastical career. The downstairs cloister is open to the public as the **Museo Arquidioscesana;** in the rear right corner, note the fabulous antique chest engraved with figures from *Don Quixote.*

The entrance to the seminary overlooks an excavated site showing the foundations of the original seafront section of the city walls—here called the **Cortina de Valdés.** (The artisans' market that formerly took up the length of Tacón moved in 2009 to a new site at the southern end of the Alameda de Paula.)

Tacón opens to a tiny *plazuela* at the junction with Empedrado, where horse-drawn cabs called *calezas* offer guided tours to tourists. From here, Tacón leads to Plaza de Armas. The **Museo de Arqueología** (Tacón #12, e/ O'Reilly y Empedrado, tel. 07/861-4469; Tues.–Sat. 9 A.M.–5 P.M., Sun.

9 A.M.–1 P.M.; CUC1), displays pre-Columbian artifacts, plus a miscellany of ceramics and other household items from the early colonial years. The museum occupies Casa de Juana Carvajal, a beautiful mansion first mentioned in documents in 1644. Its most remarkable feature is a series of eccentric floor-to-ceiling murals depicting life as it was lived in the 1700s.

PLAZA DE LA CATEDRAL

This exquisite cobbled square was the last square to be laid out in Habana Vieja. It occupied a lowly quarter where rainwater and refuse collected (it was originally known as the Plazuela de la Ciénaga—Little Square of the Swamp). A cistern was built in 1587, and only in the following century was the area drained. Its present texture dates from the 18th century.

The square is Habana Vieja at its most quintessential, the atmosphere enhanced by mulattas in traditional costume who will happily pose for your camera (for a small fee). One Saturday a month, the plaza is a venue for the **Noche en las Plazas** *espectáculo*.

Catedral San Cristóbal de la Habana

This intimate cathedral, on the north side of the plaza, is known colloquially as Catedral Colón (Columbus Cathedral) but is officially called the Catedral de la Virgen María de la Concepción Inmaculada (tel. 07/861-7771; Mon.–Sat. 10:30 A.M.–2 P.M., Sun. 9 A.M.–noon; free guided tour, tower tour CUC1), or Virgin of the Immaculate Conception, whose statue is installed in the High Altar. The cathedral was initiated by the Jesuits in 1748. The order was kicked out of Cuba by Carlos III in 1767, but the building was eventually completed in 1777 and altered again in the early 19th century. Thus the original baroque interior (including the altar) is gone, replaced in 1814 by a new classical interior.

The baroque facade is adorned with clinging columns and ripples like a great swelling sea; Cuban novelist Alejo Carpentier thought it "music turned to stone." A royal decree of December 1793 elevated the church to a cathedral. On either side of the facade are mismatched towers (one fatter and taller than the other) containing bells supposedly cast with a dash of gold and silver, said to account for their musical tone.

Columns divide the rectangular church into three naves. The neoclassical main altar is simple and made of wood; the murals above are by Italian painter Guiseppe Perovani. The chapel immediately to the left has several altars, including one of Carrara marble inlaid with gold, silver, onyx, and carved hardwoods. Note, too, the wooden image of Saint Christopher, patron saint of Havana, dating to 1633.

The Spanish believed that a casket brought to Havana from Santo Domingo in 1796 and that resided in the cathedral for more than a century held the ashes of Christopher Columbus. It was returned to Spain in 1899. All but the partisan *habaneros* now believe that the ashes were those of Columbus's son Diego.

© CHRISTOPHER P. BAKER

This *santera* in her white robes adds to the atmosphere of the Plaza de la Catedral.

Casa de los Marqueses de Aguas Claras

This splendid old mansion, on the northwest side of the plaza, was built during the 16th century by Governor General Gonzalo Pérez de Angulo and has since been added to by subsequent owners. Today a café occupies the *portico,* while the inner courtyard, with its fountain amid lush palms and clinging vines, houses the Restaurante La Fuente del Patio. The restaurant extends upstairs, where the middle classes once dwelled in apartments. Sunlight pouring in through stained-glass *mediopuntos* saturates the floors with shifting fans of red and blue.

Casa del Conde de Bayona

This simple two-story structure faces the cathedral on the south side of the square. It's a perfect example of the traditional Havana merchant's house of the period, with side stairs and an *entresuelo* (mezzanine of half-story proportions). It was built in the 1720s for Governor General Don Luis Chacón and later passed to Pancho Marty, a former smuggler-turned-entrepreneur. In the 1930s, it housed the Havana Club Bar, which was used by Graham Greene as the setting for Wormold's meeting with Captain Segura (based on Batista's real-life police chief, Ventura) in *Our Man in Havana.* Today it houses the **Museo de Arte Colonial** (San Ignacio #61, tel. 07/862-6440; daily 9:30 A.M.–5 P.M.; entrance CUC2, cameras CUC2, guides CUC1), which re-creates the lavish interior of an aristocratic colonial home. One room is devoted to colorful stained-glass *vitrales.*

Callejón de Chorro

At the southwest corner of the plaza, this short cul-de-sac is where a cistern was built to supply water to ships in the harbor. The *aljibe* (cistern) marked the terminus of the Zanja Real (the "royal ditch," or *chorro*), a covered aqueduct that brought water from the Río Almendares some 10 kilometers away. A small sink and spigot remain.

The **Casa de Baños,** which faces onto the square, looks quite ancient but was built in the 20th century in colonial style on the site of a bathhouse erected over the *aljibe.* Today the building contains the **Galería Victor Manuel** (San Ignacio #56, tel. 07/861-2955; daily 10 A.M.–9 P.M.), selling quality arts.

At the far end of Callejón de Chorro is the **Taller Experimental de la Gráfica** (tel. 07/864-7622, tgrafica@cubarte.cult .cu; Mon.–Fri. 9 A.M.–4 P.M.), where you can watch artists make prints for sale.

Casa de Conde de Lombillo

On the plaza's east side is the Casa de Conde de Lombillo (tel. 07/860-4311; Mon.–Fri. 9 A.M.–5 P.M., Sat. 9 A.M.–1 P.M.; free). Built in 1741, this former home of a slave trader houses a small post office (Cuba's first), as it has since 1821. The mansion adjoins the **Casa del Marqués de Arcos** (not open to visitors), built in the 1740s for the royal treasurer. What you see is the rear of the mansion; the entrance is on Calle Mercaderes, where the building facing the entrance is graced by the **Mural Artístico-Histórico,** by Cuban artist Andrés Carrillo.

The two houses are fronted by a wide *portico* supported by thick columns. Note the mailbox set into the outside wall; it is a grotesque face—that of a tragic Greek mask—carved in stone, with a scowling mouth as its slit. A life-size bronze statue of the late Spanish flamenco dancer Antonio Gades (1936–2004) leans against one of the columns.

Centro Wilfredo Lam

This art center (San Ignacio #22, esq. Empredado, tel. 07/861-2096 and 861-3419, wlam@artsoft.cult.cu; Mon.–Fri. 8 A.M.–5 P.M.), on cobbled Empedrado, on the northwest corner of the plaza, occupies the former mansion of the Counts of Peñalver. It displays works by the eponymous Cuban artist as well as artists from developing nations (primarily Latin America). The institution studies and promotes contemporary art from around the world. It also features a library on contemporary art.

La Bodeguita del Medio

No visit to Havana is complete without a visit to Ernest Hemingway's favorite watering hole (Empedrado #207, tel. 07/862-6121; bar daily 10:30 A.M.–midnight), half a block west of the cathedral. This neighborhood hangout was originally the coach house of the mansion next door. Later it was a *bodega,* a mom-and-pop grocery store where Spanish immigrant Ángel Martínez served food and drinks.

The bar is to the front, with the restaurant behind. Troubadours move among the thirsty *turistas.* Between tides, you can still savor the proletarian fusion of dialectics and rum. The house drink is the *mojito,* the rum mint julep that Hemingway brought out of obscurity and turned into the national drink.

Adorning the walls are posters, paintings, and faded photos of Papa Hemingway, Carmen Miranda, and other famous visitors. The walls were once decorated with the signatures and scrawlings of visitors dating back decades. Alas, a recent renovation has wiped away much of the original charm (the artwork has been erased and replaced in ersatz style, with visitors being handed blue pens; famous visitors now sign a chalkboard).

The most famous graffiti is credited to Hemingway: *"Mi Mojito en La Bodeguita, Mi Daiquirí en El Floridita,"* he supposedly scrawled on the sky-blue walls—according to Tom Miller in *Trading with the Enemy,* Martínez concocted the phrase as a marketing gimmick after the writer's death. Errol Flynn thought it "A Great Place to Get Drunk." They are there, these ribald fellows, smiling at the camera through a haze of cigar smoke and rum.

Casa del Conde de la Reunión

Built in the 1820s, at the peak of the baroque era, this home has a trefoil-arched doorway opening onto a *zaguán* (courtyard). Exquisite *azulejos* (painted tiles) decorate the walls.

Famed novelist Alejo Carpentier used the house as the main setting for his novel *El siglo de las luces* (The Enlightenment). A portion of the home, which houses the Centro de Promoción Cultural, is dedicated to his memory as the **Fundación Alejo Carpentier** (Empedrado #215, tel. 07/861-5500; Mon.–Fri. 8:30 A.M.–4:30 P.M.; free). One entire wall bears a display of Carpentier's early works. His raincoat is thrown stylishly over his old desk chair.

While here, walk one block west to **Plazuela de San Juan de Díos** (Empedrado, e/ Habana y Aguiar), a small plaza centered on a white marble life-size facsimile of Miguel de Cervantes, author of *Don Quixote,* sitting in a chair, book and pen in hand, lending the plaza its colloquial name: Parque Cervantes.

Edificio Santo Domingo

Calle San Ignacio leads 50 meters south from Plaza de la Catedral to Calle Obispo. On the southeast corner of the junction, a looming contemporary building faced in glass—the Edificio Santo Domingo—occupies the site of the early Convento de Santo Domingo, which between 1727 and 1902 housed the original University of Havana. The grotesque 1950s building was recently remodeled in eye-pleasing fashion, with a replica of the original baroque doorway and belltower containing the original bell that once tolled students to class.

The building today houses offices of the current university plus, on the ground floor, the **Museo de la Universidad** (no tel.; Tues.–Sat. 9:30 A.M.–5 P.M., Sun., Mon. 9:30 A.M.–1 P.M.) displays a model of the original structure plus miscellany related to the early university.

◖ PLAZA DE ARMAS

The most important plaza in Habana Vieja, and the oldest, this handsome square was laid out in 1519 and named Plaza de Iglesia for the church that was demolished in 1741 after an English warship, the ill-named HMS *Invincible,* was struck by lightning and exploded, sending its main mast sailing down on the church. Later, Plaza de Armas evolved to become the settlement's administrative center.

The plaza seems still to ring with the cacophony of the past, when military parades and

CUBAN COLONIAL ARCHITECTURE

Cuba boasts the New World's finest assemblage of colonial buildings. Spanning four centuries, these palaces, mansions, churches, castles, and more simple structures catalog an astonishing progression of styles. The academic classicism of aristocratic 18th-century Spanish homes blend with 19th-century French rococo, while art deco and art nouveau exteriors from the 1920s fuse into the cool, columned arcades of ancient palaces in Mudejar style. They were laid out along ruler-straight roads arranged in a grid pattern as decreed by the Laws of the Indies and usually intentionally narrow, conducive to shade.

THE COLONIAL HOME

The 17th-century home was made of limestone and modeled on the typical Spanish house, with a simple portal and balconies with lathe-turned *rejas* and tall, generously proportioned rooms and shallow-stepped staircases. By the 18th century, those houses that faced onto squares had adopted a portico and loggia (supported by arched columns) to provide shelter from sun and rain.

Colonial homes grew larger with ensuing decades and typically featured two small courtyards, with a dining area between the two, with a central hallway, or *zaguán*, big enough for carriages and opening directly from the street. Arrayed around the ground floor courtyard were warehouses, offices, and other rooms devoted to the family business, with stables and servants' quarters to the rear, while the private family quarters were sequestered above around the galleried second story reached by a stately inner stairway. The design was unique to Havana houses. Commercial activity on the ground floor was relegated to those rooms (*dependencias*) facing the street (these were usually rented out to merchants). Laundry and other household functions were relegated to the inner, second patio, or *traspatio,* hidden behind massive wooden doors often flanked by pillars that in time developed ornate arches. The formal layout of rooms on the ground floor was usually repeated on the main, upper story. Another design borrowed from Spain was the *entresuelo,* a mezzanine of half-story proportions tucked between the two stories and used to house servants.

By the 19th century, the wealthy were building summer homes in Havana's hilly suburbs. These *quintas* were typically in neoclassical style, with extensive front porticos and gardens to the rear. Many, however, were influenced by the Palladian style, fashionable in Europe.

Throughout the colonial period, windows evolved as one of the most decorative elements. Ground floor windows were full height from ground level and featured shutter-doors to permit a free flow of air. Later windows acquired ornate grilled wooden balusters, which often protruded where streets were sufficiently wide. In the 19th century, glass was introduced, though usually only for decoration in multicolored stained-glass panes inserted between or above louvered wooden panels. Meanwhile, ornate metal grills called *guardavecinos* were adopted for upper stories to

---

musical concerts were held under the watchful eye of the governor, and the gentry would take their formal evening promenade. Wednesday–Saturday the plaza is ringed by stalls selling tatterdemalion antiquarian books.

At its heart is **Parque Céspedes,** a verdant park shaded by palms and tall kapok (ceiba) trees, and pinned by a white marble **statue of Manuel de Céspedes,** hero of the Ten Years War.

The following buildings are described in clockwise order, beginning on the west side.

Palacio de los Capitanes Generales

This somber yet stately palace was completed in 1791 and became home to 65 governors of Cuba between 1791 and 1898 and, after that, the U.S. governor's residence during Uncle Sam's occupation and, in 1902–20, the early seat of the Cuban government. Between 1920 and 1967, it served as Havana's city hall.

The palace is fronted by a cool loggia supported by Ionic columns and by "cobblewood"

divide balconies of contiguous properties and so prevent intrusion.

Certain styles evolved unique to individual cities, as with the *arco mixtilíneo* (doorway lintel) and projecting turned-wood roof brackets unique to Camagüey; the mail-order gingerbread wooden homes (imported from Key West) common in Varadero; and the tromp l'oeil interior murals found in homes of Sancti Spíritus. Cuban structures were heavily influenced by traditional Spanish and Mudejar (Moorish) styles that included:

- **Alfarje:** A pitched wooden roof combining parallel and angled beams, providing a conceptual shift in emphasis to enhance a room's sense of space. Normally found in churches and smaller homes, they adopted a star pattern.

- **Antepecho:** An ornamented window guard flush with the building facade.

- **Cenefa:** Band of colored plasterwork used as decorative ornamentation on interior walls.

- **Entresuelo:** Shallow mezzanine level between ground and upper stories, housing slaves'.

- **Luceta:** Long rectangular window along the edges of a doorway or window, usually containing stained or marbled glass.

- **Mamparas:** Double-swing half doors that serve as room dividers or as partial outer doors to protect privacy. Typically they contained colored or frosted glass.

- **Mediopunto:** Half-moon stained-glass window (*vitral*) above windows or doorways.

- **Patio:** An open space in the center of Spanish buildings – a Spanish adaptation of the classic Moorish inner court – which permits air to circulate through the house. The patios of more grandiose buildings are surrounded by columned galleries.

- **Persiana:** Slatted shutter in tall, glassless windows, designed to let in the breezes while keeping out the harsh light and rain.

- **Portal:** The main doorway. Early *portales* were fairly simple but evolved to monumental proportions and featured elaborate stone molding on the lintel and bas-relief pilasters to each side.

- **Portico:** Galleried exterior walkway fronting mansions and protecting pedestrians from sun and rain. Often these stretch the length of a street, supported by stone columns dividing vaulted ceilings and arches.

- **Postigo:** Small door set at face level into massive wooden doors.

- **Reja:** Wooden window screen of rippled, lathe-turned rods called *barrotes* that served to keep out burglars (later *rejas* were made of metal).

- **Vitral:** Window of stained glass in geometric designs that diffuse the sunlight, saturating a room with shifting color.

laid instead of stone to soften the noise of carriages and thereby lessen the disturbance of the governors' sleep. The three-story structure surrounds a courtyard that contains a statue of Christopher Columbus by Italian sculptor Cucchiari amid palms and other tropical foliage. Arched colonnades rise on all sides. In the southeast corner, a hole containing the coffin of an unknown nobleman is one of several graves from the old Cementerio de Espada.

Today, the palace houses the **Museo de la Ciudad de la Habana** (City of Havana Museum, Tacón #1, e/ Obispo y O'Reilly, tel. 07/861-5001; Tues.–Sun. 9:30 A.M.–5:30 P.M., last entry at 4:30 P.M.; entrance CUC3, cameras CUC2, videos CUC10, guide CUC1). The great flight of marble stairs leads to palatially furnished rooms. The Salón del Trono (Throne Room), made for the King of Spain but never used, is of breathtaking splendor and brims with treasures. The museum also features the Salón de las Banderas (Hall of Flags), with

A WALK ALONG CALLE OBISPO

Pedestrians-only Calle Obispo links Plaza de Armas with Parque Central and is Habana Vieja's busiest street. The name means "Bishop's Street," supposedly because it was the path favored by ecclesiastics of the 18th century. It became Havana's premier shopping street early on and was given a boost when the city walls went up in the mid-1700s, linking the major colonial plaza with the Monserrate Gate, the main entranceway into the city.

Begin at Plaza Albear and walk east. Fifty yards on your left you'll pass the Infotur office and one block further, also on your left, the **Casa Natal de Félix Varela** (Obispo, e/ Aguacate y Villegas), the birthplace of the Cuban nationalist philosophy-priest.

The next few blocks are lined with boutiques, small art galleries, and simple cafés and bars.

Crossing Calle Havana, five blocks east of Plaza Albear, you arrive at Havana's erstwhile "Wall Street," centered on Calles Obispo, Cuba, and Aguiar, where the main banks were concentrated prior to the Revolution. The former neoclassical Banco Mendoza today houses the **Museo Numismático** (Coin Museum, Obispo, e/ Habana y Aguiar, tel. 07/861-5811; Tues.-Sat. 9 A.M.-4:45 P.M., Sun. 9:30 A.M.-5 P.M.; CUC1). The broad-ranging collection of coins and banknotes spans the Greco, Roman, and Phoenician epochs, as well as Spanish *reales* and *escudos*, plus Cuban money dating back to the republican era.

At Calle Aguiar, divert south one block to the **Opera y Teatro Lírico San Felipe Neri** (Aguiar esq. Obrapia, tel. 07/862-3243), a converted church – Iglesia San Felipe Neri – now hosting performances by the Coro Nacional de Cuba (National Chorus of Cuba).

At the corner of Cuba you reach the **Hotel Florida** (Obispo #252, esq. Cuba, tel. 07/862-4127), a beautifully restored colonial mansion with a fine bar and restaurant. Cater-corner to the hotel, the former **Banco Nacional de Cuba** (Obispo #211, esq. Cuba), in a splendid neoclassical building fronted by fluted Corinthian columns is occupied by the Ministerio de Finanzas y Precios (Ministry of Finance and Prices).

Havana is replete with dusty old apothecaries, but the **Museo y Farmacia Taquechel** (Obispo #155, esq. Aguiar, tel. 07/862-9286; daily 9 A.M.-6 P.M.; free) is surely the most interesting, with its mixing vases, mortars and pestles, and colorful ceramic jars full of herbs and potions. Dating from 1898, it's named for Dr. Francisco Taquechel y Mirabal.

Across the street, on the north side of Obispo, is the original site of the University of Havana, founded in January 1728. An antique bell that once tolled to call the students to class has been placed in a campanile on the north side of the new university building.

Fifty meters beyond Museo y Farmacia Taquechel you'll arrive at the rose-pink **Hotel Ambos Mundos** (Obispo, esq. Mercaderes, tel. 07/860-9530), dating from 1925. Off and on throughout the 1930s, Hemingway laid his head in Room 511, where he wrote *The Green Hills of Africa* and *Death in the Afternoon*. The room is today a museum (daily 10 A.M.-5 P.M.; CUC2). Hemingway's quarters – "a gloomy room, 16 square meters, with a double bed made of ordinary wood, two night tables and a writing table with a chair," recalled author Gabriel García Márquez – has been preserved, with furnishings from his home, Finca Vigía. The themed exhibitions change every year. Esperanza, the multi-lingual *custodio*, gives a great spiel.

One block farther brings you to Plaza de Armas.

magnificent artwork that includes *The Death of Antonio Maceo* by Menocal; plus exquisite collections illustrating the story of the city's (and Cuba's) development and the 19th-century struggles for independence. One top-floor room contains the shattered wings of the eagle that once crested the Monumento del Maine in Vedado, along with other curios suggestive of U.S. voracity. Old horse-drawn carriages and artillery are among the other exhibits.

To the south side of the palace, along a 50-meter-long cobbled pedestrian section of

Calle Obispo, is a row of ancient mansions each today hosting a unique site of interest. For example, the **Casa del Agua la Tinaja** (Obispo #111) sells mineral water (CUC0.25 a glass); and the **Museo de la Orfebrería** (Obispo #113; tel. 07/863-9861; Tues.–Sat. 9:30 A.M.–5 P.M., Sun. 9:30 A.M.–12:30 P.M.; free), or Museum of Silverwork, is crammed with silver and gold ornaments from the colonial era. Upstairs you'll find candelabras, a beautiful replica in silver of Columbus's *Santa María,* walking sticks, and a splendid collection of swords and firearms. Next door, the **Librería Navío** (Obispo #117–119; daily 10 A.M.–7 P.M.) antiquarian bookstore is housed in the oldest house in Havana, dating from around 1570. It adjoins the **Museo de Pintura Mural** (Obispo #119; tel. 07/864-2354; Tues.–Sat. 9:30 A.M.–5 P.M., Sun. 9:30 A.M.–1 P.M.), displaying colonial murals, plus a *quitrin* (traditional low-slung horse-drawn cart of the colonial nobility) in the foyer.

Palacio del Segundo Cabo

The austere, quasi-Moorish, pseudo-baroque, part neoclassical Palace of the Second Lieutenant (O'Reilly #14, tel. 07/862-8091; Mon.–Fri. 6 A.M.–midnight) dates from 1770, when it was designed as the Casa de Correos (the city post office). Later it became the home of the vice-governor general (Second Lieutenant) and, immediately after independence, the seat of the Senate. Today, it houses the **Instituto Cubano del Libro** (Cuban Book Institute), which hosts cultural events. Upstairs, the mezzanine is occupied by the **Galería Raúl Martínez** (Mon.–Fri. 10 A.M.–5 P.M., Sat. 10 A.M.– 3 P.M.) art gallery.

Immediately east of the loggia is a marble **statue of Fernando VII,** holding a scroll of parchment that from the side appears jauntily cocked and is the butt of ribald jokes among locals.

Castillo de la Real Fuerza

The pocket-size castle (O'Reilly #2; tel. 07/864-4488; Tues.–Sun. 9 A.M.– 5 P.M.; entrance CUC1, cameras CUC1) on the northeast corner of the plaza was begun in 1558 and completed in 1577. It's the oldest of the four forts that guarded the New World's most precious harbor. Built in medieval fashion, with walls 6 meters wide and 10 meters tall, the castle forms a square with enormous triangular bulwarks at the corners, their sharp angles slicing the dark waters of the moat. It was almost useless from a strategic point of view, being landlocked far from the mouth of the harbor channel and hemmed in by surrounding buildings that would have formed a great impediment to its cannons in any attack. The governors of Cuba lived here until 1762.

Visitors enter the fortress via a courtyard full of cannons and mortars. Note the royal coat of arms representing Seville, Spain, carved in stone above the massive gateway as you cross the moat by a drawbridge. The castle now houses the **Museo de Navegación** (Naval Museum), displaying treasures from the golden age when the riches of the Americas flowed to Spain. The air-conditioned Sala de Tesoro gleams with gold bars, chains, coins, toothpicks, and brooches, plus precious

Castillo de la Real Fuerza

jewels, bronze astrolabes, pewter dishes, rosary beads, clay pipes, and silver *reales* ("pieces of eight"). Labels are in Spanish only. Another *sala* has naval uniforms, swords, pistols, and model ships spanning three centuries.

You can climb to the top of a cylindrical tower rising from the northwest corner and containing a patinated brass bell. The tower is topped by a bronze weathervane called **La Giraldilla de la Habana** showing a voluptuous figure with hair braided in thick ropes; in her right hand she holds a palm tree and in her left a cross. This figure is the official symbol of Havana. The vane is a copy; the original, which now resides in the foyer, was cast in 1631 in honor of Isabel de Bobadilla, the wife of Governor Hernando de Soto, the tireless explorer who fruitlessly searched for the Fountain of Youth in Florida. De Soto named his wife governor in his absence, and she became the only female governor ever to serve in Cuba. Every afternoon for four years she scanned the horizon in vain for his return, and eventually died of sorrow.

Immediately east of the castle, at the junction of Avenida del Puerto and O'Reilly, is an obelisk to the 77 Cuban seamen killed during World War II by German submarines.

El Templete

A charming copy of a Doric temple, El Templete (daily 9:30 A.M.–5 P.M.; CUC1, including guide) stands on the square's northeast corner. It was inaugurated on March 19, 1828, on the site where the first mass and town council meeting were held in 1519, beside a massive ceiba tree. The original ceiba was felled by a hurricane in 1828 and replaced by a column fronted by a small bust of Christopher Columbus. A ceiba has since been replanted and today shades the tiny temple, whose interior features a wall-to-ceiling triptych depicting the first Mass, the first town council meeting, and the inauguration of the Templete. In the center of the room sits a bust of the artist, Jean-Baptiste Vermay (1786–1833).

Hotel Santa Isabel

The building immediately south of El Templete is the former Palacio del Conde de Santovenia (Baratillo, e/ Narciso López y Baratillo y Obispo). Its quintessentially Cuban-colonial facade is graced by a becolumned portico and, above, wrought-iron railings on balconies whose windows boast stained-glass *mediopuntos*. The *conde* (count) in question was famous for hosting elaborate parties, most notoriously a three-day bash in 1833 to celebrate the accession to the throne of Isabel II that climaxed with the ascent of a gaily decorated gas-filled balloon. Later that century it served as a hotel, as it is today. President Carter stayed here during his visit to Havana in 2002.

Half a block east of the hotel, on Calle Baratillo, is the **Casa del Café** (tel. 07/866-8061; Mon.–Sat. 9 A.M.–7 P.M., Sun. 9 A.M.–2 P.M.), serving all kinds of Cuban coffees; next door stands the **Taberna del Galeón** (tel. 07/866-8476; same hours as Casa del Café), the "House of Rum," a rum and cigar store.

Museo Nacional de Historia Natural

On the south side of the plaza, this natural history museum (Obispo #61, e/ Oficios y Baratillo, tel. 07/863-9361, museo@mnhnc. inf.cu; Tues.–Sun. 9:30 A.M.–7:30 P.M.; CUC3) shows off the rather paltry collection of the Academía de Ciencias and encompasses the Museo de Ciencias Naturales (Museum of Natural Sciences) and the Museo de Ciencias y Técnicas (Museum of Science and Technology), which covers evolution in a well-conceived display. The museum houses collections of Cuban flora and fauna—many in clever reproductions of their natural environments—plus stuffed tigers, apes, and other beasts from around the world. Children will appreciate the interactive displays.

Immediately east, the **Biblioteca Provincial de la Habana** (tel. 07/862-9035; Mon.–Fri. 8:15 A.M.–7 P.M., Sat. 8:15 A.M.–4:30 P.M., Sun. 8:15 A.M.–1 P.M.) is Havana's provincial library. The building once served as the U.S. Embassy.

Casa de los Árabes

The Arabs' House (Oficios #12, tel. 07/861-5868; Tues.–Sat. 9 A.M.–4:30 P.M., Sun. 9 A.M.–1 P.M.; free), 50 meters south of Plaza de Armas and comprising two 17th-century mansions, was formerly the Colegio de San Ambriosio, and is a fine example of Moorish-inspired architecture. It is the only place in Havana where Muslims can practice the Islamic faith (the prayer hall is decorated with hardwoods inlaid with mother-of-pearl). It now houses a small museum dedicated to the many Levantine immigrants who settled Cuba throughout the centuries.

Depósito del Automóvil

The Depository of Automobiles (Oficios #13, tel. 07/863-9942; Tues.–Sat. 9 A.M.–5 P.M., Sun. 9 A.M.–1 P.M.; entrance CUC2, cameras CUC2, videos CUC10), opposite Casa de los Árabes, includes an eclectic range of 30 antique automobiles, from a 1905 Cadillac, a 1926 Rolls-Royce Phantom, a 1924 Packard, 1926 Willys Overland Whippet, and 1930 V-6 Cadillac limousine to a pre-war Dodge hearse and Che Guevara's 1959 mint green Chevrolet Bel-Air. Classic Harley-Davidson motorcycles are also exhibited.

PLAZA DE SAN FRANCISCO

Cobbled Plaza de San Francisco, two blocks south of Plaza de Armas, at Oficios and the foot of Amargura, faces onto Avenida del Puerto. During the 16th century the area was the great waterfront of the early colonial city. Iberian emigrants disembarked, slaves were unloaded, and galleons were replenished for the passage to Spain. A market developed on the plaza, which became the focus of the annual Fiesta de San Francisco each October 3, when a gambling fair was established. At its heart is the **Fuente de los Leones** (Fountain of the Lions) by Giuseppe Gaggini, erected in 1836 and though moved to different locations at various times, finally ensconced where it began.

The five-story neoclassical building on the north side is the **Lonja del Comercio** (Goods Exchange, Amargura #2, esq. Oficios, tel. 07/866-9588; Mon.–Sat. 9 A.M.–6 P.M.), dating from 1907, when it was built as a center for commodities trading. Restored, it houses offices of international corporations, news bureaus, and tour companies. The beautiful dome is crowned by a bronze figure of the god Mercury.

Behind the Lonja and entered by a wrought-iron archway topped by a most-uncommunist fairytale crown, is the **Jardín Diana de Gales** (Baratillo, esq. Carpinetti; daily 9 A.M.–6 P.M.), a park unveiled in 2000 in memory of Diana, Princess of Wales. The 10-foot-tall column is by acclaimed Cuban artist Alfredo Sosabravo. There's also an engraved Welsh slate and stone plaque from Althorp, Diana's childhood home, donated by the British Embassy.

The garden backs onto the **Casa de los Esclavos** (Obrapía, esq. Av. del Puerto), a slave-merchant's home that now serves as the principal office of the city historian.

Iglesia y Convento de San Francisco de Asís

Dominating the plaza on the south side is this great church (Oficios, e/ Armagura y Brasil, tel. 07/862-9683; daily 9 A.M.–5:30 P.M.; entrance CUC2, guide CUC1, cameras CUC2, videos CUC10), whose construction was launched in 1719. It was reconstructed in 1730 in baroque style with a 40-meter bell tower crowned by St. Helen holding a sacred Cross of Jerusalem. The church was eventually proclaimed a Minorite Basilica, and it was from its chapel that the processions of the *Via Crucis* (Procession of the Cross) departed every Lenten Friday, ending at the Iglesia del Santo Cristo del Buen Viaje. The devout passed down Calle Amargura (Street of Bitterness), where Stations of the Cross were set up at street corners.

The Protestant English worshiped in the church during their tenure in Havana in 1762; Catholics refused thereafter to use it.

The church and adjoining convent reopened in October 1994 after a complete restoration. The main nave, with its towering roof supported by 12 columns, each topped by an apostle, features a trompe l'oeil that extends

RESTORING OLD HAVANA

Old Havana has been called the "finest urban ensemble in the Americas." The fortress colonial town that burst its walls when Washington, D.C., was still a swamp is a 350-acre repository of antique buildings in an astounding amalgam of styles. More than 900 of Habana Vieja's 3,157 structures are of historic importance. Of these, only 101 were built in the 20th century. Almost 500 are from the 19th; 200 are from the 18th; and 144 are from the 16th and 17th. Alas, many buildings are crumbling into ruins around the people who occupy them.

In 1977, the Cuban government named Habana Vieja a National Monument. In 1982, UNESCO's Inter-Governmental Committee for World Cultural and Natural Protection named Habana Vieja a World Heritage Site worthy of international protection. Cuba formalized a plan to rescue much of the old city from decades of neglect under the guidance of Eusebio Leal Spengler, the charismatic official city historian, who runs the **Oficina del Historiador de la Ciudad de La Habana** (Habana Vieja, tel. 07/861-5001, www.ohch.cu). Leal, who grew up in Habana Vieja, is a member of Cuba's National Assembly, the Central Committee of the Communist Party, and the all-important Council of State.

The ambitious plan stretches into the future and has concentrated on four squares: Plaza de Armas, Plaza de la Catedral, Plaza Vieja, and Plaza de San Francisco. The most important buildings have received major renovations; others have been given facelifts.

Priority is given to edifices with income-generating tourist value. Structures are ranked into one of four levels according to historical and physical value. The top level is reserved for museums; the second level for hotels, restaurants, offices, and schools; and the bottom levels for housing.

Restoration is being run as a self-financing business. **Habaguanex** (Calle 24 #4313, e/ 43 y 45, Rpto. Almenderes, Playa, and Calle Oficios #110, Plaza de San Francisco, Havana, tel. 07/204-9201, www.habaguanexhotels.cu) has responsibility for opening and operating commercial entities such as hotels, restaurants, cafés, and shops. The profits help finance further infrastructural improvements; 33 percent of revenues are supposedly devoted to social projects. Not every palace ends up converted for tourist use, however; some become schools, while one restored mansion is now a pediatric rehabilitation center.

Still, there is little evidence of actual homes being restored. In southern Habana Vieja, where there are relatively few structures of touristic interest, talk of restoration raises hollow laughs from the inhabitants. Because of overcrowding, some 30,000 longtime residents will be moved out for good. Many occupants have already been moved to new apartments in Alamar, the monstrous housing project east of the city; those who've been moved complain about having been transferred from ancient slum quarters to what many consider a modern and soulless slum.

the perspective of the nave. The sumptuously adorned altars are gone, replaced by a huge crucifix suspended above a grand piano. (The cathedral serves as a concert hall. Classical music performances are hosted each Saturday at 6 P.M. and Sunday at 11 A.M., except July and August.) Members of the most aristocratic families of the times were buried in the crypt; some bodies are open to view. You can climb the campanile (CUC1) for a panoramic view over Habana Vieja.

The nave opens to the cloisters of a convent that today contains the **Museo de Arte Religioso,** featuring religious silver icons, plus the lectern and armchairs used by Fidel and the pope during the latter's visit in 1998. A music school occupies part of the building.

A life-size bronze statue (by José Villa Soberón) of an erstwhile and once-renowned tramp known as **El Caballero de París** graces the sidewalk in front of the cathedral entrance. Many Cubans believe that touching his beard will bring good luck.

Calle Oficios

The west side of cobbled Calle Oficios facing the cathedral is lined with 17th-century colonial buildings that possess a marked Mudejar style, exemplified by their wooden balconies. The entire block has been magnificently restored and many of the buildings converted into art galleries. One of the gems is the **Galería de Carmen Montilla Tinoco** (Oficios #162, tel. 07/866-8768; Mon.–Sat. 9 A.M.–5 P.M.; free). Only the front of the house remains, but the architects have made creative use of the empty shell. Next door, **Estudio Galería Los Oficios** (Oficios #166, tel. 07/863-0497; Mon.–Sat. 9:30 A.M.–5 P.M., Sun. 9 A.M.–1 P.M.; free) displays works by renowned artist Nelson Domínguez.

Midway down the block, cobbled Calle Brasil extends west about 80 meters to Plaza Vieja. Portions of the original colonial-era aqueduct (the Zanja Real) are exposed. It's worth the brief detour to visit the **Aqvarium** (Brasil #9, tel. 07/863-9493; Tues.–Sat. 9 A.M.–5 P.M., Sun. 9 A.M.–1 P.M.; CUC1, children free), displaying tropical fish. Children's events are hosted each second Wednesday of the month; video screenings each third Wednesday; and lectures each fourth Wednesday. Next door, **La Casa Cubana del Perfume** (Brasil #13, tel. 07/866-3759; Mon.–Sat. 10 A.M.–6 P.M.) displays colonial-era distilleries, has aromatherapy demos, and sells handmade perfumes made on site.

Back on Oficios, you'll pass the former Casa de Don Lorenzo Montalvo, which today houses a convent and the **Hostal Convento de Santa Brígida.** Opposite the hotel, the **Coche Presidencial Mambí** (Mon.–Fri. 8:30 A.M.–4:45 P.M.; CUC1) railway carriage stands on rails at Oficios and Churruca. It served as the official presidential carriage of five presidents, beginning in 1902 with Tomás Estrada Palma. Its polished hardwood interior gleams with brass fittings.

Immediately beyond is the **Museo Palacio de Gobierno** (Oficios #211, esq. Muralla, tel. 07/863-4352; Mon.–Fri. 8:30 A.M.–4:45 P.M.). This 19th-century neoclassical building housed the Cámara de Representantes (Chamber of Representatives) during the early Republic. From 1929 on it served as the Ministerio de Educación (1929–60) and following the Revolution housed the Ministry of Education and the Poder Popular Municipal (Havana's local government office). Today it has uniforms, documents, and miscellany relating to its past official use. The interior lobby is striking for its ornate baroque and neoclassical stucco work, including a magnificent stained-glass skylight.

Cater-corner to the Palacio, on the southeast side of Oficios and Muralla, is **Casa Alejandro Von Humboldt** (Oficios #254, tel. 07/863-1144; Tues.–Sat. 9 A.M.–5 P.M., Sun. 9 A.M.–noon; CUC1), a museum dedicated to the German explorer (1769–1854) who lived here while investigating Cuba in 1800–01.

Museo de Ron

The Fundación Destilería Havana Club, or Museo de Ron (Museum of Rum, Av. San Pedro #262, e/ Muralla y Sol, tel. 07/861-8051, www.havana-club.com; Mon.–Thurs. 9 A.M.–5 P.M., Fri.–Sun. 9 A.M.–4 P.M.; CUC7 including guide and drink), two blocks south of Plaza San Francisco, occupies the former harborfront colonial mansion of the Conde de la Mortera. It's a must-see and provides an introduction to the mystery and manufacture of Cuban rum. Your tour begins with an audiovisual presentation. Exhibits include a mini-cooperage, *pailes* (sugar boiling pots), original wooden *trapiches* (sugarcane presses), and *salas* dedicated to an exposition on sugarcane, and to the colonial sugar mills and factories where the cane was pressed and the liquid processed. An operating mini-production unit replete with bubbling vats and copper stills demonstrates the process that results in some of the world's finest rums.

The highlight is a model of an early 20th-century sugar plantation at 1:22.5 scale, complete with working steam locomotives. Your tour ends in the Bar Havana Club.

On the rum theme, Hemingway once

favored **Dos Hermanos** (Av. San Pedro #304, esq. Sol, tel. 07/861-3514), a simple bar immediately south of the museum. It was closed for restoration at last visit.

CALLE MERCADERES

Cobbled Calle Mercaderes between Obispo and Plaza Vieja, four blocks south, is full of major and minor attractions. Not least is the **Maqueta de la Habana Vieja** (Mercaderes #114, tel. 07/866-4425; daily 9:30 A.M.– 6:30 P.M.; entrance CUC1, guide CUC1, cameras CUC2, videos CUC5), half a block south of Obispo. This 1:500 scale model of Habana Vieja measures eight by four meters, with every building delineated and color coded by use. Guides give a spiel.

Museo de Ásia

This charming museum (Mercaderes #111, tel. 07/863-9740; Tues.–Sat. 9 A.M.–5 P.M., Sun. 9 A.M.–1 P.M.; entrance CUC1, cameras CUC2, videos CUC10) displays a collection of Asiatica comprising gifts to Fidel from Asian nations. The best rooms are upstairs, containing an array of carved ivory, silverware, mother-of-pearl furniture, kimonos, and Oriental armaments. The museum also includes a small bonsai garden, and one of the rooms downstairs doubles as a school classroom.

Casa de la Obra Pía

One of the most important buildings hereabouts, the House of Charitable Works (Obrapía #158, tel. 07/861-3097; Tues.–Sat. 9:30 A.M.–5 P.M., Sun. 9:30 A.M.–noon; free), 20 meters west of Mercaderes, comprises two adjacent houses that were later combined. This splendid mansion with lemon-yellow walls was built in 1665 by Capitán Martín Calvo de la Puerta y Arrieta, the Cuban solicitor general (the house and street are named for the *obra pía*, or pious act, of Don Martín Calvo de la Puerta, who devoted a portion of his wealth to sponsoring five orphan girls every year). The Calvo de Puertas family built additions in baroque style. The family coat of arms, surrounded by exuberant baroque stonework, is emblazoned above the massive *portal*, brought from Cádiz in 1686. The mansion exemplifies the Spanish adaptation of a Moorish inner courtyard, with a serene coolness, illuminated by daylight filtering through *mediopuntos* fanning out like a peacock's tail. It features art galleries, plus an exhibition of works by Alejo Carpentier in the foyer (including, rather incongruously, his blue Volkswagen brought back from Paris after his tenure as Cuban ambassador to UNESCO).

Casa de África

Dedicated to a celebration of African culture, Africa House (Obrapía #157, e/ Mercaderes y San Ignacio, tel. 07/861-5798; Tues.–Sat. 9:30 A.M.–5 P.M., Sun. 9:30 A.M.–noon; CUC2), opposite Casa de la Obra Pía, is full of African artwork and artifacts. On the third floor, you'll find a collection of paraphernalia used in *santería,* including statues of the leading deities in the Yoruban pantheon. Much of the collection was contributed by various African embassies in Havana.

◖ PLAZA VIEJA AND VICINITY

The last of the four main squares to be laid out in Habana Vieja, the old commercial square (bounded by Calles Mercaderes, San Ignacio, Brasil, and Muralla) originally hosted a covered market. It is surrounded by mansions and apartment blocks from where in colonial times residents looked down on processions, executions, bullfights, and fiestas.

Time and neglect brought near ruin this century, and many of the square's beautiful buildings sank into disrepair. At last visit it was in the final stages of being restored. Even the white Carrara marble fountain—an exact replica of the original by Italian sculptor Giorgio Massari—has reappeared. Until recently, the upper stories of most buildings still housed tenement apartments, although tenants have moved out as the buildings are restored as boutiques and restaurants, etc., plus luxury apartments for foreign residents.

A WALK DOWN CALLE MERCADERES

Setting out toward Plaza Vieja from the Hotel Ambos Mundos, after 20 meters you'll pass the **Museo de Ásia** (see the main text) on your left. Next door, the **Casa de las Especias** (Mon.-Sat. 9 A.M.-5 P.M., Sun. 9 A.M.-4 P.M.) sells natural herbs, such as oregano, in cloth bags. The scent upon entering is worth the visit.

Nearby, call in to the **Maqueta de la Habana Vieja** (see main text). On the west side, 20 meters farther south, are the **Casa de Puerto Rico** and **Casa del Tabaco**, both at Mercaderes #120. Besides a fine stock of cigars, the latter houses the **Museo del Tabaco** (tel. 07/861-5795; Tues.-Sat. 10 A.M.– 5 P.M., Sun. 9 A.M.-1 P.M.; free), a cigar museum upstairs.

At the end of the block, at the corner of Obrapía, the pink building with the Mexican flag fluttering above the doorway is the **Casa de Benito Juárez** (also called Casa de México, Mercaderes #116, tel. 07/861-8186; Tues.-Sat. 9:30 A.M.-4:45 P.M., Sun. 9:30 A.M.-1 P.M.; entrance by donation), displaying artwork and costumes from Mexico, including a collection of priceless Aztec jewelry.

Turn west onto Obrapía to visit the Casa de la Obra Pía and Casa de África (see the main text). One block east, between Mercaderes and Oficios, is the **Casa de Oswaldo Guayasamín** (Obrapía #112, tel. 07/861-3843; Tues.-Sat. 9 A.M.-5:30 P.M., Sun. 9 A.M.-12:30 P.M.; free), housing a museum of art and photographs from Latin America. Guayasamín, a famous Ecuadorian painter, lived and worked here for many years; you can see his works – many are portraits of Fidel – on the upper story, where his living quarters are displayed as he left them upon his death in 1999.

Next door is the **Casa de los Abanicos** (Obrapía #107, tel. 07/863-4452, abanicos@oeetp.ohc.cu; Mon.-Sat.

10 A.M.-7 P.M., Sun. 10 A.M.-1 P.M.; free), where traditional Spanish fans (*abanicos*) are handmade and painted.

Return to Mercaderes and pop into **Habana 1791** (Mercaderes #176, tel. 07/861-3525; 10 A.M.– 6 P.M. daily), on the southwest corner of Obrapía, where traditional fragrances are made and sold. Continue south half a block to **Casa-Museo del Libertador Simón Bolívar** (Mercaderes #160, tel. 07/861-3988; Tues.-Sat. 9 A.M.-5 P.M., Sun. 9 A.M.-1 P.M.; CUC1), displaying cultural works and art from Venezuela. The collection includes portraits of the "Great Liberator," ceremonial swords, coins minted in his honor, and paintings by contemporary artists. Bolívar stayed here in March 1799 and is commemorated in the small *Plaza de Bolívar* at the corner of Mercaderes and Obrapía.

Across the street is the **Armería 9 de Abril** (Mercaderes #157, tel. 07/861-8080; Mon.-Sat. 9 A.M.-5 P.M.; CUC1), a museum that commemorates four members of Castro's 26th July Movement killed in an assault on the armory on April 9, 1958.

Crossing Lamparilla, peek in at the **Hostal Conde de Villanueva**, one of Havana's finest boutique hotels. One block south, the corner of Mercaderes and Amargura is known as the *Cruz Verde* – green cross – as it was the first stop on the annual Via Crucis pilgrimage. Today it houses the **Casa del Chocolate** (tel. 07/866-4431; daily 10 A.M.-8:30 P.M.), selling chocolate rolls and beverages and featuring a museum collection of porcelains and wall pieces relating the history of chocolate.

Midway down this curling block you'll pass **Mesón de la Flota**, a Spanish *bodega* with live flamenco. About 75 meters beyond, you'll arrive at Plaza Vieja.

The tallest building is the **Edificio Gómez Villa,** on the northeast corner. Take the elevator to the top floor for views over the plaza and to visit the **Cámara Oscura** (daily 9:30 A.M.–7 P.M.; CUC2), an optical reflection camera that revolves through 360 degrees and projects a real-time picture of Havana at 30-times magnification onto a two-meter-wide parabola housed in a completely darkened room.

Casa de los Condes de Jaruco

The most important building on the square is

A WALK AROUND PLAZA VIEJA

After visiting the **Cámara Oscura** (see the main text), begin your clockwise tour by following the shaded arcade along the east side of the plaza. Midway, you'll pass the **Casa de Juan Rico de Mata,** today the headquarters of **Fototeca** (Mercaderes #307, fototeca@ cubarte.cult.cu, tel. 07/862-2530; Tues.-Sat. 10 A.M.-5 P.M.), the state-run agency that promotes the work of Cuban photographers. It offers international photo exhibitions in the Salón Nacional de Fotografía. Note the ceramic wall mural designed by Amelia Peláez.

Next door, the **Planetario** (Mercaderes #309) was under construction in 2009, funded by the Japanese government. This will be a Cultural Center for Science and Technology, with a 70-seat planetarium, plus interactive exhibitions about the Universe. The four-level museum will top out with a state-of-the-art Goto telescope.

The old **Palacio Vienna Hotel** (also called the Palacio Cueto), on the southeast corner of Plaza Vieja, is a phenomenal piece of Gaudíesque art nouveau architecture dating from 1906. At last visit it was being restored as a deluxe hotel.

Moving to the south side, the Casa de Marqués de Prado Amero today houses the **Museo de Naipes** (Museum of Playing Cards, Muralla #101, tel. 07/860-1534; Tues.-Sat. 8:30 A.M.-5 P.M., Sun. 9 A.M.-2 P.M.; entrance by donation), displaying playing cards through the ages.

On the plaza's southwest corner, call in at the **Casa de los Condes de Jaruco** (see the main text) to view the various art galleries,

then cross San Ignacio and follow Muralla half a block to the **Tienda El Soldadito de Plumo** (Muralla #164; Mon.-Fri. 9 A.M.-5 P.M., Sat. 9 A.M.-1:30 P.M.), selling miniature metal soldiers. A large glass window lets you watch artists painting the pieces.

Return to the plaza, turn left to follow San Ignacio north, and cool off with a chilled beer brewed on-site in the **Taberna de la Muralla** (San Ignacio #364, tel. 07/866-4453; daily 11 A.M.-1 A.M.), in the former **Casa del Conde de Casa Lombillo.** The copper stills are displayed in the main bar, where a 1913 Ford delivery truck now sits and artwork by such famous Cuban artists as Kcho and Nelson Domínguez are displayed.

Fifty meters to the north, the **Casa del Conde de San Estéban de Cañongo** (San Ignacio #356, tel. 07/868-3561; Mon.-Fri. 9:30 A.M.-5:30 P.M., Sat. 9:30 A.M.-1 P.M.) opened in 2009 following restoration as a cultural center. Adjoining, on the northwest corner of the plaza, is the **Casa de las Hermanas Cárdenas,** recently restored and today housing the **Centro de Desarollo de Artes Visuales** (San Ignacio #352, tel. 07/862-2611; Tues.-Sat. 10 A.M.-6 P.M.). The inner courtyard is dominated by an intriguing sculpture by Alfredo Sosabravo. Art education classes are given on the second floor, reached via a wide wooden staircase. The top story has an art gallery.

Well worth the side trip is **Hotel Raquel** (San Ignacio, esq. Amargura, tel. 07/860-8280), one block north of the plaza. This recently restored hotel is an art deco and neoclassical jewel.

the House of the Counts of Jaruco (Muralla #107), on the southeast corner. This restored 18th-century mansion, "La Casona," as it is colloquially known, was built between 1733 and 1737 by the father of the future Count of Jaruco and is highlighted by mammoth doors opening into a cavernous courtyard surrounded by lofty archways festooned with hanging vines. Whimsical murals are painted on the walls, touched in splashy color by the undulating play of light through *mediopuntos* and by the shifting of shadows through *rejas.* It hosts offices of the Fondo Cubano de Bienes Culturales (tel. 07/860-8577). Art galleries occupy the downstairs rooms (Tues.-Sat. 9 A.M.-5 P.M.).

Museo Histórico de las Ciencias Naturales Carlos Finlay

Physicians and scientists inclined to a busman's holiday might walk one block west and one north of the plaza and check out the Museum of Natural History (Cuba #460, e/ Amargura y Brasil, tel. 07/863-4824; Mon.–Fri. 9 A.M.–5 P.M., Sat. 9 A.M.–3 P.M.; CUC2). Dating from 1868 and once the headquarters of the Academy of Medical, Physical, and Natural Sciences, today it contains a pharmaceutical collection and tells the tales of Cuban scientists' discoveries and innovations. The Cuban scientist Dr. Finlay is honored, of course; it was he who on August 14, 1881, discovered that yellow fever is transmitted by the *Aedes aegipti* mosquito. The museum also contains a medical library of 95,000 volumes and, on the third floor, a reconstructed period pharmacy.

Adjoining the museum to the north is the **Convento y Iglesia de San Francisco el Nuevo** (Cuba, esq. Amargura, tel. 07/861-8490; Mon.–Thurs. 9 A.M.–6 P.M., Sun. 8 A.M.–1 P.M.; free), completed in 1633 for the Augustine friars. It was consecrated anew in 1842 when it was given to the Franciscans, who rebuilt it in renaissance style in 1847. The church has a marvelous domed altar and nave.

SOUTHERN HABANA VIEJA

The mostly residential southern half of Habana Vieja, south of Calle Brasil, was the ecclesiastical center of Havana during the colonial era and is studded with churches and convents. Most have been restored, or are in the process of being so. Before the Revolution, this was also Havana's Jewish quarter.

Southern Habana Vieja is enclosed by Avenida del Puerto, which swings along the harborfront and becomes Avenida San Pedro, then Avenida Leonor Pérez, then Avenida Desamparados as it curves around to Avenida de Bélgica (colloquially called Egido). The waterfront boulevard is overshadowed by warehouses. Here were the old P&O docks where the ships from Miami and Key West used to dock and where Pan American World Airways had its terminal when it was still flying the old clipper flying-boats. Before World War II, when the U.S. Navy took over the docks, Calle San Isidro, which runs inland perpendicular to Desamparados, had been lined with brothels.

Calle Egido

Egido follows the hollow once occupied by Habana Vieja's ancient walls. It is a continuation of Monserrate and flows downhill to the harbor. The **Puerta de la Tenaza** (Egido, esq. Fundición) is the only ancient city gate still standing; a plaque inset within a still extant

HAVANA'S CITY WALLS

Construction of Havana's fortified city walls began on February 3, 1674. They ran along the western edge of the bay and, on the landward side, stood between today's Calle Egido, Monserrate, and Zulueta. Under the direction of engineer Juan de Siscaras, African slaves labored for 23 years to build the 1.4-meter-thick, 10-meter-tall city wall that was intended to ring the entire city, using rocks hauled in from the coast. The 4,892-meter-long wall was completed in 1697, with a perimeter of five kilometers. The damage inflicted by the British artillery in 1762 was repaired in 1797, when the thick wall attained its final shape. It formed an irregular polygon with nine defensive bastions with sections of

wall in between, and moats and steep drops to delay assault by enemy troops. In its first stage it had just two entrances (nine more were added later), opened each morning upon the sound of a single cannon and closed at night the same way.

As time went on, the *intramuros* (the city within the walls) burst its confines. In 1841, Havana authorities petitioned the Spanish Crown for permission to demolish the walls. Just 123 years after the walls went up, they came down again. The demolition began in 1863, when African slave-convicts were put to work to destroy what their forefathers had built. The demolition wasn't completed until well into the 20th century. Only fragments remain.

JEWS IN CUBA

Today, Havana's Jewish community (La Comunidad Hebrea, www.chcuba.org) is thought to number only about 1,300, about five percent of its prerevolutionary size, when it supported five synagogues and a college.

The first Jew in Cuba, Luis de Torres, arrived with Columbus in 1492 as the explorer's translator. He was followed in the 16th century by Jews escaping persecution at the hands of the Spanish Inquisition. Later, Ashkenazic Jews from Florida founded the United Hebrew Congregation in 1906, and Turkish Jews flocking to avoid World War I concentrated in southern Habana Vieja, many starting out in Cuba selling ties and cloth. Other Jews emigrating from Eastern Europe passed through Cuba en route to the United States in significant numbers until the United States slammed its doors in 1924, after which they settled in Cuba. They were relatively poor compared to the earlier Jewish immigrants and were disparagingly called *polacos*.

Sephardic Jews came later and were profoundly religious. They formed social clubs, opened their own schools, and married their own. By contrast, many Ashkenazic men married Cuban (Catholic) women and eventually were assimilated into Cuban society, says author Robert M. Levine. The Ashkenazim were fired with socialist ideals and were prominent in the founding of both the labor and Cuban Communist movements.

Cuba seems to have been relatively free of anti-Semitism (Batista was a friend to Jews fleeing Nazi Europe). Levine, however, records how during the late 1930s the U.S. government bowed to isolationist, labor, and anti-Semitic pressures at home and convinced the Cuban government to turn back European Jews. This sordid chapter in U.S. history is reflected in the tragic story of the SS *St. Louis* and its 937 passengers trying to escape Nazi Germany in 1939. The ship languished in Havana harbor for a week while U.S. and Cuban officials deliberated on letting passengers disembark; tragically, entry was refused, and the passengers were sent back to Europe and their fate.

By the 1950s, about 20,000 Jews lived in Havana, concentrated around Calle Belén and Calle Acosta, which bustled with kosher bakeries, cafés, and clothes stores. Jews knew the lessons of Nazi Germany and the totalitarian regimes of Eastern Europe and so, following the Revolution, became part of the Cuban diaspora. About 95 percent of them fled, although a few joined the Castro government; two became early cabinet members. Some 500 Cuban Jews were secretly allowed to emigrate to Israel beginning in 1994.

Although the Castro government discouraged Jews from practicing their faith, Jewish religious schools were the only parochial schools allowed to remain open after the Revolution and the government even provided school buses. The government has always made matzo available and even authorized a kosher butcher shop on Calle Acosta to supply meat for observant Jews. And Jews are the only Cubans permitted to buy beef, a nod to restrictions on pork. The Jewish community also has its own cemetery, in Guanabacoa, dating from 1910. However, the community has no rabbi and marriages and circumcisions must often wait for foreign religious officials passing through Havana.

Still, a renaissance in the Jewish faith is occurring. Synagogues have been refurbished and new ones opened. In 1994, the first bar mitzvah took place in over 12 years and the first formal bris in over five years. And the Hebrew Sunday School in the Patronato teaches Hebrew and Yiddish.

JEWISH HERITAGE SITES

The Cuban government proposes to reconstruct Habana Vieja's Jewish quarter, having made a start by rehabilitating the **Sinagoga Adath Israel** (Picota #52, esq. Acosta, tel. 07/861-3495; daily 8 A.M.–noon and 5–8 P.M.), which now sports a new wooden altar carved

HAVANA

© CHRISTOPHER P. BAKER

entrance to the United Hebrew Congregation Cemetery, Guanabacoa

with scenes from Jerusalem and historic Havana. Services are Monday-Friday 8 A.M. and 6 P.M., Saturday at 9 A.M. and 6 P.M., and Sunday at 9 A.M.

Chevet Achim (Inquisidor, e/ Luz y Santa Clara, tel. 07/832-6623) was built in 1914 and is the oldest synagogue in Cuba. The building is owned and maintained by the Centro Sefardi, but is not used for ritual or community purposes. It can be viewed by appointment.

In Vedado, the **Casa de la Comunidad Hebrea de Cuba** (Calle I #241, e/ 13 y 15, tel. 07/832-8953; Mon.-Sat. 9:30 A.M.-5 P.M.) works to preserve Cuba's Hebrew traditions and contains an active community center and a large library on Judaica. Services at the adjacent **Bet Shalon Sinagogo** are Friday at 7:30 P.M. (May-Sept.) or 6 P.M. (Oct.-Apr.) and Saturday at 10 A.M. (year-round). Nearby, the rundown **Centro Sefardí** (Calle 17 #462, esq. E, tel. 07/832-6623) is a Conservative Jewish synagogue completed in 1960.

Guanabacoa, on the east side of Havana harbor, has two Jewish cemeteries. The **Cementerio de la Comunidad Religiosa Ebrea Adath Israel** (Av. de la Independencia Este, e/ Obelisco y Puente, tel. 07/797-6644; Mon.-Fri. 8-11 A.M. and 2-5 P.M.), also known as the

United Hebrew Congregation Cemetery, is for Ashkenazim. It dates from 1912 and is entered by an ocher-colored Spanish-colonial frontispiece with a Star of David. A **Holocaust memorial** immediately to the left of the gate stands in somber memory of the millions who lost their lives to the Nazis: "Buried in this place are several cakes of soap made from Hebrew human fat, a fraction of the six million victims of Nazi savagery in the 20th century. May their remains rest in peace."

Behind the Ashkenazic cemetery is the **Cementerio de la Unión Hebrea Chevet Ahim** (Calle G, e/ 5ta y Final, tel. 07/797-5866; daily 7 A.M.-5 P.M.), for Sephardic Jews. It too has a memorial to the Holocaust victims; turn north off Avenida de la Independencia Este at Avenida de los Mártires (4ta) to reach it.

JEWISH AID ORGANIZATIONS

The following organizations send humanitarian aid to Cuba and/or offer organized trips: the **Cuban Jewish Relief Project** (1831 Murray Ave. #208, Pittsburgh, PA 15217, 412/521-2390, www.cubanjewishrelief.org); the **Cuba-America Jewish Mission** (1442A Walnut St. #224, Berkeley, CA 94709, www.thecajm.org); and **Jewish Solidarity** (100 Beacom Blvd., Miami, FL 33135, 305/642-1600, http://jewishcuba.org/solidarity).

RESOURCES

Books on the subject include *Jewish Community of Cuba: The Golden Years, 1906-1958*, by Jay Levinson (Westview Publishing, 2006); *The Chosen Island: Jews in Cuba*, by Maritza Corrales (Salsedo Press, 2005); and *Tropical Diaspora: The Jewish Experience in Cuba*, by Robert M. Levine (University Press of Florida, 1993).

Also look for screenings of the documentary films *Havana Nagila: The Jews of Cuba*, by Laura Paull, and *Next Year in Havana*, by Lori Beraha.

remnant of the wall shows a map of the old city and walls. About 100 meters south, on Avenida de Puerto, is the **Monumento Mártires del Vapor La Coubre,** made of twisted metal fragments of *La Coubre,* the French cargo ship that exploded in Havana harbor on March 4, 1960 (the vessel was carrying armaments for the Castro government). The monument honors the seamen who died in the explosion.

Egido is lined with once-beautiful buildings constructed during the mid-19th century, and today greatly dilapidated. Egido's masterpiece is the **Estación Central de Ferrocarril** (esq. Arsenal), or Terminal de Trenes, Havana's Venetian-style railway station. Designed in 1910, it blends Spanish Revival and Italian Renaissance styles and features twin towers displaying the shields of Havana and Cuba. It is built atop the former Arsenal, or Spanish naval shipyard.

On the station's north side is a small shady plaza—**Parque de los Agrimensores** (Park of the Surveyors)—pinned by a large remnant of the **Cortina de la Habana,** the old city wall. The park is now populated by ancient steam trains retired from hauling sugar cane. *Colectivo* taxis—old *yanqui* jalopies—park here, awaiting custom.

Museo Casa Natal de José Martí

The birthplace of the nation's preeminent national hero (Leonor Pérez #314, esq. Av. de Bélgica, tel. 07/861-3778; Tues.–Sat. 9 A.M.–5 P.M.; entrance CUC1, guide CUC1, cameras CUC2, videos CUC10), one block south of the railway station, sits at the end of a street named after Martí's mother. This simple house with terra-cotta tile floors is a shrine for Cubans. The national hero and leader of the independence movement was born on January 28, 1853, and spent the first four years of his life here. The house is splendidly kept, with many of his personal effects, including a beautiful lacquered *escritorio* (writing desk) and a broad-brimmed Panama hat given to him by Ecuadorian President Eloy Alfaro (Panama hats are made in Ecuador). Many of his original texts, poems, and sketches are on display.

There's even a lock of the hero's hair from when he was a child.

Plaza del Cristo

Plaza del Cristo lies at the west end of Amargua, between Lamparilla and Brasil, one block east of Avenida de Bélgica (Monserrate). It was here that Wormold, the vacuum-cleaner salesman turned secret agent, was "swallowed up among the pimps and lottery sellers of the Havana noon" in Graham Greene's *Our Man in Havana.* Wormold and his wayward daughter Millie lived at the fictional 37 Lamparilla.

The plaza is dominated by the tiny **Iglesia de Santo Cristo Buen Viaje** (Villegas, e/ Amargura y Lamparilla, tel. 07/863-1767; daily 9 A.M.–noon), dating from 1732, but with a Franciscan hermitage—called Humilladero chapel—dating from 1640. Buen Viaje was the final point of the *Via Crucis* (the Procession of the Cross) held each Lenten Friday and beginning at the Iglesia de San Francisco de Asís. The church, which was named for its popularity among sailors and travelers who used to

a 1951 Chevrolet Bel Air in Plaza del Cristo

© CHRISTOPHER P. BAKER

pray here for safe voyages, has an impressive cross-beamed wooden ceiling, stained-glass windows, and exquisite altars, including one to the Virgen de la Caridad showing three boatmen being saved from the tempest.

Iglesia y Convento de Santa Teresa de Jesús

This handsome church and adjoining convent (Brasil, esq. Compostela, tel. 07/861-1445), two blocks east of Plaza del Cristo, was built by the Carmelites in 1705, with separate baroque doorways for each. The church still performs its original function, although the convent ceased to operate as such in 1929, when the nuns were moved out and the building was converted into a series of homes.

Across the road is the **Droguería Sarrá** (Brasil, e/ Compostela y Habana, tel. 07/866-7554; daily 9 A.M.–6 P.M.; free), a fascinating apothecary—also known as Farmacia La Reunión—with paneled cabinets still stocked with herbs and pharmaceuticals in colorful old bottles and ceramic jars.

Iglesia y Convento de Nuestra Señora de Belén

The Church and Convent of Our Lady of

GRAHAM GREENE: OUR MAN IN HAVANA

No contemporary novel quite captures the tawdry intrigue and disreputable aura of Batista's Havana than does Graham Greene's *Our Man in Havana*, published in 1958 and set amid the torrid events of Havana in 1957.

The comic tale tells of Wormold, an English vacuum-cleaner salesman based in Havana and short of money. His daughter has reached an expensive age, so when approached by Hawthorne, he accepts the offer of £300 a month and becomes Agent 59200/5, MI6's man in Havana. To keep his job, he files bogus reports and dreams up military apparatuses from vacuum-cleaner parts. Unfortunately, Wormold becomes trapped by his own deceit and the workings of a hopelessly corrupt city and society.

Graham Greene (1904–91) was already a respected author when he was recruited to work for the Foreign Office, serving the years 1941–43 in Sierra Leone, Africa. In the last years of the war, he worked for the British Secret Service dealing with counterespionage on the Iberian Peninsula, where he learned how the Nazi Abwehr (the German Secret Service) sent home false reports – perfect material for his novel. He traveled widely and based many of his works, including *Our Man in Havana*, on his experiences. He visited Havana several times in the 1950s and was disturbed by the mutilations and torture practiced by Batista's police officers and by social ills such as racial discrimination: "Every smart bar and restaurant was called a club so that a Negro could be legally excluded." But he confessed to enjoying the "louche atmosphere" of Havana and seems to have savored the fleshpots completely. "I came there... for the brothel life, the roulette in every hotel," he later wrote.

Castro condoned *Our Man in Havana* but complained that it didn't do justice to the ruthlessness of the Batista regime. Greene agreed: "Alas, the book did me little good with the new rulers in Havana. In poking fun at the British Secret Service, I had minimized the terror of Batista's rule. I had not wanted too black a background for a light-hearted comedy, but those who had suffered during the years of dictatorship could hardly be expected to appreciate that my real subject was the absurdity of the British agent and not the justice of a revolution." Nonetheless, Castro permitted the screen version, starring Alec Guinness as Wormold, to be filmed in Havana in 1959.

Greene returned to Cuba in the years 1963–66. Although initially impressed by Castro's war on illiteracy (he called it "a great crusade"), he later soured after witnessing the persecution of homosexuals, intellectuals, and Catholics. Perhaps for this reason, the author isn't commemorated in Cuba in any way.

Bethlehem (Compostela y Luz, tel. 07/860-3150; Mon.–Sat. 9 A.M.–5 P.M., Sun. 9 A.M.–1 P.M. free) is the largest religious complex in Havana, occupying an entire block. The convent, completed in 1718, was built to house the first nuns to arrive in Havana and later served as a refuge for convalescents. In 1842, Spanish authorities ejected the religious order and turned the church into a government office before making it over to the Jesuits. They in turn established a college for the sons of the aristocracy. The Jesuits were the nation's official weather forecasters and in 1858 erected the Observatorio Real (Royal Observatory) atop the tower. It was in use until 1925. At last visit, the convent was still in the process of being renovated.

The church and convent are linked to contiguous buildings across the street by an arched walkway—the Arco de Belén (Arch of Bethlehem)—spanning Acosta.

Iglesia y Convento de Santa Clara de Asís

The Convent of Saint Clair of Assisi (Cuba #610, e/ Luz y Sol, tel. 07/866-9327; Mon.–Fri. 9 A.M.–5 P.M.; CUC2), two blocks east of Belén, is a massive former nunnery completed in 1644. The nuns moved out in 1922. It is a remarkable building, with a lobby full of beautiful period pieces. Its cloistered courtyard, awash in light, is surrounded by columns, one of which is entwined by the roots of a *capulí* tree. Note the 17th-century fountain of a Samaritan woman, and the beautiful cloister roof carved with geometric designs—a classic *alfarje*—in the Salón Plenario, a marble-floored hall of imposing stature. Wooden carvings abound. The second cloister contains the so-called Sailor's House, built by a wealthy ship owner for his daughter, whom he failed to dissuade from a life of asceticism.

Iglesia Parroquial del Espíritu Santo

The Parish Church of the Holy Ghost (Acosta #161, esq. Cuba, tel. 07/862-3410; Mon.–Fri. 8:30 A.M.–4 P.M.), two blocks south of Santa Clara de Asís, is Havana's oldest church, dating from 1638 (the circa-1674 central nave and facade, and circa-1720 Gothic vault are later additions), when it was a hermitage for the devotions of free *negros*. Later King Charles III issued a royal decree giving the right of asylum here to anyone hunted by the authorities, a privilege no longer bestowed.

The church reveals many surprises, including a gilded, carved wooden pelican in a niche in the baptistery. The sacristy, where parish archives dating back through the 17th century are preserved, boasts an enormous cupboard full of baroque silver staffs and incense holders. Catacombs to each side of the nave are held up by subterranean tree trunks. You can explore the eerie vault that runs under the chapel, with the niches still containing the odd bone as well as the body of Bishop Gerónimo Valdés, who remained in a kind of limbo, his whereabouts unknown, until he turned up, buried under the floor, during a restoration in 1936. The sturdy tower holds four bells; steps lead up to the gallery.

Iglesia y Convento de Nuestra Señora de la Merced

Two blocks south of Espíritu Santo is Our Lady of Mercy (Cuba #806, esq. Merced, tel. 07/863-8873; daily 8 A.M.–noon and 3–6 P.M.), a small handsome church and convent with an ornate interior containing romantic dome paintings and the Capilla de Lourdes (Lourdes Chapel), also with early-20th-century religious frescoes. The church, begun in 1755, has strong Afro-Cuban connections (the Virgin of Mercy is also Obatalá, goddess of earth and purity), and it is not unusual to see devotees of *santería* kneeling in prayer. Each September 24, scores of worshippers cram in for the Virgen de la Merced's feast day. More modest celebrations are held on the 24th of every other month.

Alameda de Paula

This 100-meter-long raised promenade runs alongside the waterfront boulevard between Luz and Leonor Pérez. It is lined with marble and iron street lamps. Midway along the Alameda stands a carved column with a fountain at its base, erected in 1847 in homage to the Spanish navy. It bears an unlikely Irish name: **Columna O'Donnell,** for the Capitán-General of Cuba, Leopoldo O'Donnell, who dedicated the monument. It is covered in relief work on a military theme and crowned by a lion with the arms of Spain in its claws.

At the southern end of the Alameda, **Iglesia de San Francisco de Paula** (San Ignacio y Leonor Pérez, tel. 07/860-4210; daily 9 A.M.–5 P.M.) studs circular Plazuela de Paula. The quaint, restored church features marvelous artworks including stained-glass pieces. It is used for baroque and chamber concerts.

On the waterfront side of the Alameda, just south of the church, is the **Feria de Artesanía,** the city's main artisans' market, which relocated in late 2009 from Calle Tacón.

Sacra Catedral Ortodoxa Rusa

Opened in October 2008, this beautiful, gleaming white, waterfront Russian Orthodox church (Avenida del Puerto and Calle San Pedro; daily 9 A.M.–5:45 P.M.), officially the Iglesia Virgen de María de Kazan, whisks you allegorically to Moscow with its bulbous, golden minarets. No photos are allowed inside, where a gold altar and chandeliers hang above gray marble floors. Exquisite!

Sights – Centro Habana and Cerro

Centro Habana (Central Havana—pop. 175,000) lies west of the Paseo del Prado and south of the Malecón. The region is a 19th-century extension of Habana Vieja and evolved following demolition of the city walls in 1863. Prior, it had served as a glacis. The buildings are deep and tall, of four or five stories, built mostly as apartment units. Hence, the population and street life are denser. Laid out in a near-perfect grid, Centro is mostly residential, with few sights of note. A notable exception is the remnants of Chinatown—Barrio Chino—delineated by Calles Zanja, Dragones, Salud, Rayo, San Nicolás, and Manrique.

The major west–east thoroughfares are the Malecón to the north, and Zanja and Avenida Salvador Allende through the center; plus Calles Neptuno and San Rafael between the Malecón and Zanja. Three major thoroughfares run perpendicular, north–south: Calzada de Infanta, forming the western boundary; Padre Varela, down the center; and Avenida de Italia (Galiano), farther east.

In prerevolutionary days, Centro Habana hosted Havana's red-light district, and prostitutes roamed such streets as the ill-named Calle Virtudes (Virtues). Then, too, Neptuno and San Rafael formed the retail heart of the city. In recent years, they have regained some of their life and the famous department stores of prerevolutionary days have reopened; many still bear prerevolutionary neon signs promoting U.S. brand names from yesteryear.

Many houses, however, are in a tumble-down state—about one in three houses has collapsed—conjuring up images of what Dresden, Germany, must have looked like after it was bombed in World War II.

South of Centro, the land rises gently to Cerro, which developed during the last century as the place to retire for the torrid midsummer months; many wealthy families maintained two homes in Havana—one in town, another on the cooler *cerro* ("hill"). The area is replete with once-stately *quintas* (summer homes) in neoclassical, Beaux-Arts, and art nouveau styles. Alas, the region is terribly deteriorated, and the majority of buildings transcend sordid.

Caution is required. Muggings commonly occur in these districts.

THE MALECÓN (CENTRO)

Officially known as Avenida Antonio Maceo, and more properly the Muro de Malecón (literally "embankment," or "seawall"), Havana's seafront boulevard winds dramatically along the Atlantic shoreline between the Castillo de San Salvador de la Punta and the Río

Almendares. The six-lane seafront boulevard was designed as a jetty wall in 1857 by Cuban engineer Francisco de Albear but not laid out until 1902 by U.S. governor General Woods. It took 50 years to reach the Río Almendares, almost five miles to the west.

The Malecón is lined with once-glorious high-rise houses, each exuberantly distinct from the next. Unprotected by seaworthy paint since the Revolution, they have proven incapable of withstanding the salt spray that crashes over the seawall in great airy clouds and then floats off in rainbows. Their facades are now decrepit, while the broad limestone walkway is pitted and broken. Many buildings have already collapsed, and those that were painted in haste for the pope's visit in 1998 have faded again. An on-going restoration seems to make little headway against the elements, although wrought-iron street lamps in classical style have gone up.

All along the shore are the worn remains of square baths—known as the "Elysian Fields"—hewn from the rocks below the seawall, originally with separate areas for men, women, and *negros*. These **Baños del Mar** preceded construction of the Malecón. Each is about 12 feet square and six to eight feet deep, with rock steps for access and a couple of portholes through which the waves wash in and out.

The Malecón offers a microcosm of Havana life: the elderly walking their dogs; the shiftless selling cigars and cheap sex to tourists; the young passing rum among friends; fishermen (*neumáticos*) tending their lines and casting off on giant inner tubes; and always, scores of couples courting and necking. The Malecón is known as "Havana's sofa" and acts, wrote Claudia Lightfoot, as "the city's drawing room, office, study, and often bedroom." All through the night, lovers' murmurings mingle with the crash of the waves.

The Malecón—the setting for spontaneous riots in the early 1990s—is also a barometer of the political state of Havana. During times of tension, the police presence is abnormally strong and the Malecón becomes eerily empty.

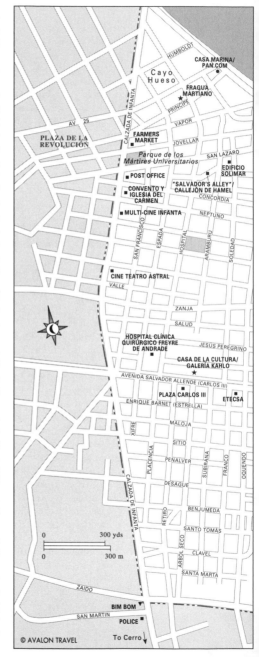

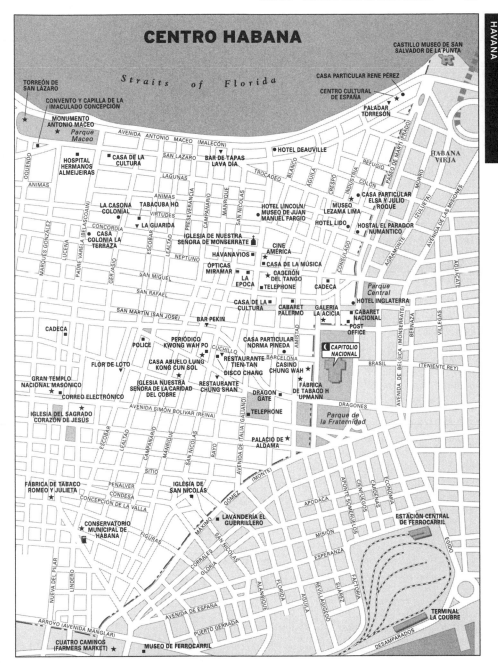

CENTRO HABANA

CASTILLO MUSEO DE SAN SALVADOR DE LA PUNTA

Straits of Florida

TORREÓN DE SAN LÁZARO

CASA PARTICULAR RENE PÉREZ

CENTRO CULTURAL DE ESPAÑA

CONVENTO Y CAPILLA DE LA IMACULADO CONCEPCIÓN

PALADAR TORRESÓN

MONUMENTO ANTONIO MACEO

Parque Maceo

AVENIDA ANTONIO MACEO (MALECÓN)

HOTEL DEAUVILLE

HABANA VIEJA

OQUENDO

REFUGIO

PASEO DE MARTÍ (PRADO)

MORRO

HOSPITAL HERMANOS ALMEIJEIRAS

CASA DE LA CULTURA

SAN LÁZARO

BAR DE TAPAS LAVA DÍA

TROCADERO

BLANCO

AGUILA

CRESPO

INDUSTRIA

COLÓN

ANIMAS

LAGUNAS

ANIMAS

TABACUBA HÚ

MANRIQUE

SAN NICOLAS

HOTEL LINCOLN/ MUSEO DE JUAN MANUEL FARGIO

MUSEO LEZAMA LIMA

CASA PARTICULAR ELSA Y JULIO ROQUE

IZQUIERDA

AVENIDA DE LAS MISIONES

LA CASONA COLONIAL

PERSEVERANCIA

CAMPANARIO

VIRTUDES

HOTEL LIDO

HOSTAL EL PARADOR NUMÁNTICO

MARQUES GONZALEZ

LUCENA

PADRE VAREA (BELASCOAIN)

CONCORDIA

CASA COLONIA LA TERRAZA

LA GUARIDA

ESCOBAR

LEALTAD

NEPTUNO

IGLESIA DE NUESTRA SEÑORA DE MONSERRATE

CONSULADO

AGRAMONTE

GERVASIO

SAN MIGUEL

HAVANAVIOS

CINE AMÉRICA

ÓPTICAS MIRAMAR

CASA DE LA MÚSICA

AGUACATE

SAN RAFAEL

LA EPOCA

CASERÓN DEL TANGO

TELEPHONE

CADECA

Parque Central

SAN MARTIN (SAN JOSÉ)

CASA DE LA CULTURA

CABARET PALERMO

GALERIA LA ACICIA

HOTEL INGLATERRA

BAR PEKIN

AMISTAD

CABARET NACIONAL

BERNAZA

VILLEGAS

CADECA

POST OFFICE

POLICE

PERIÓDICO KWONG WAH PO

CUCHILLO

CASA PARTICULAR NORMA PINEDA

BARCELONA

CAPITOLIO NACIONAL

BRASIL

(TENIENTE REY)

FLOR DE LOTO

CASA ABUELO LUNG KONG CUN SOL

RESTAURANTE TIEN-TAN

DISCO CHANG

CASINO CHUNG WAH

GRAN TEMPLO NACIONAL MASÓNICO

CORREO ELECTRÓNICO

IGLESIA NUESTRA SEÑORA DE LA CARIDAD DEL COBRE

RESTAURANTE CHUNG SHAN

DRAGON GATE

FÁBRICA DE TABACO H UPMANN

AVENIDA DE BELGICA (MONSERRATE)

IGLESIA DEL SAGRADO CORAZÓN DE JESÚS

ESCOBAR

LEALTAD

CAMPANARIO

MANRIQUE

SAN NICOLAS

RAYO

AVENIDA SIMÓN BOLIVAR (REINA)

TELEPHONE

AVENIDA DE ITALIA (GALIANO)

DRAGONES

Parque de la Fraternidad

PALACIO DE ALDAMA

SITIO

FÁBRICA DE TABACO ROMEO Y JULIETA

PENALVER

CONDESA

CONCEPCION DE LA VALLA

IGLESIA DE SAN NICOLAS

GOMEZ

(MONTE)

APODACA

CIENFUEGOS

CÁRDENAS

ECONOMIA

ESTACIÓN CENTRAL DE FERROCARRIL

CONSERVATORIO MUNICIPAL DE HABANA

FIGURAS

MAXIMO

LAVANDERÍA EL GUERRILLERO

SAN NICOLAS

MISIÓN

APONTE SOMERUELOS

NUEVA DEL PILAR

LINDERO

CORRALES

GLORIA

ESPERANZA

FACTORIA

SUÁREZ

REVILLAGIGEDO

EGIDO

ARROYO (AVENIDA MANGLAR)

AVENIDA DE ESPAÑA

PUERTO GERRADA

ALAMBIQUE

FLORIDA

AGUILA

DESAMPARADOS

TERMINAL LA COUBRE

CUATRO CAMINOS (FARMERS MARKET)

MUSEO DE FERROCARRIL

Every October 26, schoolchildren are bussed here to throw flowers over the seawall in memory of revolutionary leader Camilo Cienfuegos, killed in a mysterious air crash on that day in 1959.

Parque Maceo

Dominating the Malecón to the west, at the foot of Avenida Padre Varela, is the massive bronze **Monumento Antonio Maceo,** atop a marble base in a plaza with a fountain. The classical monument was erected in 1916 in honor of the mulatto general and hero of the Wars of Independence who was known as the "Bronze Titan." The motley tower that stands at the west end of the plaza is the 17th-century **Torreón de San Lázaro,** with loopholes for snipers aiming along the Malecón. Although it looks fairly modern, it was built in 1665 to guard the former cove of San Lázaro.

To the south, the **Hospital Hermanos Almeijeiras** looms over the park. The **Convento y Capilla de la Inmaculada Concepción** (San Lázaro #805, e/ Oquendo y Lucena, tel. 07/878-8404; Mon.–Sun. 9 A.M.–5 P.M.) is immediately west of the hospital. This beautiful church and convent was built in Gothic style in 1874 and features notable stained-glass windows and a painted altar.

BARRIO CAYO HUESO

Immediately west of the Plaza Antonio Maceo is a triangular area bordered by the Malecón, San Lázaro, and Calzada de Infanta, forming the northwest corner of Centro Habana. Known as Barrio Cayo Hueso, the region dates from the early 20th century, when tenement homes were erected atop what had been the Espada cemetery (hence the name, Cay of Bones). It boasts several art deco inspirations, such as the **Edificio Solimar** (Soledad #205, e/ San Lázaro y Ánimas) apartment complex, built in 1944.

Before the revolution, the pseudo-castle at the corner of Calle 25 and the Malecón was the **Casa Marina,** Havana's most palatial brothel. Carousing English travel writer Graham Greene was among its celebrity habitués.

Museo Fragua Martiana

Hallowed ground to Cubans, this small museum (Principe #108, esq. Hospital, tel. 07/870-7338; Mon.–Fri. 9 A.M.–4:30 P.M., Sat. 9 A.M.–1 P.M.; free) occupies the site of the former San Lázaro quarry, where national hero José Martí and fellow prisoners were forced to break rocks. The museum, whose name roughly translates as Museum of Martí's Forging, is dedicated to Martí, and displays manuscripts, and even shackles. To its rear, the quarry has been turned into a garden, with a life-size bronze statue of Martí.

"Salvador's Alley"

Almost every dance enthusiast in-the-know gravitates during their stay to **Callejón de Hamel** (e/ Aramburu y Hospital), an alley where local artist Salvador González Escalona has adorned walls with evocative murals in sun-drenched yellow, burnt orange, and blazing reds, inspired by *santería.* The alley features a *santería* shrine and fantastical totemic sculptures. González, a bearded artist with an eye for self-promotion, has an eclectic gallery, **Estudio-Galería Fambá** (Callejón de Hamel #1054, tel. 07/878-1661, eliasasef@yahoo.es; daily 9:30 A.M.–6 P.M.). On Sundays, he hosts Afro-Cuban rumbas on weekends.

Nearby, **Parque de los Mártires Universitarios** (Infanta, e/ Calles Jovellar y San Lázaro), one block west of Callejón de Hamel, honors students who were murdered or otherwise lost their lives during the fights against the Machado and Batista regimes.

Convento y Iglesia del Carmen

Soaring over Calle Infanta, about 100 meters south of San Lázaro, is one of Havana's largest and most impressive churches (Infanta, e/ Neptuno y Concordia, tel. 07/878-5168; Mon.–Sat. 8–10 A.M. and 4–7 P.M., Sun. 7:30 A.M.–12:30 P.M. and 4:30–7:30 P.M.). Built in baroque fashion, the church and convent is capped by a 60.5-meter-tall tower atop which soars a 7.5-meter-tall sculpture of Our Lady of Carmen. Inside, the church features beautiful stained glass and statuary.

GALIANO

This broad boulevard, lined with arcaded porticos, runs south from the Malecón to Avenida Salvador Allende and is Centro's main north–south artery.

The Hotel Lincoln (Galiano, e/ Ánimas y Virtudes) was where Argentina's world-champion racecar driver Fangio was kidnapped by Castro's revolutionaries in 1958 during the Cuban Grand Prix. Room #810 is today the **Museo de Juan Manuel Fangio,** with photos and magazines from the period presenting a predictably one-sided version of the affair. Also on an Argentinian theme, fans of tango might check out the **Caserón del Tango** (Neptuno #303, e/ Águila y Italia, tel. 07/863-0097; daily 10 A.M.–8 P.M.), a tiny cultural center-cum-museum run by tango lover Edmundo Daubal in honor of the Argentinian dance.

Cine América

This cinema (Galiano #253, esq. Concordia, tel. 07/862-5416) dates from 1941 and is one of the world's great art deco theaters, albeit severely deteriorated. The foyer features a terrazzo floor inlaid with zodiac motifs and a map of the world, with Cuba at the center in polished brass. Cater-corner, the rarely open **Iglesia de Nuestra Señora de Monserrate** dates from 1843, where Padre Fernando de la Vega runs Proyecto SIDA de Cuba (the Cuba AIDS Project) for HIV/AIDS patients.

Museo Lezama Lima

Literature buffs might detour to this museum (Trocadero #162, e/ Crespo y Industria, tel. 07/863-4161; Tues.–Sun. 9 A.M.–5 P.M., Sun. 9 A.M.–1 P.M.; entrance CUC2, guide CUC1), four blocks east of Galiano, in the former home of writer José Lezama Lima. The novelist is most famous for *Paradiso,* an autobiographical, sexually explicit, homoerotic baroque novel that viewed Cuba as a "paradise lost" and was eventually made into a renowned movie. Lima fell afoul of Fidel Castro and became a recluse until his death in 1975.

BARRIO CHINO

The first Chinese immigrants to Cuba arrived in 1847 as indentured laborers. Over ensuing decades, as many as 150,000 Chinese may have arrived to work the fields. They were contracted to labor for eight years for miserable wages insufficient to buy their return. Most stayed, and many intermarried with blacks. The Sino-Cuban descendants of those who worked off their indenture gravitated to Centro Habana, where they settled in the zones bordering the Zanza Real, the aqueduct that channeled water to the city. They were later joined by other Chinese fleeing persecution, including a wealthy group of California Chinese who arrived with investment opportunities in mind. In time Havana's Chinese quarter, Barrio Chino, became the largest in Latin America—a mini-Beijing in the tropics.

In the decades preceding the Revolution, Barrio Chino evolved as a center of opium dens, brothels, peep shows, and sex clubs. The vast majority of Chinese left Cuba immediately following the Revolution, after which those who stayed were encouraged to become "less Chinese and more Cuban." Today, Barrio Chino is a mere shadow of its former self, with about 400 native-born Chinese and perhaps 2,000 descendants still resident.

In 1995, the government of China funded a **Pórtico Chino** (Dragon Gate) across Calle Dragones, between Amistad and Aguila, announcing visitors' entry from the east.

Nearby, the **Iglesia Nuestra Señora de la Caridad del Cobre** (Manrique #570, esq. Salud, tel. 07/861-0945; Tues.–Fri. 7:30 A.M.–6 P.M., Sat. 7:30 A.M.–noon, Sun. 7:30 A.M.–noon and 4–6 P.M.), erected in 1802, features exquisite statuary, stained-glass, and a gilt altar.

Callejón Cuchillo

Pedestrian-only "Knife Alley" is lined with Chinese restaurants and is aglow at night with Chinese lanterns. Ernest Hemingway used to eat at the no-longer-functioning Restaurante Pacífico (San Nicolás, esq. Cuchillo), as did Fidel Castro. "To get there," recalls

the Pórtico Chino, on Calle Dragones, at the entrance to Barrio Chino

© CHRISTOPHER P. BAKER

Hemingway's son, Gregory, "you had to go up in an old elevator with a sliding iron grille for a door. It stopped at every floor, whether you wanted it to or not. On the second floor there was a five-piece Chinese orchestra blaring crazy atonal music. ... Then you reached the third floor, where there was a whorehouse. ... The fourth floor was an opium den with pitifully wasted little figures curled up around their pipes."

Chinese "Casinos"

More than one dozen social associations work to promote Chinese culture (many Cuban-Chinese, for example, worship Cuan Cung, a red-faced, long-bearded deity synchronistically akin to Changó, the African warrior saint in *santería*). Visitors are welcome. The **Casa de Artes y Tradiciones Chinas** (Salud #313, e/ Gervasio y Escobar, tel. 07/863-9632; Mon.–Fri. 8:30 A.M.–5:30 P.M., Sat. 8:30 A.M.–noon) features a small gallery, and tai chi and dance classes are offered. The **Casa Abuelo Lung Kong Cun Sol** (Dragones #364, e/ Manrique y San Nicolás, tel. 07/862-5388 or 863-2061; daily noon–midnight) exists to support elders in the Chinese community. On the third floor is the **Templo San Fan Kong**, with an exquisitely carved gold-plated altar.

AVENIDAS SIMÓN BOLÍVAR AND SALVADOR ALLENDE (CARLOS III)

Avenida Simón Bolívar (formerly Avenida Reina) runs west from Parque de la Fraternidad. Simón Bolívar is lined with once-impressive colonial-era structures gone to ruin. Beyond Avenida Padre Varela (Belascoain), it broadens into a wide boulevard called Avenida Salvador Allende. The avenue was laid out in the early 19th century by Governor Tacón, when it was known officially as Carlos III.

The **Gran Templo Nacional Masónico** (Av. Salvador Allende, e/ Padre Varela y Lucena) was established in 1951 as Havana's Grand Masonic Temple. Though no longer a Freemason's lodge, it retains a fading mural in the lobby depicting the history of Masonry in Cuba.

Iglesia del Sagrado Corazón de Jesús

One of the few structures not seemingly on its last legs, the Church of the Sacred Heart of Jesus (Simón Bolívar, e/ Padre Varela y Gervasio, tel. 07/862-4979; daily 8 A.M.– noon and 4–7 P.M.) is a Gothic inspiration in stone that could have been transported from medieval England. It was built in 1922 with a beamed ceiling held aloft by great marbled columns. Gargoyles and Christian allegories adorn the exterior, featuring a 77-meter-tall spire topped by a bronze cross. The church boasts stained-glass windows and a soaring wooden altar.

CUATROS CAMINOS AND CERRO

South of Avenidas Simón Bolívar and Salvador Allende, the down-at-the-heels neighborhoods of southern Centro Habana extend into the *municipalidad* of Cerro. Still, the area has a few sights of interest, although caution is required when walking the streets.

Several key arterial roads meet at Cuatros Caminos, an all-important junction.

Cuatros Caminos

A photogenic delight for photographers, the Four Roads Farmers Market (tel. 07/870-5934; Tues.–Sat. 7 A.M.–6:30 P.M., Sun. 7 A.M.–2 P.M.) takes up the entire block between Máximo Gómez and Cristina (also called Avenida de la México), and Manglar Arroyo and Matadero. This much-dilapidated 19th-century market hall has functioned as such for two centuries and is worth a visit for its bustling color and ambience. Here you can buy live goats, geese, pig's heads, and all manner of fruits and veggies.

Museo de Ferrocarril

On the east side of Cristina, facing the market, is the Railway Museum (tel. 07/879-3546; Mon.–Sat. 9 A.M.–4:30 P.M., Sun. 9 A.M.– 12:30 P.M.; entrance CUC2, camera CUC5), housed in the former Estación Cristina and telling the history of rail in Cuba. You'd have to be a serious rail buff to get a thrill from the exhibits (from model trains to bells, signals, and even telegraph equipment). Sitting on rails in its lobby is an 1843 steam locomotive (Cuba's first) called *La Junta*. Three other antique steam trains are displayed, along with various diesel locomotives, albeit without any information whatsoever.

Fábrica de Tabaco Romeo y Julieta

Cigar connoisseurs the world over know the name Romeo y Julieta, a fine cigar brand made at this factory (Padre Varela #852, e/ Desagüe y Peñal Verno, tel. 07/878-1058 or 879-3927; no longer open to the public), five blocks northwest of Cuatro Caminos. The factory was founded in 1875 by Inocencia Álvarez and today (as the Antonio Briones Montoto cigar factory) is a cigar-rolling school. It specializes in medium-flavored brands. Like most Havana cigar factories, duties vary by floor, with leaf handling on the ground floor, and stemming, sorting, rolling, box decorating, and ringing on the upper two floors. Tours are offered every 30 minutes. No cameras.

One block south is the **Conservatorio Municipal de Habana** (Padre Varela, esq. Carmen), a music conservatory boasting a well-preserved classical facade.

Avenida Máximo Gómez and Calzada de Cerro

Avenida Máximo Gómez (popularly called Monte; the name changes to Calzada de Cerro west of Infanta) snakes southwest from Parque de la Fraternidad and connects Habana Vieja with Cerro. During the 19th century, scores of summer homes in classical style were erected here, each more extravagantly Italianate than the next. It has been described by writer Paul Goldberger as "one of the most remarkable streets in the world: three unbroken kilometers of nineteenth-century neoclassical villas, with colonnaded arcades making an urban vista of heartbreaking beauty." Heartbreaking

HAVANA

is correct. The avenue ascends southward, marching backward into the past like a classical ruin, with once-stunning arcades and houses collapsing behind decaying facades.

One of the most splendid mansions still extant is the **Quinta del Conde de Santovenia** (Calzada de Cerro #1424, e/ Patria y Auditor), erected in 1845 in subdued neoclassical style, with a 1929 neo-Gothic chapel addition. It has served as a home for the elderly (*hogar de ancianos*) for more than a century.

Farther west, one block south of Calzada de Cerro, is the tiny **Plaza de Galicia** (Peñon, esq. Santo Tomás). Shaded by venerable ceiba trees and bougainvillea bowers, the square features the diminutive **Iglesia de Peñon,** with a Corinthian frontage and round spire. The plaza was dedicated in 1991 to the *pueblo gallego* (Galician people). Ecclesiastics on a busman's holiday might also check out the **Iglesia de San Nicolás,** on San Nicolás one block west of Monte. This splendidly restored yet tiny church has a circular bell tower.

Fábrica de Ron Bocoy

© CHRISTOPHER P. BAKER

Fábrica de Ron Bocoy

The most intriguing site in Cerro is this venerable former home turned rum factory (Máximo Gómez #1417, e/ Patria y Auditor, tel. 07/870-5642, bocoy@tuhv.cha.cyt.cu; Mon.–Fri. 7 A.M.–5 P.M., Sat. 9 A.M.–3 P.M.), facing Quinta del Conde de Santovenia. The two-tone pink facade, with the legend BOCOY above the wide, handsome door, is decorated with four dozen cast-iron swans marching wing to wing, "each standing tall and slim, its long neck bent straight down in mortal combat with an evil serpent climbing up its legs to sink its fangs," wrote James Michener, who chose this building as a setting in his book *Caribbean.* Hence the building's colloquial nickname, *Casa de Culebras* (House of Snakes). The swans were a symbol of wealth that the snakes were meant to guard. It was formerly owned by the Counts of Villanueva.

Today the mansion is a distillery and makes Cuba's famous Legendario rums and liquors. Bocoy once manufactured one of the choicest rum in Cuba, intended solely for Fidel Castro to give as gifts to notable personalities: An example of the special libation (packaged in a bulbous earthenware bottle inside a miniature pirate's treasure chest and labeled La Isla del Tesoro, or Treasure Island) is on display in the small upstairs museum that boasts an original 19th-century copper distillery.

The vaults contain great oak casks stacked in dark recesses. Free tours are offered.

Quinta las Delicias

This art nouveau mansion (Av. Santa Catalina, esq. Palatino, tel. 07/867-0205 or 841-1526; Mon.–Fri. 8 A.M.–5 P.M.), on Calzada Palatino, a westerly extension of Calzada de Cerro, was built in 1905 by Charles Brun for Rosalia Abreu, a socialite who populated the extensive grounds with almost 200 monkeys—hence the popular name, Finca de los Monos (Villa of Monkeys). The vestibule is graced by a mural by Cuban artist Arturo Mendocal, and by a gloriously decorated ceiling and stained-glass *ventrales.* The woodsy gardens contain a neo-Gothic family chapel. It functions today as a youth center. Visits by appointment only.

If you've come this far, you may as well peek at the **Pabellón de los Depósitos del Acueducto de Albear** (Fomento, e/ Chaple y Recreo), two blocks east of Calzada Palatino. This neoclassical reservoir with giant frogs in each corner was designed in 1856 by Francisco de Albear to supply gravity-fed water to the ever-expanding city. It still functions as the modern, albeit much dilapidated, waterworks, and supplies one-fifth of Havana's water. Visitors are not allowed inside.

Sights – Vedado and Plaza de la Revolución

The *municipio* of Plaza de la Revolución (pop. 165,000), west of Centro Habana, comprises the leafy residential streets of Vedado and, to the southwest, the modern enclave of Nuevo Vedado and Plaza de la Revolución.

Vedado—the commercial heart of "modern" Havana—has been described as "Havana at its middle-class best." The University of Havana is here. So are many of the city's prime hotels and restaurants, virtually all its main commercial buildings, and block after block of handsome mansions and apartment houses in art deco, eclectic, Beaux-Arts, and neoclassical styles—luxurious and humble alike lining streets shaded by stately jagüeys dropping their aerial roots to the ground.

Formerly a vast open space between Centro Habana and the Río Almendares, Vedado ("forest reserve" or "forbidden") served as a buffer zone in case of attack from the west; construction was prohibited. In 1859, however, plans were drawn up for urban expansion using. Strict building regulations, for example, defined that there should be 15 feet of gardens between building and street, and more in wider *avenidas*. Regularly spaced parks were mandated. The conclusion of the Spanish-American-Cuban War, in 1898, brought U.S. money rushing in. Civic structures, large hotels, casinos, department stores, and lavish restaurants sprouted alongside nightclubs.

The sprawling region is hemmed to the north by the Malecón, to the east by Calzada de Infanta, to the west by the Río Almendares, running in a deep canyon, and to the southeast by the Calzada de Ayestaran and Avenida de la Independencia. Vedado follows a grid pattern aligned north–northwest by south–southeast and laid out in quadrants. Odd-numbered streets (calles) run east–west, parallel to the shore. Even-numbered calles run perpendicular. (To confuse things, some "calles" are "avenidas." In addition, west of Paseo, calles are even-numbered; east of Paseo, calles run from A to P.) The basic grid is overlaid by a larger grid of broad boulevards averaging six blocks apart.

Dividing the quadrants east–west is Calle 23, which rises (colloquially) as La Rampa from the Malecón at its junction with Calzada de Infanta. La Rampa runs uphill to Calle L and continues on the flat as Calle 23. Paralleling it to the north is a second major east–west thoroughfare, Calle 9 (Línea), five blocks inland of the Malecón, which meets to the northeast.

Four major roadways divide the quadrants north–south: Calle L to the east, and Avenida de los Presidentes, Paseo, and Avenida 12 further west. Vedado slopes gently upward from the shore to Calle 23 and thence gently downward toward Nuevo Vedado and Plaza de la Revolución, connected to Vedado by three *avenidas,* which extend north to the Malecón.

THE MALECÓN (VEDADO)

The Malecón runs along the bulging, wave-battered shorefront of northern Vedado, curling east–west from La Rampa in the east to the Río Almendares in the west, a distance of three miles. The sidewalk is pitted underfoot, but a stroll its full length makes for good exercise while taking in such sites as the **Monumento Calixto García** (Malecón y Av. de los Presidentes), featuring a bronze figure of

HAVANA

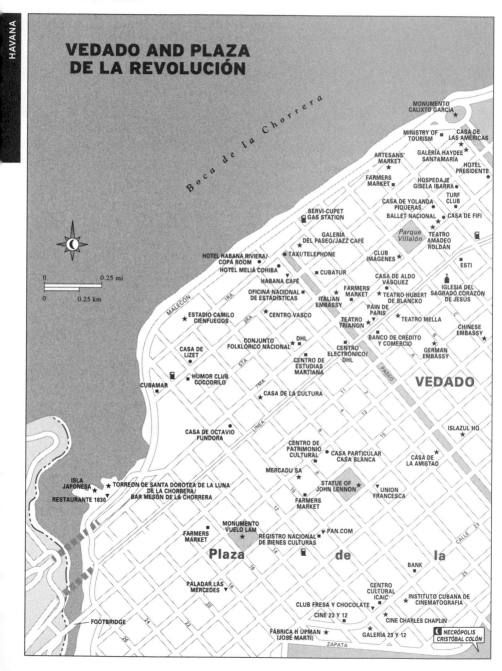

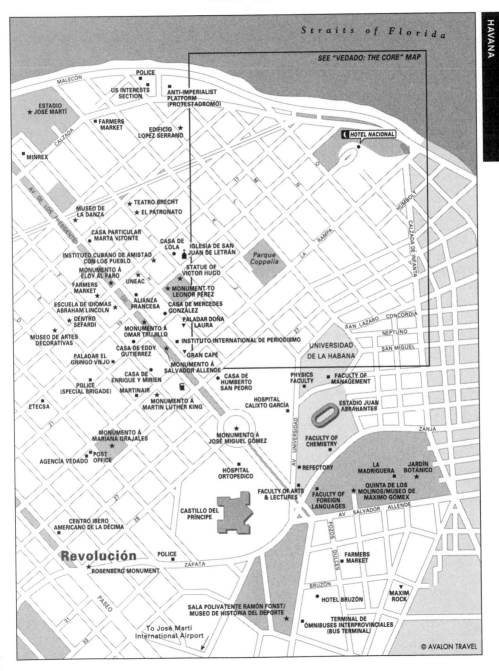

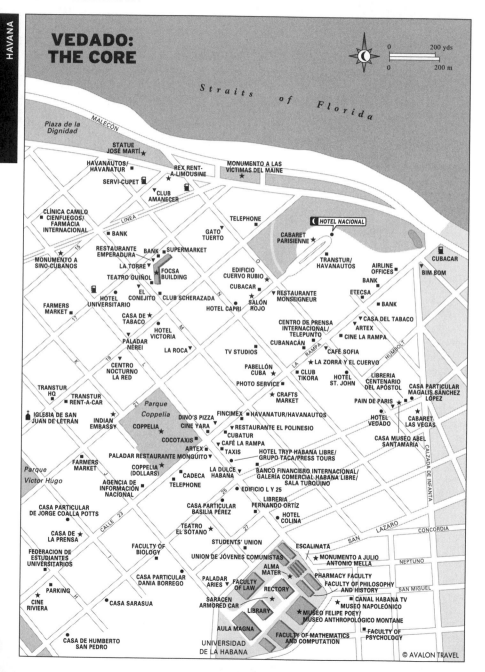

VEDADO: THE CORE

Straits of Florida

0   200 yds
0   200 m

Plaza de la Dignidad

MALECÓN

STATUE JOSÉ MARTÍ ★

MONUMENTO A LAS VICTIMAS DEL MAINE ★

HAVANAUTOS/ HAVANATUR ■

REX RENT-A-LIMOUSINE ■

SERVI-CUPET ⛽

CLUB AMANECER ▼

CLÍNICA CAMILO CIENFUEGOS/ FARMÁCIA INTERNACIONAL ■

LINEA

TELEPHONE ■

HOTEL NACIONAL

BANK ■

GATO TUERTO ▼

CABARET PARISIENNE ★

CUBACAR 🏧

MONUMENTO A SINO-CUBANOS ★

RESTAURANTE EMPERADURA ▼

BANK ■

SUPERMARKET ■

TRANSTUR/ HAVANAUTOS ■

AIRLINE OFFICES ■

BIM BOM ■

15

LA TORRE ▼

FOCSA BUILDING

EDIFICIO CUERVO RUBIO ★

BANK ■

TEATRO GUIÑOL ★

CUBACAR ■

ETECSA ■

BANK ■

FARMERS MARKET ■

HOTEL UNIVERSITARIO ■

EL CONEJITO ●

CLUB SCHERAZADA ■

▼ RESTAURANTE MONSEIGNEUR

CASA DE TABACO ★

HOTEL CAPRI ●

SALÓN ROJO ●

CASA DEL TABACO ▼

ARTEX ■

17

HOTEL VICTORIA ▼

CENTRO DE PRENSA INTERNACIONAL/ TELEPUNTO ■

CINE LA RAMPA ■

M

PALADAR NEREI ▼

LA ROCA ▼

TV STUDIOS ■

CUBANACÁN ▼

RAMPA

CAFÉ SOFIA ■

CENTRO NOCTURNO LA RED ●

19

PABELLÓN CUBA ★

LA

CLUB TIKORA ●

★ LA ZORRA Y EL CUERVO

HUMBOLT

HOTEL ST. JOHN ●

LIBRERIA CENTENARIO DEL APÓSTOL ■

CASA PARTICULAR MAGALIS SÁNCHEZ LÓPEZ ★

K

PHOTO SERVICE ■

TRANSTUR HQ ■

TRANSTUR RENT-A-CAR ■

Parque Coppelia

★ CRAFTS MARKET

PAIN DE PARIS ★

IGLESIA DE SAN JUAN DE LETRÁN 🛕

INDIAN EMBASSY ★

DINO'S PIZZA ■

FINCIMEX ■

HAVANATUR/HAVANAUTOS ■

HOTEL VEDADO ●

CABARET LAS VEGAS ■

21

COPPELIA ■

CINE YARA ■

▼ RESTAURANTE EL POLINESIO

CALZADA DE INFANTA

COCOTAXIS ■

CUBATUR ▼

CASA MUSEO ABEL SANTAMARÍA ●

ARTEX ■

▼ CAFÉ LA RAMPA

PALADAR RESTAURANTE MONGÜITO ▼

TAXIS ■

HOTEL TRYP HABANA LIBRE/ GRUPO TACA/PRESS TOURS ■

FARMERS MARKET ■

COPPELIA (DOLLARS) ★

LA DULCE HABANA ▼

BANCO FINANCIERO INTERNACIONAL/ GALERÍA COMERCIAL HABANA LIBRE/ SALA TURQUINO ■

Parque Victor Hugo

CADECA ■

Parque Victor Hugo

AGENCIA DE INFORMACIÓN NACIONAL ■

TELEPHONE ■

25

EDIFICIO L Y 25 ●

CASA PARTICULAR DE JORGE COALLA POTTS ■

CALLE 23

CASA PARTICULAR BASILIA PÉREZ ■

LIBRERIA FERNANDO ORTÍZ ■

27

HOTEL COLINA ●

LAZARO

CONCORDIA

CASA DE LA PRENSA ★

TEATRO EL SÓTANO ★

STUDENTS' UNION ■

ESCALINATA ●

SAN

FEDERACIÓN DE ESTUDIANTES UNIVERSITARIOS ■

FACULTY OF BIOLOGY ■

UNION DE JÓVENES COMUNISTAS ■

★ MONUMENTO A JULIO ANTONIO MELLA

NEPTUNO

ALMA MATER ★

PHARMACY FACULTY ■

CINE RIVIERA ★

PARKING ■

H

CASA PARTICULAR DANIA BORREGO ●

CASA SARASUA ●

PALADAR ARIES ▼

FACULTY OF LAW ■

RECTORY ■

FACULTY OF PHILOSOPHY AND HISTORY ■

SAN MIGUEL

SARACEN ARMORED CAR ●

LIBRARY ■

CANAL HABANA TV ■

MUSEO NAPOLEÓNICO ■

★ MUSEO FELIPE POEY/ MUSEO ANTHROPOLÓGICO MONTANE

CASA DE HUMBERTO SAN PEDRO ●

AULA MAGNA ●

FACULTY OF MATHEMATICS AND COMPUTATION ■

FACULTY OF PSYCHOLOGY ■

UNIVERSIDAD DE LA HABANA

© AVALON TRAVEL

HAVANA

TWENTIETH-CENTURY ARCHITECTURAL TREASURES

The turn of the 20th century spawned a desire for modernity. Cuba, a nation seeking to free itself of a parochial past, adopted North American and European influences with remarkable fervor. The arrival of U.S. architects spearheaded an American influence, while Cuba developed its own world-class Cuban School of Architecture, whose graduates showed occasional displays of genuine brilliance. The period 1925–65 was uniquely inventive. Although no uniquely Cuban architecture evolved, a subtle "Cubanization" transformed styles introduced to the island. Modernist designs with a tropical twist, from streamlined art deco apartment blocks to modernist villas, complemented Havana's astonishing trove of colonial structures.

Art nouveau arrived from Europe around 1905, with Franco-Belgian, Viennese, and Catalan versions in overlapping succession, such as the highly decorative, even whimsical, Palacio Cueto (on the southeast corner of Plaza Vieja), built in 1906 in a style influenced by Barcelona's Gaudí-inspired *modernismo*. The 1920s Beaux-Arts style, influenced by the École de Beaux-Arts in Paris, fused baroque, classical, Renaissance, and neoclassical elements. Corinthian columns, Pompeiian fresoes, with a lavish use of symbolic statues (such as those adorning the staircase to the Capitolio Nacional), conveyed a message of Havana's power and grandeur. Purely neo-Renaissance edifices – such as the legendary Hotel Nacional (1930) – also went up in quintessentially Cuban versions of Italian, French, and Spanish styles. Other structures, such as the Palacio Presidencial, completed in 1919, adopted the so-called Eclectic style, which melded revivalist trends to elements of neoclassicism, Renaissance, and Beaux-Arts forms.

Art deco followed and coincided with the heyday of Hollywood movies. Public edifices were adorned with lavish ornamentation inside and out, as with Esteban Rodríguez's masterful Edificio Bacardí (1930), on Monserrate, and the Cine América (1940), on Galiano.

This was the great age of transport and Cuban architects were inspired to infuse their art deco buildings with slick streamlined forms. Decorative panels and geometric motifs were relegated to the interiors of buildings, while exteriors were graced by gradually rounded curves and horizontally banded parapets and verandas representing bodies streaking through air. Centro Habana, in particular, boasts many apartment buildings in this streamlined style, such as the Edificio Solimar (Soledad #205, e/ San Lázaro y Ánimas).

MODERNISMO

Wed to a contemporary avant-garde style led by architects Eugenio Batista, Mario Romañach, and Max Borges Recio, "modernism" came into its glory in the 1950s and continued into the early years of the Revolution. Thousands of magnificent homes in experimental contemporary fashion blossomed in Miramar, Cubanacán, and other western suburbs. Back came stained glass, tile detailing, jalousies, and the inner patio, fused with asymmetrical cubist elements, cantilevered stairs, parabolic structures, and cast shell roofs popularized by Borges. His masterpiece is the Tropicana nightclub, combining complexity with a tropical sensuality defined by graceful curves.

Modernismo reached for the sky. Cuba's pioneering architects changed the Vedado skyline with towering hotels and apartment buildings funded, often, by Mafia money, as with the Hotel Capri (1957), Hotel Riviera (1957), and Habana Libre (1958). Meanwhile, the influence of monumentalist edifices associated with European fascist regimes was assimilated into new public structures, such as the Palace of Justice (now the Palace of the Revolution).

Following the Revolution, leading architects fled the country and the closure of the School of Architecture in 1965 spelled the end of a glorious era.

The http://havanaarchitecture.org website is a good resource.

the 19th-century rebel general on horseback; the **Hotel Habana Riviera** (Malecón y Paseo), opened by the Mafia in 1958 and recently remodeled to show off its spectacular modernist lobby; and the **Torreón de Santa Dorotea de la Luna de la Chorrera** (Malecón y Calle 20), a small fortress built in 1762 to guard the mouth of the Río Almendares. Immediately beyond "La Chorrera," the Restaurante 1830 features a Gaudíesque garden that includes a dramatic cupola and a tiny island—**Isla Japonesa**—in Japanese style.

◖ Hotel Nacional

The landmark Hotel Nacional (Calles O y 21, tel. 07/836-3564, www.hotelnacionaldecuba. com) is dramatically perched atop a small cliff at the junction of La Rampa and the Malecón. Now a national monument, this grande dame hotel was designed by the same architects who designed The Breakers in Palm Beach, which it closely resembles. It opened on December 30, 1930, in the midst of the Great Depression. In 1933, army officers loyal to Machado holed up here following Batista's coup; a gun battle ensued. More famously, in December 1946 Lucky Luciano called a mobster summit (ostensibly they were here to honor Frank Sinatra) here to discuss carving up Havana.

The elaborately detailed, Spanish-style neoclassical hotel was greatly in need of refurbishment when, in 1955, mobster Meyer Lansky persuaded General Batista to let him build a grand casino and convert some of the rooms to luxurious suites for wealthy gamblers. Luminaries from Winston Churchill and the Prince of Wales to Marlon Brando have laid their heads here, as attested by the photos in the lobby bar. It is still the preferred hotel for visiting bigwigs.

Beyond the Palladian porch, the vestibule is lavishly adorned with Mudejar patterned tiles. The sweeping palm-shaded lawns to the rear—the terrace bar is a rigueur spot to enjoy a mojito and cigar—slope toward the Malecón, above which sits a battery of cannons from the Wars of Independence. The cliff is riddled with defensive tunnels built since the 1970s.

A 1940s Cadillac sweeps along Havana's Malecón boulevard, with the Hotel Nacional behind.

© CHRISTOPHER P. BAKER

The **Edificio Cuervo Rubio** (Calles 21 y O), cater-corner to the hotel entrance, is an art deco stunner. Nip inside the lobby, which has an Italian marble statue, and look up through the "tube" of the spiral staircase augering up seven flights. The modernist **Hotel Capri** (Calles 21 y N) was built in 1958 by the American gangster Santo Trafficante and was a setting in the movie *The Godfather*. It was a shell, awaiting restoration, at last visit.

Monumento a las Víctimas del Maine

The Maine Monument (Malecón y Calle 17) was dedicated by the republican Cuban government to the memory of the 260 sailors who died when the USS *Maine* exploded in Havana harbor in 1898, creating a prelude for U.S. intervention in the Wars of Independence. Two rusting cannons tethered by chains from the ship's anchor are laid out beneath 40-foot-tall Corinthian columns dedicated in 1925 and originally topped by an eagle with wings spread wide. Immediately after the failed Bay of Pigs invasion in 1960, the monument was desecrated by an angry mob that toppled the eagle from its roost and broke its wings—its body is now in the Museum of the City of Havana, while the head hangs on the wall of the cafeteria in the U.S. Interests Section. The Castro government later dedicated a plaque that reads, "To the victims of the *Maine,* who were sacrificed by imperialist voracity in its eagerness to seize the island of Cuba."

Plaza de la Dignidad

The Plaza of Dignity (Malecón y Calzada), west of the Maine Monument, was created at the height of the Elián González fiasco in 1999–2000 from what was a grassy knoll in front of the U.S. Interests Section. A **statue of José Martí** stands at the plaza's eastern end, bearing in one arm a bronze likeness of young Elián while with the other he points an accusatory finger at the Interests Section—*habaneros* joke that Martí is trying to tell them, "Your visas are that way!"

The Cuban government also pumped US$2 million into constructing the **Tribuna Abierta Anti-Imperialista** (José Martí Anti-Imperialist Platform)—called jokingly by locals the *"protestadromo"*—at the west end of the plaza to accommodate the masses bussed in to taunt Uncle Sam. The concrete supports bear plaques inscribed with the names of Communist and revolutionary heroes, plus those of prominent North Americans—from Benjamin Spock to Malcolm X—at the fore of the fight for social reforms.

At the western end of the plaza is the **U.S. Interests Section** (formerly the U.S. Embassy), where low-profile U.S. diplomats and CIA agents serve Uncle Sam's whims behind a veil of mirrored-glass windows. A forest of 73 huge flagstaffs was erected in front of the building to block the ticker-tape anti-Castroite propaganda that the Bush administration churlishly initiated in 2007. Each black flag represents one of the Cubans killed in a bombing of a Cubana airliner in 1976; the main perpetrator, Louís Posada Carriles,

currently lives as a free man in the United States.

One block south of the plaza, the H-shaped **Edificio López Serrano** (Calle L e/ 11 y 13) *rascacielo* (skyscraper) is one of the city's most astonishing art deco apartment buildings. Built in 1932, it resembles a truncated Empire State Building. Pop inside to admire the deteriorated lobby of Moroccan red marble and the nickel-silver relief panel of *Time.*

LA RAMPA (CALLE 23)

Calle 23 rises from the Malecón to Calle L and climbs steadily past the major airline offices, nightclubs, cinemas, travel agencies, TV studios, and art deco apartment buildings mingling with high-rise office buildings. La Rampa ("the ramp") was the setting of *Three Trapped Tigers,* Guillermo Cabrera Infante's famous novel about swinging 1950s Havana, for it was here that the ritziest hotels, casinos, and nightclubs were concentrated in the days before the Revolution. Multicolored granite tiles created by Wilfredo Lam, René Portocarrero, and other leading artists are laid at intervals in the sidewalks.

Parque Coppelia

Coppelia, at the top of La Rampa (Calle 23 y L; Tues.–Sun. 10 A.M.–9:30 P.M.), is the name of a park in Havana, the flying saucer–like structure at its heart, and the brand of excellent ice cream served here. In 1966, the government built this lush park with a parlor in the middle as the biggest ice creamery in the world, serving up to an estimated 30,000 customers a day. Cuba's rich diversity is to be found standing in line at Coppelia on a sultry Havana afternoon.

The strange concrete structure that looms over the park, suspended on spidery legs, shelters a marble-topped bar where Cubans seated atop tall bar stools slurp ice cream from stainless steel bowls. A series of circular rooms is arranged overhead like a four-leaf clover, offering views out over three open-air sections where *helados* (ice cream) can be enjoyed beneath the dappled shade of lush yagüey trees. Each

A WALK ALONG VEDADO'S CALLE 17

Allow one hour for this walk along one of the most astonishing streets in the city.

From the Monumento del Maine, follow Calle 17 west toward the landmark 35-story **Focsa** (Calle 17 e/ M y N), a V-shaped apartment building built 1954–56 as one of the largest reinforced concrete structures in the world. Following the Revolution it was used to house East European and Soviet personnel.

Continue west two blocks to Calle J. Turn left and after one block turn right onto Calle 19 to view the Gothic **Iglesia San Juan de Letrán,** which dates from the 1880s. This impressive ecclesiastical edifice has fine stained-glass windows.

One block west of the church is **Parque Victor Hugo** (Calle 19, e/ I y H). Circle the park counterclockwise, passing a monument to the 19th-century French novelist (author of *Les Miserables*) on the northeast corner. At the corner of Calles 19 and H is a memorial to Leonor Pérez Cabrera, mother of José Martí, with a letter from Martí to his dearly beloved *mamá* inscribed in metal. The southeast corner (Calle 21 y I) bears a monument to Bobby Sands and nine other IRA nationalists ("martyrs" says the plaque) who died on hunger strike in Crumlin Road jail, Northern Ireland, in 1981.

Return to Calle 17 and continue westward, passing the **Instituto Cubano de Amistad con los Pueblos** (Cuban Institute for People's Friendship, Calle 17 #301, e/ H y I), occupying a palatial Beaux-Arts villa. One block west, call in at the equally magnificent mansion on the southwest corner of Calle H: The Casa de Juan Gelats, a spectacular exemplar of the Beaux-Arts style, was built in 1920 and today houses the **Unión Nacional de Escritores y Artistas de Cuba** (National Union of Cuban Writers and Artists, UNEAC, Calle 17 #351, esq. H, tel. 07/832-4551, www.uneac.co.cu), which hosts cultural events and is open to the public.

Cross Avenida de los Presidentes and detour 20 meters uphill to the **Escuela de Idiomas Abraham Lincoln** (Presidentes, e/ 17 y 19) to admire a magnificent bronze statue of the former U.S. president in the front garden.

Venerable jagüey trees provide shade as

section has its own *cola* (line) proportional in length to the strength of the sun. Even on temperate days the *colas* snake out of the park and onto nearby streets like lethargic serpents. Waitresses serve you at communal tables made of local marble.

Coppelia featured in Tomás Gutiérrez Alea's trenchant classic movie, *Fresa y chocolate,* which was based on Senel Paz's short story, "The Woods, the Wolf, and the New Man." The movie is named for the scene at Coppelia where Diego, a gay man, had ordered strawberry ice cream, much to the consternation of David, a loyal Fidelista: "Although there was chocolate that day, he had ordered strawberry. Perverse." After the success of the movie, Cuban males, concerned with their macho image, avoided ordering strawberry.

Hotel Habana Libre Tryp

The 416-foot-tall "Free Havana Hotel" (Calle L, e/ 23 y 25) was once *the* place to be after opening as the Havana Hilton in April 1958. Castro even had his headquarters here briefly in 1959. For years the hotel teemed with shady foreigners—many of them, reported *National Geographic,* "not strictly tourists" and all "watched by secret police agents from the 'ministry,' meaning MININT, the Ministry of the Interior." The hotel is fronted by a spectacular contemporary mural—**Carro de la Revolución** (the Revolutionary Car)—by ceramist Amelia Peláez, made of 525 pieces in the style of Picasso. The modernist lobby contains many fine contemporary art pieces, including a mosaic mural by René Portocarrero.

Casa Museo Abel Santamaría

Of interest primarily to students of Cuba's revolutionary history, this museum (Calle 25 #164, e/ Infanta y O, tel. 07/835-0891; Mon.–Fri. 9 A.M.–5 P.M., Sat. 10 A.M.–1 P.M.; free) occupies a simple two-room, sixth-floor

you continue west along Calle 17 two blocks to the **Museo de Artes Decorativas** (Museum of Decorative Arts, Calle 17 #502, e/ D y E, tel. 07/830-9848; Tues.-Sat. 11 A.M.-7 P.M.; entrance CUC3 with guide, cameras CUC5, videos CUC10), housed in the former mansion of a Cuban countess. It brims with a lavish collection of furniture, paintings, textiles, and chinoiserie from the 18th and 19th centuries. Upstairs, a boudoir is decorated in Asian style, its furniture inlaid with mother-of-pearl.

At Calle C, turn right and head downhill one block to Calle 15. Turn left and visit the **Galería Marianao** (Calle 15 #607, e/ B y C, tel. 07/838-2702; Tues.-Sat. 10 A.M.-5 P.M.), containing the 6,000-piece Art Collection of New America.

Return to Calle 17 and continue west four blocks to Paseo. Cross this wide boulevard. On the west side, on the left, is the **Casa de la Amistad** (Paseo #406, e/ 17 y 19, tel. 07/830-3114, an Italian Renaissance mansion **Casa de Juan Pedro Baró** – built in 1926 with a surfeit of Carrara marble. It's no longer open to the public.

Continue two blocks west along Calle 17 to Calle 6 and **"Parque Lennon."** Following John Lennon's death in 1980, a gathering of Havana bohemia took place at this small quiet park. In 2000, on the 20th anniversary of his death, a life-size bronze statue was unveiled in the presence of Fidel Castro. Lennon, who is dressed in open-neck shirt, sits on a bench, his head slightly tilted, right leg resting on his left knee, with his arm draped casually over the back of the dark-green cast-iron bench, and plenty of room for anyone who wants to join him. The sculpture was rendered by Cuban artist José Villa, who inscribed the words "People say I'm a dreamer, but I'm not the only one," at the foot of the statue. By night, a spotlight shines on Lennon, denying him sleep. A *custodio* is there 24/7; he takes care of Lennon's spectacles.

One block east, turn north one block to **Parque de Lam** (Calles 14 y 15), studded by a huge modern statue by Alberto Lescay Merencio. The bronze monument represents a human as a bird in flight – a universal element in the works of Cuban painter Wilfredo Lam.

apartment (#603) where Fidel Castro's revolutionary movement, the M-26-7, had its secret headquarters in the former home of the eponymous martyr. Abel Santamaría was brutally tortured and murdered following the attack on the Moncada barracks in 1953. The original furnishings are still in place: a sofa bed, a small bookcase, Fidel's work desk with a statue of José Martí, and a kerosene fridge. The adjoining room (#604) has a small exhibition of Abel's sister Haydee Santamaría, Fidel, and other revolutionaries.

UNIVERSIDAD DE LA HABANA AND VICINITY

The **University of Havana** (Calle L y San Lázaro, tel. 07/878-3231, www.uh.cu; Mon.–Fri. 8 A.M.–6 P.M.) was founded by Dominican friars in 1728 and was originally situated on Calle Obispo in Habana Vieja. During the 20th century, the Federación de Estudiantes Universitarios (University Students' Federation) was an extremely influential group amid the jungle of Cuban politics, and the university was an autonomous "sacred hill" that neither the police nor the army could enter—although gangsters and renegade politicians roamed the campus. (The student federation is in a beautiful Beaux-Arts mansion at the corner of Calles 27 and K.) Visitors are allowed to stroll the grounds, although peeking into the classes requires advance permission and, ostensibly, you'll need authorization to take photos (tel. 07/832-9844). The campus is off-limits on weekends, and the campus and museums are closed July–August.

From Calle L, the university is entered via an immense, 50-meter-wide stone staircase: the 88-step **Escalinata** (staircase). A patinated bronze **statue of the Alma Mater** cast by Czech sculptor Mario Korbel in 1919 sits atop the staircase. The twice-life-size statue of a woman is seated in a bronze chair with six classical bas-reliefs representing various disciplines taught at the university. She is dressed in a long-sleeve tunic and extends her bare arms, beckoning all those who desire knowledge.

The staircase is topped by a porticoed, columned facade beyond which lies a peaceful square—**Plaza Ignacio Agramonte**—surrounded by classical buildings (the tree-shaded campus was loosely modeled after New York's Columbia University). A **Saracen armored car** sits in the quadrant—it was captured in 1958 by students in the fight against Batista. The **Aula Magna** (Great Hall) features a marble urn containing the ashes of Félix Varela, plus a magnificent mural by Armando Menocal. It is usually only opened for special events.

The **Monumento a Julio Antonio Mella**, across Calle L at the base of the Escalinata, contains the ashes of Mella, founder of the University Students' Federation and, later, of the Cuban Communist Party.

Museo de Ciencias Naturales Felipe Poey

The Escuela de Ciencias (School of Sciences), on the south side of the quadrant, contains the Felipe Poey Museum of Natural Sciences (tel. 07/877-4221; Mon.–Fri. 9 A.M.–noon and 1–3 P.M.; free; no photos allowed), displaying dozens of endemic species, from alligators to sharks, stuffed or pickled for posterity. The museum dates from 1842 and is named for its French-Cuban founder. Poey (1799–1891) was versed in every field of the sciences and founded the Academy of Medical Sciences, the Anthropological Society of Cuba, and a half-dozen other societies.

The **Museo Antropológico Montane** (Montane Anthropology Museum, tel. 07/879-3488; same hours as above), on the second floor of the Escuela de Ciencias, contains a valuable collection of pre-Columbian artifacts, including carved idols and turtle shells.

Museo Napoleónico

Who would imagine that so much of Napoleon Bonaparte's personal memorabilia would end up in Cuba? But it has, housed in the Napoleonic Museum (San Miguel #1159, e/ Ronda y Masón, tel. 07/879-1460, musnap@cubarte.cult.cu; Tues.–Sat. 9 A.M.–4:30 P.M., Sun. 9 A.M–noon; entrance CUC3, guide CUC2) in a Florentine Renaissance mansion on the south side of the university. The collection (7,000 pieces) was the private work of a politician, Orestes Ferrara, one-time Cuban ambassador to France. Ferrara brought back from Europe such precious items as the French emperor's death mask, toothbrush, and the pistols Napoleon used at the Battle of Borodino. Other items were seized from Julio Lobo, the former National Bank president, when he left Cuba for exile. The museum—housed in Ferrara's former three-story home (Ferrara was also forced out by the Revolution)—is replete with portraits of the military genius. It was closed for restoration at last visit.

◖ NECRÓPOLIS CRISTÓBAL COLÓN

Described as "an exercise in pious excesses," the Columbus Cemetery (Zapata, esq. 12, tel. 07/830-4517; daily 8 A.M.–5 P.M.; entrance CUC5, including guide and right to photograph) covers 56 hectares and contains more than 500 major mausoleums, chapels, vaults, tombs, and galleries (in addition to countless gravestones) embellished with angels, griffins, cherubs, and other flamboyant ornamentation. You'll even find Greco-Roman temples in miniature, an Egyptian pyramid, and medieval castles, plus baroque, Romantic, Renaissance, art deco, and art nouveau art by a pantheon of Cuba's leading sculptors and artists. The triple-arched entrance gate, inspired by the Triumphal Arch in Rome, has marble reliefs depicting the crucifixion and Lazarus rising from the grave and is topped by a marble coronation stone representing the theological virtues: Faith, Hope, and Charity.

Today a national monument, the cemetery

© CHRISTOPHER P. BAKER

The Necrópolis Cristóbal Colón is one of the world's greatest collections of flamboyant funerary architecture.

was laid out between 1871 and 1886 in 16 rectangular blocks, or *insulae,* like a Roman military camp. The designer, a Spaniard named Calixto de Loira, divided the cemetery by social status, with separate areas for non-Catholics and for victims of epidemics. It was originally open only to nobles, who competed to build the most elaborate tombs, with social standing dictating the size and location of plots.

The cemetery is a petrified version of society of the times, combining, says the *Guía Turística* (available at the entrance gate), a "grandeur and meanness, good taste and triviality … and even an unusual black humor, as in the gravestone carved as a double-three, devoted to an emotional elderly lady who died with that domino in her hand, thus losing both game and life at a time." The *doble tres* was that of Juana Martín, a domino fanatic who indeed died as described (Calles 6 y G).

Famous *criollo* patricians, colonial aristocrats, and war heroes such as Máximo Gómez are buried here alongside noted intellectuals and politicians. The list goes on and on: José Raúl Capablanca, the world chess champion 1921–27 (his tomb is guarded by a marble queen chess piece); Alejo Carpentier, Cuba's most revered contemporary novelist; Hubert de Blanck, the noted composer; Celia Sánchez; Haydee Santamaría; and a plethora of revolutionaries killed for the cause, and even some of the Revolution's enemies. Many monuments belong to such communities as the Abakuá secret society, the Asturians, and the Galicians, and to groups such as film and radio stars. The **Galería Tobias** is one of several underground galleries; this one is 100 meters long and contains 256 niches containing human remains.

The major tombs line Avenida Cristóbal Colón, the main avenue, which leads south from the gate to an ocher-colored, octagonal neo-Byzantine church, the **Capilla Central,** containing a fresco of the Last Judgment.

La Milagrosa

The most visited grave is the flower-bedecked tomb of Amelia Goyri de Hoz (Calles 3 y F),

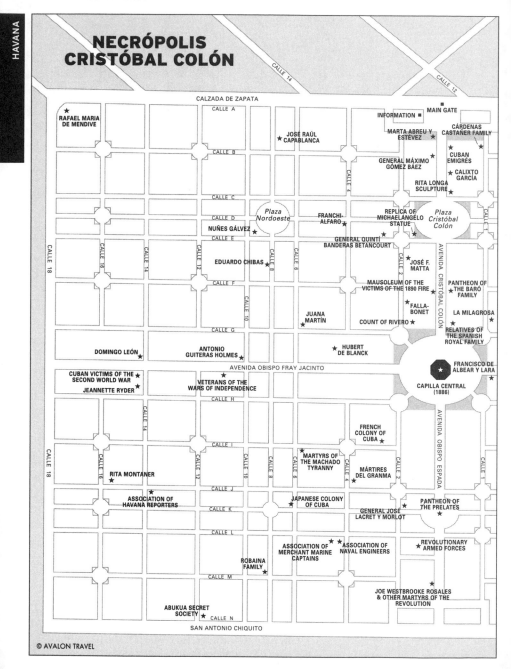

NECRÓPOLIS CRISTÓBAL COLÓN

© AVALON TRAVEL

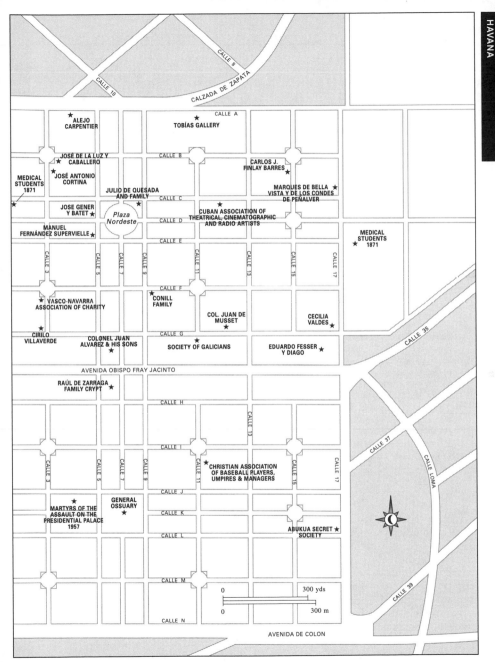

A WALK ALONG AVENIDA DE LOS PRESIDENTES

Avenida de los Presidentes (Calle G), with wide, grassy, tree-lined pedestrian medians, runs perpendicular to Calle 23 and climbs from the Malecón toward Plaza de la Revolución. The avenue is named for the statues of Cuban presidents that grace its length, along with statues of other notables in American history. (The busts of Tomás Estrada Palma and José Miguel Gómez, the first and second presidents of the Cuban republic, were toppled following the Revolution, as they were accused of being "puppets" of the U.S. government.)

Allow 40 minutes, setting out from the Malecón, where first you should admire the bas-reliefs that adorn the **Monumento Calixto García.** One block south, on your right, is the **Casa de las Américas** (Av. de los Presidentes, esq. 3ra, tel. 07/832-2706, fax 07/834-4554, www.casa.cult.cu; Mon.-Fri. 8 A.M.-4:45 P.M.), a cultural center formed in 1959 to study and promote the cultures of Latin America and the Caribbean. Housed in an astonishing, cathedral-like art deco building, the center contains the **Galería Latinamericano** art gallery (Mon.-Thur. 10 A.M.-5 P.M. and Fri. 10 A.M.-4 P.M.) and hosts concerts and cultural programs. Fifty meters south along Avenida de los Presidentes you'll pass the Casa's **Galería Haydee Santamaría** (e/ 5ta and G; closed for repair in 2009).

At 5ta you'll pass the **Hotel Presidente,** an art deco high-rise dating from 1927. Across Avenida de los Presidentes, on the east side, is the headquarters of **MINREX** (Ministerio de Relaciones Exteriores), the Foreign Rela-tions Ministry, taking up two blocks including a beautiful neo-baroque building on the north side of Calzada (7ma Calle).

At Calzada, detour west along 5ta for four blocks to **Parque Villalón** (5ta y D). On its southeast side is the Romanesque **Teatro Amadeo Roldán** (tel. 07/832-1168), recently restored to grandeur as a concert hall. Next door is the headquarters of the **Ballet Nacio-nal de Cuba** (Calzada #510 e/ D y E, Vedado, tel. 07/835-2952, www.balletcuba.cu). The facility is closed to visitors, but sometimes you can spot the dancers practicing.

Turn north onto Calle D and walk one block to Línea. On the far side, peek into the 19th-century **Iglesia del Sagrado Corazón de Jesús** (Línea, e/ C y D, tel. 07/832-6807), Vedado's parish church colloquially called Parroquia del Vedado.

Exiting the church, head east one block along Línea to Avenida de los Presidentes. On the south side of Línea note the handsome bronze **statue of Alejandro Rodríguez y Velasco** (Av. de los Presidentes y Línea), a brigadier general in the Cuban Wars of Independence, atop a granite pedestal guarded by a bronze figure of Perseus.

Cross Avenida de los Presidentes to view the **Museo de la Danza** (Calle Línea #365, esq. Av. de los Presidentes, tel. 07/831-2198, musdanza@cubarte.cult.cu; Tues.-Sat. 11 A.M.-6:30 P.M.; CUC2, guide CUC1), in a restored mansion on the southeast corner of the junction. The museum has four salons dedicated

revered as La Milagrosa ("The Miraculous One") and to whom miraculous healings are ascribed. According to legend, she died during childbirth in 1901 and was buried with her stillborn child at her feet. When her sarcophagus was later opened, the baby was supposedly cradled in her arms. Ever since, superstitious Cubans have paid homage by knocking three times on the tombstone with one of its brass rings, before touching the tomb and requesting a favor (one must not turn one's back on the tomb when departing). Many childless women pray here in hopes of a pregnancy.

Cementerio Chino

The Chinese built their own cemetery immediately southwest of Cementerio Colón (on the west side of Avenida 26, e/ 28 y 33; tel. 07/831-1645; daily 8 A.M.-4 P.M.; free). Beyond the circular gateway, traditional lions stand guard over hundreds of graves beneath highly pitched

to Russian ballet, modern dance, the National Ballet of Cuba, and other themes. Exhibits include wardrobes, recordings, manuscripts, and photographs relating to the history of dance. From here, walk south along the central median. Ascending the avenue, you'll pass statues to Ecuadorian president Eloy Alfaro (e/ 15 y 17), Mexican president Benito Juárez (e/ 17 y 19), Venezuelan Simón Bolívar (e/ 19 y 21), Panamanian strongman president Omar Torrijos (e/ 19 y 21), and Chilean president Salvador Allende (e/ 21 y 23).

Cross Calle 23 and walk west one block to Calle F, where on the southwest corner of the junction the **Monumento a Martin Luther King** is a marble tableaux with a bas-relief bronze of the Afro-American civil rights leader.

Return to Avenida de los Presidentes and continue south (the park on the southeast corner of Calle 23 is colloquially named **Parque de los Roqueros** for the goths and *roqueros* – "rockers" – who gather at night in black leather, black eyeliner, and pink-tinted hair). The tree-shaded boulevard climbs two blocks to the **Monumento a José Miguel Gómez** (Calle 29), designed by Italian sculptor Giovanni Nicolini and erected in 1936 in classical style to honor the former Republican president (1909–13). Beyond, the road drops through a canyon lined with giant jagüey trees, which form a glade over the road. Hidden from sight on the bluff to the west is the **Castillo del Príncipe,** built between 1767 and 1779 following the English invasion. The castle is off-limits as it is now a military zone and houses a prison.

Arriving at the junction with Avenida Salvador Allende, Zapata, and Avenida Rancho Boyeros, turn left onto Salvador Allende. After 100 meters, on the north side of the road, you'll arrive at the once-graceful **Quinta de los Molinos** (e/ Infanta y Luaces), reached via a decrepit cobbled, gladed drive. The mansion, built between 1837 and 1840, is named for the royal snuff mills that were built here in 1791 to take advantage of the waters of Zanza Real; you can still see part of the original aqueduct inaugurated in 1592 to the rear of the time-worn *quinta*. The mansion originated as a summer palace for the captains-general and in 1899 was granted as the private residence of General Máximo Gómez, the Dominican-born commander-in-chief of the liberation army. It now houses the motley **Museo de Máximo Gómez** (tel. 07/879-8850; closed for restoration at last visit). His sword and a few other personal effects are on display.

The *quinta* grounds now form the **Jardín Botánico** (Botanical Gardens; Tues.-Sun. 7 A.M.-7 P.M.). Following the Revolution, the once exquisite pleasure gardens of the governor's summer palace were transferred to the University of Havana and are now an overgrown mess littered with tumbledown statues, fountains, and grottoes with giant jagüeys and other trees twining around them, many with voodoo dolls and other *santería* offerings stuffed in their interstices.

burial chapels with upward-curving roofs of red and green tile in the traditional *xuan-shan* (hanging mountain) gabled style.

Galería 23 y 12

The northwest corner of Calles 23 and 12, one block north of Cementerio Colón, marks the spot where on April 16, 1961, Castro announced (on the eve of the Bay of Pigs invasion) that Cuba was henceforth socialist. The anniversary of the declaration of socialism is marked each April 16th, when Castro speaks here. The facade bears a bronze bas-relief showing Fidel surrounded by the heroes who were killed in the U.S.-sponsored strike on the airfield at Marianao that was a prelude to the invasion.

PLAZA DE LA REVOLUCIÓN

Havana's largest plaza, which occupies the Loma de los Catalanes (Hill of the Catalans), is an ugly tarred square accurately described

JOSÉ MARTÍ

A knowledge of José Martí is an absolute prerequisite to understanding contemporary Cuba. He is the most revered figure in Cuban history... the canonical avatar of Cuba's independence spirit and the "ideological architect" of the Cuban Revolution, claims Castro. His works have been seized upon by Cubans on both sides of the Straits of Florida, being "full of the lament of exile and the passion for the lost homeland," thought Claudia Lightfoot. "Cubans take José Martí into their consciousness with their first breath and their mother's milk." Cubans of every stripe quote their saintly hero by heart. So important is Martí within the Cuban psyche that foreigners who admit to never having heard of him are usually met with a wide-mouthed, uncomprehending stare. There is hardly a quadrant in Havana that does not have a street, square, or major building named in his honor. Every year on January 28 the entire country honors Martí's birth.

José Julian Martí de Pérez was born in 1853 in a small house on Calle Paula (today known as Leonor Pérez, to honor his mother) in Habana Vieja. His father was from Valencia, Spain, and became a policeman in Cuba; his mother came from the Canary Islands. He spent much of his youth in Spain before his parents returned to Cuba. When the War of Independence erupted in 1868, Martí was 15 years old. Already he sympathized with the nationalist cause.

At the age of 16, he published his first newspaper, *La Patria Libre* (Free Fatherland). He also wrote a letter denouncing a school friend for attending a pro-Spanish rally. The letter was judged to be treasonous, and Martí was sentenced to six years' imprisonment, including six months' hard labor. Martí suffered a hernia, and gained permanent scars from his shackles. In 1871, his sentence was commuted to exile on the Isla de Pinos, and briefly thereafter he was exiled to Spain, where he earned a degree in law and philosophy and gravitated to the revolutionary circles then active in Madrid.

Later, he settled in Mexico, where he became a journalist, and Guatemala, where he taught, but was expelled for incendiary activities. In 1878, as part of a general amnesty, he was allowed to return to Cuba but was then deported again. He traveled through France and Venezuela and, in 1881, to the United States, where he settled in New York for the next 14 years with his wife and son. Here he worked as a reporter and acted as a consul for Argentina, Paraguay, and Uruguay.

THE PEN AND THE SWORD

Dressed in his trademark black frock coat and bow tie, with his thick moustache waxed into pointy tips, Martí devoted more and more of his time to winning independence for Cuba. He wrote poetry heralding the liberation of his homeland, wedding the rhetoric of nationalism to calls for social justice and fashioning a

---

by P. J. O'Rourke as "a vast open space resembling the Mall in D.C., but dropped into the middle of a massive empty parking lot in a tropical Newark." The trapezoidal complex spanning 11 acres was laid out during the Batista era, when it was known as the Plaza Cívica. It forms the administrative center for Cuba, and all the major edifices date back to the 1950s. Huge rallies are held here on May 1. The plaza is under close surveillance and loitering is discouraged.

Among the important buildings are the **Biblioteca Nacional** (tel. 07/855-5442; Mon.–Sat. 8:30 A.M.–5:30 P.M.), Cuba's largest library, built 1955–1957 on the east side of the plaza in a similar monumental style as the Palace of Justice; the 21-story **Ministerio de Defensa,** originally built as the municipal seat of government on the plaza's southeast side; and the **Teatro Nacional** (Paseo y Av. Carlos M. de Céspedes, tel. 07/879-6011), one block to the northwest of the plaza, built 1954–60 with a convex glazed facade. Paseo climbs northwest from the plaza to Zapata, where in the middle of the road rises the **Memorial**

vision of a free Cuba that broke through class and racial barriers. He was one of the most prolific and accomplished Latin American writers of his day, unsurpassed in the inspiration he ignited. Martí's writing helped define the school of modern Latin American poetry.

He admired the liberty of America but became an arch-anticolonialist, and his voluminous writings are littered with astute critiques of U.S. culture and politics. He despised the expansionist nature of the United States, arguing that U.S. ambitions toward Cuba were as dangerous as the rule of Spain. "It is my duty... to prevent, through the independence of Cuba, the USA from spreading over the West Indies and falling with added weight upon other lands of Our America. All I have done up to now and shall do hereafter is to that end."

Prophetically, Martí's writings are full of invocations to death. It was he who coined the phrase "La Victoria o el Sepulcro" (Victory or the Tomb), which Fidel Castro has turned into a call for "Patria o Muerte" (Patriotism or Death) and more recently "Socialismo o Muerte."

THEORY INTO ACTION

In 1892, Martí presented his "Fundamentals and Secret Guidelines of the Cuban Revolutionary Party," outlining the goals of the nationalists: independence for Cuba, equality of all Cubans, and establishment of democratic processes. That year, Martí began publishing *Patria*. Having established himself as the acknowledged political leader of the independence cause, he melded the various exile factions together and integrated the cause of Cuban exile workers into the crusade – they contributed 10 percent of their earnings to his cause. He also founded a revolutionary center, Cuba Libre (Free Cuba), and La Liga de Instrucción, which trained revolutionary fighters.

In 1895, Martí was named major general of the Armies of Liberation; General Máximo Gómez was named supreme commander. On April 11, 1895, Martí, Gómez, and four followers landed at Cajobabo, in a remote part of eastern Cuba. Moving secretly through the mountains, they gathered supporters and finally linked up with Antonio Maceo and his army of 6,000. The first skirmish with the Spanish occurred at Dos Ríos on May 19, 1895. Martí was the first casualty. He had determined on martyrdom and committed sacrificial suicide by riding headlong into the enemy line. Thus, Martí – the "Apostle of the Nation" – brought the republic to birth, says Guillermo Cabrera Infante, "carrying a cadaver around its neck."

The **Centro de Estudios Martiana** (Calzada. e/ Calles 2 y 4, Vedado, Havana, tel. 07/833-2203, cem@josemarti.co.cu; Mon.-Fri. 9 A.M.-4 P.M.) studies the life and works of Martí.

---

a **Ethel y Julius Rosenberg,** bearing cement doves and an inset sculpture of the U.S. couple executed in Sing Sing Prison, New York, in 1953 for passing nuclear secrets to the Soviet Union. An inscription reads, "Assassinated June 19, 1953." The Cuban government holds a memorial service here each June 19.

To the rear of the library is the **Monumento El Legado Cultural Hispánico,** a larger-than-life bronze statue by American sculptor Anna Hyatt Huntington of two naked men (one on horseback) passing a baton.

One block northeast of the plaza is the **Museo de História del Deporte** (Av. Rancho Boyeros, e/ 19 de Mayo and Bruzón, tel. 07/881-4696; Tues.–Sun. 10 A.M.–5 P.M.; CUC1), the sports museum, in the **Sala Polivatente Ramón Fonst** stadium.

To get from Vedado to the plaza, you can take bus #84 from the bottom of La Rampa, at Calle 0 and Humboldt.

Monumento y Museo José Martí

This massive monument on the south side of the square sits atop a 30-meter-tall base

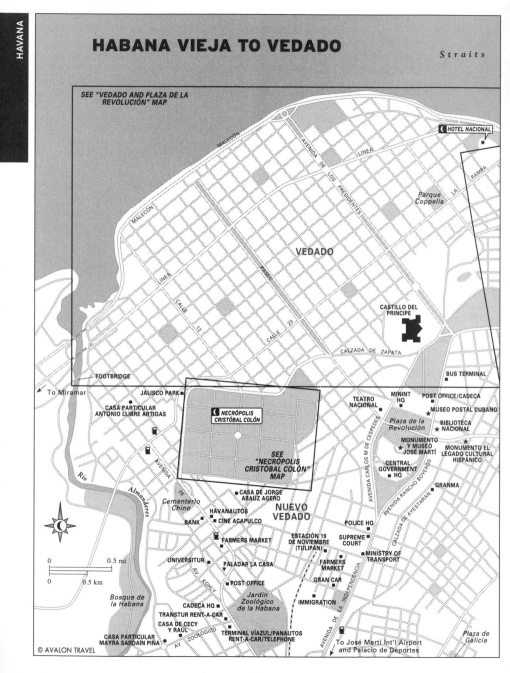

HABANA VIEJA TO VEDADO

Straits

SEE "VEDADO AND PLAZA DE LA
REVOLUCIÓN" MAP

HOTEL NACIONAL

MALECÓN
AVENIDA DE LOS PRESIDENTES
LINEA
LA RAMPA

Parque
Coppelia

MALECÓN

VEDADO

LINEA

CALLE

12

CALLE 23

CASTILLO DEL
PRINCIPE

CALZADA DE ZAPATA

FOOTBRIDGE

BUS TERMINAL

To Miramar

JALISCO PARK

CASA PARTICULAR
ANTONIO LLIBRE ARTIGAS

NECRÓPOLIS
CRISTÓBAL COLÓN

TEATRO
NACIONAL

MININT
HQ

POST OFFICE/CADECA

MUSEO POSTAL CUBANO

Plaza de la
Revolución

BIBLIOTECA
NACIONAL

SEE
"NECRÓPOLIS
CRISTÓBAL COLÓN"
MAP

MONUMENTO
Y MUSEO
JOSÉ MARTÍ

MONUMENTO EL
LEGADO CULTURAL
HISPÁNICO

CENTRAL
GOVERNMENT
HQ

AVENIDA CARLOS M DE CESPEDES

AVENIDA RANCHO BOYEROS

GRANMA

CASA DE JORGE
ARAUZ AGERO

Cementerio
Chino

NUEVO
VEDADO

CALZADA DE AYESTARAN

HAVANAUTOS

BANK

CINE ACAPULCO

POLICE HQ

Río

Almendares

AVENIDA

FARMERS MARKET

ESTACIÓN 19
DE NOVIEMBRE
(TULIPÁN)

SUPREME
COURT

MINISTRY OF
TRANSPORT

0   0.5 mi

UNIVERSITUR

PALADAR LA CASA

FARMERS
MARKET

0   0.5 km

AV. KOHLY

POST OFFICE

GRAN CAR

AVENIDA DE LA INDEPENDENCIA

Bosque de
la Habana

CADECA HQ

Jardín
Zoológico
de la Habana

IMMIGRATION

TRANSTUR RENT-A-CAR

CASA DE CECY
Y RAÚL

CASA PARTICULAR
MAYRA SARDAÍN PIÑA

AV. ZOOLÓGICO

TERMINAL VÍAZUL/PANAUTOS
RENT-A-CAR/TELEPHONE

To José Martí Int'l Airport
and Palacio de Deportes

Plaza de
Gálica

© AVALON TRAVEL

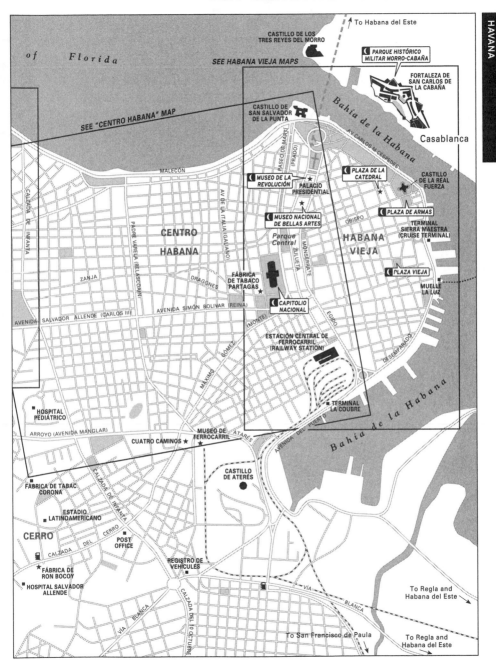

that is shaped as a five-pointed star. It is made entirely of gray granite and marble and was designed by architect Enrique Luis Varela. Completed in 1958, it predates the Revolution. To each side, arching stairways lead to an 18-meter-tall (59-foot) gray-white marble statue of national hero José Martí sitting in a contemplative pose, like Rodin's *The Thinker*.

Behind looms a 109-meter-tall marble edifice stepped like a soaring ziggurat from a sci-fi movie. It's the highest point in Havana. The edifice houses the **Museo José Martí** (tel. 07/859-2351; Mon.–Sat. 9 A.M.–5 P.M.; entrance CUC3, cameras CUC5, videos CUC10). Among the exhibits are first-edition works, engravings, drawings, and maps, as well as reproductions of significant artifacts in Martí's life. New Age music plays in the background, drawing you to a multiscreen broadcast on the Wars of Independence and the Revolution. An art gallery features portraits of Martí. For an additional CUC2 you can take an elevator to the top of the tower for a 360-degree view over Havana.

Palacio de la Revolución

The center of government is the Palace of the Revolution (tel. 07/879-6551), immediately south of the José Martí monument. This monumental structure was inspired by the architecture then popular in Fascist Europe and was built 1954–57 as the Palace of Justice. Today, it is where the Castro brothers and Council of Ministers work out their policies of state. The labyrinthine, ocher-colored palace adjoins the buildings of the Central Committee of the Communist Party. Before the revolution, the buildings served as the Cuban Supreme Court and national police headquarters. No visitors are allowed.

Ministerio del Interior

Commanding the northwest side of the plaza is the seven-story Ministry of the Interior (the ministry in charge of national security), built in 1953 to be the Office of the Comptroller. On its east side is a windowless horizontal block that bears a soaring **"mural" of Che Guevara**—the image is from Alberto "Korda" Gutiérrez's world-renowned photo—and the words Hasta la Victoria Siempre ("Always Toward Victory"), erected in 1995 from steel railings donated by the French government.

Ministerio de Comunicaciones

Immediately east of the Interior Ministry is the Ministry of Communications, with the **Museo Postal Cubano** (Av. Rancho Boyeros, esq. 19 de Mayo, tel. 07/882-8255; Mon.–Thurs. 8 A.M.–5:30 P.M., Fri. 8 A.M.–5:30 P.M.; entrance CUC1) on the ground floor. The well-cataloged philatelic collection displays a complete range of Cuban postage stamps (including the first, dating from 1855), plus a large collection of stamps from almost 100 other countries. A *filatelica* sells stamps.

NUEVO VEDADO

Nuevo Vedado, which stretches south from Cementerio Colón and southwest of Plaza de la Revolución, is a sprawling complex of mid-20th-century housing, including high-rise, postrevolutionary apartment blocks. There are also some magnificent modern edifices, notably private homes built in modernist style in the 1950s, plus the **Palacio de Deportes** (Sports Palace, but colloquially called "El Coliseo"), on the southeast side of the traffic circle at Avenida 26, Avenida de la Independencia (Rancho Boyeros), and Vía Blanca.

Jardín Zoológico de la Habana

The disgracefully managed Havana Zoological Garden (Av. 26 y Zoológico, tel. 07/881-9926 or 881-8915, zoohabana@ch.gov.cu; Wed.–Sun. 9:30 A.M.–5:30 P.M.; CUC2) is heartbreaking. The hippopotamus, crocodiles, caimans, flamingos, and other water-loving species wade and wallow in polluted lagoons. Garbage is everywhere. Cuban visitors taunt the animals and throw them processed food. And there are neither informational panels nor custodians to instruct Cubans on politically correct

© CHRISTOPHER P. BAKER

Visitors admire a leopard in the Jardín Zoológico de la Habana.

behavior. Other species on view include Andean condors, water buffalo, jaguars, leopards, lions, and a gorilla.

Bosque de la Habana and Parque Metropolitano de la Habana

From the zoo, you can follow Avenida Zoológica west to the bridge over the Río Almendares to enter the Bosque de la Habana (Havana Forest). This wild woodland stretches alongside the river, forming a ribbon of vine-draped virgin forest. There is no path—you must walk along Calle 49C, which parallels the river—and going alone is not advised, as robberies occur.

North of Bosque de la Habana, and accessed from Avenida 47, the motley riverside Parque Metropolitano de la Habana has pony rides, row boats (don't fall in; the river stinks of sewage), mini-golf, and an excellent children's playground (donated by the British Embassy).

To the south, the woods extend to **Los Jardines de la Tropical** (Calle Rizo, tel. 07/881-8767; Tues.–Sun. 9 A.M.–6 P.M.), a landscaped park built 1904–10 on the grounds of a former brewery for promotional purposes. The park found its inspiration in Antoni Gaudí's Parque Güell in Barcelona. Today it is in near-derelict status and looks like an abandoned set from *Lord of the Rings*. The Polar brewing company competed by opening the smaller **Jardines de la Polar,** on the north side of Calzada de Puentes Grandes.

The headquarters is at **Aula Ecológica** (Ciclovía, tel. 07/881-9979; Mon.–Fri. 9 A.M.–5 P.M.), which features a meager visitor center with a 1:2,000 scale model of the project.

Museo Camilo Cienfuegos

Southeast of Nuevo Vedado the residential district of Vibora extends to Lawton, where the house where Camilo Cienfuegos (a future Comandante in Fidel's revolutionary army) was born is now a museum (Calle Pocito #228, esq. Calle Lawton, no tel.; Tue.–Sat. 9 A.M.–5 P.M., Sun. 9 A.M.–noon). It displays suitably revolutionary miscellany recalling the life of this popular leader, who died mysteriously in an air crash in 1959.

Sights – Playa (Miramar and Beyond)

West of Vedado and the Río Almendares, the *municipio* of Playa extends to the western boundary of Havana as far as the Río Quibu. Many of the areas were renamed following the Revolution. Gone are Country Club and Biltmore, replaced with politically acceptable names such as Atabey, Cubanacán, and Siboney, in honor of Cuba's indigenous past.

MIRAMAR

Leafy Miramar is Havana's upscale residential district, laid out in an expansive grid of tree-shaded streets lined by fine mansions. Most of their original owners fled Cuba following the Revolution and many of the mansions have fallen into ruin. Nonetheless, Miramar is at the forefront of Cuba's quasi-capitalist remake. The best-stocked stores are here, as are the international schools and foreign embassies.

Avenida Primera runs along the shore, comprised of raised coral outcrops and lacking beaches, except to the extreme west. Time-worn *balnearios* (bathing areas) are found all along Miramar's waterfront, cut into the coral shore. Of limited appeal to tourists, they draw Cubans on hot summer days.

Inland, running parallel at intervals of about 200 meters, are 3ra Avenida, 5ta Avenida (the main thoroughfare), and 7ma Avenida.

Tunnels under the Río Almendares connect Miramar to Vedado. The first connects the Malecón with 5ta Avenida; the second connects Línea (Calle 9) with 7ma Avenida and Avenida 31, which leads to the Marianao district. In addition, Calle 23 crosses the river via the Puente Almendares bridge to become Avenida 47, linking Vedado with the Kohly district and Marianao. You can also cross via a steel footbridge (the Puente de Hierro) at the west end of Calle 11.

Buses #132 and 232 run to Miramar from

Bathers cool off in the summer heat at *balnearios* (bathing areas) lining 1ra Avenida, Miramar.

© CHRISTOPHER P. BAKER

Dragones y Industria, on the northwest side of Parque de la Fraternidad, Habana Vieja. Bus #264 runs to Miramar from Desamparados (e/ Compostela y Picota), near the railway station in Habana Vieja. In Vedado, the P1 runs along Calle 23 to Miramar (you can board at Coppelia, esq. L), where it runs along 4ra Avenida; and the P4 runs along Línea.

Pabellón de la Maqueta de la Habana

The Model of Havana (Calle 28 #113, e/ 1ra y 3ra, tel. 07/206-1268, maqueta@gdic.cu; Tues.–Sat. 9:30 A.M.–5 P.M.; adults CUC3; students, seniors, and children CUC1; guided tour CUC1, cameras CUC2) is a 1:1,000 scale model of the city housed in a hangar-sized, air-conditioned building. The 144-square-meter model represents 144 square kilometers of Havana and its environs. The *maqueta* took more than 10 years to complete and shows Havana in the most intimate detail. It is color-coded by age. A visit here puts the entire city in accessible 3-D perspective.

Acuario Nacional

The National Aquarium (3ra Av., esq. 62, tel. 07/203-6401 or 202-5872, www.acuarionacional.cu; Tues.–Sun. 10 A.M.–6 P.M.; adults CUC7, children CUC5) exhibits 450 species of sealife, including anemones, corals, exotic tropical fish, sharks, hawksbill turtles, sea lions, and dolphins. Most of the tanks are bare and the displays are disappointing by international standards. Daily activities are offered. A sea lion show is held daily at noon, 2:15 P.M., and 4 P.M.; and dolphin show daily at 11 A.M., 3 P.M., and 5 P.M.

Museo del Ministerio del Interior

The Museum of the Ministry of the Interior (5ta Av., esq. 14, tel. 07/203-4432; Tues.–Fri. 9 A.M.–5 P.M., Sat. 9 A.M.–3 P.M.; entrance CUC2, guide CUC1) is dedicated to the CIA's inept efforts to dethrone Fidel. The seal of the CIA looms over a room full of photos and gadgets straight from a spy movie, small arms,

bazookas, and the like. It also features exhibits honoring MININT's good work in solving homicides—there's even a stuffed German shepherd that was used by police in their sleuthing. To make things easier for the CIA should it ever take another stab at Fidel, the museum shows a video giving details of Castro's security plans, including tunnels that lead from his residence (one of many) in Jaimanitas to the nearby Ciudad Libertad military airstrip.

Fundación Naturaleza y El Hombre

This institution, the Foundation of Man and Nature (Av. 5B #6611, e/ 66 y 70, tel. 07/209-2885, halcma@fanj.cult.cu; Mon.–Fri. 8:30 A.M.–4:30 P.M.; CUC2) honors Cuban naturalist and explorer Antonio Nuñez Jiménez and features his personal collection. Much of the fascinating and eclectic exhibit is dedicated to the 10,889-mile journey by a team of Cubans (led by Nuñez) that paddled from the source of the Amazon to the Bahamas in dugout canoes in 1996. A replica of the canoe is there, along with a large photo collection, indigenous artifacts such as weapons, headdresses, and a vast collection of ceramics, many showing figures copulating and masturbating.

NÁUTICO, FLORES, AND JAIMANITAS

Beyond Miramar, 5ta Avenida curls around the half-moon Playa Marianao, and passes through the Náutico and Flores districts, setting for Havana's elite prerevolutionary social clubs and *balnearios*. Following the Revolution they were reopened to the hoi polloi and rechristened. The beaches—collectively known as Playas del Oeste—are popular with Cubans on weekends, when they get crowded. There was even an eponymous mini-version of New York's famous Coney Island theme park; re-created in 2008 as Isla de Coco Parque Temático, Havana's only amusement park.

Commanding the scene is the palatial Mudejar-style former **Balneario de la Concha** (5ta e/ 112 and 146), and immediately west,

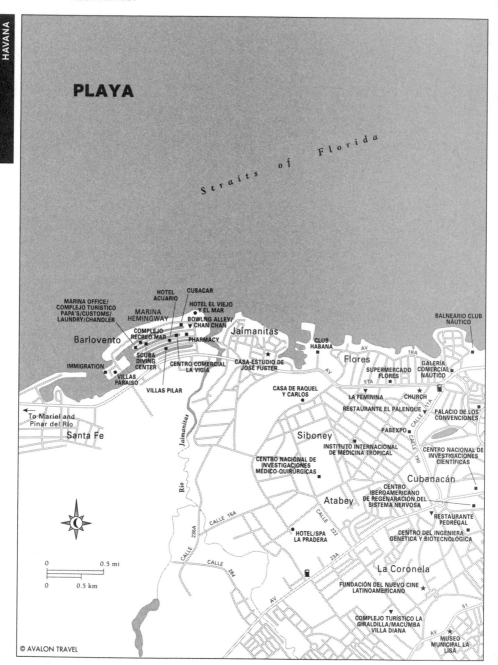

PLAYA

Straits of Florida

MARINA OFFICE/
COMPLEJO TURÍSTICO
PAPA'S/CUSTOMS/
LAUNDRY/CHANDLER

HOTEL
ACUARIO

CUBACAR

HOTEL EL VIEJO
Y EL MAR

MARINA
HEMINGWAY

BOWLNG ALLEY/
CHAN CHAN

COMPLEJO
RECREO MAR

Jaimanitas

CLUB
HABANA

BALNEARIO CLUB
NÁUTICO

Barlovento

PHARMACY

SCUBA
DIVING
CENTER

Flores

IMMIGRATION

CENTRO COMERCIAL
LA VIGÍA

CASA-ESTUDIO DE
JOSÉ FUSTER

SUPERMERCADO
FLORES

GALERÍA
COMERCIAL
NÁUTICO

VILLAS
PARAISO

VILLAS PILAR

CASA DE RAQUEL
Y CARLOS

LA FEMININA

CHURCH

To Mariel and
Pinar del Río

RESTAURANTE EL PALENQUE

PALACIO DE LOS
CONVENCIONES

Santa Fe

Siboney

PABEXPO

INSTITUTO INTERNACIONAL
DE MEDICINA TROPICAL

CENTRO NACIONAL DE
INVESTIGACIONES
CIENTÍFICAS

CENTRO NACIONAL DE
INVESTIGACIONES
MÉDICO-QUIRÚRGICAS

Cubanacán

Atabey

CENTRO
IBEROAMERICANO
DE REGENERACIÓN DEL
SISTEMA NERVOSA

RESTAURANTE
PEDREGAL

HOTEL/SPA
LA PRADERA

CENTRO DEL INGENIERA
GENÉTICA Y BIOTECNOLÓGICA

La Coronela

FUNDACIÓN DEL NUEVO CINE
LATINOAMERICANO

0   0.5 mi

0   0.5 km

COMPLEJO TURÍSTICO LA
GIRALDILLA/MACUMBA
VILLA DIANA

MUSEO
MUNICIPAL LA
LISA

© AVALON TRAVEL

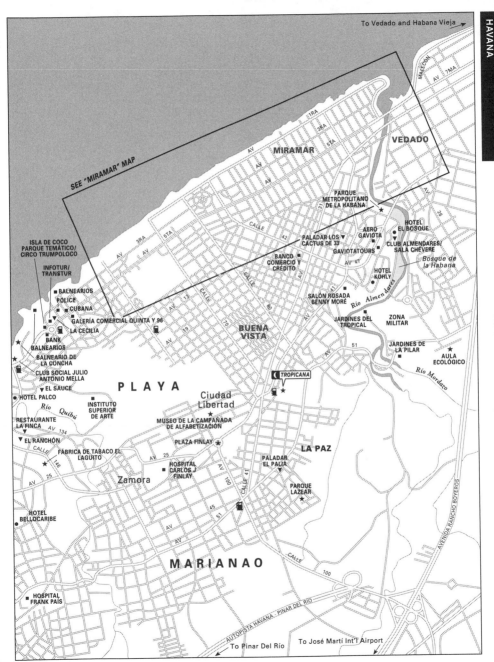

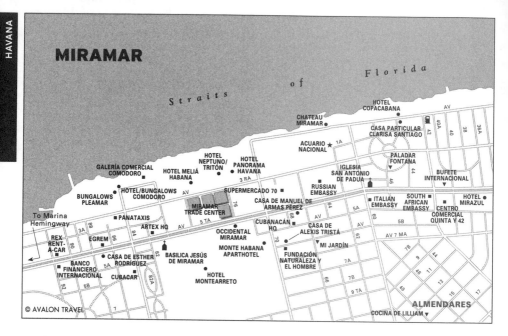

the former **Havana Yacht Club** (5ta y 146). The "Yacht," as the latter was colloquially called, was founded in 1886 and became the snootiest place in Havana (it was here that mulatto President Fulgencio Batista was famously refused entry for being too "black") until the Revolution, when it became the Club Social Julio Antonio Mella, for workers.

Beyond the Río Quibu, 5ta Avenida passes into the Flores district. Here was the Havana-Biltmore Yacht and Country Club, dating from 1928 and fronting Havana's most beautiful expanse of white sand. After the Revolution the beach was opened to all Cubans and the former casino and hotel became a workers' social club. Today, as the **Club Habana** (5ta Av., e/ 188 y 192, Playa, tel. 07/204-5700; dircom@clubhaba.club-hana.get.cu), it has reverted to its former role as a private club for the social (mostly foreign) elite. Nonmembers are welcome (Mon.–Fri. 9 A.M.–7 P.M.; entrance CUC20, including CUC10 consumo mínimo).

Havana's huge yachting marina, **Marina** **Hemingway** (5ta Av. y Calle 248, tel. 07/204-1150, fax 07/204-1149, comercial@comermh. cha.cyt.cu) is in the Jaimanitas district, 15 kilometers west of downtown.

Buses #9 and 420 run to Marina Hemingway from 5ta Avenida and Calle 0.

Casa-Estudio de José Fuster

Artist José R. Fuster, a world-renowned painter and ceramist nicknamed the "Picasso of the Caribbean," has an open-air workshop-gallery at his home (Calle 226; esq. Av. 3A; tel. 07/271-2932 or cell 05264-6051; www. josefuster.com; daily 9 A.M.–5 P.M.). You step through a giant doorway—La Puerta de Fuster—to discover a surreal world made of ceramics. Many of the naive, childlike works are inspired by farmyard scenes, such as *El torre del gallo* (Rooster's Tower), a 12-foot-tall statement on male chauvinism that also doubles as an oven. Other allegorical creations—puppet-like forms, buses bulging with people—pay tribute to Compay Segundo (of Buena Vista Social Club fame) and other

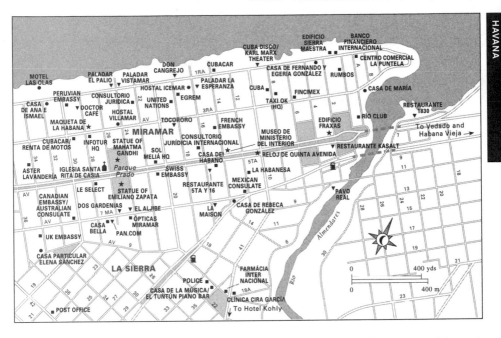

provincial figures. Call ahead to arrange a visit.

Fuster's creativity now graces the entryways, benches, roofs, and facades of houses throughout his local community.

(Fidel Castro's main domicile is nearby, but you can't see it. The home, complete with tennis and basketball courts, is set in an expansive compound surrounded by pine trees and electrified fences and heavy security. All streets surrounding it are marked as one-way, heading away from the house.)

CUBANACÁN AND VICINITY

Cubanacán is—or was—Havana's Beverly Hills, a reclusive area on either side of the Río Quibú. It was developed in the 1920s with winding tree-lined streets and enormous lots on which the most grandiose of Havana's mansions arose. An 18-hole golf course at the Havana Country Club served Havana's wealthy classes, lending the name Country Club Park to what is now called Cubanacán, still the swankiest address in town.

Following the Revolution, most of the area's homeowners fled Cuba. Their mansions were dispensed to Communist Party officials, many of whom live in a lap of luxury that the vast majority of Cubans can only dream of and, of course, never see. Castro maintains several homes here, and the area is replete with military camps and security personnel. Other homes serve either as "protocol" houses—villas where foreign dignitaries and VIPs are housed during visits—or as foreign embassies and ambassadors' homes, among them the U.S. Residency (even the U.S. Marines have a house).

One of the swankiest mansions was built in 1910 for the Marquís de Pinar del Río (it was later adorned with 1930s art deco glass and chrome, a spiral staircase, and abstract floral designs). Today it is the **Fábrica El Laguito** (Av. 146 #2302, e/ 21 y 21A, tel. 07/208-4654), the nation's premier cigar factory, making Montecristos and the majority of Cohibas, *the* premium Havana cigar. Visits by appointment only.

Havana's impressive convention center, the

A WALK ALONG QUINTA AVENIDA

The wide fig-tree-lined boulevard called Fifth Avenue, or "Quinta," runs ruler-straight through the heart of Miramar. It is flanked by mansions, many of which have been restored and are now occupied by various Cuban commercial agencies or leased to foreign corporations. Quinta Avenida is also "Embassy Row." The broad central median is tailor-made for walking the boulevard's eight-kilometer length.

Begin at the **Edificio Fraxas**, a restored Beaux-Arts mansion on the north side of 5ta at Calle 2. Walking west you'll arrive, after four blocks, at Calle 10, pinned by **Reloj de Quinta Avenida**, a large clock erected in 1924 in the central median. At Calle 12, cross to the north side of the street to visit the **Museo del Ministerio del Interior** (see main text); then, one block west, cross to the south side to admire the stained glass and large cigar collection in the **Casa del Habano** (5ta, e/ 14 y 16).

Continue west four blocks to Calle 24, where **Parque de los Ahorcados** (Park of the Hanged), spanning 5ta between Calles 24 and 26, is shaded by massive jagüey trees, seemingly supported by their aerial roots dangling like cascades of water. On the south side of the road is **Plaza Emiliano Zapata,** with a life-size stone statue of Zapata, Mexico's revolutionary hero; on the north side is **Parque Prado,** with a Romanesque temple and a bronze bust to Mahatma Gandhi.

Rising over the west side of Parque Prado is **Iglesia de Santa Rita de Casia** (5ta, esq. Calle 26, tel. 07/204-2001). This exemplar of modernist church architecture dates from 1942 and mixes neocolonial and modern features. Its main feature is a modernist statue of Santa Rita by Rita Longa.

The next 10 blocks are lined with gracious mansions, many of them foreign embassies.

Crossing Calle 60, call in at the modernist-style Romanesque **Iglesia San Antonio de Padua** (Calle 60 #316, esq. 5ta, tel. 07/203-5045), which dates from 1951 and boasts a magnificent, albeit non-functional, organ.

One block west, on the south side of the street, you finally pass a monstrous Cubist tower that can be seen virtually the length of the avenue. Formerly the Soviet Embassy, it is now the **Russian Embassy** (5ta, e/ 62 y 66).

At Calle 70, on your left is the **Occidental Miramar** hotel and, on your right, the **Miramar Trade Center.**

One block farther, on the south side of 5ta, rises the massive Roman-Byzantine-style **Basilica Jesús de Miramar** (5ta #8003, e/ 80 y 82, tel. 07/203-5301; daily 9 A.M.-noon and 4-6 P.M.), built in 1953 with a magnificent organ with 5,000 pipes. The restored church features 14 splendid oversize paintings of the Stations of the Cross by Spanish artist César Hombrados Oñativa.

Palacio de las Convenciones (Calle 146, e/ 11 y 13, tel. 07/202-6011, fax 07/208-4329, www.cpalco.com), was built in 1979 for the Non-Aligned Conference. The main hall (one of 15), seating 2,200 delegates, hosts twice-yearly meetings of the Cuban National Assembly. To its rear is **Pabexpo** (Av. 17 y 180, tel. 07/271-6775), with four exhibition halls for hosting trade shows.

Cuba's biotechnology industry is also centered here and extends westward into the districts of Atabey and Siboney, earning the area the moniker Scientific City. The **Centro de Ingeniería Genética y Biotecnología**

(Center for Genetic Engineering and Biotechnology, Av. 31, e/ 158 y 190, Havana; tel. 07/271-6022; http://gndp.cigb.edu.cu), Cuba's main research facility, is perhaps the most sophisticated research facility in any developing nation.

The convoluted roads of Siboney and Cubanacán follow no logical order.

Bus #32 operates between La Rampa in Vedado and Cubanacán (five pesos).

Instituto Superior de Arte

Following the Revolution, Fidel Castro and Che Guevara famously played a few rounds

THE CIA'S ATTEMPTS TO KILL CASTRO

The bitter taste left by the CIA's botched Bay of Pigs invasion led to an all-out secret war against Castro, an effort code-named Operation Mongoose and headed by Bobby Kennedy. Mongoose eventually involved 500 caseworkers handling 3,000 anti-Castro Cubans at an expense of more than US$100 million a year. The CIA's attempts (now defunct) to oust Castro were set in motion by President Eisenhower as early as March 1959. In *Inside the Company: CIA Diary*, ex-CIA agent Philip Agee described how the dirty-tricks campaign included bombings of public venues meant to discredit Cuba (the CIA claims that Agee later worked for Cuban intelligence; he settled in Havana, where he died in 2008). The agency also invented protest demonstrations, sowed discord in Cuban intelligence by fingering top officials as CIA agents, and even recruited Cuban Embassy staff by "dangling stunning beauties... exceptionally active in amorous adventures."

The CIA's plans read like a James Bond novel... or a comedy of errors. Some plots were straightforward, like the attempt to kill Castro with a bazooka. The CIA's Technical Services Division (TSD) was more imaginative. It impregnated a box of cigars with botulism (they were tested on monkeys and "did the job expected of them") and hoped – in vain – to dupe Castro into smoking one. No one knows whether they reached Castro or whether some innocent victim smoked them. The spooks also tried to damage Castro's image by sprinkling his shoes with thallium salts (a strong depilatory), hoping that his beard would fall out.

Eventually the CIA turned to the Mob. It hired assassins hand-picked by Johnny Rosselli, who had run the syndicate's Sans Souci casino in Havana. The killers were on both the FBI's 10 Most Wanted and Bobby Kennedy's target list of organized crime figures. The marksmen disguised as Marxmen didn't fool Castro – he correctly assumed the CIA would hire assassins, whom he considered inefficient. Several assassins were caught and executed.

---

of golf at the exclusive Havana Country Club before tearing it up and converting the grounds to house Cuba's leading art academy, the National Art Schools (Calle 120 #1110, esq. 9na, tel. 07/208-0017 or 208-0288, isa@cubarte.cult.cu, visits by appointment only), featuring the Escuela de Música (School of Music), Escuela de Ballet (Ballet School), Escuela de Baile Moderno (School of Modern Dance), and Escuela de Bellas Artes (School of Fine Arts). The school was designed by three young "rebel" architects: Italians Roberto Gottardi and Vittorio Garatti, and Cuban Ricardo Porro. Porro's art school was a deliberate evocation of the female form complete with fountain shaped as a *mamey,* or papaya—an overt reference to the female vulva. Gradually, as the five main buildings emerged, they were thought too sensual, too avant-garde for grim Communist tastes. The project was halted before completion, though

the school did open. The ghostly complex fell into ruin, with long tentacles of branches and roots creeping into the buildings. Amazingly, in 2001 the Cuban government approached the three architects and asked them to complete the project. Restoration was completed in 2009.

For the best views, drive along Calles 15 and 134. In summer the facility is closed.

MARIANAO AND LA CORONELA

This dilapidated *municipio,* on the heights south of Miramar, evolved in the mid-19th century, when wealthy Cubans built fine summer homes along newly laid streets. During the 1920s, Marianao boasted the Marianao Country Club, the Oriental Park racetrack, and Grand Nacional Casino, and was given a further boost on New Year's Eve 1939 when the Tropicana nightclub opened

A BIOTECH SUCCESS STORY

Cuba is a biotech minipower. Under Fidel Castro's personal patronage, Cuba has evolved one of the world's most advanced genetic engineering and biotechnology industries, with large-scale investment coming from public sources such as the Pan American Health Organization and the World Food Program.

Cuba has developed some 200 products, both innovative and derivative. It invented and manufactures vaccines for cerebral meningitis, cholera, Hepatitis B, interferon for the treatment of AIDS and cancer, and a skin growth factor to speed the healing of burns. For years, Cuba has touted a cure for the skin disease vitiligo. Recently it developed PPG, a "wonder drug" that reputedly washes cholesterol out of blood (and, incidentally, is Cuba's equivalent of Viagra). Other advances have been made in agriculture and industrial bioengineering. Unfortunately, U.S. law prevents these lifesaving wonders from being sold in the United States.

as the ritziest establishment Havana had ever seen. Marianao remained a pleasure center until the Revolution, when the cabarets were shut down.

Following the U.S. occupation of Cuba in 1898, the U.S. military governor, General Fitzhugh Lee, established his headquarters in Marianao and called it Camp Columbia: Campamento Columbia later became headquarters for Batista's army; it was from here that the sergeant effected his *golpes* in 1933 and 1952. Camp Columbia was bombed on April 15, 1960, during the prelude to the CIA-run Bay of Pigs invasion. Five of Castro's planes were destroyed, but the bombers also struck houses in the neighborhood, killing 7 people and wounding 52, giving Castro a grand political victory in his calls for solidarity against U.S. aggression. The following day he announced for the first time that Cuba was "socialist."

A tower in the center of the traffic circle— **Plaza Finlay**—outside the main entrance, at Avenida 31 and Avenida 100, was erected in 1944 as a beacon for the military airfield. In 1948 a needle was added so that today it is shaped like a syringe in honor of Carlos Finlay, the Cuban who in 1881 discovered the cause of yellow fever.

Bus #34 departs Dragones y Industria, on the northwest side of Parque de la Fraternidad, Habana Vieja, for Marianao.

Museo de la Campaña de Alfabetización

Following the Revolution, Castro turned the barracks of Camp Columbia into a school complex—Ciudad Escolar Libertad—which in 1961 became the headquarters for Castro's national literacy campaign. The Museum of the Literacy Campaign (Av. 29E, esq. 76, tel. 07/260-8054; Mon.– Fri. 8 A.M.–5 P.M.; free) is dedicated to the amazing campaign initiated on January 1, 1960, when 120,632 uniformed *brigadistas,* mostly comprising students, spread out across the country to teach illiterate peasantry to read and write.

Tropicana

The Tropicana nightclub (Calle 72 between 41 and 45, tel. 07/207-0110, fax 07/207-0109) is one of Havana's most astonishing exemplars of modernist architecture. Most of the structures date from 1951, when the club was restored with a new showroom—the **Salon Arcos de Cristal** (Crystal Bows)—designed by Max Borges Recio with a stupendous roof of five arcing concrete vaults and curving bands of glass to fill the intervening space. Built in decreasing order of height, they produce a telescopic effect that channels the perspective toward the orchestra platform. Borges also added the famous geometric sculpture that still forms the backdrop to the main stage, in the outdoor *Salón Bajo las Estrellas.*

Visitors can only view the exterior features by day, when the dancers practice. To admire the Salon Arcos de Cristal, you must visit at night, when the lavishly costumed, statuesque showgirls perform beneath the stars.

A ballet dancer (shown pirouetting on the tips of her toes) by the renowned Cuban sculptor Rita Longa dances amid the lush foliage in front of the entrance. The statue, which has become Tropicana's motif, is joined by a fittingly sensuous statue of the Greek maenads by Longa, with the bacchants performing a wild ritual dance to honor Dionysius.

Sights – Across the Harbor

The harbor channel and Bahía de la Habana (Havana Bay) separate Habana Vieja from the communities of Casablanca, Regla, and Guanabacoa. Although run-down, and with relatively few sights of interest, the districts draw tourists interested in *santería* and Afro-Cuban music and dance, while Casablanca is an access point to the Parque Histórico Militar Morro-Cabaña.

Little ferries bob their way across the harbor, connecting Casablanca and Regla with each other and with Habana Vieja.

◖ PARQUE HISTÓRICO MILITAR MORRO-CABAÑA

Looming over Habana Vieja, on the north side of the harbor channel, is the rugged cliff face of the Cabaña, dominated by two great fortresses that constitute El Morro-La Cabaña Historical Military Park (Carretera de la Cabaña, Habana del Este). Together, the castles comprise the largest and most powerful defensive complex built by the Spanish in the Americas.

Visitors arriving by car reach the complex via the harbor tunnel (no pedestrians or motorcycles without sidecars are allowed) that descends beneath the Máximo Gómez Monument off Avenida de Céspedes. Buses from Parque de la Fraternidad pass through the tunnel and stop by the fortress access road.

Castillo de Los Tres Reyes del Morro

This handsome castle (tel. 07/863-7941; daily 8 A.M.–8 P.M.; entrance CUC5, children under 12 free, guide CUC1, cameras CUC2, videos CUC5) is built into the rocky palisades of Punta Barlovento, crowning a rise that drops straight to the sea at the entrance to Havana's narrow harbor channel. Canted in its articulation, the fort—designed by Italian engineer Bautista Antonelli and initiated in 1589—forms an irregular polygon that follows the contours of the rocky

THE CAÑONAZO

The Ceremonía del Cañonazo (Cannon-Firing Ceremony, CUC6) is held nightly at 8:30 P.M. at the Fortaleza de San Carlos de la Cabaña, where troops dressed in 18th-century military garb and led by fife and drum light the fuse of a cannon to announce the closing of the city gates, maintaining a tradition going back centuries. You are greeted at the castle gates by soldiers in traditional uniform, and the place is lit by flaming lanterns. About 8:50 P.M. a cry rings out, announcing the procession of soldiers marching across the plaza bearing muskets, while a torchbearer lights flaming barrels. The soldiers ascend to the cannon, which they prepare with ramrod and live charge. When the soldier puts the torch to the cannon, you have about three seconds before the thunderous boom. Your heart skips a beat. But it's all over in a millisecond, and the troops march away.

Be sure to get there no later than 8 P.M. if you wish to secure a place close to the cannon. Hotel tour desks offer excursions.

headland on which it was built, with a sharp-angled bastion at the apex, stone walls 10 feet thick, and a series of batteries stepping down to the shore. Hundreds of slaves toiled under the lash of whip and sun to cut the stone in situ, extracted from the void that forms the moats. El Morro took 40 years to complete and served its job well, repelling countless pirate attacks and withstanding for 44 days a siege by British cannon in 1762.

Originally the castle connected with the outside world principally by sea, to which it was linked via the **Plataforma de la Estrella,** the wharf at the southern foot of the cliff. Today you enter via a drawbridge across the deep moat that leads through the **Túnel de Aspillerado** (Tunnel of Loopholes) to vast wooden gates that open to the **Camino de Rondas,** a small parade ground (Plaza de Armas) containing a two-story building atop the cisterns that supplied the garrison of 1,000 men with water.

To the right of the plaza, a narrow entrance leads to the **Baluarte de Austria** (Austrian Bastion), with cannon embrasures for firing down on the moat. A cobbled ramp leads up to other *baluartes.* Various plaques commemorate heroic figures of the siege—even the Royal Navy is honored.

To the left of the Plaza de Armas, the **Sala de História del Faro y Castillo** profiles the various lighthouses and castles in Cuba. Beyond is the **Surtida de los Tinajones,** where giant earthenware vases are inset in stone. They once contained rapeseed oil as lantern fuel for the 15-meter-tall **Faro del Morro** (8 A.M.–7 P.M.; CUC2 extra), a lighthouse constructed in 1844. Today an electric lantern still flashes twice every 15 seconds. You can climb to the top for a bird's-eye view of the castle—the last leg of the climb is tight, and not for claustrophobics.

All maritime traffic in and out of Havana harbor is controlled from the **Estación Semafórica,** the semaphore station atop the castle, accessed via the Baluarte de Tejeda.

Below the castle, facing the city on the landward side and reached by a cobbled ramp, is the **Batería de los Doce Apóstoles** (Battery of the

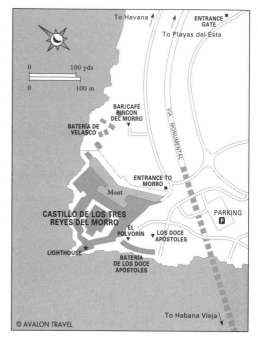

Twelve Apostles). It boasts massive cannons and a little bar—El Polvorín (The Powderhouse).

Fortaleza de San Carlos de la Cabaña

This massive fortress (Carretera de la Cabaña, tel. 07/862-4095; daily 10 A.M.–10 P.M.; entrance CUC5 adults, children under 12 free, CUC8 for the *cañonazo* ceremony, guide CUC1), half a kilometer east of the Morro, enjoys a fantastic strategic position, with a clifftop balcony over the city and harbor. It is the largest fort in the Americas, covering 10 hectares and stretching 700 meters in length. It was built 1763–1774 following the English invasion, and cost the staggering sum of 14 million pesos—when told the cost, the king after whom it is named reached for a telescope; surely, he said, it must be large enough to see from Madrid. The castle counted some 120 bronze cannons and mortars, plus a permanent garrison of 1,300 men. While never actually used in battle, it has been claimed that its

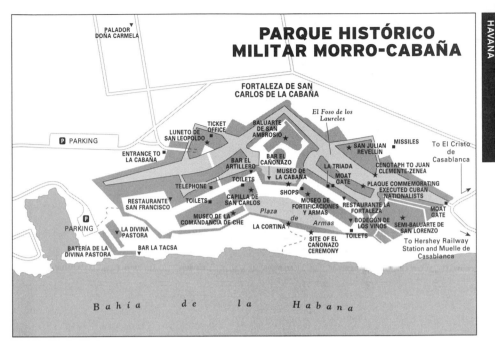

PARQUE HISTÓRICO MILITAR MORRO-CABAÑA

PALADOR DOÑA CARMELA

FORTALEZA DE SAN CARLOS DE LA CABAÑA

El Foso de los Laureles

P PARKING

LUNETO DE SAN LEOPOLDO

TICKET OFFICE

BALUARTE DE SAN AMBROSIO

ENTRANCE TO LA CABAÑA

SAN JULIAN REVELLIN

MISSILES   To El Cristo de Casablanca

BAR EL ARTILLERO

BAR EL CAÑONAZO

LA TRIADA

CENOTAPH TO JUAN CLEMENTE-ZENEA

MUSEO DE LA CABAÑA

MOAT GATE

TELEPHONE

TOILETS

SHOPS

PLAQUE COMMEMORATING EXECUTED CUBAN NATIONALISTS

RESTAURANTE SAN FRANCISCO

TOILETS

CAPILLA DE SAN CARLOS

MUSEO DE FORTIFICACIONES Y ARMAS

RESTAURANTE LA FORTALEZA

MOAT GATE

P PARKING

LA DIVINA PASTORA

MUSEO DE LA COMANDANCIA DE CHE

Plaza de Armas

LA CORTINA

BODEGÓN DE LOS VINOS

SEMI-BALUARTE DE SAN LORENZO

BATERÍA DE LA DIVINA PASTORA

BAR LA TACSA

SITE OF EL CAÑONAZO CEREMONY

TOILETS

To Hershey Railway Station and Muelle de Casablanca

B a h í a   d e   l a   H a b a n a

---

dissuasive presence won all potential battles—a tribute to the French designer and engineer entrusted with its conception and construction. The castle has been splendidly restored.

From the north, you pass through two defensive structures before reaching the monumental baroque portal flanked by great columns with a pediment etched with the escutcheon of Kings Charles III, and a massive drawbridge over a 12-meter-deep moat, one of several moats carved from solid rock and separating individual fortress components.

Beyond the entrance gate, a paved alley leads to the **Plaza de Armas,** centered on a grassy, tree-shaded park fronted by a 400-meter-long curtain wall. The wall—**La Cortina**—runs the length of the castle on its south side and formed the main gun position overlooking Havana. It is lined with cannons engraved with lyrical names such as *La Hermosa* (The Beautiful). The *cañonazo* (cannon-lighting) ceremony is held here nightly.

Opening to the plaze is a small **chapel** with

baroque facade and charming vaulted interior. Facing it is the **Museo de la Comandancia de Che,** where Che Guevara had his headquarters in the months following the Triunfo del Revolución. Here he set up his revolutionary tribunals for "crimes against the security of the state." The small museum salutes the Argentinian doctor-turned-revolutionary who played such a key part in the Cuban Revolution. His M-1 rifle, submachine gun, radio, and rucksack are among the exhibits.

A cobbled street leads west from the entrance gate to a large cannon-filled courtyard, from where steps lead down to **La Divina Pastora** restaurant, beside the wharf where supply ships once berthed. The adjoining **Bar La Tasca** (tel. 07/860-8341; daily noon–11 P.M.) overhangs the harbor and is a great place to relax with a mojito and cigar.

On the north side of the plaza, the **Museo Monográfico de la Fortaleza** traces the castle's development. The museum features uniforms and weaponry from the colonial epoch, including a representation of the *cañonazo* ceremony. A portal here leads into a garden—**Patio de Los Jagüeyes**—that once served as a *cortadura,* a defensive element packed with explosives that could be ignited to foil the enemy's attempts to gain entry.

Farther east is the **Museo de las Maquetas,** featuring 3-D *maquetas* of each of Cuba's castles, including a detailed model of the Cabaña. Next door, the **Museo de Fortificaciones y Armas** contains suits of armor and weaponry that spans the ancient Arab and Asian worlds and stretches back through medieval times to the Roman era.

The museums open to the north to cobbled **Calle de la Marina,** where converted barracks, armaments stores, and prisoners' cells now contain restaurants and the **Casa del Tabaco y Ron,** displaying the world's longest cigar (11 meters long).

Midway down Marina, a gate leads down to **El Foso de los Laureles,** a massive moat containing the execution wall where nationalist sympathizers were shot during the Wars of Independence. A cenotaph is dedicated to Juan Clemente Zenea, executed in 1871. Following the Revolution, scores of Batista supporters and "counterrevolutionaries" met a similar fate here.

On the north side of the moat, a separate fortress unit called **San Julián Revellín** contains examples of Soviet missiles installed during the Cuban Missile Crisis (called the October 1962 Crisis or the Caribbean Crisis by Cubans). The rest of the fortress grounds is still used as a military base and is off-limits. It includes the domed **Observatorio Nacional** (National Observatory).

A ferry (10 centavos) runs to Casablanca every 20 minutes or so from the Muelle Luz (Av. del Puerto y Calle Santa Clara) in Habana Vieja. You can walk uphill from Casablanca to an easterly entrance gate to the Foso de los Laureles. This gate closes at dusk, so don't take this route if you plan on seeing the *cañonazo*.

Estatua Cristo de la Habana

A great statue of Jesus Christ (daily 9 A.M.–8 P.M.; entrance CUC1, children under 12 free) on Carretera del Asilo looms over Casablanca, dominating the cliff face immediately east of the Fortaleza. The 15-meter-tall statue, which was unveiled on December 25, 1958, was hewn from Italian Carrara marble by female Cuban sculptor Jilma Madera. From the *mirador* surrounding the statue, you have a bird's-eye view of the harbor. The views are especially good at dawn and dusk, and it is possible, with the sun gilding the waters, to imagine great galleons slipping in and out of the harbor, laden with treasure en route to Spain.

Adjoining, the **Casa del Che** (daily

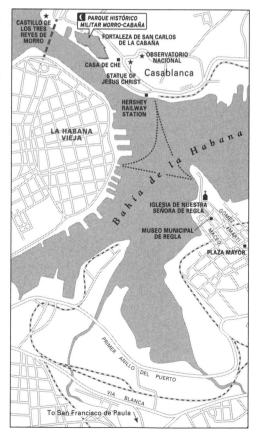

9 A.M.–8 P.M.) café/restaurant has a small museum dedicated to the revolutionary, with personal effects (entrance CUC4, guide CUC1, camera CUC2).

The statue is a 10-minute uphill walk from the Casablanca dock.

REGLA

Regla, a working-class *barrio* on the eastern shore of Havana harbor, evolved in the 16th century as a fishing village and eventually became Havana's foremost warehousing and slaving center. It developed into a smugglers' port in colonial days, a reputation it maintained until recent days, when pirates (who made their living stealing off American yachts anchored in the harbor) were known as *terribles reglanos*. Havana's main electricity-generating plant is here, along with petrochemical works, both of which pour bilious plumes over town.

Many slaves settled here, infusing Regla with a profound African heritage. Regla is a center of *santería;* walking its streets, note the tiny shrines outside many houses. Calle Calixto García has many fine examples. Many *babalawos* (*santería* priests) live here and will happily dispense advice for a fee; try **Eberardo Marero** (Nico López #60, e/ Coyola y Camilo Cienfuegos).

The **Museo Municipal de Regla** (Martí

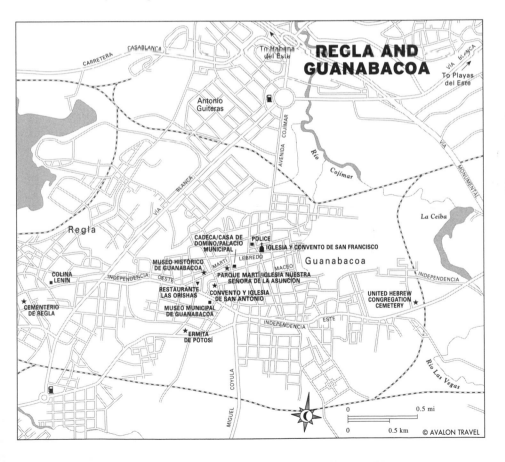

#158, e/ Facciolo y La Piedra, tel. 07/797-6989; Tues.–Sat. 9 A.M.–5 P.M., Sun. 9 A.M.–1 P.M.; entrance CUC2, guide CUC1), two blocks east of the harborfront, tells the tale of the town's *santería* associations. Other displays include colonial-era swords, slave shackles, and the like.

Ferries (10 centavos) run between Regla and the Muelle Luz (Av. San Pedro y Santa Clara) in Habana Vieja.

Bus #6 departs for Regla from Agramonte (Zulueta) and Genios in Habana Vieja; bus #106 departs from Agramonte and Refugio.

Iglesia de Nuestra Señora de Regla

The Church of Our Lady of Regla (Sanctuario #11, e/ Máximo Gómez y Litoral, tel. 07/797-6228; daily 7:30 A.M.–5:30 P.M.), built in 1810 on the harborfront, is one of Havana's loveliest churches. Its inner beauty is highlighted by a fabulous gilt altar beneath an arched ceiling. On holy days, the altar is sumptuously lit with votive candles. Dwelling in alcoves in the wall are figurines of miscellaneous saints, including a statue of St. Anthony leading a wooden suckling pig wearing a dog collar and a large blue ribbon. *Habaneros* flock to pay homage to the black Virgen de Regla, patron saint of sailors and Catholic counterpart to Yemayá, the African goddess of the sea in the Yoruba religion. Time your visit for the seventh of each month, when large masses are held; or September 7, when a pilgrimage draws the devout of Catholicism and *santería* and the Virgin is taken down from her altar and paraded through town.

Outside, 20 meters to the east and presiding over her own private chapel, is another statue of the Virgen de Regla, with a statue of the Virgen de la Caridad del Cobre, Cuba's patron saint. Syncretized as the *orisha* Ochún, the Virgen de la Caridad del Cobre also draws adherents of *santería*.

Colina Lenin

Calle Martí, the main street, leads east to the city cemetery where turning north, after two blocks, steps lead up to Lenin Hill (Calle Vieja, e/ Enlase y Rotaria), where a three-meter-tall bronze face of the Communist leader is carved into the cliff face, with a dozen life-size figures (in cement) cheering him from below. A rather pitiful museum (tel. 07/797-6899; Tues.–Sat. 9 A.M.–5 P.M.; free) atop the hill is dedicated to Lenin and various martyrs of the Cuban revolution.

The Colina is more directly reached from Parque Guaycanamar (Calle Martí, six blocks east of the harborfront) via Calle Albuquerque and 24 de Febrero; you'll reach a metal staircase that leads to the park. Bus #29 will also take you there from the Regla dock.

GUANABACOA

Guanabacoa, about three kilometers east of Regla, was founded in 1607 and developed in colonial days as the major trading center for slaves. Thus, an Afro-Cuban culture evolved here, expressed not least in a strong musical heritage. The **Casa de la Trova** (Martí #111, e/ San Antonio y Versalles, tel. 07/797-7687; Tues.–Sun. 9 A.M.–11 P.M.; entrance one peso) hosts performances of Afro-Cuban music and dance, as does **Restaurante Las Orishas** (Calle Martí, e/ Lamas y Cruz Verde, tel. 07/794-7878; daily noon–midnight).

Guanabacoa is also Cuba's most important center of *santería*. So strong is the association that all over Cuba, folks facing extreme adversity will say "I'm going to have to go to Guanabacoa," implying that only the power of a *babalawo* can fix the problem.

Guanabacoa also boasts several important religious sites (most are tumbledown and await restoration), including two Jewish cemeteries on the east side of town. Combined with a visit to Regla, it makes an intriguing excursion from downtown Havana.

Getting There: Bus #29 runs to Guanabacoa from the Regla dock. Bus #3 departs for Guanabacoa from Máximo Gómez and Aponte, on the south side of Parque de la Fraternidad, in Habana Vieja; and bus #95 from the corner of Corrales and Agramonte (Zulueta). From Vedado, you can take bus #195; from the Plaza de la Revolución, take bus #5.

Parque Martí

The sprawling town is centered on this small tree-shaded plaza (Calles Martí, División Pepe Antonio, y Adolfo del Castillo Cadenas). Parque Martí is dominated by the recently restored **Iglesia Nuestra Señora de la Asunción** (División #331, e/ Martí y Cadenas, tel. 07/797-7368; Mon.–Fri. 8 A.M.– noon and 2–5 P.M.; Sun. 8–11 A.M.), commonly called the Parroquial Mayor. Completed in 1748, it features a lofty Mudejar-inspired wooden roof and baroque gilt altar dripping with gold, plus 14 Stations of the Cross. If the main doors are locked, try the side entrance on Calle Enrique Güiral.

The **Museo Histórico de Guanabacoa** (Historical Museum of Guanabacoa, Martí #108, e/ Valenzuela y Quintín Bandera, tel. 07/797-9117; Tues.–Sat. 10 A.M.–6 P.M., Sun. 9 A.M.–1 P.M.; entrance CUC2), one block west of the plaza, tells the tale of Guanabacoa's development and outlines the evolution of Afro-Cuban culture and *santería*.

One block southwest of the park is the **Convento y Iglesia de San Antonio** (Máximo Gómez, esq. San Antonio, tel. 07/797-7241), begun in 1720 and completed in 1806. The convent is now a school but the *custodio* may let you in to admire the exquisite *alfarje* ceiling.

Convento de Santo Domingo

This convent (Santo Domingo #407, esq. Rafael de Cadena, tel. 07/797-7376; Tues.–Fri. 9–11:30 A.M. and 3:30–5 P.M. but often closed), dating from 1728, has an impressive neo-baroque facade. Its church, the **Iglesia de Nuestra Señora de la Candelaria,** boasts a magnificent blue-and-gilt baroque altar plus an intricate *alfarje*. The door is usually closed, in which case ring the doorbell to the left of the main entrance.

Ermita de Potosí

The only ecclesiastical edifice thus far restored is the tiny hilltop Potosí Hermitage (Calzada Vieja Guanabacoa, esq. Calle Potosí, tel. 07/797-9867; daily 8 A.M.–5 P.M.), the highlight of a visit to Guanabacoa. The simple hermitage dates back to 1644, and is the oldest religious structure still standing in Cuba. It has an intriguing cemetery.

Entertainment and Events

Don't believe anything you've read about Communism having killed the capital city's zest. Yes, the city has lost the Barbary Coast spirit of prerevolutionary days, but *habaneros* love to paint the town red (so to speak) as much as their budgets allow. Many venues are seedier (albeit without the strippers) than they were four decades ago; in many the decor hasn't changed!

The scene is fluid. Nightlife is a lot tamer than it was just a decade ago, not least because pricey entrance fees dissuade Cubans from attending. *Habaneros* mostly socialize impromptu, on the street, although afternoon discos keep up some of the old abandon. And though Havana has scores of bars, Cubans are even priced out of most bars (one beer can cost the equivalent of a week's salary),

and few have any energy. Habana Vieja is relatively quiet; most of the top venues are in Vedado.

For theater, classical concerts, and other live performances it's often difficult to make a reservation by telephone. Instead, you should go to the venue and buy a ticket in advance or just before the performance. Comedy and theater are exclusively in Spanish.

Resources

Havana lacks a reliable, widely circulated forum for announcements of upcoming events. Word of mouth is the best resource. Call ahead to double-check dates, times, and venue.

A good Internet source (in Spanish only, alas) is **Egrem** (tel. 07.204-4685, http://promociones.egrem.co.cu), which maintains a

© CHRISTOPHER P. BAKER

Karl Marx theater, formerly known as the Blanquita theater

weekly update of live concerts nationwide on its website.

Cartelera (www.lajiribilla.cu/cartelera_cultural.html) also has weekly updates on its website; a weekly publication with information on exhibitions, galleries, performances, and more in both Spanish and English. is available in many hotel lobbies, as is the monthly *Guía Cultural de la Habana,* which provides up-to-date information on what's on in town. *Granma,* the daily Communist Party newspaper, also lists the forthcoming week's events.

Radio Taíno (1290 AM and 93.3 FM), serving tourists, offers information on cultural happenings with nightly broadcasts 5–7 P.M., as does Radio Habana (94.9 FM); the TV program Hurón Azul (Cubavision) gives a preview of the next week's top happenings every Thursday at 10:25 P.M.

EVENTS

For a list of forthcoming festivals, conferences, and events, visit www.cubaabsolutely.com/events.html or contact **Paradiso** (Calle 19 #560, esq. C, Vedado, Havana, tel. 07/836-2124, www.paradiso.cu), or the **Buró de Convenciones** (Hotel Neptuno, 3ra Ave., e/ 70 y 74, 3er. piso, Miramar, tel. 07/204-8273, fax 07/204-8162, http://buro.get.tur.cu).

Annual Events
JANUARY
The **Cabildos** festival is held on January 6, when Habana Vieja resounds with festivities recalling the days when Afro-Cuban *cabildos* danced through the streets in vivid costumes. Contact Agencia de Viajes San Cristóbal (Oficios #110, e/ Lamparilla y Amargura, tel. 07/861-9171, www.viajessancristobal.cu).

FEBRUARY
The star-studded **Festival Internacional de Jazz** (International Havana Jazz Festival, Calle 15, esq. F, Vedado, tel. 07/862-4938, romeu@cubarte.cult.cu) is now held in February and is highlighted by the greats of Cuban jazz, such as Chucho Valdés and Irakere and Juan

CINEMAS

Most of Havana's cinemas are mid-20th-century gems that have been allowed to deteriorate to the point of near-dilapidation. Movie houses on La Rampa, in Vedado, tend to be less rundown than those in Habana Vieja and Centro Habana. *Granma* and *Cartelera* list what's currently showing. Children under 16 years of age are not allowed in, regardless of movie content. Entrance usually costs two pesos; foreigners are sometimes charged in dollars.

The **Sala Glauber Rocha** (Av. 212, esq. 31, La Coronela, tel. 07/271-8967), in the Fundación del Nuevo Cine Latinoamericano, shows mostly Latin American movies Tuesday–Friday at 3 P.M. and 5:30 P.M. (CUC2).

The most important cinemas are:

Cine Acapulco (Av. 26, e/ 35 y 37, Vedado, tel. 07/833-9573).

Cine-Teatro Astral (Calzada de Infanta #501, esq. San Martín, Centro Habana, tel. 07/878-1001) is the comfiest *cine* in Havana. It functions mostly as a theater for political features.

Cine Charles Chaplin (Calle 23 #1155, e/ 10 y 12, Vedado, tel. 07/831-1101) shows Wednesday–Sunday at 5 and 8 P.M.

Cine La Rampa (Calle 23 #111, e/ O y P, Vedado, tel. 07/878-6146) shows daily from 4:40 P.M. except Wednesday; it mostly shows Cuban and Latin American films, plus the occasional obscure foreign movie.

Cine Payret (Prado #503, esq. San José, Habana Vieja, tel. 07/863-3163) is Havana's largest cinema and has as many as six showings daily, beginning at 12:30 P.M. It has midnight shows Friday–Sunday.

Cine Riviera (Calles 23, e/ H y G, Vedado, tel. 07/832-9564), has predominantly Hollywood movies daily from 4:40 P.M.

Cine Yara (Calle 23 y Calle L, Vedado, tel. 07/832-9430) opens at 12.30 P.M. and is Havana's "main" theater.

Multi-Cine Infanta (Infanta, e/ Neptuno y San Miguel, tel. 07/878-9323), with four up-to-date auditoriums, shows Monday–Friday at 5 and 8 P.M., Saturday and Sunday at 2 P.M., 5 P.M., and 8 P.M.

Formell and Los Van Van. Concerts are held at various venues.

The **Habanos Festival** (tel. 07/204-0510, www.habanos.com), for big-spenders, celebrates Cuban cigars and opens at the Tropicana nightclub. The high point is an elegant dinner and auction.

Bookworms should time their visit to coincide with the **Feria Internacional del Libro de la Habana** (Havana Book Fair), organized by the Instituto Cubano del Libro (Cuban Book Institute, Calle O'Reilly #14, Habana Vieja, tel. 07/862-4789, www.cubaliteraria.cult.cu) and held in Plaza de Armas.

APRIL

The **Festival Internacional de Percusión** (International Percussion Festival, tel. 07/203-8808, percuba@mail.com) is held each April.

The prestigious **Bienal de la Habana** (Havana Biennial, tel. 07/209-6569, www.

bienaldelahabana.cu), hosted in even-numbered years by the Centro Wilfredo Lam (Calle San Ignacio #22, tel. 07/861-2096, www.cnap.cult.cu), features artists from more than 50 countries. It offers workshops and other activities.

MAY

On May 1, head to the Plaza de la Revolución for the **Primero de Mayo** (May Day Parade). The day is meant to honor workers and is intended to appear as a spontaneous demonstration of revolutionary loyalty. In reality it is a carefully choreographed affair. While loyalists display genuine enthusiasm, the majority of attendees are bused in and attend for fear of being black-marked by CDRs and party officials at work. Stooges use loudspeakers to work up the crowd with chants of *"¡Viva Fidel!"* and *"¡Viva Raúl!"* Each year's theme reflects the anti–United States flavor of the day. You'll be surrounded by as many as 500,000 people waving colorful banners and placards and wearing T-shirts painted with revolutionary slogans.

The **Festival Internacional de Guitarra** (International Guitar Festival and Contest) is held at the Teatro Roldán in even-numbered years.

The **Festival de Danzón** (tel. 07/838-3113, promeven@uneac.co.cu) celebrates the traditional dance form.

JUNE

The **Festival Internacional Boleros de Oro** (International Boleros Festival, UNEAC, Calle 17 #351, e/ G y H, Vedado, tel. 07/832-4551, www.uneac.co.cu), features traditional Latin American folk music.

JULY

Coloquio Internacional Hemingway (International Hemingway Colloquium) takes place in early July every odd-numbered year. The venue changes each year.

AUGUST

The amateurish **Carnaval de la Habana** (Carnival in Havana, tel. 07/832-3742, atic@cubarte.cult.cu) is now held in the first or second week of August.

Every odd year sees the **Festival Internacional de Música Popular Benny Moré,** featuring a panorama of popular Cuban music. The festival takes place in Havana concurrently with events in Cienfuegos.

SEPTEMBER

The 10-day biennial **Festival Internacional de Teatro** (International Theater Festival of Havana), sponsored by the Consejo Nacional de Artes Escénicas (National Council of Scenic Arts, Calle 4 #257, Miramar, tel. 07/832-4126), is held in odd-numbered years and features international theater companies covering drama, street theater, musicals, and dance.

OCTOBER

The **Festival Internacional de Ballet** (International Ballet Festival) features ballet corps from around the world, plus the acclaimed

Ballet Nacional de Cuba (BNC, Calzada #510, e/ D y E, Vedado, Ciudad Habana, tel. 07/832-4625, www.balletcuba.cult.cu).

NOVEMBER

ExpoCanino (tel. 07/641-9006, balance@minag.cu) is Havana's answer to the Crufts and Westminster dog shows. It also has a show in April.

The annual **Festival de la Habana de Música Contemporánea** (Havana Festival of Contemporary Music, c/o UNEAC, Calle 17 #351, e/ G y H, Vedado, tel. 07/832-0194, www.uneac.com.cu) spans a week in early October, with performances ranging from choral to electro-acoustic.

DECEMBER

The **Festival del Nuevo Cine Latinoamericano** (Festival of New Latin American Cinema, c/o the Instituto de Cinematografía Calle 23 #1155, Vedado, tel. 07/838-2354, www.habanafilmfestival.com or www.cubacine.cu) is one of Cuba's most glittering events. Cuban actors and directors schmooze with Hollywood counterparts at parties in the Hotel Nacional and Hotel Habana Libre. Movies from throughout the Americas and Europe are shown at cinemas and theaters across the city and the festival culminates with Cuba's own version of the Oscar, the Coral prizes. You buy your tickets for particular cinemas well before the programming is announced; or you can buy a pass (CUC25) good for the duration of the festival.

BARS
Habana Vieja

Every tourist in town wants to sip a *mojito* at **La Bodeguita del Medio** (Empredado #207, e/ Cuba y Tacón, tel. 07/862-6121; daily noon–midnight), as Ernest Hemingway did almost daily. However, the *mojitos* are weak and far too small for the CUC4 tab. Go for the ambience, aided by troubadors.

Another Hemingway favorite—and one offering far better and cheaper (CUC3) *mojitos*—is the **Dos Hermanos** (Av. San Pedro #304, esq. Sol, tel. 07/861-3514; 24 hours), a down-

---

CONSUMO MÍNIMO

You'll come across this term everywhere for entry to nightclubs and many other facilities. The term means "minimum consumption" and can be a source of scams and confusion. Basically, it means that patrons have a right to consume up to a specified amount of food and/or beverage. For example, entry to the swimming pool at the Hotel Sevilla costs CUC20, but includes a consumo mínimo of up to CUC16 of food and beverage. There are no refunds for unused portions of the fee.

---

to-earth wharf-front saloon where Hemingway bent elbows with sailors and prostitutes at the long wooden bar, open to the street through wooden *rejas*. There's often live music and usually more Cubans than tourists.

Hemingway enjoyed his daily daiquiri at **El Floridita** (Obispo, esq. Monserrate, tel. 07/867-9299; bar daily 11:30 A.M.–1 A.M.). It may not quite live up to its 1950s aura, when *Esquire* magazine named it one of the great bars of the world, but to visit Havana without sipping a (weak) daiquiri here would be like visiting France without tasting the wine.

The wood-paneled **Bar Monserrate** (Monserrate, esq. Obrapía, tel. 07/860-9751; daily noon–midnight), just south of El Floridita, is popular with Cubans and is noted for its Coctel Monserrate (one teaspoon of sugar, two ounces of grapefruit juice, five drops of grenadine, two ounces of white rum, ice, and a sprig of mint; CUC2.50). It's a good spot to while away the afternoon listening to live music. It also draws *jiniteros* and *jiniteras*. The staff is no less trustworthy: Count your change!

I love the **Café Barrita** (Monserrate #261, esq. San Juan de Díos, tel. 07/862-9310 ext. 131; daily 9 A.M.–6 P.M.), in Edificio Bacardí. Formerly the private bar of the Bacardí family, it casts you right back to the 1930s. Snacks are served. It's popular with a cigar-smoking foreign crowd, and the *mojitos* are strong.

Lluvia de Oro (Obispo #316, esq. Habana, tel.

07/862-9870; daily 9 A.M.–midnight) is a lively, down-to-earth bar popular with foreigners come to sample the live music and meet wayward *cubanas* and *cubanos*. It serves cheap but strong *mojitos* (CUC2.50), and features live *son* music. Nearby, the once-rocking **Café París** (San Ignacio #202, esq. Obispo, tel. 07/862-0466; daily 9 A.M.–midnight) a few years back fell afoul of the police for the lively mixing of Cubans and tourists; it has yet to reignite its former spark.

Hotel bars get few clients (except a sprinkling of tourists) and are generally boring. The 24-hour lobby piano-bar in the **Hotel Ambos Mundos** (Obispo, esq. Mercaderes, tel. 07/860-9530) is a delightful place to tipple, as is the **Bar La Marina** (Av. San Pedro, esq. Luz, tel. 07/862-8000) in the Hotel Armadores de Santander. The latter has an upscale mood and nautical motif (including staff in mariners' uniforms). The chicest bars are in the **Hotel Saratoga** (Paseo del Prado #603, esq. Dragones, tel. 07/868-1000; noon–midnight); and the art deco **Bar Lejaim** (San Ignacio, esq. Amargura, tel. 07/860-8280) in the Hotel Raquel, which has an open bar each Wednesday evening, with Cuban cocktails and *bocas* (snacks).

Beer lovers should head to Plaza Vieja, where the **Taberna de la Muralla** (San Ignacio #364, tel. 07/866-4453; daily 11 A.M.–1 A.M.) is a Viennese-style brewpub producing delicious Pilsen (light) and Munich (dark) beer. You can order half-liters (CUC2), liters, or a whopping three-liter dispenser, called a *dispensa*. This tall glass cylinder is fitted with a tap and filled with beer kept chilled by a thinner center tube filled with ice.

Vedado and Plaza de la Revolución

The Hotel Nacional's **Bar Vista del Golfo** (Calle O, esq. 21, tel. 07/874-3564) has a jukebox and walls festooned with photos of such famous visitors as Errol Flynn and assorted mobsters. It rarely has patrons, however; they prefer the hotel's airy **Bar La Terraza,** where you can sit in a sofa chair with a cigar and cocktail while musicians entertain with live music.

The small **El Relicario Bar** (Paseo, e/ 1ra y 3ra, tel. 07/204-3636; 1 P.M.–1 A.M.), in the mezzanine of the Hotel Meliá Cohiba, is popular with a monied, cigar-loving crowd and offers an elegant Edwardian ambience and relative serenity. It has a pool table. I also like the small lobby bar in the **Hotel Habana Riviera** (Malecón y Paseo, tel. 07/836-4051), and the sedate lobby bar of the **Hotel Habana Libre Tryp.**

For superb views of the city, try the Habana's Libre's **Salón Turquino** (tel. 07/834-6100), on the 25th floor; or **La Torre** (Calle 17 #55, e/ M y N, tel. 07/832-2451), atop the Focsa building.

Penny-pinchers wanting to sup with Cubans should head to **Gran Café** (Calle 23, esq. Av. de los Presidentes, tel. 07/830-9375; daily 10 A.M.–2 A.M.), serving CUC1 *mojitos* and CUC0.50 rum shots. The surrounds are simple.

Also popular with Cubans is **Mesón de la Chorrera** (Malecón y Calle 20, tel. 07/838-3896; daily noon–midnight), upstairs in the old fortress at the mouth of the Río Almendares; this atmospheric place even has cannons pointing through the windows.

Playa (Miramar and Beyond)

This district has very few bars. The most sophisticated are in the Hotel Meliá Habana and Occidental Miramar hotels, though these are devoid of Cubans and lifeless.

Classier **Paleta Bar** (tel. 07/204-7311; daily 11:30 A.M.–midnight), in the Miramar Trade Center, draws in-the-know expats. This hip, minimalist place is trendy and has occasional live music.

Two piano bars to consider are at **Dos Gardenias** (7ma Av. y 26, tel. 07/204-2353) and **Piano Bar Piel Canela** (Calle 16 #701, esq. 7ma, tel. 07/204-1543; nightly 3–8 P.M. and 10 P.M.–3 A.M.; entrance CUC1), at La Maison.

TRADITIONAL CUBAN MUSIC AND DANCE

Habana Vieja

Agencia de Viajes San Cristóbal (Oficios #110, e/ Lamparilla y Amargura, tel. 07/861-9171, www.viajessancristobal.cu) hosts **Noche en las Plazas** (Night in the Plazas) one Saturday per month at 9 P.M. in the Plaza de la Catedral or Plaza de San Francisco, with folkloric *espectáculos* (CUC22 with dinner). Reservations can be made at hotel tour desks.

Every last Saturday of the month at 3 P.M., the **Peña de Heydi Igualada** features the eponymous trova singer in the Palacio de Segundo Caballo (O'Reilly #14, tel. 07/862-8091), on Plaza de Armas.

The **Asociación Cultural Yoruba de Cuba** (Prado #615, e/ Dragones y Monte, tel. 07/863-5953) hosts the Peña Oyú Obbá, with traditional Afro-Cuban music and dance, each Thursday at 6–8 P.M. and Friday at 9–8 P.M. (CUC5).

Centro Habana

The place to be on Sunday is "Salvador's Alley" for **Rumba del "Salvador's Alley"** (Callejón de Hamel, e/ Aramburo y Hospital, tel. 07/878-1661, eliasasef@yahoo.es), where Salvador González Escalona hosts a rumba with Afro-Cuban music and dance, Sunday noon–3 P.M.; and traditional music each last Friday of the month at 9 P.M.

The **Casa de la Trova** (San Lázaro #661, e/ Padre Varela y Gervasio, tel. 07/879-3373l; Mon.–Fri. 8:30 A.M.–4:30 P.M.; CUC5) has live music—everything from *filin* to *son* and *nueva trova*. Friday evening is best. Adherents of *filin* music flock on Friday 10 P.M.–1 A.M. for **La Peña de Joya** (San Lázaro #667, Apto. 9, e/ Padre Varela y Gervasio), two doors down.

Centro Cultural Comunitario (San Nicolás #220, e/ Concordia y Virtudes) hosts country music every Monday at 6 P.M.

Folkloric groups practice *bolero, danzón,* and *guanguancó* at **Salón de Ensayo Benny Moré** (Neptuno #960, e/ Aguila y Galiano, tel. 07/878-8827; Tues.–Sat. 9:30 A.M.–noon and 2–5 P.M.).

Vedado and Plaza de la Revolución

My favorite hangout in Havana is **Café Concierto Gato Tuerto** (Calle O #14, e/ 17 y

19, tel. 07/833-2224; CUC5 cover), a cramped and moody 1950s-style nightclub that hosts *música filin*, *trova*, and *bolero* nightly until 3 A.M. It gets packed, mostly with middle-aged Cubans (and a smattering of expats and trophy Cuban women) packed cheek-to-jowl up to the postage-size stage tucked in one corner. The show normally doesn't begin until 11 P.M. It's the kind of place Sinatra and his Rat Pack might have hung out. Don't miss the Voces Negras, a quintet that sings everything from Aretha Franklin and Frank Sinatra to salsa.

In a similar vein, try **Club Imágenes** (Calzada #602, esq. C, tel. 07/833-3606; daily 11 P.M.–3 A.M.; CUC5 cover), a stylish piano bar hosting *boleros* and other traditional music for the late-night (and more mature) crowd. It also has karaoke and comedy (Fri.–Sun. 3:30–8 P.M.; CUC2).

El Hurón Azul (UNEAC, Calle 17 #351, esq. H, tel. 07/832-4551; daily 5 P.M.–2 A.M.) hosts a *peña* with Afro-Cuban music and dance on Wednesday at 5 P.M. (CUC5), *trovas* on Thursday at 5 P.M. (CUC1), plus *boleros* each Saturday at 9 P.M. (CUC1). This is ground zero for bohemian intellectual life in Havana, and many of Cuba's top writers and artists hang out here.

The acclaimed **Conjunto Folklórico Nacional** (National Folklore Dance Group, Calle 4 #103, e/ Calzada y 5ta, tel. 07/830-3060; CUC5) performs *Sábado de rumba* alfresco each Saturday at 3 P.M. This is Afro-Cuban music and dance at its best.

Casa de las Américas (3ra Calle, esq. Av. de los Presidentes, tel. 07/832-2706, www.casa.cult.cu), hosts an eclectic range of concerts, Mon.–Fri. 8 A.M.–4:30 P.M.

On the third Sunday of each month, head to the Centro Iberoamericano de la Décima (Calle A, e/ 25 y 27, tel. 07/837-5383, decimal@cubarte.cult.cu) for **El Jardín de la Gorda** (5 P.M.), when Sara González—the *gorda* (fat lady)—belts out *nueva trova*. And at 6 P.M. on the last Saturday of every month, Frank Delgado performs *nueva trova* live at the **Cine Riviera** (Calle 23, e/ F y G, tel. 07/830-9564).

Playa (Miramar and Beyond)

For *boleros*, head to **Rincón de Boleros** (7ma Av., esq. 26, tel. 07/204-2353; daily 10:30 P.M.–3 A.M.; CUC10), in the Dos Gardenias complex.

CABARETS ESPECTÁCULOS
Habana Vieja

The **Hotel Telégrafo** (Paseo del Prado #408, esq. Neptuno, tel. 07/861-1010; CUC5) has a small *cabaret espectáculo* on Fridays at 5 P.M. and Saturday at 9 P.M.

Centro Habana

Cabaret Nacional (San Rafael, esq. Prado, tel. 07/863-2361; CUC5), in the dingy basement of the Gran Teatro, has a modest *espectáculo* nightly at 10 P.M. The campy show normally doesn't begin until later, and is followed by a disco. It packs in Cubans on weekends for steamy dancing. A dress code applies, and ostensibly only couples are admitted.

Vedado and Plaza de la Revolución

The most lavish show is the **Cabaret Parisien** (Calle O, esq. 21, tel. 07/836-3863; CUC35), in the Hotel Nacional. The *Cubano cubano* show is offered nightly at 10 P.M. The dinner special (CUC50–70) is best avoided. The place is cramped and gets filled with smoke, and while the show is nowhere near the scale of the Tropicana, it has plenty of feathers and flesh and sexual energy, and it's handily right in the heart of Vedado and thus beats the long trek out to Marianao for the Tropicana.

The **Cabaret Copa Room** (Paseo y Malecón, tel. 07/836-4051; CUC20, or CUC45 with dinner and cocktail), in the Hotel Riviera, hosts a cabaret Thurs.–Sun. at 10 P.M. The venue specializes in the Latin beat and often features the top names in live Cuban music, such as Los Van Van. It's one of Havana's top spots for serious salsa fans.

Catering mostly to a tourist crowd, the contrived **Habana Café** (Paseo, e/ 1ra y 3ra, tel. 07/833-3636, ext. 147; nightly 8 P.M.–

3 A.M.), adjoining the Hotel Meliá Cohiba, offers cabaret. A classic Harley-Davidson, an old Pontiac, and a 1957 open-top canary-yellow Chevy add a dramatic effect, as does an airplane suspended from the ceiling (suddenly the car horns beep and the headlamps flash, you hear the roar of an airplane taking off, then the curtains open and—voilà—the show begins). Entrance is free but a CUC5 *consumo mínimo* applies; entrance costs CUC20 when top bands such as Los Van Van and Charanga Habanera play. It has a disco on Friday nights. You can make a night of it by dining on reasonable quality but overpriced burgers (from CUC5) and even a "banana split" (CUC5). Check your bill carefully, as scams are frequent. It relies heavily on the tourist trade, and there's no shortage of *jiniteras*.

Primarily serving impecunious Cubans, the **Cabaret Las Vegas** (Infanta #104, e/ 25 y 27, tel. 07/870-7939) was closed for remodeling at last visit and was slated to reopen with folkloric rumbas and less gratuitous skin. Author Tom Miller summed up the erstwhile mood well: "The *chicas* danced in earnest but seldom in sync, their tattered fishnet stockings running before our eyes" while the solo singer "singing off-key into her cordless mike… would have been better served had she carried a mikeless cord."

Similar third-tier venues catering mostly to Cubans are **Karachi Club** (Calles 17 y K, tel. 07/832-3485; nightly 10 P.M.–4 A.M.; CUC5); **Centro Nocturno La Red** (Calle 19 #151, esq. L, tel. 07/832-5415; 10 P.M.–4 A.M.; CUC1–2), with karaoke on Monday, Latin music on Wednesday, comedy on Thursday–Saturday, followed by disco; and the dingy **Club Amanecer** (Calle 15, e/ O y N; 10 P.M.–3 A.M.; CUC5), with a small *cabaret espectáculo* on Monday and Tuesday, karaoke on Wednesday and Thursday, and live music Friday and Saturday.

Playa (Miramar and Beyond)
The small open-air cabaret at **La Cecilia** (5ta Av. #11010, e/ 1110 y 112, tel. 07/204-1562; Fri. and Sat. 9:30 P.M.; Fri. CUC5, Sat.

CUC10) has been improved and draws monied foreign residents and Cuba's youthful hipsters for the disco that follows. Top bands often perform (CUC20–25).

Macumba Habana (Calle 222, e/ 37 y 51, tel. 07/273-0568; Sat. 5 P.M.–midnight, Sun. 5–11 P.M., Sun. 5–11 P.M.; CUC5–15), in the La Giraldilla complex in the La Coronela district, offers a small but classy *espectáculo* at 9:30 P.M. with a different theme nightly.

Other Second-tier venues include the **Hotel Comodoro** (1ra Av. y Calle 84, tel. 07/204-5551); **Hotel Kohly** (Av. 49 y 36A, Rpto. Kohly, Playa, tel. 07/204-0240; free), on Monday and Wednesday at 9 P.M.

◖ Tropicana
Cuba's premier Las Vegas–style nightclub is the Tropicana (Calle 72 #4504 y Línea del Ferrocarril, Marianao, tel. 07/267-1717, fax 07/267-0119, www.cabaret-tropicana.com; entrance CUC70–90; cameras CUC5, videos CUC15, dinner CUC10), boasting more than 200 performers, a fabulous orchestra, and astonishing acrobatic feats. Famous international entertainers occasionally perform. The cabaret takes place in the open-air Salón Bajo Las Estrellas Tuesday–Sunday at 10 P.M. A superb violin octet—the Violines de Tropicana—entertains early arrivals. The entrance fee is outrageous, but includes a quarter bottle of rum with cola, a glass of cheap champagne, and a cheap cigar. You can purchase tickets at the reservation booth (10 A.M.–6 P.M.) or directly at the entrance from 8:30 P.M. (call ahead to check availability), but it's best to book in advance through your hotel tour desk, as the show often sells out, and it's also a 20-minute ride downtown. Whole or partial refunds are offered if the show is rained out. Cocktails cost CUC5, but it's usually best to buy a bottle of rum and a can of Coke to last you all night. (Beware rip-offs by the waiters, who typically wait until the end of the show to bill you for any incidentals, then disappear without giving you your change as you get caught in the rush to depart.) The Tropicana also has two eateries: the elegant

sky-lit Los Jardines, serving tasty continental fare (6 P.M.–1 A.M.); and the 1950s diner–style Rodney Café (noon–2 A.M.).

DISCOTHEQUES AND NIGHTCLUBS

Habana Vieja

Disco Karaoke, atop the Hotel Plaza (Zulueta #267, esq. Neptuno, tel. 07/860-8583; nightly 11 P.M.–5 A.M.; CUC5), packs Cubans in thick as sardines.

Centro Habana

The hottest spot in town at last visit was **Casa de la Música** (Galiano #253, e/ Concordia y Neptuno, tel. 07/862-4165; daily 4–7 P.M. and 10 P.M.–2 A.M.; CUC10–20), a modern theater known as "Dos" (for Casa de la Música 2, or *dos*) that packs in a mostly Cuban crowd for concerts and dancing. It's run by Egrem, the state recording company.

A bit more raw and rough around the edges, **Cabaret Palermo** (San Miguel esq. Amistad, tel. 07/861-9745; Thurs.–Sun. 10 P.M.–4 A.M. CUC2–5) is one of Havana's major rap scenes. Shows are sometimes preceded by a *cabaret espectáculo*.

Vedado and Plaza de la Revolución

Salón Turquino (Calle L, e/ 23 y 25, tel. 07/834-4011; nightly 10:30 P.M.–3 A.M.; CUC10 cover), atop the Hotel Habana Libre, offers a medley of entertainment varying nightly, followed by salsa dancing. Top bands often perform, and the place often closes for VIP parties. This popular venue draws tourists and Cubans with dollars to spend. No single Cubans are allowed, so foreigners are propositioned at the door by females seeking admission.

In 2008, the **Salón Rojo** (Calle 21, e/ N y O, tel. 07/833-3747 or 832-0511; nightly 10 P.M.–2 A.M.; CUC10–25), beside the Hotel Capri, emerged from a remake and has ditched its cabaret in favor of a nightclub venue hosting Havana's hottest acts, such as Los Van Van and Bandolero. It's now the hottest spot in town for sexy dancing and searing sounds.

Penny-pinchers might head to the **Cabaret Pico Blanco** (Calle O #206, e/ 23 y 25, tel. 07/833-3740; nightly 9 P.M.–3 A.M.; CUC5–10), in the glass-enclosed top floor of the Hotel St. John. It hosts salsa, *boleros,* and *trova,* though the mood runs hot and cold. Occasionally a top name is featured; other times you may have to suffer through karaoke. A disco follows.

Around the corner, Calle 23 between Calles O y N has several dingy clubs drawing a young Cuban crowd for merengue and salsa.

Cubans also flock to **Café Cantante** (Paseo, esq. 39, tel. 07/879-0711; Tues.–Sat. 9 P.M.–5 A.M.; CUC3, or CUC10–20 when top groups perform), one of the city's hottest spots, in the basement of the Teatro Nacional. No hats, T-shirts, or shorts for men, and no photos allowed. Go on Friday afternoons for live salsa (4–6 P.M.), only Cubans go and with luck you'll be charged in pesos. The plusher **Delirio Habanero** (tel. 07/873-5713), a lounge on the third floor of the Teatro Nacional, also has afternoon *peñas* (3–7 P.M.) and live music Tuesday–Sunday (10 A.M.–2 A.M.; CUC5–CUC15), when the place can rock to everything from *boleros* to *timba.* Also in the Teatro Nacional, **Mi Habana** has music and dance the same hours.

Playa (Miramar and Beyond)

The **Casa de la Música** (Av. 25, esq. 20, tel. 07/204-0447; Wed.–Sun. 5–9 P.M. and 11 P.M.–3:30 A.M.; CUC10–20), run by Egrem, the state recording company, sometimes has sizzling-hot afternoon salsa sessions as well as nightly (except Monday) performances by such legends as Bamboleo and Chucho Valdés. This place is preferred by Cubans with some money to burn, and the fact that the audience usually includes some of Cuba's hottest performers says it all. The headliner normally doesn't come on until 1 A.M. Also here is the **Disco Tun Tún** (nightly 11 P.M.–6 A.M.; CUC10), which keeps in the groove until dawn.

The hippest spot in town on my last visit was **Don Cangrejo** (1ra Av., e/ 16 y 18, tel. 07/204-

4169; daily noon–midnight; entrance CUC5), a most unlikely venue. This restaurant's open-air oceanfront pool complex hosts live music and packs in the chic in-crowd (mostly well-heeled foreign males, monied white Cubans with high-positioned parents, and beautiful *habaneras*, many of them with their eyes on the well-heeled foreign males). There's no room to dance.

Cubans of lesser means head to **Club Río** (Calle A #314, e/ 3ra y 5ta, tel. 07/209-3389; Tues.–Sun. 10 P.M.–3 A.M.; CUC5), colloquially called Johnny's. DJs spin up-to-date tunes. It also has a cabaret on the sunken dance floor. Couples only are permitted. It has a reputation for pickpockets, violence, and scams.

Salón Chévere (Club Almendares, Calle 49C y 28A, Rpto. Kohly, tel. 07/204-4990; daily noon–4 A.M.) has live music and dancing alfresco, with the real action beginning after 10 P.M. The CUC15 entrance includes an open bar.

Cubans without dollars also find their fun at **Teatro Karl Marx** (1ra Av., e/ 8 y 10, tel. 07/203-0801; Fri.–Sun. 9 P.M.–2 A.M.; CUC10–20). Los Van Van, Isaac Delgado, and other big names play here. The vast theater also plays host to many of the city's big-ticket events (such as the closing galas of the Latin American Film Festival).

Farther out, **Salón Rosado Benny Moré** (Av. 41, esq. 48, tel. 07/209-1281; Fri.–Mon. 7 P.M.–2 A.M. with live groups; Tues.–Wed. for cabaret; CUC5–10), an open-air concert arena known as El Tropical, is immensely popular on weekends, when top-billed Cuban salsa bands perform. Probably the wildest place in town on Saturday night, with kick-ass music and dancing, it gets jam-packed, the dancing is salacious, and rum-induced fights often break out. For better or worse, foreigners are sometimes kept apart from *habaneros*.

Another popular venue for Cubans is **El Sauce** (9ta #12015, e/ 120 y 130, tel. 07/204-6248), hosting live bands, from rock (such as the Cuban group Dimensión Vertical, every Sunday at 4 P.M.) to salsa.

JAZZ
Habana Vieja
Jazz trios perform upstairs nightly in **Café del**

Oriente (Oficios #112, esq. Amargura, tel. 07/860-6686), and in the lobby of the **Hotel NH Parque Central** (Neptuno, e/ Prado y Zulueta, tel. 07/866-6627) five nights a week.

However, the key jazz venue is the **Bar Chico O'Farrill** (Cuba #102, esq. Chacón; tel. 07/860-5080), in the Hotel Palacio O'Farrill, hosting Cuba's top performers every Fri.–Sun. evening.

Vedado and Plaza de la Revolución
The **Jazz Café** (1ra at the base of Paseo, tel. 07/838-3556; daily noon–2 A.M.; CUC10 *consumo mínimo*), on the third floor of the Galería del Paseo, is a classy supper-club with some of the best live jazz in town, including from resident maestro Chucho Valdés. The music doesn't get going until about 11:30 P.M., though the seats usually fill up well before then.

La Zorra y el Cuervo (Calle 23, e/ N y O, tel. 07/833-2402, zorra@cbcan.cyt.cu; 10 P.M.–2 A.M.; CUC10) is a jazz club in a dreary basement setting. Occasional foreign bands perform here, as do the Cuban greats such as Chucho Valdés. It has "blues" on Thursdays. The first set normally kicks off at 10:30 P.M.

UNEAC's **El Hurón Azul** (Calle 17 #351, e/ G y H, Vedado, tel. 07/832-4551, www.uneac.com) has *tardes del jazz* (jazz afternoons) every second Thursday of the month at 5 P.M. And the **Peña de Rembert Duharte** is hosted in the garden adjoining the Teatro Mella (Linea e/ A y B, tel. 07/830-4987) each last Friday of the month at 5 P.M.

Playa (Miramar and Beyond)
A jazz group performs at the **Tocororo** (Calle 18 y 3ra Av., tel. 07/202-2209) restaurant; and the piano bar at the **Hotel Panorama Havana** (Calle 70, esq. 3ra, tel. 07/204-0100; 9 P.M.–2 A.M.) hosts jazz nightly.

TANGO AND FLAMENCO
Habana Vieja
Flamenco is hosted at **Centro Andaluz en**

Cuba (Prado #104, e/ Genios y Refugio, tel. 07/863-6745; free) each Wednesday, Friday, and Saturday at 9 P.M. Lessons are offered Tuesday–Thursday 9–11 A.M. (CUC15 per hour).

The touristy **El Mesón de la Flota** (Mercaderes #257, e/ Amargura y Brasil, tel. 07/863-3838; free) hosts flamenco 1:30–3 P.M. and 9–11 P.M. daily; you can even watch from the street through the bars.

The **Caserón de Tango** (Calle Justíz #21, e/ Baratillo y Oficios, tel. 07/861-0822) has tango *peñas* on Wednesday and Friday at 5 P.M.; shows on Saturday at 10 P.M. and Sunday at 9:30 P.M.; and tango lessons (CUC5) Thursday at 4–6 P.M. and Saturday 2–4 P.M., and other days by arrangement.

Centro Habana
Caserón del Tango (Neptuno #303, e/ Águila y Italia, tel. 07/863-0097) hosts tango *peñas* on Monday, 7–8 P.M.

THEATER, CLASSICAL MUSIC, AND BALLET
Habana Vieja
The most important theater in Havana is the **Gran Teatro de la Habana** (Paseo de Martí #458, e/ San Rafael y San Martín, Habana Vieja, tel. 07/861-3077; CUC20 for best orchestra seats), on the west side of Parque Central. It's the main stage for the acclaimed Ballet Nacional de Cuba, Ballet Español de la Habana, and the national opera company. The ballet is usually performed to taped music. The building has three theaters—the Teatro García Lorca, where ballet and concerts are held, and the smaller Sala Alejo Carpentier and Sala Antonin Artaud, for less commercial, experimental performances. Performances are Thursday–Saturday at 8:30 P.M. and Sunday at 5 P.M. A dress code applies.

On Friday, a symphony band strikes up at 4 P.M. in **Plaza de Armas.**

The **Basílica de San Francisco de Asís** (Calle Oficios, e/ Amargura y Brasil, tel. 07/862-9683) hosts classical irregular weekly concerts at 6 P.M. (CUC2–10).

the baroque facade of the Gran Teatro — each corner is tipped by an angel

© CHRISTOPHER P. BAKER

For choral music, head to **Hostal Frailes** (Brasil, e/ Oficios y Mercaderes, tel. 07/862-9383; daily 10 A.M.–5 P.M.), hosting sacred music in the lobby. Classical and ecclesiastical concerts are also featured in the **Iglesia de San Francisco de Paula** (Av. del Puerto, esq. Leonor Pérez, tel. 07/860-4210, free or CUC5) on Fridays and Saturdays at 7 P.M.; and in the **Oratorio San Felipe Neri** (Calle Aguiar esq. Obrapía) daily at 7 P.M.

Vedado and Plaza de la Revolución
Performances of the National Symphony and Danza Contemporanea de Cuba are hosted at the **Teatro Nacional** (Av. Carlos M. de Céspedes, esq. Paseo, tel. 07/879-6011, tnc@cubarte.cult.cu) every Friday–Saturday at 8:30 P.M. and Sunday at 5 P.M. (CUC1.80–8.90). The ticket office is open Tuesday–Thursday 10 A.M.–6 P.M. and Friday–Sunday 3–9 P.M.

The **Teatro Mella** (Línea #657, e/ A y B, Vedado, tel. 07/833-5651) is noted for contemporary dance, theater, and ballet (CUC5–10), and hosts the Conjunto Folklórico Nacional.

For something more intimate, head to the monthly **Peña de Manuel Argudín** (Agencia Cubana de Derecho de Autor Musical, Calle 6 #313, e/ 13 y 15, Vedado, tel. 07/830-0724, www.acdam.cu) each last Saturday at 6 P.M. The renowned eponymous guitarist is often accompanied by such renowned performers as pianist Frank Fernández.

And every last Thursday of the month, UNEAC (Calle 17 #351, e/ G y H, Vedado, tel. 07/832-4551, www.uneac.com) hosts an open *peña* for chamber musicians at 6 P.M.

Teatro Cine Trianón (Línea #706, e/ Paseo y A, tel. 07/832-9648; five pesos) often features foreign classics, such as the works of Tennessee Williams, performed by the Teatro el Público company.

The **Teatro Amadeo Roldán** (Calzada y D, Vedado, tel. 07/832-1168; CUC5–10), which has two *salas,* features classical concerts year-round. The Orquesta Sinfónica Nacional is based here, with concerts each Thursday–Sunday at 5 P.M. in season, and many lesser classical groups perform.

Nearby is the **Teatro Hubert de Blanck** (Calzada #657, e/ A y B, tel. 07/830-1011; CUC5), known for both modern and classical plays. Shows (in Spanish) are usually Friday–Saturday at 8:30 P.M. and Sunday at 5 P.M.

The 150-seat **Teater Buendía** (Calle Loma y 38, Nuevo Vedado, tel. 07/881-6689; five pesos), in a converted Greek Orthodox church, hosts performances by the eponymous theater company, considered to be Cuba's most innovative and accomplished. It performs here Friday–Sunday at 8:30 P.M.

OTHER ENTERTAINMENT
Habana Vieja
Comedy: The **Casa de la Comedia** (Calle Justíz #18, esq. Baratillo, tel. 07/863-9282; CUC2), one block southeast of Plaza de Armas, hosts comic theater on weekends at 7 P.M.

Cine-Teatro Fausto (Prado #201, esq. Colón, Habana Vieja, tel. 07/862-5416) has

---

HAVANA'S CIRCUS AND THEME PARK

Named for a famous but deceased Cuban clown, **Havana's Circo Trompoloco** (Calle 112 esq. 5ta Av., Miramar, tel. 07/206-5609 or 206-5641; Thurs.-Sun. 7 P.M. and Sat.-Sun. 4 P.M.; CUC10) opened in 2007 to much fanfare as the headquarters of the National Circus of Cuba, which performs beneath a red-and-white-striped "big top" on Thursday and Friday at 4 P.M. and Saturday and Sunday at 4 P.M. and 7 P.M.

Adjoining the circus is **Isla del Coco Parque Temático** (tel. 07/208-0330; Wed.-Fri. 4-10 P.M., Sat. and Sun. 10 A.M.-10 P.M.). This theme park can't quite match Disneyworld, but it's still an admirable venue for kids to thrill to go-karts, a big-dipper, carousels, etc.

---

comedy Friday–Saturday at 8:30 P.M. and Sunday at 5 P.M. Bar Monserrate (Av. de Bélgica, Monserrate, esq. Obrapía, tel. 07/860-9751) has comedy each Saturday at 10 P.M. (CUC5.30 consumo mínimo).

Poetry Readings and Literary Events: The **La Moderna Poesía** (Calle Obispo #525, esq. Bernaza, Habana Vieja, tel. 07/861-5600) bookshop hosts literary events, as do UNEAC's **Casa de la Poesía** (Calle Muralla #63, e/ Oficios y Inquisidor, Habana Vieja, tel. 07/861-8251) and the **Fundación Alejo Carpentier** (Empedrado #215, Habana Vieja, tel. 07/861-3667).

Centro Habana
Comedy is a staple at **Teatro América** (Av. de Italia #253, e/ Concordia y Neptuno, tel. 07/862-5416) every Saturday at 8:30 P.M. and Sunday at 5 P.M.

Vedado and Plaza de la Revolución
Centro Cultural Fresa y Chocolate

HAVANA'S GAY SCENE

Gay life in Havana has expanded noticeably in recent years, although homosexual venues remain subject to police crackdowns. There are no established gay bars or clubs, which are banned, and the gay "scene" typically is relegated to "hangout" street locales. Most venues attract male prostitutes, called *pingueros* (from the Spanish word *pinga*, or prick). Several recent unreported murders of foreigners in Havana have been linked to transvestites and the homosexual underground. Be careful who you give a ride to on 5ta Avenida, Miramar, as *transvesti* prostitutes trawl for clients by night.

Most nights there's one or more gay parties known as *fiestas de diez pesos* at private venues (entrance typically costs 10 pesos, or sometimes CUC1-2). Havana society is non-exclusionary, however; everyone is welcome, and the mix usually includes a sprinkling of straight, lesbian, and even *transvestis*. Private parties often feature drag shows. The "floating party" venues change nightly as they try to stay one step ahead of the police.

To find out where the night's gay party is, head to the **Cine Yara** (La Rampa y L, Ve-

dado). However, in 2009 this area had cooled and Havana's main nighttime cruising spot is now the Malecón, opposite Fiat Café near the foot of La Rampa.

Cine Yara is the sole public venue for lesbians, who are less tolerated in this macho society.

BARS, CAFÉS, AND CLUBS

A *transvesti* show is hosted at the **Sociedad Cultural Rosalía de Castro** (Av. de Bélgica #504 altos, e/ Máximo Gómez y Dragones, tel. 07/862-3193).

In Vedado, **La Arcada** (Calle M y 23; 24 hours) is effectively the only gay bar in town and is always packed. The cramped, humid **Club Tropical** (Línea, esq. F, tel. 07/832-7361; daily 10 p.m.–3 a.m.) occasionally acts as a gay venue, as does the steamy cellar bar, **Club Saturno** (Línea, e/ 10 y 12, tel. 07/833-7942; daily 11 p.m.-2:30 a.m.).

Bar de las Estrellas (Calle A #507, e/ 15 y 16), in the Lawton district, south of Cerro, is a *paladar* (private restaurant) with a transvestite cabaret at 10 p.m.

(Calle 23 y 12, tel. 07/833-9278; Fri.–Sun. 6 P.M.–2 A.M.), attached to the INEAC film institute, hosts films, live music, and poetry. It typically has *trova* on Fridays, jazz on Saturdays, and comedy on Sundays.

Comedy: The hot spot at last visit was **La Roca** (Calle 21 esq. M, tel. 07/834-4501; Tues., Wed., Fri. and Sun. 10 P.M.–2 A.M.; CUC5), which packs in Cubans for slapstick comedy; dine here first to secure a good seat.

Comedy is also performed at the **Humor Club Cocodrilo** (Av. 3ra and 10, Vedado, tel. 07/837-0305; nightly 10 P.M.–3 A.M.; CUC5). Magicians perform there as well. And the **Teatro Bertolt Brecht** (Calle 13, esq. I, tel. 07/832-9359) specializes in comedy, offered Tuesday at 8:30 P.M.

The **Teatro Guiñol** (Calle M, e/ 17 y 19, tel. 07/832-6262; CUC2), on the west side of the Focsa building, is Cuba's leading children's

theater with comedy and puppet shows on Friday at 3 P.M., Saturday at 5 P.M., and Sunday at 10:30 A.M. and 5 P.M.

Rap and Rock: If ever you doubted that Cuba has a rock scene, head to **Maxim Rock** (Bruzón, e/ Almendares y Ayasterán, tel. 07/877-5925), which hosts live concerts Wed.–Sat. 8 P.M.–midnight.

Roqueros also gravitate to **Patio de María** (Calle 37 #262, e/ Paseo y 2, Vedado, tel. 07/881-0722; daily 7:30 A.M.–11 P.M.; five pesos), one block west of Teatro Nacional, where rock concerts and varied peñas are hosted. Meanwhile, the theater hosts the **Peña de Los Kents** in the Café Cantante (Sun. 4 P.M.), when the eponymous and aging rock band play oldster classics.

Rap, reggaeton, and other innovative avante-garde music concerts are hosted at **La Madriguera** (Av. Salvador Allende, e/ Infanta

PARADISE UNDER THE STARS

Tropicana, the prerevolutionary extravaganza now in its sixth decade of Vegas paganism has been in continuous operation since New Year's Eve 1939, when it opened (in the gardens of a mansion – Villa Mina – that once housed the U.S. ambassador) as the most flamboyant nightclub in the world. The club quickly won the favor of the elite of society and soon eclipsed all other clubs in the grandeur and imagination of its productions. The Congo Pantera revue, which simulated a panther's nocturnal hunt in lush jungle, established the Tropicana's trademark, with dancers in the thick vegetation illuminated by colored spotlights – the name Tropicana melds the world *trópico* (tropics) with *palma cana* (fan palm).

In its heyday, the Tropicana spent more than US$12,000 nightly on its flamboyant shows. International celebrities such as Nat "King" Cole, Josephine Baker, and Carmen Miranda headlined the show, which was so popular that a 50-passenger "Tropicana Special" flew nightly from Miami for an evening of entertainment that ended in the nightclub's casino, where a daily US$10,000-bingo jackpot was offered and a new automobile was raffled every Sunday.

Talent scouts scoured Cuba for the most beautiful models and dancers. The more than 200 performers are still handpicked from the crème de la crème of Cuba's singers and dancers, though the latter no longer dance topless. Patrons watch mesmerized as rainbow-hued searchlights sweep over the hordes of long-legged showgirls, gaudily feathered with sensational headdresses more ostentatious than peacocks, parading 20 feet up among the floodlit palm trees, quivering beseechingly like tropical birds.

In 2005, however, the Ministry of Tourism, headed by a new, austere military figure, took control of Tropicana. Immediately, it was announced that the infamously erotic show would be tamed down and replaced with "Drums in Concert," a theatrical show with more emphasis on stage sets and high-tech lighting. Even the dancers bemoan the change, which meant goodbye to much of the gratuitous skin marked by the opening act, when a troupe of near-naked showgirls paraded down the aisles wearing see-through body stockings and glowing chandeliers atop their heads.

y Luaces, tel. 07/879-8175; 5–10 pesos; Mon.–Wed. and Fri.–Sat. 9 A.M.–7 P.M. and Thurs. until midnight), an unlikely spot in the overgrown botanical gardens, entered off Infanta. A disco is hosted on Thursdays. La Madriguera is home to the Asociación Hermanos Saíz, or youth group of UNEAC.

Poetry Readings and Literary Events: The **Unión Nacional de Escritores y Artistas de Cuba** (UNEAC, Calle 17, esq. H, Vedado, tel. 07/832-4551) and the **Casa de las Américas** (3ra Calle, esq. Av. de los Presidentes, tel. 07/832-2706, www.casa.cult.cu) host literary and other cultural events.

Aguas Espectáculos: Choreographed water ballets are offered at the **Hotel Meliá Cohiba** nightly at 9:30 P.M. (CUC10) and at the **Hotel Nacional** Sunday at 9 P.M. (CUC10).

Playa (Miramar and Beyond)

Cuba's catwalk divas strut at **La Maison** (Calle 16 #701, esq. 7ma, Miramar, tel. 07/204-1543; CUC5), renowned for its *desfiles de modas* (fashion shows) and *cabaret espectáculo* held Thursday–Sunday at 10 P.M. in the terrace garden of an elegant old mansion. Reservations are recommended. A 4 P.M. matinee show is offered on Wednesday–Thursday and Saturday–Sunday.

Shopping

Havana offers superb shopping for art and crafts, as well as hand-crafted scents, Spanish fans, and rum and cigars.

ANTIQUES

Havana's museums and private homes overflow with colonial-era antiques. However, the government bans the sale and export of antiques. Hence, there are no longer any stores selling antiques to tourists.

Colección Habana (Mercaderes, esq. O'Reilly, Habana Vieja, tel. 07/861-3388; daily 9 A.M.–6 P.M.) sells antique reproductions and decorative items.

ARTS AND CRAFTS

For information on formal galleries, contact the **Fondo Cubano de Bienes Culturales** (Av. 47 #4702, esq. 38, Rpto. Kohly, tel. 07/204-8005, fcbc@cubarte.cult.cu).

Habana Vieja

The largest market is the **Feria de la Artesanía** (Avenida Desamparados at San Ignacio; daily 8:30 A.M.–7 P.M.), selling everything from little ceramic figurines, miniature bongo drums, and papier-mâché 1950s autos, to banana-leaf hats, crocheted bikinis, straw hats, and paintings. In late 2009, it moved from Calle Tacón to the waterfront in southern Habana Vieja.

Habana Vieja contains dozens of galleries, many selling naive works by the artists themselves; these galleries, called *expo-ventas* (commercial galleries representing freelance artists), concentrate along Calle Obispo. The **Asociación Cubana de Artesana Artistas** (Obispo #411, tel. 07/860-8577; Mon.–Sat. 10 A.M.–8 P.M., Sun. 10 A.M.–6 P.M.) represents various artists.

The **Fondo Cubano de Bienes Culturales** (Muralla #107, Habana Vieja, tel. 07/862-2633, galeriahab@cubarte.cult.cu; Mon.–Fri. 10 A.M.–5 P.M., Sat. 10 A.M.–2 P.M.), in Plaza Vieja, sells quality work in its **Génesis Galerías.** The best works are upstairs.

Nearby, experimental art is for sale at the **Centro de Desarrollo de las Artes Visuales** (Casa de las Hermanas Cárdenas, Plaza Vieja, tel. 07/862-2611; Tues.–Sat. 10 A.M.–6 P.M.).

One of the best galleries is **Galería La Acacia** (San José #114, e/ Industria y Consulado, tel. 07/863-9364; Mon.–Sat. 9 A.M.–5 P.M.), selling artwork of international standard by many of Cuba's leading artists. Similar pieces can be found at **Galería Victor Manuel** (San Ignacio #46, e/ Callejón del Chorro y Empedrado, tel. 07/861-2955; daily 10 A.M.–9 P.M.), on the west side of Plaza de la Catedral. Around the corner is the **Taller Experimental de la Gráfica** (Callejón del Chorro, tel. 07/867-7622, tgrafica@cubarte. cult.cu; Mon.–Fri. 9 A.M.–4 P.M.), which has exclusive lithographic prints for sale.

Vedado and Plaza de la Revolución

Vedado has an artisans' market on La Rampa, e/ M y N (8 A.M.–6 P.M.) and the **Feria del Malecón** (Malecón, e/ D y E; Tues.–Sun. 8:30 A.M.–6 P.M.).

The **Casa de las Américas** (Av. de los Presidentes, esq. 3ra, tel. 07/832-2706, www. casa.cult.cu; Mon.–Fri. 8 A.M.–4:45 P.M.) hosts exhibitions with works for sale. The small gallery in the lobby of the **Hotel Nacional** and the Hotel Meliá Cohiba's **Galería Cohiba** also sell quality artwork.

BOOKS AND STATIONERY

Havana is desperately in need of a Barnes & Noble, and newspapers or magazines are sold only in a few tourist hotels.

Habana Vieja

The **Instituto Cubano del Libro** (Cuban Book Institute, O'Reilly #4, esq. Tacón, tel. 07/863-2244; Mon.–Sat. 10 A.M.–5 P.M.), in the Palacio del Segundo Cabo, on Plaza de Armas, has three small bookshops; most books are in Spanish. The plaza is also the setting for the **Mercado de Libros** (Wed.–Sat. 9 A.M.–7 P.M.), a secondhand book fair where you can rummage through a dreary collection of tattered tomes.

Librería La Internacional (Obispo #528, Habana Vieja, tel. 07/861-3238; daily 10 A.M.–5:30 P.M.) stocks a limited selection of texts in English, plus a small selection of English-language novels. **La Moderna Poesía** (Obispo #527, esq. Bernaza, tel. 07/861-6983; Mon.–Sat. 10 A.M.–8 P.M.) is Cuba's largest bookstore, although virtually the entire stock is in Spanish.

La Papelería (O'Reilly #102, esq. Tacón, Habana Vieja, tel. 07/863-4263; 9 A.M.–6:30 P.M.), cater-corner to the Plaza de Armas, sells pens and other office supplies.

Vedado and Plaza de la Revolución

Librería Fernando Ortíz (Calle L, esq. 27, tel. 07/832-9653; Mon.–Sat. 10 A.M.–5:30 P.M.) is your best bet for English-language books. Its meager collection spans a wide range.

Librería Centenario del Apóstol (Calle 25 #164, e/ Infanta y O, tel. 07/870-7220; daily 9 A.M.–9 P.M.) has a broad selection of used texts.

RUM AND CIGARS

Havana has about two dozen Casas del Habano (the official cigar stores). Buy here; if you buy off the street, you're almost certainly going to be sold fakes, although you'll be hard-pressed to know this.

The airport departure lounge has the best-stocked rum and liquor stock in town, as well as a fine cigar selection and a full range of Cuban and import scents and colognes, though don't expect better prices.

Habana Vieja

The best cigar store is the **Casa del Habano** (Industria #520, e/ Barcelona y Dragones, tel. 07/862-0086; Mon.–Fri. 9 A.M.–7 P.M., Sat. 9 A.M.–5 P.M., Sun. 10 A.M.–4 P.M.), in the Partagás factory. It has a massive walk-in humidor, plus

a hidden lounge with a narrow humified walk-in cigar showcase for serious smokers.

My other favorites are the **Casa del Habano** (Mercaderes #202, esq. Lamparilla, tel. 07/862-9682; daily 10:30 A.M.–7 P.M.), in the Hostal Conde de Villanueva; and **Salón Cuba** (Neptuno, e/ Prado y Zulueta, tel. 07/866-6627; daily 8:30 A.M.–9:15 P.M.), in the Hotel NH Parque Central. Each has a sumptuous smoker's lounge.

The **Casa del Habano** (Mercaderes #120, esq. Obrapía, tel. 07/861-5795; daily 9 A.M.–5 P.M.) has a limited selection. And the **Casa del Ron y Tabaco** (Obispo, e/ Monserrate y Bernaza, tel. 07/866-0911; daily 10 A.M.–6 P.M.), above El Floridita, has knowledgeable staff. This store also lets you sample the rums before buying, as does the **Fundación Havana Club** (Av. del Puerto #262, e/ Churruca y Sol, tel. 07/861-8051; daily 9 A.M.–9 P.M.), adjoining the Museo de Ron.

Taberna del Galeón (Baratillo, esq. Obispo, tel. 07/33-8476; Mon.–Fri. 9 A.M.–7 P.M.), off the southeast corner of Plaza de Armas, is well stocked with rums.

Centro Habana and Cerro

Fábrica de Ron Bocoy (Máximo Gómez #1417, e/ Patria y Auditor, Cerro, tel. 07/877-5781; Mon.–Fri. 7 A.M.–5 P.M., Sat. 9 A.M.–3 P.M.) has a well-stocked store, plus a bar for tasting as a prelude to buying.

Vedado and the Plaza de la Revolución

The **Casas del Habano** in the Hotel Nacional, Hotel Habana Libre Tryp, the Hotel Meliá Cohiba, and the Hotel Riviera are well-stocked.

Playa (Miramar and Beyond)

Miramar has some of the best cigar stores in town. The **Casa del Habano** (5ta Av., esq. 16, tel. 07/204-7975; Mon.–Sat. 10 A.M.–6 P.M.) boasts a vast humidor, executive rooms, bar and lounge, and good service.

Club Habana's **Casa del Habano** (5ta Av. e/ 188 y 192, tel. 07/204-5700; daily 9 A.M.–

5 P.M.) is run by Enrique Mons, whom *Cigar Aficionado* magazine has termed "the maestro of cigar merchants in Havana," and who for most of the 1970s and '80s was in charge of quality control for the Cuban cigar industry.

Other sources include **Tabaco El Aljibe** (7ma Av., e/ 24 y 26, tel. 07/204-1012); **Tabaco La Giraldilla** (Calle 222 y Av. 37, La Coronela, tel. 07/33-1155); and the tobacco stores in the Hotel Comodoro, Hotel Meliá Habana, and Hotel Occidental Miramar.

MUSIC AND MUSICAL INSTRUMENTS
Habana Vieja
Longina Música (Obispo #360, tel. 07/862-8371; Mon.–Sat. 10 A.M.–7 P.M., Sun. 10 A.M.–1 P.M.) sells musical instruments, and has a large CD collection.

Centro Habana and Cerro
You can buy instruments at their source at **Industria de Instrumentos Musicales Fernando Ortíz** (Pedroso #12, esq. Nueva, Cerro, tel. 07/879-3161), where guitars, drums, claves, etc. are made.

Playa (Miramar and Beyond)
For the widest CD selection in town, head to the **Casa de la Música Egrem** (Calle 10 #309, tel. 07/202-6900, www.egrem.com.cu), the sales room of EGREM, the state recording agency. The **Casa de la Música** (Calle 20 #3309, e/ 33 y 35, tel. 07/204-0447; daily 10 A.M.–12:30 P.M.) also has a large selection.

PERFUMES, TOILETRIES, AND JEWELRY
Habana Vieja
Havana 1791 (Mercaderes #156, esq. Obrapía, tel. 07/861-3525; daily 10 A.M.–6 P.M.) sells locally made scents (CUC6–18) in exquisite engraved bottles with not entirely trustworthy cork tops, in an embossed linen bag. The twelve fragrances—*aromas coloniales*—include Tabaco, which smells surprisingly unlike cigars. It also sells brand-name French

perfumes at duty-free prices. Yanelda, the official "Alchemist of Old Havana," will make up a fragrance to order.

In a similar vein is **La Casa Cubana del Perfume** (Brasil #13, tel. 07/866-3759; Mon.–Sat. 10 A.M.–6 A.M.), on the south side of Plaza Vieja.

Farmacia Taquechel (Obispo #155, e/ Mercaderes y San Ignacio, tel. 07/862-9286; daily 9 A.M.–5 P.M.) sells face creams, lotions, and other natural products made in Cuba.

Perfumería Prado (Prado, e/ Refugio y Colón, Habana Vieja; 10 A.M.–6 P.M.) has a large selection of imported perfumes, as do boutique stores in most of the city's upscale hotels.

Playa (Miramar and Beyond)
Most upscale hotels have quality jewelry stores, as do **La Maison** (Calle 16 #701, esq. 7ma, Miramar, tel. 07/204-1543) and **Le Select** (5ta Av., esq. 30, Miramar, tel. 07/204-7410), plus **Joyería La Habanera** (Calle 12 #505, e/ 5ta y 7ma, tel. 07/204-2546; Mon.–Sat. 10 A.M.–6 P.M.) and the Club Habana's **Joyería Bella Cantando** (5ta Av. y 188, tel. 07/204-5700).

CLOTHING AND SHOES
Habana Vieja
Men seeking a classic *guayabera* shirt should head to **El Quitrín** (Obispo #163, e/ San Ignacio y Mercaderes, tel. 07/862-0810; daily 9 A.M.–5 P.M.), or **Guayabera Habana** (Calle Tacó #20, e/ O'Reilly y Empedrado; Mon.–Sat 9 A.M.–6 P.M.). For ladies, El Quitrín also sells embroideries and lace, plus chic blouses, skirts, and so on. Most items are Cuban-made and of merely average quality. Items can be made to order.

Nearby, **Sombreros Jipi Japa** (Obispo, esq. Compostela) is the place to go for hats of every shade, and **La Habana** (Obispo, e/ Habana y Compostela, tel. 07/861-5292; and Obispo, esq. Aguacate) offers a reasonable stock of shoes and leather goods.

For hip Italian items head to **Paul & Shark** (Muralla #105, e/ San Ignacio y Mercaderes, tel. 07/866-4326, www.paulshark.it; Mon.–Sat.

10 A.M.–7 P.M., Sun. 10 A.M.–1 P.M.), on Plaza Vieja. This upscale boutique sells quality silk blouses, skirts, and other designer wear, including jackets and pants for men.

Vedado and Plaza de la Revolución

Galerías Amazonas (Calle 12, e/ 23 y 25, tel. 07/66-2438; Mon.–Sat. 10 A.M.–7 P.M., Sun. 10 A.M.–2 P.M.) is a mall with several shops devoted to fashion, including designer labels. For quality imported shoes, try the gallery's **Peletería Claudia.**

Adidas and **Nike** have their own well-stocked branches selling sportswear in the **Galería Habana Libre** (Calle 25, e/ L y M).

Playa (Miramar and Beyond)

The **Complejo Comercial Comodoro** (3ra Av., esq. 84, tel. 07/204-5551), adjoining the Hotel Comodoro, has outlets for United Colors of Benetton, Givenchy, Versace, and other name-brand designers.

La Maison (Calle 16 #701, esq. 7ma, tel. 07/204-1543; Mon.–Sat. 10 A.M.–6:45 P.M.) has boutiques selling upscale imported clothing, shoes, and duty-free items. Likewise, **Le Select** (5ta Av., esq. 30, tel. 07/204-7410; Mon.–Sat. 10 A.M.–8 P.M., Sun. 10 A.M.–2 P.M.), with its ritzy chandeliers and marble statues, is as close as you'll come to Bond Street or Rodeo Drive. This little Harrods in the tropics even has a ground-floor delicatessen, plus an array of boutiques selling high-fashion, cosmetics, and the like.

Casa Verano (Calle 18 #4706, e/ 41 y 43, tel. 07/204-1982; Mon.–Fri. 10:30 A.M.–6:30 P.M., Sat. 9:30 A.M.–1 P.M.) sells Cuban-designed clothes, including beautiful one-of-a-kind Verano dresses and straw hats; upstairs sells men's fashion, including shoes.

Adidas (3ra Av., e/ 70 y 82; Mon.–Sat. 9:30 A.M.–7 P.M., Sun. 9:30 A.M.–1:30 P.M.), in the Miramar Trade Center, sells sportswear. The Miramar Trade Center also has a dozen or so upscale boutiques selling imported designer clothing.

DEPARTMENT STORES AND SHOPPING CENTERS

Habana Vieja

Harris Brothers (Monserrate #305, e/ O'Reilly y Progreso, Habana Vieja, tel. 07/861-1644; daily 9 A.M.–6 P.M.) has four stories of separate stores that sell everything from fashions and children's items to toiletries.

Centro Habana and Cerro

The **Plaza Carlos III** (Av. Salvador Allende, e/ Árbol Seco y Retiro, Centro Habana, tel. 07/873-6370; Mon.–Sat. 9:30 A.M.–6:30 P.M.) is intended for Cubans, not tourists. Its many stores range from electronics and clothing to a take on the original Woolworth's dime store (with separate stores where everything costs CUC1, CUC5, or CUC10, respectively).

Calle San Rafael—a pedestrian-only shopping zone, known colloquially as "El Bulevar"—east of Av. de Italia (Galiano) is Havana's main shopping street and retains many department stores that were located in prerevolutionary days. **La Época** (Av. de Italia, esq. Neptuno, Centro Habana, tel. 07/66-9414; Mon.–Sat. 9:30 A.M.–7 P.M., Sun. 9:30 A.M.–2 P.M.) is a good place for clothing, including kiddie items and designer fashions. The former Woolworth's, today called **Variedades Galiano** (Av. de Italia, esq. San Rafael, tel. 07/862-7717), still has its original lunch counter.

Vedado and Plaza de la Revolución

Galerías de Paseo (1ra Calle, e/ Paseo y A, tel. 07/833-9888; Mon.–Sat. 9 A.M.–6 P.M., Sun. 9 A.M.–1 P.M.), at the foot of Paseo, has more than two dozen stores of varying kinds.

Playa (Miramar and Beyond)

La Puntilla Centro Comercial (1ra Av., esq. 0, tel. 07/204-7309) has four floors and stores covering electronics, furniture, clothing, and more; similarly there's **Quinta y 42** (5ta Av. y 42, Miramar, tel. 07/204-7070; Mon.–Sat. 10 A.M.–6 P.M., Sun. 9 A.M.–1 P.M.) and **Complejo Comercial Comodoro** (3ra Av., esq. 84, Miramar, tel. 07/204-5551).

The largest supermarket is **Supermercado 70** (3ra Av., e/ 62 y 70), with all manner of imported foodstuffs.

MISCELLANY
Habana Vieja
You can buy handmade Spanish fans (*abanicos*) for CUC2–150 at the **Casa del Abanicos** (Obrapía #107, e/ Mercaderes y Oficios, tel. 07/863-4452; Mon.–Sat. 10 A.M.–7 P.M., Sun. 10 A.M.–1 P.M.).

The **Tienda El Soldadito de Plano** (Muralla #164, tel. 07/866-0232; Mon.–Fri. 9 A.M.–5 P.M., Sat. 9 A.M.–1:30 P.M.) sells miniature metal soldiers, including a 22-piece Wars of Independence collection, for CUC5.45 apiece.

The **Tienda Muñecos de Leyendas** (Mercaderes, e/ O'Reilly y Empedrado; Tues.–Sat. 10 A.M.–5:30 P.M., Sun. 10 A.M.–1 P.M.) sells dolls of *duendes* (goblins).

Vedado and Plaza de la Revolución
The **Centro Cultural Cinematográfico** (Calle 23 #1155, e/ 10 y 12, tel. 07/833-6430; Mon.–Sat. 9 A.M.–5 P.M.) sells posters and videos of Cuban films; it's on the fourth floor of the Cuban Film Institute (ICAIC).

Playa (Miramar and Beyond)
Ofimatica (tel. 07/204-0632), in Edificio Habana in the Miramar Trade Center, sells computer and office accessories.

Sports and Recreation

Havana has many *centros deportivos* (sports centers). The largest are the **Complejo Panamericano** (Vía Monumental Km 1.5, Ciudad Panamericano, Habana del Este, tel. 07/795-4140), with an Olympic athletic stadium, tennis courts, swimming pool, and even a velodrome for cycling; and **Ciudad Deportiva** (Vía Blanca, esq. Av. Rancho Boyeros, tel. 07/854-5022), or Sports City, colloquially called "El Coliseo," in Nuevo Vedado.

PARTICIPATORY ACTIVITIES
Bowling
You can practice your 10-pin bowling in the **Hotel Kohly** (Av. 49, esq. 36A, Rpto. Kohly, Vedado, tel. 07/204-0240; 3 P.M.–3 A.M.; CUC2 per game); or at **La Bolera,** at the **Club de Golf Habana** (tel. 07/649-8918), in the Capdevilla area, 20 km south of Havana, with a fully mechanized two-lane bowling alley and full-size pool tables.

Golf
The **Club Habana** (5ta Av., e/ 188 y 192, Rpto. Flores, tel. 07/204-5700; Mon.–Fri.

7:30 A.M.–7 P.M.; nonmembers CUC20) has a practice range. Nonmembers are welcome.

Club de Golf Habana (Carretera de Vento Km 8, Boyeros, tel. 07/649-8918) has a nine-hole course.

Gyms and Spas
Upscale hotels have tiny gyms and/or spas, though most are a letdown by international standards. Recommended gyms include those in the Hotel Raquel (CUC5 for use of gym, CUC5 for the sauna; or CUC20 per month); Hotel NH Parque Central; Hotel Nacional (nonguests CUC15); Hotel Meliá Cohiba; and Hotel Meliá Habana.

One of the best facilities is at **Club Habana** (5ta Av., e/ 188 y 192, Rpto. Flores, tel. 07/204-5700; Mon.–Fri. 7:30 A.M.–7 P.M.; nonmembers CUC20).

Running
The Malecón is a good place to jog, although you need to beware the uneven surface and massive potholes. For wide open spaces, head to Parque Lenin, where the road circuit provides a perfect running track. Runners in search of a track

might head to the **Estadio José Martí** (Calle I, e/ 5ta y Malecón, Vedado), **Estadio Juan Abrahantes** (Zapata), south of the university; or **Ciudad Deportiva** (Vía Blanca, esq. Av. Rancho Boyeros, Nuevo Vedado, tel. 07/54-5022).

Annual road races include the 5K International Terry Fox Race (February), the 98K Ultra Marabana (April), the 5K Día de la Madre (Mother's Day Race; May), the 10K Clásico Internacional Hemingway (May), and the Habana Marabana (Havana Marathon; November; CUC40 entry fee). Contact the **Comisión Marabana** at the Ciudad Deportiva for information.

Sailing

Club Habana (5ta Av., e/ 188 y 192, Rpto. Flores, tel. 07/204-5700, dircom@clubhaba.clubhana. get.cu; Mon.–Fri. 7:30 A.M.–7 P.M.) has Hobie Cats for rent. Full-size yachts and motor vessels can be rented at **Marina Hemingway** (5ta Av., esq. 248, Santa Fe, tel. 07/204-1150, comercial@ comermh.cha.cyt.cu).

Scuba Diving

There's excellent diving offshore of Havana. The Gulf Stream and Atlantic Ocean currents meet west of the city, where many ships have been sunk through the centuries. The so-called "Blue Circuit," a series of dive sites, extends east from Bacuranao, about 10 kilometers east of Havana, to the Playas del Este, where there's a decompression chamber at Hospital Luis Díaz Soto (Vía Monumental y Carretera, Habana del Este, tel. 07/95-4251).

Centro de Buceo La Aguja (Marina Hemingway, 5ta Av. y 248, Santa Fe, tel. 07/204-5088 or 07/271-5277, fax 07/204-6848; 8:30 A.M.–4:30 P.M.) rents equipment and charges CUC30 for one dive, CUC50 for two dives, CUC60 for a "resort course," and CUC360 for an open-water certification.

The **Centro Internacional Buceo Residencial Club Habana** (5ta Av., e/ 188 y 192, Rpto. Flores, tel. 07/204-5700; Mon.–Fri. 7:30 A.M.–7 P.M.; nonmembers CUC20) also has scuba.

Sportfishing

Marlin, S.A. (Canal B, Marina Hemingway, tel. 07/204-1150, ext. 735) charges from CUC275 for four hours and from CUC375 for eight hours, including skipper and tackle.

Swimming

Most large tourist hotels have pools that permit use by nonguests. Many are popular with Cubans in summer and can be noisy and crowded on weekends.

In Habana Vieja, head to the small rooftop pool of the Hotel NH Parque Central or that of the Hotel Saratoga, or to **Piscina Hotel Sevilla** (Prado, esq. Ánimas; 10 A.M.–6 P.M.; entrance CUC20, including CUC16 *consumo mínimo*; free to guests of the hotel).

In Vedado, the **Hotel Nacional** (CUC18 *consumo mínimo* for nonguests) and **Hotel Habana Libre Tryp** (CUC15 *consumo mínimo*) have excellent pools. The Hotel Victoria charges CUC3 to use its small pool.

In Miramar, the Occidental Miramar and Hotel Meliá Habana have excellent pools, and **Club Habana** (5ta Av., e/ 188 y 192, Rpto. Flores, tel. 07/204-5700, dircom@clubhaba. clubhana.get.cu; Mon.–Fri. 7:30 A.M.–7 P.M.; nonmembers CUC20, including CUC10 *consumo mínimo*) has a large swimming pool, plus a splendid beach that shelves gently into calm waters. The pool at **Club Almendares** (Av. 49C, esq. 28A, Rpto. Kohly, tel. 07/204-4990; daily 11 A.M.–6 P.M.; adults CUC10 including CUC8 *consumo mínimo*, children CUC5) gets packed with Cubans on weekends.

Farther west, the **Complejo Turístico La Giraldilla** (Calle 222, e/ 37 y 51, tel. 07/273-0568; daily 10 A.M.–6 P.M.; CUC5 including CUC3 *consumo mínimo*), in La Coronela, has a nice and relatively peaceful pool, while that at Papa's in **Marina Hemingway** (5ta Av., esq. 248, Santa Fe, tel. 07/204-1150) can get crowded with Cubans.

SPECTATOR SPORTS
Baseball

Havana has two teams: the Industriales (colloquially called "Los Azules," or "The Blues"), considered the best team in the National League; and the Metropolitanos (known as "Los Metros"). Both teams play at the 60,000-seat **Estadio Latinoamericano** (Consejero Aranjo y Pedro Pérez, Cerro, tel. 07/870-6526), the main baseball stadium. Games are played November–May, Tuesday–Thursday and Saturday at 8 P.M., and Sunday at 2 P.M. (CUC3). Tickets are sold on a first come first served basis, although a few seats are reserved for foreigners.

For further information, contact the **Federación Cubana de Béisbol** (tel. 07/879-7980).

Basketball

The Liga Superior de Baloncesto (National Basketball League) comprises four teams—Havana's team is the Capitalinos and runs September–November. Games are played at the **Coliseo de Deportes** (Vía Blanca, esq. Av. Rancho Boyeros, Nuevo Vedado, tel. 07/40-5933; Mon.–Fri. 8 A.M.–5 P.M.), at Ciudad Deportiva; and at the **Sala Polivalente Ramón Fonst** (Av. de la Independencia, esq. Bruzón, Plaza de la Revolución, tel. 07/882-0000; Mon.–Sat. 8:30 P.M., Sun. 3 P.M.).

For further information, contact the **Federación Cubana de Baloncesto** (tel. 07/857-7156).

Boxing

Championship matches are hosted at the **Coliseo de Deportes** (Vía Blanca, esq. Av. Rancho Boyeros, Nuevo Vedado, tel. 07/40-5933), base for the **Federación Cubana de Boxeo** (tel. 07/857-7047, www.cendecomb.cu).

The main training center is the **Centro de Entrenmiento de Boxeo** (Carretera Torrens, Wajay, tel. 07/202-0538), in the Boyeros district, south of Havana.

You can also watch boxing and martial arts at the **Gimnasio de Boxeo Rafael Trejo** (Calle Cuba #815, Habana Vieja, tel. 07/862-0266; Mon.– Fri. 8 A.M.–5 P.M.) and at **Sala Polivalente Kid Chocolate** (Prado, e/ San Martín y Brasil, Habana Vieja, tel. 07/862-8634).

OTHER SPORTS
Volleyball

Voleibol is a major sport in Cuba; the national women's team—Las Morenas del Caribe (the Caribbean Brown Sugars)—is the best in the world. Volleyball games are hosted at the **Sala Polivalente Kid Chocolate** and **Sala Polivalente Ramón Fonst** (Av. de la Independencia, esq. Bruzón, Plaza de la Revolución, tel. 07/882-0000). Major tournament games are held at the **Coliseo de Deportes,** which hosts the Liga Mundial de Voleibol (World Volleyball League) each spring. For further information, contact the **Federación Cubana de Voleibol** (tel. 07/841-3557).

Roller Skating

The **Complejo de Pelota Vasca y Patinodromo,** at Ciudad Deportiva (Vía Blanca, esq. Av. Rancho Boyeros, tel. 07/854-5022), has a roller skating track.

Soccer

Fútbol has been adopted as the sport of choice when baseball season ends. Cuba's soccer league is not well developed, although there *is* a national league. Havana's team is Ciudad Havana (nicknamed "Los Rojos"—"The Reds"). Games are played at the **Estadio Pedro Marrero** (Av. 41 #4409, e/ 44 y 50, Rpto. Kohly, tel. 07/203-4698).

Squash and Tennis

The national *equipo* (team) trains at **Complejo Panamericano** (Vía Monumental Km 4, Ciudad Panamericano, tel. 07/797-4140), where six tennis courts (*canchas de tenis*) can be rented. **Club Habana** (5ta Av., e/ 188 y 192, Rpto. Flores, tel. 07/204-5700, dircom@clubhaba.clubhana.get.cu; Mon.– Fri. 7:30 A.M.–7 P.M.; nonmembers CUC20) has squash and tennis courts, as do the **Hotel Copacabana** (squash and tennis); **Hotel Meliá Habana** (tennis); **Hotel Nacional** (tennis); and **Hotel Occidental Miramar** (squash and tennis).

For information, contact the **Federación Cubana de Ténis** (tel. 07/97-2121).

HAVANA

Accommodations

Havana is blessed with accommodations of every stripe. All are run by one of the Cuban government's five hotel groups, which assigns at least one star too many to all its hotel ratings (thus a "four-star" hotel would be considered a three- or even two-star in Europe or North America). Following a few years of being overpriced, most hotels are now fairly priced. However, even the most upscale hotels suffer from indifferent staffing, unresponsive management, and a litany of miscellanous issues (in many, constant refurbishings still fail to bring the hotels up to par). Scams by staff are endemic. For these reasons we strongly recommend *casas particulares* (private room rentals).

All properties listed have private bathrooms unless noted.

Which District?

Location is important in choosing your hotel.

Habana Vieja puts you in the heart of the old city, within walking distance of Havana's main touristic sights. A dozen or so colonial-era mansions administered by Habaguanex (www.habaguanexhotels.com) have opened after splendid makeovers. And there are some good upscale business-oriented hotels behind colonial facades.

Centro Habana, although offering few sites of interest, has three budget-oriented hotels close to the Prado and Habana Vieja; Cuba's state tour agencies push the Hotel Deauville, used by many budget package-tour companies, but this gloomy cement tower is terrible and everyone who stays here has a complaint. This predominantly run-down residential district also has many *casas particulares,* but safety on the rubble-strewn streets is a concern.

Vedado and Plaza de la Revolución offer mid-20th-century accommodations well situated for sightseeing and including several first-class modernist hotels with modest decor. Vedado also has the best *casas particulares.*

Playa (Miramar and Beyond) has a number of moderate hotels popular with tour groups, as well as modern deluxe hotels aimed at business travelers. All are far away from the main tourist sights and you'll need wheels to get around. Otherwise be prepared to spend your money on taxi rides to and fro. One hotel to avoid is the Hotel Neptuno/Triton, dreary siblings that face consistent plumbing and other infrastructural problems.

HABANA VIEJA
Casas Particulares
Casa de Daniel Carrasco Guillén (Cristo #16, 2ndo piso, e/ Brasil y Muralla, tel. 07/866-2106, carrascohousing@yahoo.com; CUC25) is recommended. The owner and his friendly family rent two lofty-ceilinged rooms with modest furnishings. Take a pick from rooms in the colonial home. Modern rooms atop the roof can get hot during midday, but are cross-ventilated. All have air-conditioning and hot water, but only one has a private bathroom.

A stone's throw north, **Casa de Raquel y Ricardo** (Calle Cristo #12, e/ Brasil y Muralla, tel. 07/867-5026, casaraquel@cubacaribemail. com; CUC25–30) is a gracious upstairs home with a spacious, airy lounge with rockers and *mediopuntos.* It has two rooms with lofty ceilings. One is air-conditioned and has its own bathroom.

Casa de Eugenio Barral García (San Ignacio #656, e/ Jesús María y Merced, tel. 07/862-9877; CUC30), in southern Habana Vieja, is one of the best private room rentals with two air-conditioned bedrooms with fans, refrigerators, and modern hot-water bathrooms in an old home graciously and eclectically appointed with antiques and precious ornaments. **Casa de Paula y Norma** (San Ignacio #654, e/ Merced y Jesús María, tel. 07/863-1279; CUC25–30), next door, is an identical home but much more simply furnished.

For historic ambience, I like **Casa de**

Luis Batista (Amargura #255, e/ Habana y Compostela, tel. 07/863-0622; CUC30). Beyond its nail-studded door, this 1717 colonial gem has *vitrales* and a stunning *alfarje* ceiling. Four air-conditioned rooms with fans open to a long narrow patio where you can relax on rockers, shaded by an arbor of vines. Two have private hot water bathrooms.

I also recommend **Casa Chez Nous** (Brasil #115, e/ Cuba y San Ignacio, tel. 07/862-6287, cheznous@ceiai.inf.cu; CUC30), one block from Plaza Vieja. This delightful upstairs colonial home has two large air-conditioned rooms with *vitral* windows, fridges, simple antique furnishings, and balconies. They share a spacious bathroom with hot water. There's an airy TV lounge, plus a shaded patio with songbirds. Adjoining, in the same building, **Casa do Marta o Israel** (tel. 07/862-0948, martha@secomar.telemar.cu; CUC30) is similar, though rooms are smaller, darker, and more simply furnished.

Casa de Pepe y Rafaela (San Ignacio #454, e/ Sol y Santa Clara, tel. 07/867-5551; CUC30), on the second floor of a colonial home, has a spacious lounge full of antiques and songbirds. The owners rent two air-conditioned rooms with tall ceilings, fridges, fans, antique beds and furniture, glass chandeliers, and heaps of light pouring in from the balcony windows. Modern bathrooms have large showers.

In 2009, I enjoyed a stay at **Casa de Irma y Roly** (Compostela #117, e/ Tejadillo y Empedrado, tel. 07/861-1004). The hosts are a delight and make filling breakfasts (CUC4–5). The two upstairs rooms are small and lack windows, but are air-conditioned and have private bathrooms with hot water.

A stone's throw away from Casa de Irma y Roly, **Casa de Luis y Mirtha** (Compostela #119, esq. Empedrado, tel. 07/860-0650; CUC30) has one room up and one down; they have double-pane windows, a/c, modern private bathrooms with hot water, and firm mattresses.

Around the corner from Casa de Luis y Mirtha, and perhaps the best bet in Habana Vieja, is ◖ **Casa de Alina Peña** (Calle San Juan de Díos #154, Apto. 9, e/ Villegas y Aguacate, tel. 07/862-1533, adrpa1955@yahoo. com; CUC25 low season, CUC30 high season). On the seventh floor, this lovely, spacious, well-lit, and beautifully furnished home has fabulous views over Habana Vieja, including from the single rented room with high ceiling with fan. The small but modern bathroom is across the lounge. There's even a computer with Internet.

Run by a pleasant couple, **Casa de Alexis y Aleida** (Compostela #310B, e/ Obispo y Obrapia, tel. 07/861-0637; CUC30) has one room with a private bathroom and a small window opening to a private patio.

Around the corner from Casa de Alexis y Aleida, I like the clinically clean **Casa de Juana** (Lamparilla #254, e/ Habana y Compostela, tel. 07/862-6797; CUC25), festooned with colorful tiles, marble, and limestone. The two upstairs rooms with a/c have external bathrooms.

Also to consider are **Casa Jesús y María** (Aguacate #518, e/ Sol y Muralla, tel. 07/861-1378, jesusmaria2003@yahoo.com; CUC25) and **Casa de Nancy Pérez** (Jesús María #23, Apt. F, e/ San Ignacio y Inquisidor, tel. 07/860-1898; CUC20), two places with simply furnished air-conditioned rooms. Bathrooms are shared at Casa de Nancy Pérez.

Hotels Under CUC50
Residencia Académica Convento de Santa Clara (Cuba #610, e/ Luz y Sol, tel. 07/861-3335, fax 07/866-5696, reaca@cencrem.cult. cu; CUC25 per person, CUC35 suite, including breakfast), in a former 17th-century convent, is a bargain. It has nine charming, modestly furnished but well-kept dorm rooms plus some private rooms. However, the rooms lack air-conditioning and can be stifling, especially in summer. A café serves refreshments.

Seeking silent repose in a *real* convent? Try **Hotel Convento de Santa Brígida** (Oficios #204, e/ Teniente Rey y Muralla, tel. 07/866-4064, fax 07/866-4066, brigidahabana@enet. cu; CUC35 pp including breakfast), attached to the still-functioning nunnery.

Hotel Caribbean (Prado #164, e/ Colón y Refugio, tel. 07/860-8241, reservas@lidocaribbean.hor.tur.cu; CUC33 s, CUC48 d low

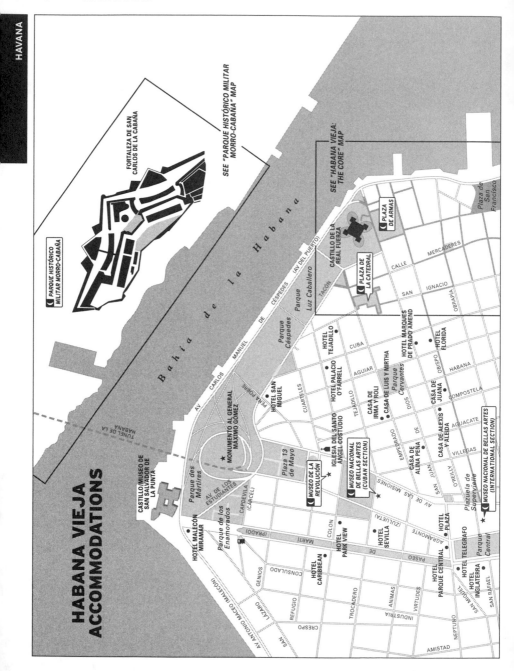

HABANA VIEJA ACCOMMODATIONS

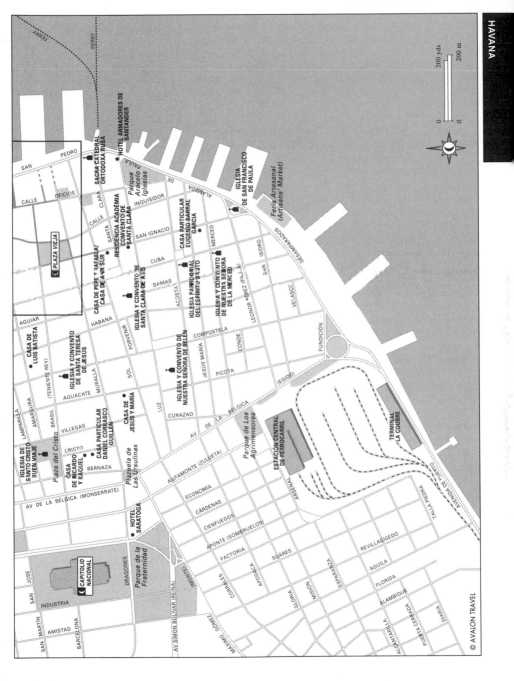

HAVANA

200 yds
200 m

FERRY

SAN PEDRO

CALLE OFICIOS

PLAZA VIEJA

SACRA CATEDRAL ORTODOXA RUSA

HOTEL ARMADORES DE SANTANDER

Parque Aracelo Iglesias

IGLESIA DE SAN FRANCISCO DE PAULA

ALAMEDA DE PAULA

Feria Artesanal (Artisans' Market)

CALLE SANTA CLARA

RESIDENCIA ACADEMIA CONVENTO DE SANTA CLARA

INQUISIDOR

SAN IGNACIO

CASA PARTICULAR EUGENIO BARRAL GARCIA

CASA DE PEPE "ZAFAELA"/CASA DE AMISUR

CUBA

DAMAS

MERCED

SAN ISIDRO

DESAMPARADOS

AGUIAR

CASA DE LUIS BATISTA

IGLESIA Y CONVENTO DE SANTA CLARA DE ASÍS

IGLESIA PARROQUIAL DEL ESPÍRITU SANTO

IGLESIA Y CONVENTO DE NUESTRA SEÑORA DE LA MERCED

LEONOR PÉREZ (PAULA)

VELASCO

HABANA

PORVENIR

ACOSTA

(TENIENTE REY)

IGLESIA Y CONVENTO DE SANTA TERESA DE JESÚS

MURALLA

SOL

COMPOSTELA

CONDE

JESÚS MARÍA

FUNDICIÓN

AGUACATE

IGLESIA Y CONVENTO DE NUESTRA SEÑORA DE BELÉN

PICOTA

AMARGURA

LAMPARILLA

BRASIL

VILLEGAS

CRISTO

CASA PARTICULAR DANIEL CORRASCO GUILLÉN

CASA DE JESÚS Y MARÍA

LUZ

CURAZAO

AV. DE LA BÉLGICA

(EGIDO)

Parque de Los Agrimensores

IGLESIA DE SANTO CRISTO BUEN VIAJE

Plaza del Cristo

CASA DE RICARDO Y RAQUEL

BERNAZA

Plazuela de Las Ursulinas

AGRAMONTE (ZULUETA)

ARSENAL

ESTACIÓN CENTRAL DE FERROCARRIL

TERMINAL LA COUBRE

AV. DE LA BÉLGICA (MONSERRATE)

HOTEL SARATOGA

ECONOMÍA

CÁRDENAS

CIENFUEGOS

APONTE (SOMERUELOS)

FACTORÍA

SUÁREZ

REVILLAGIGEDO

AGUILA

TALLA PIEDRA

AVENIDA DEL PUERTO

SAN JOSÉ

CAPITOLIO NACIONAL

DRAGONES

Parque de la Fraternidad

MONTE

AV. SIMÓN BOLÍVAR (REINA)

APODACA

CORRALES

GLORIA

MISIÓN

ESPERANZA

FLORIDA

ALAMBIQUE

DIARIA

INDUSTRIA

SAN MARTÍN

AMISTAD

BARCELONA

SAN NICOLÁS

MÁXIMO GÓMEZ

ALCANTARILLA

PUERTA CERRADA

© AVALON TRAVEL

season, CUC36 s, CUC54 d high season, including breakfast) serves budget travelers with 38 small air-conditioned rooms, meagerly yet adequately furnished in lively colors, with tiny satellite TVs, telephones, safes, and small yet pleasant bathrooms. There's a simple bar and the café.

Hotels CUC50-100

Hostal Valencia (Oficios #53, e/ Obrapía y Lamparilla, tel. 07/857-1037, fax 07/860-5628, www.habaguanexhotels.com; CUC70 s, CUC110 d standard, CUC77 s, CUC130 d junior suite low season; CUC80 s, CUC130 d standard, CUC87 s, CUC150 d junior suite high season) might induce a flashback to the romantic *posadas* of Spain. The 18th-century mansion-turned-hotel originated as the home of Governor Count Sotolongo. It exudes charm, with its lobby of hefty oak beams, Spanish tiles, and wrought-iron chandeliers. The 12 spacious rooms (some air-conditioned) have cool marble floors, are simply furnished, and have satellite TVs, telephones, refrigerators, and safes (hot water is said to be unreliable). The La Paella restaurant is a mega-bonus.

Attached to Hostal Velencia, the **Hotel El Comendador** (Obrapía #55 e/ Baratillo y Oficios; tel. 07/857-1037, fax 07/860-5628, www.habaguanexhotels.com; CUC70 s, CUC110 d standard, CUC77 s, CUC130 d junior suite low season; CUC80 s, CUC130 d standard, CUC87 s, CUC150 d junior suite high season) is another endearingly restored colonial home. Its 14 exquisite rooms feature marble floors, iron-frame beds, antique reproduction furnishings, safe deposit boxes, local TVs, old-style phones, and mini-fridges. Modern bathrooms have claw-foot bathtubs, hairdryers, and toiletries. Rooms on the mezzanine are cramped; take an upper-story room with lofty ceilings.

El Mesón de la Flota (Mercaderes #257, e/ Amargura y Brasil, tel. 07/863-3838, www.habaguanexhotels.com; CUC55 s, CUC86 d low season; CUC64 s, CUC105 d high season) is a classic Spanish *bodega* bar-restaurant with five intimate rooms. Each has antique

reproductions; one has a magnificent *vitral*. It's overpriced, despite its charm.

Hotel Park View (Colón, esq. Morro, tel. 07/861-3293, fax 07/863-6036, www.habaguanexhotels.com; CUC57 s, CUC86 d low season; CUC57 s, CUC90 d high season, including breakfast), in a sober green-and-ocher color scheme, has 55 lofty-ceilinged rooms, nicely furnished with green marble highlights. Some bathrooms have stand-up showers; others have tubs. Third-floor rooms have balconies. It has minimal facilities, but the Hotel Sevilla is around the corner.

Hotels CUC100-150

Hotel Plaza (Zulueta #267, esq. Neptuno, tel. 07/860-8583, fax 07/860-8869, www.gran-caribe.com; CUC84 s, CUC120 d standard, CUC115 s, CUC145 d suites, year-round), built in 1909, occupies the northeast corner of Parque Central. The lobby is supported by Corinthian columns. A marble stairway leads upstairs to 188 lofty-ceilinged, air-conditioned rooms and suites furnished with simple antique reproductions, satellite TVs, radios, safes, and heaps of closet space. Some rooms are gloomy, and those facing the street can be noisy. It was refurbished for its 100th anniversary in 2009. A pianist hits the ivories in the gracious lobby bar lit by stained-glass skylights and gilt chandeliers. It has a chic restaurant, a gift store, and solarium.

The overpriced **Hotel Inglaterra** (Prado #416, esq. San Rafael, tel. 07/860-8594, fax 07/860-8254, www.gran-caribe.com; CUC84 s, CUC120 d year-round), on the west side of Parque Central, has an extravagant lobby bar and restaurant that whisk you off to Morocco with their arabesque details. It has 83 air-conditioned rooms with telephones, satellite TVs, safes, hairdryers, and minibars. Noise from the square can be a problem, and many rooms are dark.

Overpriced, **Hotel Ambos Mundos** (Obispo #153, e/ San Ignacio y Mercaderes, tel. 07/860-9530, fax 07/860-9532, www.habaguanexhotels.com; CUC80 s, CUC130 d standard, CUC110 s, CUC180 d junior suites low season;

CUC100 s, CUC160 d standard, CUC125s, CUC210 d junior suites high season), one block west of Plaza de Armas, lets you rest your head where Ernest Hemingway found inspiration in the 1930s. The hotel offers 59 air-conditioned rooms and three junior suites arranged atrium style, each with satellite TV and direct-dial telephone. Most rooms are small, dark, and have undistinguished furnishings, for which room rates are double what is justified. Those facing the interior courtyard are quieter. It has a pleasant lobby bar, plus rooftop restaurant and solarium. Avoid the fifth floor—a thoroughfare for sightseeing gawkers.

I like the **Hotel del Tejadillo** (Tejadillo, esq. San Ignacio, tel. 07/863-7283, fax 07/863-8830, www.habaguanexhotels.com; CUC70 s, CUC110 d standard; CUC85 s, CUC140 d suites low season; CUC80 s, CUC130 d standard, CUC97 s, CUC160 d suites high season), another converted colonial mansion. Beyond the huge doors is an airy marble-clad lobby with a quaint dining area. It offers 32 air-conditioned rooms around two courtyards with fountains. The cool, high-ceilinged rooms are graced by *mediopuntos* and modern furniture, and feature safes, minibars, and simple bathrooms.

On the harborfront, **Hotel Armadores de Santander** (Luz #4, esq. San Pedro, tel. 07/862-8000, fax 07/862-8080, www.habaguanexhotels.com; CUC85 s, CUC130 d standard, CUC110 s, CUC180 d junior suite low season; CUC100 s, CUC160 d standard, CUC125 s, CUC210 d junior suite high season; CUC300 s/d suite year-round) has 39 spacious rooms, including three duplexes, a junior suite, and a fabulous contemporary suite with a whirlpool tub in the center of the mezzanine bedroom with a four-poster bed. All rooms feature lush hardwoods, colonial tile floors, and handsome furnishings, including state-of-the-art bathrooms. One room is accessible for travelers with disabilities. It has a 24-hour bar, billiards room, and a fine restaurant.

Playing on a monastic theme, the **Hostal Los Frailes** (Brasil, e/ Oficios y Mercaderes, tel. 07/862-9383, fax 07/862-9710, www .habaguanexhotels.com; CUC70 s, CUC110 d standard, CUC85 s, CUC140 d junior suite low season; CUC80 s, CUC130 d standard, CUC95 s, CUC160 d junior suite high season), another restored historic property, has staff dressed in monks' habits, plus lots of heavy timbers, stained glass, wrought-iron, murals, and earth-tone decor. It has 22 air-conditioned rooms around a patio with an *aljibe* and fountain. The rooms have patterned terra-cotta tile floors, sponge-washed walls, religious prints, plus TVs, period telephones, minibars, safes, and spacious bathrooms. It has Internet and a bar, but no restaurant.

Hotel Beltrán de Santa Cruz (San Ignacio #411, e/ Muralla y Sol, tel. 07/860-8330, fax 07/860-8363, reserva@bsantacruz.co.cu, www. habaguanexhotels.com; CUC70 s, CUC110 d standard, CUC77 s, CUC130 d junior suite low season; CUC80 s, CUC135 d standard, CUC87 s, CUC150 d junior suite high season) is a handsome conversion of an elegant, three-story 18th-century mansion with exquisite *mediopuntos* and other architectural features (the atrium still features the original *aljibe*). Its 11 air-conditioned rooms and one junior suite exude historic ambience courtesy of gracious antique reproductions; all have direct phone lines, satellite TVs, minibars, safes, and modern bathrooms.

Another fine colonial conversion, the romantic **Hotel Palacio O'Farrill** (Cuba #102, esq. Chacón, tel. 07/860-5080, fax 07/860-5083, www.habaguanexhotels.com; CUC85 s, CUC130 d standard, CUC100 s, CUC180 d suite low season; CUC100 s, CUC160 d standard, CUC125 s, CUC210 d suite high season) is centered on a three-story atrium courtyard lit by a skylight and adorned with antique marble plus bronze statues. It has 38 graciously furnished rooms on three floors, with decor reflecting the 18th century (mezzanine), 19th century (3rd floor), and 20th century (fourth floor). All have satellite TV, safe, minibar, and modern bathrooms. Facilities include a cybercafé, elegant restaurant, and a jazz café.

Hotel Raquel (San Ignacio, esq. Amargura, tel. 07/860-8280, fax 07/860-8275, www.habaguanexhotels.com; CUC85

HAVANA

s, CUC130 d standard, CUC110 s CUC180 d junior suite low season; CUC100 s, CUC160 d standard, CUC125 s, CUC210 d junior suite high season, including breakfast), dating to 1905, is a dramatic exemplar of art nouveau styling. The lobby gleams with marble columns and period detailing, including Tiffany lamps and a mahogany bar. The theme carries into the charming air-conditioned rooms featuring tile floors, wrought-iron beds, direct-dial phones, satellite TVs, safes, minibars, and hairdryers. It has an elegant restaurant, and there's a rooftop solarium plus gym. On the edge of the old Jewish quarter, the Hotel Raquel incorporates its location with richly illustrated passages from the Old Testament covering the walls, rooms on the second floor named for Biblical patriachs, kosher food served in the restaurant, and chandeliers in the lobby inspired by the Star of David.

Other historic hotels to consider include the pleasant 10-room **Hotel San Miguel** (Calle Cuba #52, esq. Peña Pobre, tel. 07/862-7656, www.habaguanexhotels.com; CUC85 s, CUC130 d standard, CUC110 s, CUC180 d junior suite low season; CUC100 s, CUC160 d standard, CUC125 s, CUC210 d junior suite high season); and **Hotel Marqués de San Felipe y Santiago de Bejucal** (www.habaguanexhotels.com), a restored 1771 building slated to open on Plaza San Francisco in 2010 with minimalist decor, and wifi, DVDs, and hot tubs in its suites. Meanwhile, work is advancing on rebuilding the old **Hotel Packard** (Paseo del Prado esq. Carcel, www.habaguanex.com), due to open in 2011. An entirely new interior will arise behind a preserved historic facade.

Hotels CUC150-250

Entered via giant brass-studded carriage doors, **(Hotel Conde de Villanueva** (Mercaderes #202, esq. Lamparilla, tel. 07/862-9293, fax 07/862-9682, www.habaguanexhotels.com; CUC95 s, CUC140 d standard, CUC110 s, CUC180 d junior suite, CUC125 s, CUC210 d suite low season; CUC110 s, CUC175 d standard, CUC135 s, CUC230 d junior suite,

CUC150 s, CUC260 d suite high season) is an exquisite conversion of the mansion of the Conde de Villanueva. The spacious lobby-lounge, with its bottle-green sofas and blood-red cushions, terra-cotta floor, and beamed ceiling with chandeliers, opens to an intimate courtyard, with caged birds and tropical foliage. It has nine large, airy, simply appointed air-conditioned rooms and one suite (with whirlpool tub) with 1920s reproduction furnishings, TVs, safes, and minibars. There's a small restaurant and bar, plus Internet. The hotel aims at cigar smokers with a Casa del Habano outlet and smokers' lounge.

(Hotel Florida (Obispo #252, esq. Cuba, tel. 07/862-4127, fax 07/862-4117, www.habaguanexhotels.com; CUC85 s, CUC130 d standard, CUC135 s, CUC230 d suite low season; CUC100 s, CUC160 d standard, CUC150 s, 260 d suite high season) is a compact colonial charmer built around an atrium courtyard with rattan lounge chairs, planters, stained-glass skylight, and black-and-white checkered marble floors. Sumptuously furnished, its 25 rooms feature tasteful colonial decor, including marble floors and wrought-iron beds, plus phones, satellite TVs, minibars, and safes. The restaurant is elegant and has above-average cuisine, while the upstairs piano bar is a marvelous place for evening cocktails.

Immediately behind the Hotel Florida, and part of it, is the upscale **Hotel Marqués de Prado Ameno** (Mercaderes #202, esq. Lamparilla, tel. 07/862-9293, fax 07/862-9682, www.habaguanexhotels.com; CUC95 s, CUC140 d standard, CUC110 s, CUC180 d junior suite, CUC125 s, CUC210 d suite low season; CUC110 s, CUC175 d standard, CUC135 s, CUC230 d junior suite, CUC150 s, CUC260 d suite high season), a restored 18th-century mansion with 16 stylishly furnished rooms, all with satellite TV, safes, minibars, and modern bathrooms; and a *bodega* (colonial-style bar-restaurant) that whisks you back 200 years. Lovely!

On Parque Central, **Hotel Telégrafo** (Paseo del Prado #408, esq. Neptuno, tel. 07/861-1010, fax 07/861-4744, www.habaguanexhotels.com;

CUC80 s, CUC130 d standard, CUC105 s, CUC180 d suite low season; CUC95 s, CUC160 d standard, CUC150 s, CUC220 d suite high season) melds its classical elements into an exciting contemporary vogue. It has 63 rooms with beautiful furnishings and trendy color schemes, including sponge-washed walls and bare stone, plus marble floors and classy bathrooms. The hip lobby bar is skylit within an atrium framed by colonial ruins.

The **Hotel Mercure Sevilla** (Trocadero #55, e/ Prado y Zulueta, tel. 07/860-8560, fax 07/860-8875, www.accorhotels.com; CUC99 s, CUC149 d low season; CUC154 s, CUC201 d high season), built in 1924, is famous as the setting for Graham Greene's *Our Man in Havana* (Wormold stayed in room 501). The lobby is straight out of *1,001 Arabian Nights*. Its 178 rooms—recently done up in ocher and red color schemes, with antique reproductions, but still rather modest and overpriced—each has a safe, minibar, telephone, and satellite TV. The sumptuous top-floor restaurant serves continental fare. There's a tour and car rental desk, swimming pool, four bars, assorted shops, plus an Internet café and wifi in the lobby.

Hotel Santa Isabel (Baratillo #9, e/ Obispo y Narciso López, tel. 07/860-8201, fax 07/860-8391, www.habaguanexhotels.com; CUC190 s, CUC240 d standard, CUC230 s, CUC340 d junior suite, CUC315 s CUC400 d suite), a small and intimate hostelry in the former 18th-century palace of the Count of Santovenia, enjoys a fabulous setting overlooking Plaza de Armas (some rooms face the harbor). The hotel has 27 lofty-ceilinged, air-conditioned rooms furnished with marble or stone floors, plus four-poster beds, reproduction antique furniture, satellite TVs, direct-dial telephones, and safes, plus leather recliners on wide balconies. Suites have whirlpool tubs. There's an elegant restaurant and two bars. The recent guest list reads like a *Who's Who*: not least President Jimmy Carter, Jack Nicholson, Robert Redford, and Sting. Still, plumbing has been an issue, many rooms have mold, and readers report that staff are indifferent, which makes the rates all the more outrageous.

Hotels CUC250 and Up

◖ Hotel NH Parque Central (Neptuno, e/ Prado y Zulueta, tel. 07/866-6627, fax 07/866-6630, www.nh-hotels.cu; CUC205 s, CUC270 d standard, CUC225 s, CUC325 d superior, CUC330 s/d junior suite; CUC375–420 s/d suite year-round) occupies the north side of Parque Central and fuses colonial and contemporary styles. This modern, Dutch-managed hotel is one of the most sophisticated in town and is popular with businessfolk. Its 281 air-conditioned rooms are tastefully appointed with antique reproduction furnishings, king-size beds, direct-dial phones, satellite TVs, Internet modems, plus marble-clad bathrooms. For views, ask for an exterior room. Facilities include two choice restaurants, rooftop grill, cigar lounge-bar, meeting rooms, business center, boutiques, plus rooftop swimming pool, and fitness room. At press time, a 150-room annex was being built.

The finest rooms in Havana are at the **◖ Hotel Saratoga** (Paseo del Prado #603, esq. Dragones, tel. 07/868-1000, fax 07/868-1001, reservaciones@saratoga.co.cu, www.habaguanexhotels.com; CUC170 s, CUC235 d standard, CUC205 s, CUC280 d junior suite low season; CUC200 s CUC275 d standard, CUC235 s, CUC300 d junior suite high season; CUC424–715 suite year-round), which opened in late 2005. European architects and designers have turned this colonial edifice into a visual stunner inside. Imbued throughout with a hip aesthetic, the hotel effuses sophistication on a par with New York or London. Guest-room decor varies from colonial inspired to thoroughly contemporary. Most rooms have king-size four-poster beds; all have rich color schemes, gorgeous halogen-lit bathrooms, and 21st-century amenities. A rooftop pool, spa, and gym offer fabulous views over the city. And the bar and restaurantrestaurant are New York chic (although the food is disappointing).

CENTRO HABANA
Casas Particulares

In a high-rise overlooking the Malecón, **Casa de René Pérez** (Malecón #51, e/ Tenios y

© CHRISTOPHER P. BAKER

a standard room in the Hotel Saratoga

Carcel, tel. 07/861-8108, rmichelpd@yahoo. com; CUC40) is an unusually lavish option with two spacious, windowless yet romantic air-conditioned rooms decorated with antiques. They share a mediocre hot-water bathroom. The vast lounge is sumptuously appointed and has a TV/VCR plus views along the Malecón. Entry is to the rear, via the parking lot (CUC1).

I also recommend **Casa de Elsa y Julio Roque** (Consulado #162, Apto. 2, e/ Colón y Trocadero, tel. 07/861-8027, julioroq@yahoo. com; CUC20, CUC25 with fridge and TV), with a pleasant lounge with leather sofas. Run by erudite and delightful owners, it has two rooms with air-conditioning, fans, wicker furniture, modern bathrooms, and each with an independent entrance.

Hostal el Parador Numantino (Consulado #223, e/ Ánimas y Trocadero, tel. 07/863-8733; CUC30) is a contemporary conversion with a spacious air-conditioned lounge with gleaming ceramic floor and comfy leather sofas. The two air-conditioned bedrooms upstairs are small and feature fans, TV, and mini-fridge.

La Casa Colonial (Gervasio #216, e/ Concordia y Virtudes, tel. 07/862-7109; CUC25) is a gracious place with two spacious and pleasantly furnished bedrooms with fans and air-conditioning, and filled with antiques. It has a nice courtyard.

There are several other room rentals in the area, including **Casa Colonial La Terraza** (Calle Belascoain #207, e/ Concordia y Neptuno, tel. 07/864-1275, www.casaterraza.com).

Hotels Under CUC50

Hotel Lincoln (Av. de Italia #164, esq. Virtudes, tel. 07/862-8061, www.islazul.cu; CUC30 s, CUC40 d low season; CUC39 s, CUC46 d high season) dates from 1926 and features graceful public arenas, including a lobby boasting chandeliers and Louis XVI–style furnishings. The 135 clean, air-conditioned rooms have radios, telephones, satellite TVs, and mini-fridges. Facilities include two eateries, a rooftop bar, and entertainment.

The budget **Hotel Islazul Lido** (Consulado, esq. Ánimas, tel./fax 07/867-1102; CUC26 s, CUC36 d low season; CUC36 s, CUC46 d high season) has 63 air-conditioned rooms with lackluster utility furniture, satellite TVs, telephones, radios, and tiny balconies. Safes can be rented (the Lido has a reputation for theft), and the dreary, overly air-conditioned lobby has a snack bar and Internet service. The rooftop restaurant is open 24 hours.

VEDADO AND PLAZA DE LA REVOLUCIÓN
Casas Particulares

C **Casa de Jorge Coalla Potts** (Calle I #456, Apto. 11, e/ 21 y 23, Vedado, tel. 07/832-9032 or cell 5283-1237, www.havanaroomrental.com, jorgepotts@yahoo.co.uk; CUC30–35) is my favorite *casa particular* in Havana and where I stay, if possible, when in town. This delightful home is run by Jorge and his wife, Marisel, who offer a large, well-lit, well-furnished air-conditioned bedroom to the rear of their spotless ground-floor apartment home, only two blocks from the Hotel Habana Libre Tryp. The room has a telephone, refrigerator, double bed with a firm orthopedic mattress, a lofty ceiling with fan, and a spacious tiled bathroom with plentiful hot water. There's a TV lounge with rockers. The couple and their daughter Jessica (fluent in English) go out of their way to make you feel at home. There's secure parking nearby.

The remarkable art deco Edificio Cuervo Rubio, at the corner of Calles 21 and O, has 14 *casas particulares*. They're more or less identical in layout. Take an east-facing apartment for ocean views. One such is **Casa de Alejandria García** (#42, tel. 07/832-0689; CUC35), on the fourth floor.

Also on Calle 21, and highly recommended by a reader, is **Casa Mercedes González** (Calle 21 #360, Apto. 2-A, e/ G y H, tel. 07/832-5846; CUC30). This graciously furnished abode has a mix of antique and utility furnishings, a modern bathroom, and its own balcony. I like it too!

Casa de Magalis Sánchez López (Calle 25 #156, e/ Infanta y O, tel. 07/870-7613, magalissanlop@correosdecuba.cu; CUC30 low season; CUC35 high season) has two air-conditioned rooms to the rear of a patio. Both have a TV, fridge, and radio-cassette player. Guests get use of the centenary home with lofty ceilings, a kitchen, and TV lounge. There's secure parking.

Casa de Basilia Pérez (Calle 25 #361, Apto. 7, e/ K y L, tel. 07/832-3953, basiliapcu@yahoo.es; CUC25–30) has two air-conditioned rooms in a pleasant home secluded behind an apartment block. Each has an independent entrance, fridge, fan, TV, and telephone.

Casa de Dania Borrego (Calle J #564B, e/ 25 y 27, tel. 07/832-9956; CUC20–25) has two upstairs air-conditioned rooms in the home of this pleasant family. Each has fans and modern furnishings. Guests get use of a well-lit lounge, plus secure parking.

I also like **Casa de Enrique y Mirien** (Calle F #509, e/ 21 y 23, tel. 07/832-4201, mirien@enet.cu; CUC30), a beautiful option with an independent entrance, security box, a nice modern bathroom, a delightful bedroom with TV, and a patio with rockers and a shade tree. Another independent apartment nearby is **Casa de Humberto San Pedro** (Calle 25 #567 e/ G y H, tel. 07/833-9670, sanpalbearcuba@yahoo.es; CUC30), tucked behind a massive vine. It has a small kitchen and tiny lounge downstairs; the air-conditioned bedroom and small modern bathroom are upstairs; the only drawback is the low ceiling, and it can get hot. I've stayed here twice with no regrets.

I also stayed at **Casa de Lola** (Calle I #355, e/ 17 y 19, tel. 07/832-1525; CUC25–30), on the third floor of a 1920s mansion. The owners are a tad aloof, the mattress is tired, and you don't get a key to the apartment, but the air-conditioned room is spacious and well ventilated and has its own modern bathroom with hot water. A terrace has rockers.

Casa de Eddy Gutiérrez (Calle 21 #408, e/ F y G, tel. 07/832-5207; CUC35) has two

HAVANA

HOTELS FOR STUDENTS

Various state agencies operate accommodations for visiting students and educators, all charging CUC15-25 s, CUC20-38 d.

In Vedado, **Villa Residencial Estudiantil** (Calle 2, e/ 15 y 17, tel. 07/830-5250), run by the Ministry of Public Health (MINSAP), is in a converted mansion with simple rooms. It has a small restaurant and a broad, breeze-swept veranda with rockers.

Hotel Universitario (Calle L y 17, tel. 07/838-2373, hoteluni@enet.cu), run by the Ministerio de Educación (MINED), is a basic, wood-paneled affair with a gloomy student union-style bar and a pleasant restaurant downstairs behind the glum lobby. Its 21 rooms offer the bare essentials.

At last visit, the following were being used exclusively for Venezuelan medical staff:

In Miramar, **Hostal Icemar** (Calle 16, e/ 1 y 3, tel. 07/203-7735 or 203-6130), operated by MINED, is a 1950s Miami-style hotel with 54 large air-conditioned rooms with TV and hot water. Rooms facing the sea have more light. Six minimally furnished apartments across the road sleep up to eight people apiece.

MINED also operates **Hotel Universitaria Ispaje** (1ra, esq. 22, tel. 07/203-5370), with eight rooms with private baths, plus a swimming pool and bar; **Villa Universitaria Miramar** (Calle 62 #508, e/ 5ta-A y 5ta-B Av., tel. 07/832-1034), with 25 rooms with private baths; **Hostal Costa Sol** (3ra y Calle 60, tel. 07/209-0828), with 11 air-conditioned rooms, plus a restaurant; and **Hotel Mirazúl** (5ta #3603, e/ 36 y 40, tel. 07/204-0088, fax 07/204-0045, hotelmi@enet.cu), with eight spacious rooms with modest bamboo furnishings, satellite TV, air-conditioning, telephone, and hot-water bathroom.

independent apartments to the rear of the owner's colonial mansion with secure parking. Both are air-conditioned and have fans and refrigerators; one has its own small kitchen, while the other is larger and has higher ceilings.

Casa de Marta Vitorte (Av. de los Presidentes #301, e/ 17 y 19, tel. 07/832-6475, martavitorte@hotmail.com; CUC40) is a splendid two-room, two-bath apartment that takes up the entire 14th floor and boasts wraparound glass windows on a balcony that offers fabulous views. The lounge has plump leather sofas, lounge chairs, and antiques. The beautifully maintained rooks feature antique beds. Martha is an engaging conversationalist who speaks fluent English. The only drawback is the rickety elevator.

Hospedaje Gisela Ibarra (Calle F #104 altos, e/ 5ta y Calzada, tel. 07/832-3891, latinhouse@enet.cu; CUC30) is a beautiful colonial-era home decorated with antiques and modern art. The delightful owners, Gisela and her daughter, Marta, have two air-conditioned rooms with antiques (including antique double beds), safety deposit boxes, and refrigerators. There's a roof terrace, plus parking, and a TV lounge gets the breezes. Meals are served in a gracious dining room.

I also like **Casa de Fifi** (Calzada #508, e/ D y E, tel. 07/832-3133, fifiacosta@yahoo.com; CUC30), an 1892 house in colonial style entered via a dramatic carriage door and opening to an arched terrace with planters. The two air-conditioned rooms, simply furnished with aged pieces, are spacious and have lofty ceilings and large modern bathrooms. The hostess is a delight.

A marvelous option, **Casa de Yolanda Piqueras** (Calle E #104, e/ Calzada y 5ta, tel. 07/832-3025; CUC30) is a pleasant colonial home with a shaded patio with rockers and swing chair and an interior with marble columns. The English-speaking family rents two rooms. One has a delightful modern bathroom. The second, a modern addition with its own entrance, is up a dangerous staircase.

Run by a savvy, politically well-placed owner, **Casa de Aldo Vásquez** (Calle B

#154, e/ Línea y Calzada, tel. 07/832-3223; CUC30) is another well-kept colonial home with a wide front porch with rockers, plus a TV lounge full of antiques. The two spacious air-conditioned bedrooms each have TV, fan, and modern clean private bathroom. There's secure parking.

Two pleasant independent apartments to recommend in this area are **Casa de Lizet** (Calle 3ra #580 bajos, e/ 8 y 10, tel. 07/832-1226; CUC30) and **Casa de Octavio Fundora** (Calle 10 #152, Apto. 1-D, e/ Calzada y Línea, Vedado, tel. 07/833-9769; CUC30).

One of the best options in town, **Casa Blanca** (Calle 13 #917, e/ 6 y 8, tel. 07/833-5697; CUC25), in the heart of western Vedado, is a gracious colonial home with a front garden riotous with bougainvillea. The home is replete with antiques. It has an air-conditioned room with two double beds, stereo, safe deposit box, and a clean, modern bathroom. It also email service for guests.

Casa de Antonio Llibre Artigas (Calle 24 #260, e/ 17 y 19, tel. 07/833-7156; CUC30) offers two rooms in a well-kept, cross-ventilated house with lofty ceilings in western Vedado. There's also a two-bedroom air-conditioned apartment with a small kitchen and TV. It has secure parking. Sr. Llibre was formerly aide-de-camp to Fidel in the Sierra Maestra.

In Nuevo Vedado, **Casa Mayra Sardaín Piña** (Av. Zoológico #160, e/ 38 y 40, tel. 07/881-3792; CUC40 low season; CUC50 high season), close to the Víazul bus station, is a graciously decorated house with a sun-kissed lounge with wicker furnishings and modern art. Two pleasingly furnished air-conditioned rooms reached by a spiral staircase have TVs and fridges. There's a small swimming pool in the rear courtyard.

Casa de Cecy y Raul (Av. Zoológico #112, e/ 36 y 28, tel. 07/881-3727, ceciraul@enet. cu; CUC40) is a pleasant 1950s home with an independent air-conditioned apartment with lounge and kitchen. And **Casa Jorge Araoz Agero** (Calle San Juan Bautista #62, e/ 35 y 37, tel. 07/883-7378 or 05/270-3364; CUC35–45) is another lovely property with two rooms.

Hotels Under CUC50

Handy for the nearby bus station, **Hotel Bruzón** (Calle Bruzón, e/ Av. Rancho Boyeros y Pozos Dulces, tel. 07/877-5682; CUC16 s, CUC24 d low season, CUC18 s, CUC28 d high season), just north of Plaza de la Revolución, offers the cheapest digs in town. Its 48 rooms are barebones, with utility furniture.

Hotels CUC50-100

Hotel St. John's (Calle O #206, e/ 23 y 25, tel. 07/833-3740, fax 07/833-3561, reserva@ stjohns.gca.tur.cu, www.gran-caribe.com; CUC38 s, CUC60 d low season; CUC56 s, CUC80 d high season) is a popular bargain. Beyond the chill lounge, this 14-story property has 87 air-conditioned rooms, each with radio, telephone, and TV. A cabaret is offered in the rooftop nightclub, plus there's a rooftop swimming pool, a tourism bureau, and the Steak House Toro.

Hotel Vedado (Calle O #244, e/ 23 y 25, tel. 07/836-4072, fax 07/834-4186, reserva@ vedado.gca.tur.cu, www.gran-caribe.com; CUC45 s, CUC60 d low season; CUC63 s, CUC80 d high season) is of similar standard. It has a tiny, uninspired lounge. Its 203 air-conditioned pastel-hued rooms are small, with satellite TV, telephone, tile floors, and small bathrooms; remodeled in 2008, however, they have firm mattresses and are eye-pleasing. There's a restaurant, piano bar, disco and cabaret, and swimming pool.

Hotel Victoria (Calle 19 #101, esq. M, tel. 07/833-3510, fax 07/833-3109, reserva@victo ria.gca.tur.cu, www.gran-caribe.com; CUC65 s, CUC80 d low season; CUC80 s, CUC100 d high season; CUC130 suites year-round) is a charming Victorian-style, neoclassical hotel that focuses on a business clientele. It has 31 elegant, albeit small air-conditioned rooms with antique reproduction furnishings, plus Internet modems. There's a small swimming pool, intimate lobby bar, and elegant restaurant. In 2009 the hotel awaited a restoration by England's Escencia hotel group.

For unfussy budget-minded travelers, my last resort would be the lackluster **Hotel Colina**

(Calle L esq. 27, tel. 07/836-4071, reservas@ colina.gca.tur.cu; CUC40 s, CUC50 d), near the Hotel Habana Libre Tryp.

Hotels CUC100-150

The art deco high-rise **Hotel Presidente** (Calzada #110, esq. Av. de los Presidentes, tel. 07/855-1801, fax 07/833-3753, reserva@hpdte .gca.tur.cu; CUC90 s, CUC140 d standard, CUC200 s/d suites year-round) was inaugurated in 1927 and retains its maroon and pink interior, with sumptuous Louis XIV–style furnishings and Grecian urns and busts that rise from a beige marble floor. It has 160 spacious rooms with tasteful contemporary furnishings, including marble bathrooms. One suite is appointed in Louis XIV style. It has an elegant restaurant, an outdoor swimming pool, plus gym and sauna.

Mobster Meyer Lansky's 23-story **Hotel Habana Riviera** (Malecón y Paseo, tel. 07/836-4051, fax 07/833-3739, reserva@gcrivie.gca.tur. cu, www.gran-caribe.com; CUC50 s, CU80 d standard, CUC150 junior suite low season; CUC71 s, CUC130 d standard, CUC150 s/d junior suite high season; CUC300 suite year-round) recently underwent refurbishing to recapture its 1950s luxe, but the hotel is still badly deteriorated. The fabulous modernist lobby, with acres of marble and glass and original furnishings, is the high point and has a pleasant cocktail lounge. The 352 spacious air-conditioned rooms, with direct-dial phones, satellite TV, safes, and minibars, have jaded and conservative furniture, cleanliness and bad plumbing are of concern, and some rooms have mildew. The hotel has two mediocre restaurants, a 24-hour snack bar, mediocre swimming pool (packed with noisy Cubans and clamorous with piped-in music), gym with sauna and massage service, tour desk, boutique, cigar store, and the swank Copa Room nightclub. Theft from guest rooms is a problem.

Hotels CUC150-250

◖ **Hotel Nacional** (Calle O y 21, tel. 07/873-3564, fax 07/873-5054, reserva@gcnacio .gca.tur.cu, www.hotelnacionaldecuba.com;

CUC120 s, CUC170 d standard, CUC215 s/d one-bedroom suite, CUC390 two-bedroom suite, CUC400–CUC1,000 special suites; all rooms CUC25 more in peak season) is Havana's flagship hotel, to which celebrities flock. A recent restoration revived much of the majesty of this 1930s eclectic-style gem, perched overlooking the Malecón. The 475 large air-conditioned rooms each have satellite TV, telephone, safe, and minibar, although furnishings are dowdy. The Executive Floor has 63 specially appointed rooms and suites. The Comedor de Aguiar (one of four restaurants) is one of the city's most elegant eateries, and the Cabaret Parisien, the top-floor cocktail lounge, and the open-air terrace bar are high points. Plus it has two swimming pools, upscale boutiques, a beauty salon, spa, tennis courts, bank, and business center. Theft from guest rooms is a problem.

Hotel Habana Libre Tryp (Calle L, e/ 23 y 25, tel. 07/834-6100, fax 07/834-6365, www .solmeliacuba.com; CUC140 s, CUC150 d standard, CUC170 s/d junior suite low season; CUC190 s, CUC200 d standard, CUC230 s/d junior suite high season; CUC440 s/d suite year-round), managed by the Spanish Grupo Sol Meliá, is Havana's landmark high-rise hotel. It was built in the 1950s by the Hilton chain and soon became a favorite of mobsters. The modernist atrium lobby with glass dome exudes a '50s retro feel. Although the 533 rooms feature satellite TVs, direct-dial telephones, minibars, safes, and hairdryers, furnishings are dowdy, plumbing is finicky to the point of breakdown, and guests complain about poor housekeeping. The hotel is loaded with facilities: tour desks, bank, airline offices, boutiques, international telephone exchange, plus 24-hour café, four restaurants (the Polinesio and El Baracón are dismal; the rooftop Las Antillas is recommended), an excellent open-air swimming pool, plus business center, underground parking, and one of Havana's best nightclubs.

Also managed by Spain's Sol Meliá, the deluxe postmodern, 22-story ◖ **Meliá Cohiba** (Paseo, esq. 1ra, tel. 07/833-3636, fax 07/834-

4555, www.solmeliacuba.com; CUC175 s/d standard, CUC200 s/d junior suite, CUC225 s/d suite low season; CUC225 s/d standard, CUC250 s/d junior suite, CUC275 s/d suite high season) is perhaps the city's finest all-round hotel. Its 462 spacious and elegant air-conditioned rooms feature brass lamps, marble floors, and Romanesque chairs with contemporary fabrics. The bathrooms dazzle with halogen lights and huge mirrors, bidets, hairdryers, and fluffy towels. South-facing rooms can get hot. It has first-rate executive services, plus a magnificent swimming pool, gym, squash court, solarium, boutiques, five top-ranked restaurants, four bars, and the Habana Café nightclub.

PLAYA (MIRAMAR AND BEYOND)
Casas Particulares

Casa de Fernando y Egeria González (1ra #205, e/ 2 y 4, Miramar, tel. 07/203-3866, egeria@finagri.co.cu; CUC35) is a superb property. This gracious family home offers two spacious and airy air-conditioned rooms with huge and exquisite tiled bathrooms. The family is a delight. There's secure parking, and a patio to the rear.

Further west, **Casa de Clarisa Santiago** (1ra #4407, e/ 44 y 46, tel. 07/209-1739; CUC30) is another excellent option, with an independent air-conditioned apartment in the rear patio. It's modern throughout and has a nicely decorated bedroom with TV and fan, plus a bathroom with a small hot water shower. A separate, well-stocked kitchen (by Cuban standards) has a tall refrigerator. There's secure parking and daily maid service.

Inland, **[Casa de Elena Sánchez** (Calle 34 #714, e/ 7ma y 17, tel. 07/202-8969, gerardo@enet.cu; CUC100) is one of the nicest 1950s-style rentals in town. You rent the entire two-story modernist home. It has two air-conditioned rooms, each with TV, fridge, private hot-water bathrooms, and a mix of antiques, 1950s modernist pieces, and contemporary furniture. A large TV lounge with leather sofas opens to a shaded garden patio with rockers. There's secure parking.

Casa de María (3ra #37, esq. B, Miramar, tel. 07/209-5297, fffmiramar@yahoo.com; CUC200–300) is a four-bedroom modernist home circa 1950s that's rented out in its entirety. Downstairs it has a large TV lounge and separate dining room with period pieces. The two upstairs bedrooms, reached by a spiral staircase, each have a large marble-clad bathroom from the era, plus huge walk-in closet with wall safe. The rear garden even has its own swimming pool overlooking the mouth of the Río Almendares. It has secure parking.

If you want to know how Communist bigwigs live, check out **Casa de Raquel y Carlos** (7ma #21602, e/ 216 y 218, Siboney, tel. 07/271-4319, fax 07/469-5404, figueredos@hotmail.com; CUC300 daily, CUC5,000 monthly). This fantastic modernist home, built in 1958 and confiscated when its original owner fled Cuba following the revolution, is graciously furnished with rattan furnishings, original Tiffany lamps, plus paintings and eclectic items such as antique pistols. The vast kitchen features contemporary appliances and would do Betty Crocker proud. It has two huge air-conditioned bedrooms, each with fabulous rattan king-size beds, large satellite TVs, and fans, plus humongous bathrooms with his and hers sinks. The vast garden has a swimming pool with heated whirlpool tub. How is all this permitted? Well, the new owner is a former head of MININT, the Ministry of the Interior.

Others to consider include **Casa de Manuel de Armas Pérez** (5ta #6607, e/ 66 y 68, tel. 07/203-7429; CUC50), a beautiful old home with a huge, pleasantly furnished, independent apartment with a patio and parking; **Casa de Esther Rodríguez** (5ta #8609, e/ 86 y 88, tel. 07/203-8480; CUC30), a 1950s home with one room simply furnished with period pieces, plus secure parking; **Casa de Ana e Ismael** (Calle 32 #101, esq. 1ra, tel. 07/202-9486; CUC120), a two-story 1950s home full of antique furnishings and enclosed in spacious, well-kept grounds with secure parking; and **Casa de Alexis Tristá** (5taB Av. #6612, e/ 66 y 70, tel. 07/203-2388 or 05/283-3392, angelad@

infomed.sld.cu; CUC100 up to four people), a lovely home that rents an entire floor with kitchen and patio garden.

Hotels CUC50-100

Hotel Kohly (Av. 49 y 36A, Rpto. Kohly, Playa, tel. 07/204-0240, fax 07/204-1733, comercial@kohly.gav.tur.cu, www.gaviota-grupo.com; CUC50 s, CUC65 d) is a 1970s-style property popular with budget tour groups despite its out-of-the-way location. The 136 air-conditioned rooms have tasteful albeit simple furniture, satellite TVs, radios, telephones, minibars, and safes. Most have a balcony. Facilities include two modest restaurants, a tour desk, car rental, bar, and 10-pin bowling alley, plus a twice-weekly cabaret.

Run jointly with the Hotel Kohly, the **Hotel el Bosque** (Calle 28A, esq. Av. 47, tel. 07/204-9232, fax 07/204-5637, comercial@kohly.gav.tur.cu, www.gaviota-grupo.com; CUC45 s, CUC60 d) has 62 modestly furnished air-conditioned rooms with satellite TVs, telephones, safes, and French windows opening to balconies (some rooms only). It has car rental, a laundry, and a tour desk. There's no restaurant; guests must walk downhill to Club Almendares.

Used principally by package-tour groups, the bargain-priced **Hotel Copacabana** (1ra Av., e/ 34 y 36, tel. 07/204-1037, fax 07/204-2846, comercial@copa.gca.tur.cu, www.hotelescubanacan.com; CUC58 s, CUC70 d year-round) is an oceanfront hotel with a Brazilian flavor: the Itapoa steak house, the Caipirinha bar and grill, and more. The hotel, including 168 rooms, was undergoing a total refurbishing at my last visit. Facilities include a swimming pool (popular with locals on weekends), discotheque, tourism bureau, car rental, and boutique.

Refurbished in 2008, the beachfront **Hotel Comodoro** (1ra Av. y Calle 84, tel. 07/204-5551, fax 07/204-2089, reservas@comodor.cha.cyt.cu, www.hotelescubanacan.com; CUC61 s, CUC76 d standard, CUC86 s, CUC108 d suite year-round) has 134 spacious air-conditioned rooms, including 15 suites, with modern furnishings plus satellite TV and telephone. Some have a balcony. The contemporary lobby lounge opens to four restaurants, several bars, plus a meager bathing area. The adjacent shopping complex has boutiques, a clinic, and beauty salon. A shuttle runs to Habana Vieja five times daily. The Comodoro's **Bungalows Pleamar** (CUC61 s, CUC76 d one-bedroom, CUC122 s/d two-bedroom, CUC150 s/d three-bedroom year round) are the closest thing to a beach resort in the city. The 320 aesthetically striking two-story, one-, two-, and three-bedroom villas are built around two sinuous amoeba-shaped swimming pools. Rooms have a balcony or patio, plus kitchen, living room, and minibar.

Way out west, **Hotel y Villas Marina Hemingway** (5ta Av. y Calle 248, Santa Fe, tel. 07/204-7628, fax 07/204-4379, comercial@comermh.cha.cyt.cu), in the Marina Hemingway complex, offers modestly attractive waterfront suites and villas with terrace, TV and video, safe, and kitchen. Also here, the **Hotel El Viejo y El Mar** (tel. 07/204-7628) was closed for restoration at last visit.

Hotels CUC100-150

The lonesome **Hotel Chateau Miramar** (1ra Av., e/ 60 y 62, tel. 07/204-1951, fax 07/204-0224, reservas@chateau.cha.cyt.cu, www.hotelescubanacan.com; CUC95 s, CUC120 d standard; CUC150 s/d junior suite; CUC170 s/d suite), on the shorefront, aims at business clientele. The handsome five-story hotel has 50 nicely furnished rooms with satellite TV, minibar, radio, and safe; suites have whirlpool tubs. Facilities include a pool, elegant restaurant, two bars, and business center.

The **Hotel Palco** (Av. 146, e/ 11 y 13, tel. 07/204-7235, fax 07/204-7236, info@hpalco.gov.cu; CUC74 s, CUC94 d low season; CUC91 s, CUC111 d high season; CUC130–150 junior suites year-round), adjoining the Palacio de Convenciones, aims at convention traffic. The 144 air-conditioned rooms and 36 junior suites are spacious and have modern decor in lively colors. Facilities include a business center, elegant restaurant, split-level pool, and small sauna and gym. It sometimes has low season specials that include car rental.

Hotels CUC150-250

Directly across from the Miramar Trade Center, **Meliá Habana** (3ra Av., e/ 76 y 80, tel. 07/206-9406, fax 07/204-8505, www.solmeliacuba.com; CUC225 s/d standard, CUC500 suites), with its huge atrium lobby, is a luxury hotel that aims at a business clientele. The 405 air-conditioned, marble-clad rooms and four suites are up to international standards and feature satellite TVs, telephones with fax and modem lines, and safes. The executive floor offers more personalized service plus data ports. Facilities include five restaurants, five bars, a cigar lounge, a beautiful swimming pool, plus tennis courts, gym, and business center.

The Spanish-managed **[Occidental Miramar** (5ta Av., e/ 72 y 76, tel. 07/204-3584, fax 07/204-9227, www.occidental-hoteles.com; CUC100 s, CUC130 d standard; CUC160 d deluxe; CUC160 s junior suite; CUC300 s/d suite year-round) lives up to its deluxe billing. This beautiful modern property features a mix of neoclassical wrought-iron furniture and hip contemporary pieces in the vast, marble-clad lobby. Its 427 cavernous rooms, including eight junior suites, eight suites, and five rooms rigged for travelers with disabilities, are done up in regal dark blue and gold. Cabarets are held beside a huge swimming pool. It has a beauty salon, squash court, health

center, tennis courts, business center, and three restaurants.

Tucked behind the Occidental, the garish **Montehabana Aparthotel** (tel. 07/206-9595, www.gaviota-grupo.com; CUC80 s/d standard, CUC90 s/d studio, CUC100 s/d one-bedroom apartment, CUC175 s/d two-bedroom apartment) has pleasantly furnished rooms, notwithstanding its tasteless architecture and lack of facilities. At least the atrium lobby is flooded with light, and you have the Occidental Miramar at hand for restaurants and services. Nearby, and slated to open in 2010, the Spanish-run **Barceló Habana Ciudad** (5ta Av. e/ 78 y 80, www.barcelo.com) will have 186 rooms with colorful contemporary decor.

With an exterior of blue-tinted glass, the mammoth and contemporary **Hotel Oasis Panorama** (Calle 70, esq. 3ra, tel. 07/204-0100, fax 07/204-4969, comercial@panorama.co.cu; CUC90 s, CUC120 d standard, CUC110 s, CUC160 d executive room, CUC180 s, CUC240 d suite) might be too gauche for some tastes. Still, I like the decor in its 317 rooms with ceramic floors, mini-bars, safes, direct-dial phones, interactive TVs, and Internet modems. The executive rooms and suites get their own top floor restaurant. Other facilities include a piano bar, squash court, Internet room, and Italian- and German-themed restaurants, and the swimming pool and deck, plus top-floor piano bar with live jazz are highlights.

Food

Havana reflects all the horror stories about Cuban dining. Fortunately it *does* have some fine restaurants, many in the top-class hotels. The number of private restaurants (*paladares*) had fallen from 600 to fewer than 40 at last visit, when the four state-run vegetarian restaurants launched in 2004 were no longer functioning as such. Some establishments mentioned in this book may be closed by the time you arrive.

HABANA VIEJA
Breakfasts

Most hotel restaurants are open for breakfast to non-guests. I recommend the buffet in the **Mediterráneo** (tel. 07/860-6627; daily 7–10 A.M.), in the Hotel NH Parque Central.

If all you want is a croissant and coffee, head to **Pastelería Francesca** (Prado #410, e/ Neptuno y San Rafael, tel. 07/862-0739;

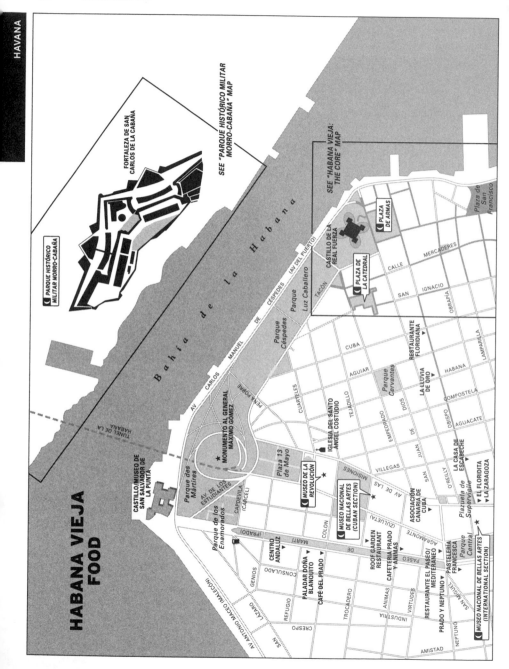

HABANA VIEJA FOOD

PARQUE HISTÓRICO MILITAR MORRO-CABAÑA

FORTALEZA DE SAN CARLOS DE LA CABAÑA

SEE "PARQUE HISTÓRICO MILITAR MORRO-CABAÑA" MAP

SEE "HABANA VIEJA: THE CORE" MAP

B a h i a   d e   l a   H a b a n a

TÚNEL DE LA HABANA

CASTILLO/MUSEO DE SAN SALVADOR DE LA PUNTA

CASTILLO DE LA REAL FUERZA

PLAZA DE ARMAS

PLAZA DE LA CATEDRAL

Plaza de San Francisco

MERCADERES

CALLE

SAN   IGNACIO

OBRAPIA

RESTAURANTE FLORIDIANA

LAMPARILLA

HABANA

COMPOSTELA

AGUACATE

LA LLUVIA DE ORO

Parque Cervantes

OBISPO

LA CASA DE LA BECHE

EL FLORIDITA

LA ZARAGOZA

Parque Céspedes

Parque Luz Caballero

MANUEL   DE   CÉSPEDES   (AV. DEL PUERTO)

CUBA

AGUIAR

TEJADILLO

EMPEDRADO

DIOS

JUAN   DE

SAN

O'REILLY

VILLEGAS

Plazuela de Santa Vieja

ASOCIACIÓN CANARIA DE CUBA

IGLESIA DEL SANTO ANGEL COSTÚDIO

CUARTELES

PEÑA POBRE

AV. CARLOS

MANUEL

Parque de los Mártires

Parque de los Enamorados

MONUMENTO AL GENERAL MÁXIMO GÓMEZ

AV. DE LOS ESTUDIANTES

Plaza 13 de Mayo

MUSEO DE LA REVOLUCIÓN

MUSEO NACIONAL DE BELLAS ARTES (CUBAN SECTION)

CAPDEVILA

(CÁRCEL)

COLON

(ZULUETA)

AGRAMONTE

AV. DE LAS   MISIONES

ROOF GARDEN RESTAURANT

CAFETERIA PRADO Y ANIMAS

PASEO   DE

PASTELERIA FRANCESCA

Parque Central

RESTAURANTE EL PASEO MEDITERRANEO

PRADO Y NEPTUNO

MUSEO NACIONAL DE BELLAS ARTES (INTERNATIONAL SECTION)

CENTRO ANDALIZ

MARTÍ   (PRADO)

PALADAR DOÑA BLANQUITO

CAFÉ DEL PRADO

GENIOS

CONSULADO

TROCADERO

ANIMAS

VIRTUDES

INDUSTRIA

SAN MIGUEL

NEPTUNO

AMISTAD

LAZARO

REFUGIO

CRESPO

SAN

AV ANTONIO MACEO (MALECÓN)

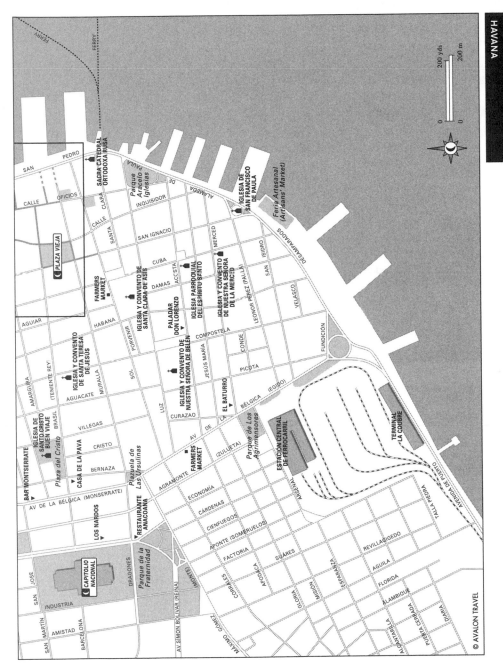

© AVALON TRAVEL

daily 8 A.M.–11 P.M.), on the west side of Parque Central; be aware this is a pick-up spot for *jineteras* and foreign males. The **€ Café El Escorial** (Mercaderes #317, tel. 07/868-3545; daily 9 A.M.–9 P.M.), on Plaza Vieja, is the closest you'll come in Havana to a European-style coffee shop. This atmospheric venue with a Tuscan mood sells croissants, truffle cream cakes, ice creams, and gourmet coffees and coffee liqueurs. It's a lovely spot to relax.

Paladares

The pocket-size **La Moneda Cubana** (San Ignacio #77, e/ O'Reilly y Plaza de la Catedral, tel. 07/867-3852; daily noon–11 P.M.) is a tiny, well-run place with speedy service and huge portions. The menu offers Cuban staples such as grilled chicken or fried fish (CUC9) and even pork chops (CUC10) served with rice and beans, mixed salad, and bread.

Paladar Don Lorenzo (Acosta #260A, e/ Habana y Compostela, tel. 07/861-6733; daily noon–midnight), a rooftop restaurant with thatched bar and musicians, has a large and creative menu that includes stuffed tomatoes (CUC2.50) and octopus vinaigrette (CUC5) appetizers, and main dishes such as squid in ink (CUC14), crocodile in mustard sauce (CUC18), and roast chicken in cider (CUC15).

Criollo

€ La Bodeguita del Medio (Empedrado #207, e/ San Ignacio y Cuba, tel. 07/862-1374, comercial@bdelm.gca.tur.cu; daily noon–midnight; bar 10:30 A.M.–midnight; CUC10–20), one block west of Plaza de la Catedral, specializes in traditional Cuban dishes—most famously its roast pork, steeped black beans, flat-fried bananas, garlicky yucca, and sweet guava pudding "overflowing," thought Nicolás Guillén (Cuba's national poet), "with surges of aged rum." Though Ernest Hemingway liked to drink *mojitos* here, today they are the worst in Havana. You may have to wait for an hour or more to be seated, but a tip or friendly banter with Tito or Caesar, the "house captains,"

should get you a good table. The service is relaxed to a fault, and the atmosphere bohemian and lively. Troubadours entertain. The food is generally fresher at lunch than at dinner. Reservations are advised.

Restaurant El Patio (tel. 07/867-1035; café 8 A.M.–midnight, restaurant noon–midnight), on Plaza de la Catedral, has heaps of ambience, as you dine at tables spilling into the plaza, with live music. It serves sandwiches (CUC3.50), hamburger (CUC3), and gazpacho (CUC4.50), plus hot dishes such as roasted pork leg (CUC9). The main restaurant has three air-conditioned dining rooms, and an upstairs grill where the overpriced dishes (CUC16–28) include shrimp *al ajillo* (in garlic) and T-bone steak.

Similar, but facing onto Plaza de Armas, the touristy and always packed **Café/Restaurante La Mina** (Obispo #109, esq. Oficios, tel. 07/862-0216; noon–midnight) offers shaded patio dining and a menu featuring snacks and salads (CUC3–5) and Cuban dishes (CUC4–12). The waiters are efficient, the setting is wonderful, and there's always live music. The courtyard to the rear has free-roaming peacocks.

Penny-pinchers once knew to head to the former **Restaurante Hanoi,** now the **Casa de la Pava** (Brasil, esq. Bernaza, tel. 07/867-1029; 11:45 A.M.–midnight), which promoted Vietnamese cuisine, but is, in reality, limited to a typical Cuban menu. It offers "combination specials" for below CUC5. *Mojitos* cost a mere CUC2.

To dine with Cubans, you can't beat **€ Los Nardos** (Paseo de Prado #563, e/ Teniente Rey y Dragones, tel. 07/863-2985; daily 11:30 A.M.–11:30 P.M.), upstairs in a run-down building opposite the Capitolio. The long lines at night hint at how good this place is. It has restaurants on three levels; be sure to dine in the atmospheric Los Nardos, not the more ascetic El Trofeo or El Asturianito, on the upper levels. Los Nardos has a soaring ceiling, fabulous wooden furnishings, and a wall lined with soccer trophies plus a wine cellar. The huge meals include

SELF-CATERING

Farmers markets (*agromercados* or *mercados agropecuarios*) selling fresh produce exist throughout the city. State-run hard-currency groceries charge exorbitantly for packaged goods, but you have no other option.

HABANA VIEJA

The *agromercado* is on Avenida de la Bélgica (Egido), e/ Apodaca y Corrales.

Imported meats are sold at **La Monserrate** (Monserrate, e/ Brasil y Muralles), an air-conditioned butcher shop; and at **Harris Brothers** (Monserrate #305, e/ O'Reilly y Progreso, Habana Vieja, tel. 07/861-1644), a department store with various foodstuff sections.

Supermercado Isla de Cuba (Máximo Gómez #213, esq. Factoria, tel. 07/33-8793; Mon.- Sat. 10 A.M.-6 P.M., Sun. 9 A.M.-1 P.M.), on the south side of Parque de la Fraternidad, is reasonably well stocked.

CENTRO HABANA

Havana's largest *agromercado* is **Cuatro Caminos** (Máximo Gómez, esq. Manglar, tel. 07/870-5934; Tues.-Sat. 7 A.M.-6:30 P.M., Sun. 7 A.M.-2 P.M.).

Almacenes Ultra (Av. Simón Bolívar #109, esq. Rayo; Mon.-Sat. 9 A.M.-6 P.M., Sun. 9 A.M.-1 P.M.) is a reasonably well-stocked grocery. Similarly, try the basement supermarket in

La Época (Galiano, esq. Neptuno; Mon.-Sat. 9:30 A.M.-9:30 P.M., Sun. 9 A.M.-1 P.M.).

VEDADO

There are **agromercados** at Calle 15, esq. 10; at Calle 17, e/ K y L; at Calle 19, e/ F y Av. de los Presidentes; at Calle 21, esq. J; Calle 16 e/ 11 y 13; and Pozos Dulces e/ Ave. Salvador Allende and Bruzón.

There's a grocery stocking Western goods, plus a bakery, on Calle 17, e/ M y N (Mon.-Sat. 9 A.M.-6 P.M., Sun. 9 A.M.- 1 P.M.). Also try **Supermercado Meridiano** (1ra, esq. Paseo, in the Galería del Paseo; Mon.-Sat. 10 A.M.-5 P.M., Sun. 10 A.M.-2 P.M.).

PLAYA (MIRAMAR AND BEYOND)

Supermercado 70 (3ra Av., e/ 62 y 70, Miramar, tel. 07/204-2890; Mon.-Sat. 9 A.M.-6 P.M., Sun. 9 A.M.-1 P.M.) is Cuba's largest supermarket selling imported foodstuffs. The next best-stocked grocery is **Diplo Mercado Miramar** (Mon.-Sat. 10 A.M.-6 P.M., Sun. 9 A.M.-1 P.M.), in the Havana Trade Center.

You can buy delicious pastries and breads at **Doña Neli Panadería Dulcería** (5ta Av., esq. 42; Mon.-Sat. 7 A.M.-6 P.M., Sun. 7 A.M.-1 P.M.), in the Quinta y 42 shopping complex; and at **La Francesa del Pan** (Calle 42, esq. 19, tel. 07/204-2211).

---

garlic shrimp, lobster in Catalan sauce, paella, and Cuban staples such as pork dishes. For drinks, opt for the house sangría, served in a pitcher. Service is on the ball. The place is run by Cuba's Spanish Asturian association. Best yet, it's bargain priced, and a pianist sometimes performs. No credit cards.

Similar, but less atmospheric than Los Nardos is the hidden restaurant in the **Asociación Canaria de Cuba** (Monserrate #258, e/ Neptuno y Ánimas, tel. 07/862-5284; Wed.–Sun. noon–8:30 P.M.). It serves fruit cocktails (CUC0.50), shredded beef stew (CUC2), shrimp enchiladas (CUC5), and the like amid garish surrounds. It's tucked into

the rear at the top of the stairs. Completing the Spanish social club tripytich, the **Centro Andaluz** (Prado #104, e/ Genios y Refugio, tel. 07/863-6745, Tues.–Sat. 10 A.M.–10 P.M.) is another bargain-priced, albeit no-frills *criollo* restaurant. I recommend the paella (CUC8) followed by a *locura flamenco* cocktail (CUC1.75). On Thursday and Saturday, stick around for the flamenco show at 9 P.M.

Café Taberna (Mercaderes #531, esq. Brasil, tel. 07/861-1637; daily 10 A.M.–midnight), on the northeast side of Plaza Vieja, is a lively place serving creative *criollo* fare (CUC5–15), and the long bar is a handsome place to bend an elbow. A nine-piece band performs. Inspect your bill; I've been scammed by the waiters *every* visit!

Taberna de la Muralla (San Ignacio #364, tel. 07/866-4453; daily 11 A.M.–1 A.M.) is a great place to sit on the shaded patio overlooking Plaza Vieja. It serves a good cheese and onion soup (CUC1.50), shrimp skewer (CUC9), and grilled sausage (CUC4), plus burgers.

Nouvelle Cuban

The Moorish-themed **Restaurante Anacaona** (Paseo del Prado #603, esq. Dragones, tel. 07/868-1000; daily noon–11 P.M.), in the Hotel Saratoga, exudes chic. The menu promises mixed sushi (CUC7), oysters Rockefeller (CUC13.50), chicken supreme marsala (CUC13.50.50), and fondues (CUC23). You'd expect this deluxe hotel to perform kitchenwise, but both my meals here were total duds! Perhaps Canadian chef Michel Cascione wasn't in the house those nights.

◖ **Restaurante Santo Ángel** (Brasil, esq. San Ignacio, tel. 07/861-1626; café daily 9 A.M.–11 P.M., restaurant noon–midnight), on the northwest corner of Plaza Vieja, is one of my favorite restaurants. The menu features gazpacho (CUC2), garlic mushrooms (CUC3.75), curried shrimp (CUC15), and pork chops in mustard (CUC10). Fresh-baked breads come with a superb *comport de champiñones* (mushroom paté) in olive oil; the bread is charged extra on your bill, which includes a 10 percent service charge. A large wine list includes California labels (CUC14–25). It has live music.

The ballroom **Roof Garden Restaurant** (Trocadero #55, e/ Prado y Zulueta, tel. 07/860-8560; daily 6:30–10 P.M.), atop the Hotel Sevilla, offers a Renaissance paneled ceiling and marble floors, and tall French doors open to balconies—a great spot to catch the breeze. One reader raves about the food—a fusion of Cuban and French (CUC5–30), but my experience was mediocre, as was service.

The elegant **Restaurante El Paseo** (Neptuno, e/ Prado y Zulueta, tel. 07/866-6627; daily 6–11 P.M.), in the Hotel NH Parque Central, has a creative menu that includes such starters as salmon carpaccio (CUC12.50) and lobster casserole (CUC24) for a main course. An alternative is the hotel's **Restaurante Mediterráneo** (7–10 A.M. and noon–4 P.M. and 6–11 P.M.), which in 2009 had turned to offering *tapas fusión* cuisine. The cuisine is well executed, if overpriced, but service can be indifferent.

The elegant **Restaurante Floridiana** (7–10 P.M.), in the Hotel Florida, also offers well-prepared dishes, such as roast pork (CUC8) and an overpriced lobster with orange (CUC27).

Arabic

Restaurante al Medina (Oficios, e/ Obispo y Obrapía, tel. 07/861-1041; daily noon–11 P.M.), in the Casa de los Árabes, one block south of Plaza de Armas, offers predominantly *criollo* items such as fish and rice (CUC3), salsa chicken (CUC2.50), and vegetarian specialties. But you'll also find couscous and lamb dishes (CUC6), as well as kebabs (CUC5.50), kibbe (minced meatballs, CUC5), and hummus (CUC3). It has value-priced set meals for CUC9–12.

Continental

Italian: The best Italian restaurant in Habana Vieja is **Dominica** (O'Reilly #108, esq. Mercaderes, tel. 07/860-2918; daily 9 A.M.–6 P.M.; CUC7–24), serving pastas, pizzas, spaghettis, and more in elegant air-conditioned surroundings. Live musicians perform. The place is foreign managed and the food and service above average.

The modern **Restaurante Prado y Neptuno** (Prado esq. Neptuno, tel. 07/860-9636; daily 11 A.M.–5 P.M. and 6:30–11:30 P.M.) is popular with expats in Havana for its reasonable Italian fare and pizzas. The contemporary decor is jazzy, and there's a bar with high-stools.

Spanish: I love the rustic ambience at **El Mesón de la Flota** (Mercaderes #257, e/ Ama-rgura y Brasil, tel. 07/863-3638; daily noon–11 P.M.; bar 24 hours), a classic Spanish *bodega* with Iberian decor and *tapas,* tortillas, *criollo* entrees (CUC4–18), and Spanish wines (CUC1.50 a glass). It hosts flamenco shows.

Similarly, the *bodega*-style **❰ La Paella** (Oficios #53, esq. Obrapía, tel. 07/867-1037; daily noon–11 P.M.), in the Hostal Valencia, serves paella for two people only (although one person could ostensibly eat a double serving), for CUC7–15. The *caldo* (soup) and bread is a meal in itself (CUC3). You can also choose steak, grilled fish, and chicken dishes (CUC2–10), washing them down with Spanish wines (CUC6–12). Try the excellent house vegetable soup. The kitchen also serves the **Bodegón Ouda** (Obrapía, esq. Baratillo, tel. 07/867-1037; Mon.–Sat. noon–7 P.M.), a quaint tapas bar around the corner in the Hotel El Comendador. It serves empanadas, tortillas (CUC1–2), *piquillos* (fried green peppers, CUC1.50), pizza, etc., washed down with sangria.

La Zaragoza (Monserrate #352, e/ Obispo y Obrapía, tel. 07/867-1040; daily noon–midnight), a moody Spanish-style *bodega,* serves mostly *criollo* fare but offers seafood such as squid rings (CUC6), garlic shrimp (CUC12), and *ceviche peruano* (CUC2.50), plus lamb stew (CUC9), tortillas (CUC3), and pizza (from CUC2).

The **Restaurant Jardin del Éden** (San Ignacio, esq. Amargura, tel. 07/860-8280; noon–midnight), in the Hotel Raquel, offers old-world elegance and an eclectic menu that includes Hungarian goulash (CUC10.50), curried fish (CUC12), and mushroom sirloin (CUC15), plus Jewish dishes such as potatoe latkes, red-beet borscht, and matzoball soup.

Asian

Torre de Márfil (Mercaderes #121, e/ Oficios y Obrapía, tel. 07/867-1038; daily noon–midnight) has all the trappings: the Chinese lanterns, screens, and even a banquet table beneath a pagoda. It's staffed by Chinese waiters, but the service can be excruciatingly slow. The menu includes authentic spring rolls and reasonable chop suey, chow mein, fried wontons

(CUC1.50), and shrimp and lobster dishes (CUC14). It has set dinners from CUC6.

Surf and Turf

El Floridita (Obispo #557, esq. Monserrate, Habana Vieja, tel. 07/867-1300; daily noon–11 P.M.) has a fantastic fin de siècle ambience—the sole reason to dine here, due to the excessive air-conditioning, ridiculous prices, and surly service. A shrimp cocktail costs CUC15; oyster cocktails cost CUC5. The house special is *langosta mariposa* (lobster grilled with almonds, pineapple, and butter; CUC42). Many of the dishes are disappointing; stick with simple dishes such as prawns flambéed in rum. The wine list is impressive.

The simple **La Casa del Escabeche** (Obispo, esq. Villegas, tel. 07/863-2660; daily noon–11 P.M.), open to the street, serves delicious *escabeche* (cube chunks of fish marinated with lime and salsa) for pennies. You can opt for a modern air-conditioned area.

The ritzy **❰ Café del Oriente** (Oficios, esq. Amargura, tel. 07/860-6686; daily noon–midnight), on Plaza de San Francisco, serves some of the best food in town. It has a marble-top bar, tux-clad waiters (service here is top notch), and a jazz pianist downstairs in the Bar Café (heck, you could be in New York or San Francisco). Upstairs is even more elegant, with sparkling marble and antiques, French drapes, and a magnificent stained-glass ceiling. It offers mostly steaks and seafood dishes (CUC12–30), including calf's brains with mustard and brandy cream sauce and a diving filet mignon.

❰ Restaurante El Templete (Av. del Puerto, esq. Narciso López, tel. 07/866-8807; daily noon–midnight) is recommended for its harborfront position, where it receives the breezes. Housed in a restored colonial mansion, this seafood restaurant with rustic decor has heaps of ambience, plus a diverse menu that ranges from oyster cocktail (CUC5) to overpriced lobster (CUC28) and a delicious chocolate brownie dessert, all prepared by Gallego chef Arkaitz Etxarte. The sibling

Restaurante La Barca (Av. del Puerto, esq. Narcisco López, tel. 07/866-8807; daily noon–midnight), adjoining, serves pastas and continental dishes.

CENTRO HABANA
Breakfasts
The best of your meager choices is **Pan.com** (Malecón y Calle 25, tel. 07/878-1853; daily 11 A.M.–11 P.M.), serving sandwiches and pastries.

Paladares
Private restaurants are few and far between in residential Centro, yet the area boasts the best *paladar* in town: **La Guarida** (Concordia #418, e/ Gervasio y Escobar, Centro Habana, tel. 07/866-9047, www .laguarida.com; daily noon–4 P.M. and 7 P.M.–midnight), on the third floor of a once glamorous, now dilapidated, 18th-century townhouse-turned-crowded *ciudadela* (tenement). Don't be put off by the near-derelict staircase, lent an operatic stage-set air by hanging laundry. The place is run jointly with the Ministry of Culture, explaining why there are vastly more seats than the officially permitted 12 for *paladares*. The walls are festooned with period Cuban pieces and giant prints showing famous personages who've dined here, plus fashion shoots on the crumbling stairway. You may recognize it as a setting for scenes in the Oscar-nominated 1995 movie *Fresa y Chocolate*. Owners Enrique and Odeysis Nuñez serve up such treats as gazpacho (CUC5) and *tartar de pargo* (CUC7) for starters; and tuna with sugarcane and coconut (CUC13), chicken breast with honey and lemon (CUC13), and desserts such as lemon pie (CUC5). The couple knows how to make their food dance, although quality is far from consistent and there are some duds (the Caesar salad needs work). It has a large wine list, but only house wine by the glass (CUC3). La Guarida is usually jam-packed with diplomats, foreign businessmen, glamorous models, and and occasional sprinkling of Hollywood figures, from Jack Nicholson to Jody Foster. Reservations are essential.

The popular **Paladar Doña Blanquita** (Prado #158, e/ Colón y Refugio, tel. 07/867-4958; daily noon–midnight) offers a choice of dining in the elegant *sala* or on a balcony overlooking the Prado. The *criollo* menu delivers large portions for CUC5–10. The place overflows with whimsical Woolworth's art such as cheap *muñequitas* (dolls), plastic flowers, animals, and cuckoo clocks.

Criollo
Restaurant Colonial (Galiano #164, esq. Virtudes, tel. 07/861-0702; daily 11 A.M.–midnight), in the Hotel Lincoln, is one of the better restaurants in Centro and serves soups, fish, shrimp, and chicken dishes for less than CUC4. The service is swift and conscientious.

Continental
Remarkable for its sensational modernist architecture (the façade features trifold Gothic-inspired curving peaks, like those of an Indonesian temple), the glass-fronted **Bar de Tapas Lava Día** (Malecón #407, e/ Manrique y Campanario, tel. 07/864-4432; daily noon–midnight) is a bit yuppyish, but I like its ambience. No surprise, it serves tapas and sangría.

Asian
Barrio Chino boasts a score of Chinese restaurants, many with waitstaff in traditional costumes. Most are concentrated along Calle Cuchillo and offer both indoor and patio dining. However, this isn't Hong Kong or San Francisco, so temper your expectations.

Restaurante Tien-Tan (Cuchillo #17, tel. 07/861-5478, taoqi@net.cu; daily 11 A.M.–midnight) is the best of a dozen options on Cuchillo. The extensive menu includes such tantalizing offerings as sweet-and-sour fried fish balls with vinegar and soy, and pot-stewed liver with seasoning. The budget-minded will find many dishes for around CUC2; but dishes run to CUC18 (medium and large portions are offered). Wash them down with a chilled Xing Tao. Chef Tao Qi hails from Shanghai. A 20 percent service fee is charged.

One of the best bargains in town is **Flor**

de Loto (Salud #313, e/ Gervasio y Escobar, tel. 07/860-8501; daily noon–midnight). Though the staff dress in Chinese robes, about the only Asian item on the menu is *maripositas* (fried wontons). However, the *criollo* fare, such as spicy shrimp (CUC6.50) and grill lobster (CUC7.50), is tasty and filling.

Casa Abuelo Lung Kong Cun Sol (Dragones #364, e/ Manrique y San Nicolás, tel. 07/862-5388; daily noon–midnight) has a restaurant upstairs serving classics such as *maripositas chinas* (fried wontons), (CUC0.40–2.70). This is the real McCoy: Chinese staff, Chinese ambience, Chinese patrons. Likewise, **Sociedad Chang Weng Chung Tong** (San Nicolás #517, e/ Zanja y Dragones, tel. 07/862-1490) has an all-you-can-eat buffet (CUC12) Mon.–Fri. 6 P.M.–midnight and Sat.–Sun. 12:30–5 P.M. and 6:30 P.M.–midnight).

VEDADO AND PLAZA DE LA REVOLUCIÓN
Breakfasts

Late-risers (and budget hounds seeking to shun other tourists) might head to the **Café TV** (Calle 17, e/ M y N, tel. 07/832-4499; daily 10 A.M.–9 P.M.), tucked in the depths of the Edificio Focsa skyscraper. Entered via a tunnel, this classic (and chilly) café space has TV-related decor and serves a North American breakfast for CUC2. It also has burgers, salads, pastas, and *uruguayano* (stuffed with ham and cheese) dishes. It rocks at night, with karaoke, comedy, etc.

Café La Rampa (Calle 23, esq. L, tel. 07/838-4011 ext. 125; 24 hours), outside the Hotel Habana Libre Tryp, serves American-style breakfasts (CUC3–6), plus tortillas (CUC3–5), and has a breakfast special of toast, eggs, bacon, coffee, and juice for CUC7. The burgers here are surprisingly good (CUC5), as are the sandwiches. The hotel also offers a varied breakfast buffet (CUC9) in its mezzanine restaurant.

Pain de Paris (Línea, e/ Paseo y A; and at Calle 25 #164, esq. O, tel. 07/833-3347; 24 hours) sells excellent croissants, pastries, etc.

Most hotels have buffet breakfasts open to non-guests.

Paladares

Two of my favorite *paladares,* the Hurón Azul (Humboldt #153, esq. P) and Le Chansonnier (Calle J #259, e/ 15 y Línea) had been closed by authorities at last visit, leaving only a handful of options.

Restaurante Gringo Viejo (Calle 21 #454, e/ E y F, Vedado, tel. 07/831-1946; daily noon–11 P.M.) is favored by Cuban celebrities and is granted extensive leeway by the authorities. However, I've been scammed frequently by the staff (check your bill carefully), so I recommend it only because it has a consistently great *ropa vieja* (CUC11), and the *flan de la casa* is delicious.

Another place where the owners sometimes scam patrons is **Paladar Nerei** (Calle 19, esq. L, tel. 07/832-7860; Mon.–Fri. noon–midnight, Sat.–Sun. 6 P.M.–midnight), which I'm recommending for its terrace dining and filling fish filet in garlic (CUC12–18). The once-wide-ranging menu was limited at last visit to standard Cuban fare.

The tiny **Paladar Restaurante Monguito** (Calle L, e/ 23 y 25; Fri.–Wed. 11 A.M.–10 P.M.), directly opposite the Hotel Habana Libre Tryp, is a bargain and for that reason almost always full. "China," your hostess, serves simple but filling Cuban dishes such as *pollo asado,* grilled fish, and pork dishes (CUC3–6).

Further west, **Paladar Las Mercedes** (Calle 18 #204, e/ 15 y 17, tel. 07/831-5706; daily noon–midnight) is a charming option in the style of a thatched rural *bohío.* Excellent quality *criollo* dishes with an imaginative twist are served, along with tapas and pastas. I recommend the *pescado a la Mercedes* (two types of fish with cheese sauce, plus calamari. The *brocheta* (kebab) is also good. All dishes cost CUC17, including a set menu. It has a student special for CUC5 before 7 P.M.

A last resort is **Paladar Aries** (Ave. Universidad #456, e/ J y K, tel. 07/832-4118; daily noon–midnight). Not personally reviewed, but recommended by a reader is **Casa Sarasua** (Calle 25 #510, e/ H y I, tel. 07/832-

2114; Mon.-Sat. noon–11 P.M.), serving traditional Cuban fare; the place is adorned with antique weaponry.

In Nuevo Vedado, **⦗** **La Casa** (Calle 30 #865, e/ 26 y 41, tel. 07/881-7000; daily noon–midnight) is worth the drive. This 1950s modernist house still has its original modish decor and is lush with tropical plantings. An indoor-outdoor patio features waterfalls and pools full of drowsy terrapins. La Casa serves such delicious dishes as octopus and onions (CUC9), ceviche (CUC5), and caramel flan (CUC1.20). Matt Dillon and the Kennedys are among the famous clientele.

Criollo

El Conejito (Calle M #206, esq. Av. 17, tel. 07/832-4671; daily 10 A.M.–11 P.M.) is a good option, not least for its Teutonic ambience. A pianist plays while you dine on *conejo* (rabbit) served any of a dozen ways. It also serves beef, chicken, and pasta dishes, plus a decent grilled fish. Entrées average CUC8. It has "student nights" on Wednesday and weekends.

La Roca (Calle 21 esq. M, tel. 07/836-3219; daily noon–midnight) has set meals for CUC3.25–4.50, including beer. It's perhaps the best bargain in town. And the retro-1950s decor is a plus. A comedy show is hosted at 10:30 P.M.

Continental

There's no shortage of little in-house cafeterías around the university serving *cajitas* (boxed lunches) for CUC1 or so, or the equivalent in pesos. Try **Cajitas** (Calle L, esq. 25; go down the stairs into the home). **Doña Laura's** (Calle H, e/ 21 y 23; 11 A.M.–4 P.M.) is a porch-based cafeteria serving sandwiches for five pesos, *cajitas* (25 pesos), and splendid *batidos* (shakes).

Penny-pinching pizza hounds should head to **Pizza Celina** (Infanta y San Rafael), alias "Pie-in-the-Sky." Reports student Bridget Murphy: "Celina the capitalist genius hasn't let the fact that she lives on the third floor stop her from running a successful pizza business. Scream up your order from across the street, and then

in a few minutes pick up your pizzas from, and drop your pesos into, the plastic basket (complete with red bows) that comes crashing down." It's pretty good pizza, too.

The **Comedor de Aguiar** (Calle O, esq. 21, tel. 07/873-5054; daily 7 A.M.–midnight), in

---

ICE-CREAM PARLORS

Street stalls sell ice-cream cones for about 2.50 pesos. However, the milk may not be pasteurized, and hygiene is always a question.

Habana Vieja: The **Cremería el Naranjal** (Obispo, esq. Cuba) sells ice-cream sundaes, including a banana split (CUC1.50-3), as does **Heladería La Mina** (Oficios, esq. Obispo). A better bet is **Cremería Obispo** (Obispo, esq. Villegas), selling various flavors for pesos.

Vedado: An institution in its own right, **Coppelia** (Calle 23, esq. Calle L, tel. 07/832-6149; Tues.-Sun. 10 A.M.-9:30 P.M.) serves ice cream of excellent quality. Tourists are normally steered toward a special section that, though offering immediate service, charges CUC2.60 for an *ensalada* (three scoops), while the half a dozen communal peso sections for Cubans (choose from indoor or outdoor dining) offer larger *ensaladas* (five scoops) for only five pesos, a *jimagua* (two scoops) for two pesos, and a *marquesita* (two scoops plus a sponge cake) for 2.50 pesos. Be prepared for a *long* wait, in summer. Some lines are for inferior (lower fat) Veradero ice cream (closed Monday).

Bim Bom (Calle 23, esq. Infanta, tel. 07/879-2892; 11 A.M.-11 P.M.), at the bottom of La Rampa, is run along the lines of Baskin-Robbins and charges accordingly, as does **Dulce Habana** (Calle 25; daily 10 A.M.-9 P.M.), on the south side of the Hotel Habana Libre Tryp.

Playa (Miramar and Beyond): Try **Bosque de la Habana** (3ra Av., e/ 78 y 80, tel. 07/204-8500; 24 hours), in the Hotel Meliá Habana; or **La Casa de Helado** (Calle 84, 3ra Av., noon-7 P.M.) in the Galería Comercial Comodoro.

the Hotel Nacional, fairly glitters with chandeliers and silverware and appeals to those with money to burn. The waiters are liveried to the T and trained to provide top-notch service. The well-executed menu featuring creative international cuisine is highlighted by shrimp with rum flambé, and smoked salmon with capers and onion for starters. Main courses are priced CUC13–40.

❰ La Torre (Calle 17 #155, e/ M y N, tel. 07/832-2451; daily noon–11:30 P.M.; bar 11:30 A.M.–12:30 A.M.), atop the Focsa building, offers splendid all-around views of the city. Its French-inspired nouvelle cuisine is of higher than usual standard: I recommend the prawns and mushrooms in olive oil and garlic starter (CUC9), and I enjoyed a fish filet poached in white wine, butter and cream, roasted with cheese and served with mashed potatoes and crisp vegetables (CUC14). Order the mountainous and delicious profiteroles (CUC5) for dessert! Only one wine is served by the glass (CUC3.50), and it's tiny and not very good.

Competing for the loftiest views in town, the **Sierra Maestra** (Calle 23 y L, tel. 07/834-6100; noon–midnight), atop the Hotel Habana Libre Tryp, is virtually unknown to tourists (other than the hotel guests). I haven't dined here, but both the service and continental dishes are said to rank highly.

If you want to experience Havana's gauche 1950s-redux decor, dine at either **Restaurante Monseigneur** (Calle O esq. 21, tel. 07/832-9884; daily 11:30 A.M.–1 A.M.), with its black marble bar and kitsch; or the **El Emperador** (Calle 17 e/ M y N, tel. 07/832-4998; daily noon–2 A.M.), with its blood-red curtains and Louis XIV-style furnishings. Both serve such dishes as carpaccio (CUC5), grilled shrimp (CUC10), and rabbit in creole sauce (CUC8), but you really come for the ambience.

The Meliá Cohiba's **El Abanico Restaurante Gourmet** (Paseo, esq. 1ra, tel. 07/833-3636; daily 7–11 P.M.) is one of the most elegant in town. Its nouvelle dishes might seem a bit ambitious, but execution is accomplished. I recommend the medallions of caramelized trout

with tarragon starter (CUC7), followed by walnut sole with risotto (CUC17).

Also in the mezzanine of the Meliá Cohiba, the best place for Italian fare is the baseball-themed **La Piazza Ristorante** (tel. 07/833-3636; daily 1 P.M.–midnight). It offers 17 types of pizza (CUC7–20) but also has minestrone (CUC7.50), gnocchi (CUC10), and seafoods (from CUC11). It even has pizza to go!

The Basque cultural center's **Centro Vasco** (Calle 4 esq. 3ta, tel. 07/833-9354; noon–midnight) serves grilled shrimp (CUC7), paella (CUC7.50), and lamb stew (CUC7).

PLAYA (MIRAMAR AND BEYOND)
Breakfasts

All the tourist hotels have buffet breakfasts. Those of the Meliá Habana and Occidental Miramar are recommended.

For fresh-baked croissants and good coffee, I like **Pain de Paris** (Calle 26 e/ 5ta y 7ma; daily 8 A.M.–10 P.M.).

Paladares

❰ La Esperanza (Calle 16 #105, e/ 1ra y 3ra, tel. 07/202-4361; Fri.–Wed. 7–11:30 P.M.) is an exceptional *paladar* inside a 1930s middle-class home with a *sala* full of art nouveau furnishings, antiques, books, and intriguing miscellany. Jazz or classical music is normally playing. Your waiter will read off the day's French inspirations, served with lively sauces. On my last visit, I enjoyed a superb eggplant *de ochún* (in honey) stuffed with chicken. The service is friendly and professional, and prices are fair (budget CUC25 for a meal), although a 10 percent service charge is automatically added. A reservation is essential.

Reservations are also essential at **❰ Cocina de Lilliam** (Calle 48 #1311, e/ 13 y 15, Miramar, tel. 07/209-6514; Sun.–Fri. noon–3 P.M. and 7–10 P.M.), in the lush grounds of a 1939s era mansion romantically lit at night. The brick-lined patio is shaded by trees, with colonial lanterns and wrought-iron tables and chairs. Lilliam Domínguez conjures up tasty nouvelle Cuban. Her appetizers include tartlets of tuna and onion, and a savory dish of garbanzo beans and ham with onion and red and green peppers. Entrées include such Cuban classics as simmered lamb with onions and peppers; chicken breast with pineapple; plus fresh fish dishes and oven-roasted meats served with creamy mashed potatoes. Budget CUC15–25 apiece. The place has been jam-packed ever since President Jimmy Carter dined here in May 2002. The house often runs out of more popular dishes by 9 P.M. and closes for two weeks in summer and the month of December.

By the shore, **Paladar Vistamar** (1ra Av. #2206, e/ 22 y 24, tel. 07/203-8328; noon–midnight), in a modern house on the seafront, is popular for its high-quality cuisine and has the advantage of ocean views. It serves continental fare as well as Cuban staples. Starters include fish cocktail (CUC3) and mushroom soup (CUC3.50), while main dishes include *pescado milanesa* (CUC12), and grilled fish with garlic (CUC11.50). One block west, **Paladar Ristorante El Palio** (1ra Av. #2402, esq. 24, tel. 07/202-9869; noon–midnight) serves Italian-*criollo* cuisine and is popular with elite Cubans. You dine on a shaded patio, with suitably Italian decor.

Near Paladar Ristorante El Patio, but not reviewed personally, is **Doctor Café** (Calle 28 #111, e. 1ra y 3ra, tel. 07/203-4718; daily noon–midnight), which has been recommended. By reservation only.

La Fontana (3ra Av. #305, esq. 46, tel. 07/202-8337; noon–midnight; CUC2–15) specializes in barbecued meats from an outdoor grill serving T-bone steak. Starters include salads, *escabeche* (ceviche), and onion soup; main dishes include a greasy fillet grilled with garlic. Rice and extras cost additional. Review your bill closely. Choose cellar or garden seating in a traditional country *bohío* setting. It has caged birds and animals. Service is hit or miss.

Mi Jardín (Calle 66 #517, esq. 5ta Av. B, tel. 07/203-4627; noon–midnight), in a beautiful 1950s home full of antiques, is run by an affable and conscientious Mexican and his Italian wife. They serve genuine Mexican fare—well,

as much as the government prohibition on beef allows. The chicken *molé mexicano* and house special fish Veracruz are recommended. You'll also find enchiladas, *totopos* (nachos), plus Italian and *criollo* dishes. You can dine inside or on a patio beneath an arbor. Budget CUC10 per person.

Named for the huge cactus in the front garden, **Paladar Los Cactus de 33** (Av. 33 #3405, e/ 34 y 36, Rpto. Kohly, tel. 07/203-5139; noon–midnight) justifies the price with splendid fare—they do have off nights, however—such as the grilled snapper with creole sauce, and the house chicken breast with olives, mushrooms, and cheese, plus baked custard enjoyed in a Gothic-style home with a garden garlanded with fairy lights. Budget CUC25 per head.

Out in Marianao, **Paladar El Paila** (Av. 51A #8827, esq 88B, tel. 07/267-0282; noon–3 P.M. and 6–11 P.M.), handily close to the Tropicana nightclub, has tables in a lantern-lit garden. Imagine octopus and mango salad, or tomato bruschetta, and grilled wahoo filets with shrimp! You can dine with a drink for less than CUC15.

Criollo

I find myself returning time and again to (**El Aljibe** (7ma Av., e/ 24 y 26, tel. 07/204-1583; daily noon–midnight), my favorite state-run restaurant in Havana, serving the best Cuban fare in town and popular with tour groups and with the Havana elite and foreign expats showing off their trophy Cuban girlfriends. You dine beneath a soaring thatch roof. The superb house dish, the *pollo asado el aljibe,* is glazed with a sweet orange sauce, then baked and served with fried plantain chips, rice, French fries, and black beans served until you can eat no more. It's a tremendous bargain at CUC12; desserts and beverages cost extra. Other *criollo* dishes are served (CUC10–20), but you really should order the house chicken. The bread and side salad delivered to your table will be charged to your bill even if you didn't order it, and a 10 percent service charge is automatically billed. The wine cellar has almost 27,000 bottles! Service is prompt and efficient.

Restaurant 5ta y 16 (5ta Av., esq. 16, tel. 07/206-9509; daily noon–1 A.M.) is acclaimed as one of Havana's best restaurants for traditional Cuban cooking, notably grilled fish and meats (the grilled pork chops are particularly good) from a *churrasquería*. More creative dishes include a delicious appetizer of stuffed red peppers with tuna, plus a daily special, from roast beef to lamb chops. The food is well prepared and the portions are huge. Choose from a downstairs buffet or à la carte upstairs. Budget CUC10–25.

The Communist elite can often be found dining at **El Rancho Palco** (Av. 19, esq. 140, tel. 07/208-9346; daily noon–11 P.M.), in jungly surroundings in the heart of Cubanacán, is a handsome, open-sided *bohío* with terra-cotta floor, Tiffany-style lamps, decor featuring saddles, and wooden toucans and parrots on swings. You can opt to dine on a patio or beneath thatch, or in an air-conditioned dining room. It serves meat dishes (CUC10–30), seafood (CUC12–26), and the usual *criollo* fare. Quality is hit or miss, depending on your timing; on a good night it serves the best filet mignon (CUC11) in Cuba. It has floor shows at night. Scan your bill carefully as scams are frequent.

Seafood

Don Cangrejo (1ra Av., e/ 16 y 18, tel. 07/204-4169; daily noon–midnight) offers some of the finest seafood in town, served in a converted colonial mansion offering views out to sea. It's popular with the monied Cuban elite. The menu features crab cocktail (CUC6), crab-filled wontons (CUC3), house specialties such as crab claws (CUC15), and garlic shrimp (CUC13); plus paella, lobster, and fish dishes. The wine list runs to more than 150 labels. An open bar is offered on Monday (CUC10). You can use the swimming pool 10 A.M.–6 P.M. (CUC10 with CUC7 *consumo mínimo*).

Continental

A favorite of the Cuban elite, the overpriced **Tocororo** (Calle 18 #302, esq. 3ra, tel. 07/204-2209; noon–midnight), housed in a classical mansion, has an antique decor extending into a garden patio with furniture, Tiffany lamps, potted plants, wooden parrots hanging from gilt perches, plus real parrots in cages. A pianist (by day) and jazz ensemble (by night) entertain. The food is typical Cuban fare with an exotic international twist; crocodile and ostrich occasionally feature. Expect to pay CUC25 and up (I ask you, CUC40 for a lobster?). Even the bread will be charged, and a 10 percent service charge is automatic. Although El Aljibe and other upscale restaurants have stolen Tocororo's thunder, in 2009 it attempted a comeback with a new tapas bar (noon–2 A.M.).

The bigwigs in town also dine at **La Ferminia** (5ta Av. #18207, e/ 182 y 184), which serves disappointing fare at outrageous prices.

Paleta Bar y Amelia Restaurante (3ra Av., e/ 70 y 82, tel. 07/204-7311; daily 11:30 A.M.–midnight), on the ground floor of the Miramar Trade Center, is an elegant contemporary restaurant decorated with modern art. The hip marble-topped bar is a fine place to bend your elbow. The fairly simple menu includes sandwiches, burgers (CUC3), steaks, and the likes of shrimp enchiladas (CUC7).

For jungly ambience try **La Cecilia** (5ta Av. #11010, e/ 110 y 112, tel. 07/204-1562; daily noon–midnight), another elegant option in the middle of a large garden surrounded by bamboo, although it has an air-conditioned section. It serves typical Cuban dishes such as *ajiaco* (a stew, and the national dish), *tasajo* (jerked beef), *churrasco* (broiled steak), and *pollo con mojo* (chicken with onion and garlic), as well as grilled lobster. Entrées cost CUC12–25. It hosts a *cabaret espectáculo* Friday and Saturday night, and there's live music on other nights.

The **Complejo Turístico La Giraldilla** (Calle 222, e/ 37 y 51, tel. 07/27-0568; 10 A.M.–5 A.M.), in La Coronela, has gone downhill since the disco here was canceled, but is worth the visit if you're this far west. Choose from a selection of dining rooms in the Patio Los Naranjos. I enjoyed a superb creamed vegetable soup (CUC4), sautéed prawns in garlic

UC17), and sautéed salmon (CUC19), but that was a few years ago. On Saturdays it hosts a CUC18 "La Noche del Búfalo" special for groups only. La Bodega del Vino basement tapas bar serves everything from tacos to chicken mole, washed down with sangria. It has an extensive wine list.

Asian

For sushi and traditional Japanese fare, head to **Sakura** (Calle 18, esq. 3ra, tel. 07/204-2209; daily noon–midnight), in the Tocororo. The sushi menu is restricted, but quality is surprisingly good. Miso soup (CUC3), tempura (CUC12), and sashimi (CUC12) are served, as are sake and Japanese beers. Likewise, the **Fusion El Abanico,** in the Hotel Meliá Cohiba, offers Japanese fare, including sushi.

Other

Pan.Com (Calle 26, esq. 7ma; Mon.–Fri. 8 A.M.–2 A.M., Sat.–Sun. 10 A.M.–2 A.M.), pronounced pahn POOHN-to com, makes every kind of sandwich. It also has omelettes, burgers, and tortillas, all for less than CUC5, plus yogurts, fruit juices, *batidos,* and cappuccinos.

ACROSS THE HARBOR

You'll be hard-pressed to find anywhere worthy of dining in Regla and Guanabacoa (one wonders how the locals get by). However, Parque Histórico Militar Morro-Cabaña has several good touristy restaurants, described in the sightseeing sections.

Surprisingly, there's even a private restaurant here: **Paladar Doña Carmela** (Calle B #10, tel. 07/863-6048; daily 7–11 P.M.), serving *criolla* fare in an outdoor setting.

Information and Services

MONEY
Banks

The **Banco Financiero Internacional** is the main bank, with eight branches throughout Havana (Mon.–Fri. 8 A.M.–3 P.M., but 8 A.M.–noon only on the last working day of each month), including in Edificio Jerusalem in the Miramar Trade Center (3ra Av., e/ 70 y 82, Miramar). Its main outlet, in the Hotel Habana Libre Tryp, has a special desk handling travelers checks and credit card advances up to US$5,000 for foreigners. The Banco de Crédito y Comercio (Bandec), Banco Internacional de Comercio, and Banco Metropolitano also have services for foreigners. Banco Popular serves Cubans.

The foreign exchange agency, **Cadeca** (Obispo, e/ Cuba y Aguiar, Habana Vieja, tel. 07/866-4152; daily 8 A.M.–10 P.M.), represents Western Union (Mon.–Sat. 8 A.M.–5 P.M., Sun. 8:30 A.M.–noon). Cadeca has outlets through the city, including a branch on the mezzanine level of the Hotel Nacional (daily 10 A.M.–7 P.M.), good on Sunday when banks are closed.

ATM Cards

ATMs allowing cash advances of Cuban convertible pesos from Visa cards (but not MasterCard or U.S.-issued Visa cards) are located at Cadeca on Calle Obispo (see above); in Etecsa (Obispo esq. Habana, tel. 07/866-0089; daily 8:30 A.M.–9 P.M.); and at the Hotel NH Parque Central, Hotel Cohiba, Hotel Nacional, and Miramar Trade Centre; plus the Banco Internacional de Comercio (3ra Av., esq. 78, Miramar) and Banco Metropolitano (5ta Av., esq. 113, Miramar). All of which dispense up to CUC300.

COMMUNICATIONS
Post Offices

Most major tourist hotels have small post offices and will accept your mail for delivery. In Habana Vieja, there are post offices on the east side of Plaza de la Catedral; at Obispo #102, on the west side of Plaza de San Francisco; at Obispo #518; next to the Gran Teatro on Parque Central; and on the north side of the railway station on Avenida de Bélgica.

In Vedado, there's a 24-hour post office in the lobby of the Hotel Habana Libre Tryp. Havana's main post office is **Correos de Cuba** (tel. 07/879-6824; 24 hours) on Avenida Rancho Boyeros, one block north of the Plaza de la Revolución.

Servi-Postal (Havana Trade Center, 3ra Av., e/ 76 y 80, Miramar, tel. 07/204-5122; Mon.–Sat. 10 A.M.–6 P.M.) has a copy center and Western Union agency.

Express Mail Services

DHL Worldwide Express (1ra Av. y Calle 26, Miramar, tel. 07/204-1578, fax 07/204-0999, commercial@dhl.cutisa.cu; Mon.–Fri. 8 A.M.–8 P.M., Sat. 8:30 A.M.–4 P.M.) also has offices at Calzada #818, e/ 2 y 4, Vedado (tel. 07/832-2112), and Edificio Habana in the Miramar Trade Center (3ra Av., e/ 76 y 80, Miramar).

Telephone and Fax Service

The **Empresa de Telecomunicaciones de Cuba** (Etecsa) is headquartered at the Miramar Trade Center (3ra Av., e 76 y 80, Miramar). The main international telephone exchange (tel. 07/834-6106; 24 hours) is in the lobby of the Hotel Habana Libre Tryp.

Key *centros telefónicos* (telephone kiosks) are on the ground floor of the Lonja del Comercio (Mon.–Fri. 8:30 A.M.–5:30 P.M.) on Plaza de San Francisco and at Obispo, esq. Habana, in Habana Vieja; and, in Vedado, at the foot of Paseo.

Cellular Phones: You can rent or buy (CUC49–CUC331) cellular phones from **Cubacel** (Calle 28 #510, e/ 5 y 7, Miramar, tel. 05/264-2266 or 07/880-2222, www.cubacel. com; daily 8:30 A.M.–7:30 P.M., Sat. 8 A.M.– noon), which can also activate your own cell-pone for CUC40. The main Havana office is in Edificio Santa Clara in the Miramar Trade Center (3ra Av., e/ 70 y 82), but you may be sent to the office at Desamparados esq. Habana (Mon.–Thur. 8:30 A.M.–5 P.M., Fri. 8:30 A.M.–4 P.M.).

Internet Access

Most *correos* (post offices) and *telecorreo* (telephone offices) offer Internet service to the public; as of July 2009 you must buy a prepaid card (CUC6 for one hour). Most tourist hotels also have Internet access for guests; shop around, as hourly rates vary. Upscale hotels usually have DSL feed; inexpensive hotels are slower.

Habana Vieja: The best outlets are **Cibercorreo** (Obispo #457, esq. Aguacate; Mon.–Sat. 9 A.M.–8:30 P.M., Sun. 10 A.M.– 6:30 P.M.); **Etecsa** (Obispo, esq. Habana, tel. 07/866-0089; daily 8:30 A.M.–9 P.M.); and thebusiness center at the Hotel NH Parque Central (Mon.–Fri. 8 A.M.–8 P.M., Sat.–Sun. 8 A.M.–4 P.M.; CUC12 per hour). Most other hotels have Internet service in the lobby, at cheaper rates; those at the Hotel Plaza and Hotel Inglaterra cost CUC6 per hour.

Centro Habana: The **telecorreo** at Salvador Allende, esq. Padre Varela (tel. 07/879-5795; 24 hours) and Zanja e/ Infanta y San Francisco (8:30 A.M.–7 P.M.) offer Internet access.

Vedado: All tourist hotels offer Internet service. The business center in the **Hotel Nacional** (Calle O y 21; daily 8 A.M.–8 P.M.) charges CUC4 per 15 minutes; that in the **Hotel Habana Libre Tryp** (Calle L, e/ 23 y 25; daily 7 A.M.–11 P.M.) charges CUC10 per hour; and that in the **Hotel Meliá Cohiba** (Paseo, e/ 1ra y 3ra; Mon.–Sat. 8 A.M.–10 P.M.) charges CUC12 per hour.

Correos de Cuba (Av. Rancho Boyeros, tel. 07/866-8249), the main post office, on the northeast side of Plaza de la Revolución, has 24-hour Internet service; as does the **telecorreo** (Línea, esq. Paseo, tel. 07/830-0809), but expect a long wait for access.

Students at the University of Havana have free Internet service in the Biblioteca Central (San Lázaro, esq. Ronda, tel. 07/878-5573), at the faculty of Artes y Letras (you need to sign up the day before), and at the faculty of Filosofía y História, with long lines for use.

Miramar: The **Servi-Postal** in the Miramar Trade Center (3ra Av., e/ 70 y 82) has an Internet Center (CUC6 per hour).

All the hotels have a cybercafé.

Photography

The best resource is **Photo Obispo** (Obispo

#307, esq. Habana; Mon.–Sat. 9 A.M.–9 P.M., Sun. 9 A.M.–1 P.M.), which develops film, sells digital cameras, and makes CDs.

Also try **Agfa Photo Center,** in the Miramar Trade Center (3ra Av., e/ 76 y 80, Miramar).

GOVERNMENT OFFICES
Immigration and Customs

Requests for visa extensions (*prórrogas*) and other immigration issues relating to foreigners are handled by **Inmigración** (Calle Factor final, Nuevo Vedado, tel. 07/206-3218; Mon.–Wed., Fri. 8 A.M.–5 P.M., Thur., Sat. 8:30 A.M.–noon). Journalists and others requiring special treatment are handled by the **Ministerio de Relaciones Exteriores** (Ministry of Foreign Relations, Calzada #360, e/ G y H, Vedado, tel. 07/830-9775, www.cubaminrex.cu).

The main Customs office is on Avenida del Puerto, opposite Plaza San Francisco.

Consulates

The following nations have embassies/consulates in Havana. Those of other countries can be found in the local telephone directory under Embajadas, and at the Ministerio de Relaciones Exteriores' website (www.cubaminrex.cu/DirectorioDiplomatico/Articulos/Cuba/A.html).

- **Australia:** c/o Canadian Embassy
- **Canada:** Calle 30 #518, esq. 7ma, Miramar, tel. 07/204-2516, fax 07/204-2044
- **United Kingdom:** Calle 34 #702, e/ 7ma y 17-A, Miramar, tel. 07/204-1771, fax 204-8104
- **United States:** Interests Section, Calzada, e/ L y M, Vedado, Havana, tel. 07/833-3551 to 07/833-3559, emergency/after hours tel. 07/833-3026, http://havana.usinterestsection.gov

TRAVEL AGENCIES

There are no independent travel agencies. Hotel tour bureaus can make reservations for excursions, car rental, and flights, as can **San Cristóbal Agencia de Viajes** (Oficios #110, e/ Lamparilla y Amargura, tel. 07/861-9171, fax 07/860-9586, ventas@viajessancristobal.cu; Mon.–Sat. 9 A.M.–6 P.M., Sun. 9:30 A.M.–1 P.M.) specializes in excursions in Havana.

TOURIST INFORMATION
Information Bureaus

Infotur (tel. 07/204-0624, www.infotur.cu), the government tourist information bureau, has nine information bureaus in Havana, including in the arrivals lounges at José Martí International Airport.

Maps

Tienda de los Navegantes (Mercaderes #115, e/ Obispo y Obrapía, Habana Vieja, tel. 07/861-3625; Mon.–Fri. 8:30 A.M.–5 P.M., Sat. 8:30 A.M.–noon) has a wide range of tourist maps of Havana and provinces.

MEDICAL SERVICES

Most large tourist hotels have nurses on duty. Other hotels will be able to request a doctor for in-house diagnosis.

Hospitals

Tourists needing medical assistance are usually steered to the **Clínica Internacional Cira García** (Calle 20 #4101, esq. Av. 41, Miramar, tel. 07/204-4300 or 204-2811, fax 07/204-2660, ciragcu@infomed.sld.cu; 24 hours), a full-service hospital dedicated to serving foreigners.

The **Centro Internacional Oftalmológica Camilo Cienfuegos** (Calle L, e/ Línea y 13, Vedado, tel. 07/832-5554, fax 07/833-3536, www.retinosis.sld.cu) specializes in eye disorders but also offers a range of medical services.

Pharmacies

Local pharmacies serving Cubans are meagerly stocked. For homeopathic remedies, try **Farmacia Ciren** (Calle 216, esq. 11B, Playa, tel. 07/271-5044) and **Farmacia las Praderas** (Calle 230, e/ 15A y 17, Siboney, tel. 07/273-7473).

Your best bets are the foreigners-only *farmacias internacionales,* and stocked with imported medicines. They're located at the **Hotel Sevilla** (Trocadero #55, e/ Prado y Zulueta, tel.

INFOTUR BUREAUS

Infotur (www.infotur.cu), the government tourist information bureau, has 24-hour bureaus in the José Martí International Airport (Terminal Three, tel. 07/641-6101, infoaereo@enet.cu); at the Terminal de Cruceros (Cruise Terminal); plus the following outlets in Havana (8:30 A.M.–8:30 P.M.):

HABANA VIEJA

Calle Obispo, e/ Bernazas y Villegas, tel. 07/866-3333, obispodir@enet.cu
Calle Obispo, esq. San Ignacio, tel. 07/863-6884

MIRAMAR

5ta Avenida, esq. Calle 112, tel. 07/204-3977, miramar@enet.cu

07/861-5703), **Hospital Camilo Cienfuegos** (Calle L, e/ Línea y 13, Vedado, tel. 07/832-5554, fax 07/33-3536, cirpcc@infomed.sid.cu; 8 A.M.–8 P.M.); the **Galería Comercial Habana Libre** (Calle 25 y L, Vedado; Mon.–Sat. 10 A.M.–7:30 P.M.); the **Clínica Internacional Cira García** (Calle 20 #4101, esq. Av. 41, Miramar, tel. 07/204-2880; 24 hours); the **Farmacia Internacional** (Av. 41, esq. 20, Miramar, tel. 07/204-4350; daily 8:30 A.M.–8:30 P.M.); and in the Edificio Habana at the **Miramar Trade Center** (3ra Av., e/ 76 y 80, Miramar; Mon.–Fri. 8 A.M.–6 P.M.).

Opticians

Ópticas Miramar (Neptuno #411, e/ San Nicolás y Manrique, Centro Habana, tel. 07/863-2161; and 7ma Av., e/ Calle 24 y 26, Miramar, tel. 07/204-2990) provides full-service optician and optometrist services.

SAFETY

A rash of muggings and petty crime that erupted some years back has been drastically reduced since January 1999, when thousands of policeman took to the streets on a 24-hour basis. Still, Havana is not entirely safe despite this policing. Most crime is opportunistic, and thieves seek easy targets. Be wary of darker back streets at night.

Bad apples hang out at major tour-isted haunts. Be wary around the Capitolio Nacional and Parque Central, the Paseo de Martí (Prado), and Plaza 13 de Marzo in front of the Museo de la Revolución, once a favorite spot for nocturnal muggings. Other areas that require special caution by day or night are the back streets of southern Habana Vieja and Centro Habana, and anywhere in the Cerro district and other slum districts or wherever police are not present. I was mugged on a main street in Centro!

Be cautious and circumspect of all *jiniteros*.

MISCELLANEOUS PRACTICALITIES

Haircuts

I recommend the **Barbería de Plaza de Armas** (Obispo, e/ Oficios y Mercaderes, Habana Vieja, tel. 07/863-0943; Mon.–Sat. 8 A.M.–noon and 2–5 P.M.) or **Salón Correo Barbería** (Brasil, e/ Oficios y Mercaderes, Habana Vieja; Mon.–Sat. 8 A.M.–6 P.M.), two old-style barber shops.

Laundry

In Habana Vieja, **Lavandería El Guerrillero** (Máximo Gómez #521, e/ San Nicolás y Indio, tel. 07/863-7585; daily 6 A.M.–6 P.M.) offers a wash and dry service for 3 pesos. Another small launderette is at the corner of Villegas and Lamparilla. You drop off your clothes and, hey presto, they're usually ready a few hours later, crisp and folded, for CUC3 a load.

In Miramar, **Aster Lavandería** (Calle 34 #314, e/ 3ra y 5ta, Miramar, tel. 07/204-1622; Mon.–Fri. 8 A.M.–5 P.M., Sat. 8 A.M.–noon) has a wash-and-dry service (CUC3 per load) and dry cleaning (CUC2 for pants, CUC1.50 for shirts for three-day service; same-day service costs more). There's also a laundry in the **Complejo Comercial Comodoro** (3ra Av., esq. 84, tel. 07/204-5551).

Most upscale hotels offer dry-cleaning and laundry service. Many locals will wash your clothes for a few dollars, but be prepared to have them stretched, beaten, and faded.

Legal Services

Consultoría Jurídica Internacional (CJI, International Judicial Consultative Bureau, Calle 16 #314, e/ 3ra y 5ta, Miramar, tel. 07/204-2490, fax 07/204-2303, www.cji.co.cu) provides legal advice and services, as does the **Bufete Internacional** (5ta Av. #16202, esq. 162, Miramar, tel. 07/204-6749, bufete@bufeteinternacional.cu).

Libraries

The **Biblioteca Nacional** (Av. de la Independencia, esq. 20 de Mayo, tel. 07/881-5442, fax 07/881-6224, aponce@jm.lib.cult.cu; Mon.–Fri. 8:15 A.M.–6 P.M., Sat. 8:15 A.M.–4 P.M.), on the east side of Plaza de la Revolución, has about 500,000 texts. Getting access, however, is another matter. Five categories of individuals are permitted to use the library, including students and professionals, but not lay citizens. Foreigners can obtain a library card valid for one year (CUC3) if they have a letter from a sponsoring Cuban government agency, and/or ID establishing academic credentials, plus two photographs and a passport, which you need to hand over whenever you wish to consult books. The antiquated, dilapidated file system makes research a Kafkaesque experience. There is no open access to books. Instead, individuals must request a specific work, which is then brought to you; your passport or (for Cubans) personal ID is recorded along with the purpose of your request.

The University of Havana, in Vedado, has several libraries, including the **Biblioteca Central** (San Lázaro, esq. Ronda, tel. 07/878-5573 or 878-3951, ranero@dict.uh.cu).

The **Biblioteca Provincial de la Habana** (Obispo, Plaza de Armas, tel. 07/862-9035; Mon.–Fri. 8:15 A.M.–7 P.M., Sat. 8:15 A.M.–4 P.M.) is a meagerly stocked affair. It's closed the first Monday of each month.

Toilets

The only modern public toilet to Western standards is in the ground floor of the Lonja del Comercio, Plaza de Armas.

Most hotels and restaurants will let you use their facilities. An attendant usually sits outside the door dispensing a few sheets of toilet paper for pocket change (also note the bowl with a few coins meant to invite a tip).

Getting There

BY AIR
José Martí International Airport

José Martí International Airport (switchboard tel. 07/206-4644, www.airportcuba.com/?Action=Airport_JM) is 25 kilometers southwest of downtown Havana, in the Wajay district. It has five terminals spaced well apart and accessed by different roads (nor are they linked by a connecting bus service).

Terminal One: This terminal (tel. 07/275-1200) serves domestic flights.

Terminal Two: Charter flights originating in Los Angeles, Miami, and New York arrive at Terminal Two carrying passengers with OFAC licenses. Occasionally other flights pull in here, although the outbound flight will invariably depart Terminal Three.

Terminal Three: All international flights except United States–Havana charters arrive at Terminal Three (tel. 07/642-6225, or tel. 07/266-4133 for arrivals and departures) on the north side of the airport. For information on arrivals and departures call 07/266-4133 or 07/33-5666.

Immigration and Customs: Immigration proceedings are slow. Travelers arriving without prebooked accommodations are usually made to book—and pay for—at least three nights' hotel stay before being granted entry. You'll be escorted to a tour desk where representatives sell hotel rooms at full price.

Beware porters who grab your bags outside; they'll expect a tip for hauling your bag the few yards to a taxi.

Information and Services: A 24-hour Infotur (tel. 07/266-4094) tourist information office is outside the customs lounge. Check in here if you have prepaid vouchers for accommodations or transfers into town.

A foreign exchange counter is also ouside the customs lounge.

Terminal Four: This serves the military.

Terminal Five: Aero Caribbean flights arrive here.

Getting into Town

There's no public bus service from either of the international terminals. A public bus marked "Aeropuerto" departs from Terminal One (domestic flights) for Vedado and Parque Central (one peso). The bus is intended for Cubans, and foreigners may be refused. It runs about once every two hours.

Alternately, you can catch Metrobus P12 (originating in Santiago de las Vegas) or Ómnibus #480 from the east side of Avenida de la Independencia, about a 20-minute walk east of the terminal—no fun with baggage. The bus goes to Parque de la Fraternidad on the edge of Habana Vieja. The journey takes about one hour, but the wait can be just as long; the bus gets incredibly crowded, is renowned for pickpockets, and is a hassle that will appeal to only the most seasoned, penny-pinching travelers. You'll need 20 pesos for the fare.

Cubataxi taxis await outside the arrivals lounges. Official rates are CUC15–20 to downtown hotels, but some taxi drivers will not want to use their meter and may ask you how much you're prepared to pay (they reset their meter at a discount rate and pocket the difference); quote below the fares given here. Avoid private (illegal) taxis, as several foreigners have been robbed.

Car Rental: The following have booths at Terminal Three: **Cubacar** (tel. 07/649-9800); **Havanautos** (tel. 07/649-5197); and **Rex** (tel. 07/266-6074). The following have booths at

Terminal Two: **Cubacar** (tel. 07/649-5546); **Havanautos** (tel. 07/649-5215), and **Rex** (tel. 07/649-0306).

BY SEA
By Cruise Ship

Havana's **Terminal Sierra Maestra** (Av. del Puerto, tel. 07/862-1925) is a natty conversion of the old customs building. Passengers step through the doorways directly onto Plaza de San Francisco, in the heart of Havana.

By Private Vessel

Private yachts berth at **Marina Hemingway** (Av. 5ta y Calle 248, Santa Fe, tel. 07/204-5088, fax 07/204-5280, comercial@prto. mh.cyt.cu, www.nauticamarlin.com), 15 kilometers west of downtown. The harbor coordinates are 23° 5'N and 82° 29'W. You should announce your arrival on VHF Channel 16, HF Channel 68, and SSB 2790.

If you plan to dock for less than 72 hours, visas are not required (your passport will suffice). For longer stays you'll need a tourist card (CUC20), issued at the marina. The harbormaster's office (tel. 07/204-1150, ext. 2884), in Complejo Turístico Papa's, at the end of channel B, will facilitate your entry and exit, and visa extensions can be arranged for CUC25.

Docking fees (CUC0.35 per foot per day) include water, electricity, and custodial services. Gasoline and diesel are available 8 A.M.–7 P.M. (tel. 07/204-1150, ext. 450).

The 24-hour medical post (ext. 737) is in Complejo Turístico Papa's, as are a 24-hour launderette (ext. 451), bathrooms with showers, soda bar, and TV lounge, storage room (security boxes can be rented), ship chandler (ext. 2344), plus a beach volleyball court and tennis courts. The post office (ext. 448) is at the entrance of Intercanal C, where you'll also find the Hemingway International Nautical Club (ext. 701), which offers fax and telephone facilities. The shopping mall is at the east end of Intercanal B (ext. 739).

Rental cars are also available (ext. 87), as are microbuses and taxis (ext. 85).

Getting Around

ON FOOT

Havana is a walker's city, easily and best explored on foot. Only when traveling between districts will you need transport. Except in the restored section of Habana Vieja, sidewalks are in atrocious repair. Beware potholes, broken curbs, and dog excrement. And be wary of walking beneath corroded porticos. If *habaneros* are walking in the street to avoid certain arcades, so should you.

BY BUS
Tourist Bus

Since May 2008, Havana has a double-decker tourist bus service, the **HabanaBusTour** (tel. 07/835-0000, www.transtur.cu; daily 9 A.M.–9 P.M.), perfect for first-time visitors who want to get their bearings and catch the main sights of Havana. For just CUC5 you can hop on and off the buses as many times as you wish in a day at any of the 44 stops, currently served by a fleet of 12 buses (three are open-top double-deckers) covering 95 miles of route. Although there are three routes, the red-and-blue, Chinese-made double-deckers only serve one route. The other two routes are by minibus, which takes away the fun.

The T1 route (double-decker) begins on the west side of Parque Central and does a figure eight around the perimeter of Habana Vieja, and then through Vedado as far as Plaza de la Revolucion via the Hotel Habana Libre. At Plaza de la Revolucion you can hop aboard the T2 minibus for a sightseeing tour of Nuevo Vedado and Miramar and as far afield as Marina Hemingway, on the western fringe of the city. The T3 minibus is a great way to get out to the Playas del Este beaches.

Public Bus

Hurrah! Havana's formerly crowded and uncomfortable public buses, or *guaguas* (pronounced WAH-wahs), have been replaced with modern imported buses. No buses operate within Habana Vieja except along the major peripheral thoroughfares. Buses are often packed to the gills, especially during rush hours—7–10 A.M. and 3–6 P.M.

Public transportation comes to a halt on May 1 and other days of major political celebrations, as buses are redirected to transporting the masses to the demonstrations.

Bus service is the responsibility of three agencies: Asociación de Transportes de Servicios de Ómnibus (Astro), Transmetro, and Ómnibus Metropolitano.

Schedules and Fares: Most *guaguas* run 24 hours, at least hourly during the day but on reduced schedules 11 P.M.–5 A.M. The standard fare for any journey throughout the city is 20 centavos, or 40 centavos on smaller buses called *ómnibuses ruteros,* which have the benefit of being uncrowded. *Taxibuses*—buses that ply a fixed, non-stop route to the airport and bus and train stations—charge one peso.

Routes and Route Maps: Many buses follow a loop route, traveling to and from destinations along different streets. Few routes are a circle. If you find yourself going in the wrong direction, don't assume that you'll eventually come around to where you want to get to. Most buses display the bus number and destination above the front window. Many buses arrive and depart from Parque Central and Parque de la Fraternidad in Habana Vieja and La Rampa (Calle 23) in Vedado, especially at Calle L and at Calzada de Infanta.

BY TAXI

Modern taxis—including top-of-the-line Mercedes—serve the tourist trade while locals make do with wheezing jalopies. Most taxis lack seatbelts or are otherwise in a poor state of repair.

Dollar Taxis

Since 2008, the various competing state-run taxi companies have been amalgamated. Now,

Transtur operates all *turistaxis* as **Cubataxi** (tel. 07/855-5555), which can be hailed outside hotels or by calling for radio dispatch. Taxis range from modern Mercedes to beat-up Ladas, the Russian-made Fiat described by Martha Gellhorn as "tough as a Land Rover, with iron-hard upholstery and, judging by sensation, no springs." Only the most modern vehicles have functioning seat belts.

Some taxis are metered (CUC1 at flag drop, then CUC0.45 a kilometer), but not all. Few drivers will use the meter, but will ask you how much you want to pay. You will rarely pay more than CUC10 or so for any journey within town. Expect to pay about CUC5 between Habana Vieja and the Hotel Tryp Habana Libre. A light above the cab signifies if the taxi is *libre* (free).

Classic Cars: Fancy tooling around in a 1950 Studebaker or 1959 Buick Invicta convertible? **Gran Car** (Calle Marino esq. Santa María, Nuevo Vedado, tel. 07/855-5567, grancardp@transnet.cu) rents classic-car taxis for CUC30 per hour (20-km limit the first hour, with shorter limits per extra hour). Daily rates decline from CUC90 for one day to CUC70 per

day for five days (120-km daily limit). Set prices apply for provincial touring. They can be found outside major hotels.

You can rent a taxi and driver (CUC13 per person two hours, CUC25 four hours, CUC50 eight hours, CUC85 14 hours).

Peso Taxis

The workhorses of the taxi system, the privately owned 1950s-era *colectivos* or *máquinas* run along fixed routes, much like buses, and charge 10 or 50 pesos for a ride anywhere along the route. Parque de las Agrimensores, on the north side of the railway station, is the official starting point for set routes throughout the city. They are officially barred from accepting foreigners, but occasionally will do so.

Bici-taxis

Hundreds of homespun tricycle taxis with shade canopies ply the streets of Habana Vieja and Vedado. The minimum fare is usually CUC1 (or five pesos for Cubans on peso-only *bici-taxis*). You can go the full length of the Malecón, from Habana Vieja to Vedado, for CUC3–5. Always agree to a fare before setting off.

© CHRISTOPHER P. BAKER

Tourists embark on a tour of Habana Vieja by horse-drawn cab from outside the Capitolio.

METROBUSES

About half of the one million trips that *habaneros* make daily are aboard "Metrobuses," which formerly carried the "M" designation (for Metrobus), but since 2008 have been designated with "P." Most services originate from Parque de la Fraternidad. Formerly operated by *camellos* (uncomfortable and crowded homemade articulated bodies hauled by trucks), the Metrobus service now uses modern and comfortable Chinese-made articulated buses. Seventeen routes span Havana and the most distant suburbs. Two key routes to know are the P11 (Vedado to Habana del Este) and P12 (Parque de la Fraternidad to Santiago de las Vegas via the international airport).

Most begin operation at 4 A.M., with the last departure at 10 or 11 P.M. A standard 20 centavo fare applies.

PC: Hospital Naval to Playa
Route: Ciudad Panamericano – Circunvalación – Rpto. San Pedro – Rpto. Eléctrico – Cujae – 51 y 114 – Hospital Militar – Escuela Nacional de Artes – Playa

P1: La Rosita to Playa
Route: Carretera Central – (Cotorro) – (San Francisco de Paula) – Calzada de Güines – Vía Blanca – Cuatro Caminos – Arroyo – Infanta – La Rampa – Calle L – Linea – 3ra Av. – Playa

P2: Alberro (Cotorro) to Vedado
Route: Carretera Central – (Cotorro) – (San Francisco de Paula) – Av. Camilo Cienfuegos – Ciudad Deportivo – Av. Independencia – Av. Rancho Boyeros – Av. G – Linea

P3: Alamar to Vedado
Route: Alamar – Rpto. Antonio Guiteras – Semaforo Guanabacoa – Vía Blanca – Av. de Acosta – La Vibora – Av. Santa Catalina – Av. Boyeros – Ciudad Deportiva – Av. 26 – Tunel Linea

P4: San Agustín (Lisa) to Parque Fraternidad
Route: Naútico – Playa – 19 y 70 – 41 y 42 – Kohly – Calle 23 – La Rampa – Av. Infanta – Av. Salvador Allende – Parque Fraternidad

P5: San Agustín (Lisa) to Terminal de Trenes
Route: Calle 270 (e/ 25 y 27) – La Lisa – 51 y 114 – Hospital Militar – La Ceguera – 31 y 66 – 31 y 56 – 31 y 30 – Linea – La Rampa – Hospital Hermanos Ameijenas – Malecón – Av. del Puerto – Terminal de Trenes

P6: Eléctrico to Playa
Route: 13 de Mayo – Lacret y 10 de Octubre – Cuatro Caminos – Av. Padre Varela – Hospital Hermanos Ameijanes – Malecón – La Rampa – Calle L – Linea – 3ra Av. – Playa

These jalopies are barred from certain streets, so you might end up taking a zigzagging route to your destination.

Coco-taxis

These cutesy three-wheeled eggshells on wheels whiz around the touristed areas of Havana and charge CUC0.50 per kilometer. However, they are inherently unsafe.

Horse-Drawn Buggies

Horse-drawn coaches offer a popular way of exploring the Malecón and Old Havana, although the buggies are barred from entering the pedestrian-only quarter. They're operated by **San Cristóbal Agencia de Viajes** (Oficios #110, e/ Lamparilla y Amargura, Habana Vieja, tel. 07/861-9171). Their official starting point is the junction of Empedrado and Tacón, but you can hail them wherever you see them. Others can be hailed outside the Hotel Inglaterra, on Parque Central, and at Plaza de la Revolución. They charge CUC10 per person for one hour.

BY CAR

The narrow one-way streets in Habana Vieja are purgatory for motor vehicles. The main plazas and the streets between them are barred to traffic.

P7: Alberro (Cotorro) to Parque de la Fraternidad
Route: Av. 99 (y Final) – Carretera Central – Av. 101 – Calzada de Güines – Lindero – Calzada de Luyanó – 10 de Octubre – Cuatro Caminos – Máximo Gómez (Monte) – Industria – Dragones – Parque de la Fraternidad

P8: Rpto. Eléctrico to Ciudad Panoráica
Route: 13 de Mayo – Lacret y 10 de Octubre – Cuatro Caminos – Máximo Gómez – Parque Fraternidad – Tunel – La Cabaña – Ciudad Panamericano

P9: Vibora to Hospital Militar
Route: Lacret y 10 de Octubre – Cuatro Caminos – Padre Varela – Hospital Hermanos Ameijanos – La Rampa – Calle 23 – Kohly – 41 y 42 – Hospital Militar

P10: Vibora to Naútico
Route: Ciro Frias – Poey – 100 y Aldabas – Autopista Pinar del Río – 100 y 51 – 19 y 70 – Av. 3ra y 70 – Naútico

P11: Alamar to Av. de los Presidentes (Hospitals)
Route: Micro X – Calle 168 – Rpto. Guiteras – Vía Monumental – La Cabana – Tunel – Zulueta – Parque Fraternidad – Simón Bolívar (Reina) – Salvador Allende – Av. G

P12: Santiago de las Vegas (Boyeros) to Parque de la Fraternidad
Route: Av. 349 (y Final) – Calle 17 – Calle 2 – Av. Boyeros – Salvador Allende – Simón Bolívar (Reina) – Parque de la Fraternidad

P13: Santiago de las Vegas (Boyeros) to Vibora
Route: Parque Santiago – Calabazar – Vibora

P14: San Agustín to Parque Fraternidad
Route: Rpto. Barbosa – Novia del Mediodia – 51 y 250 – La Lisa – 51 y 114 – 100 y 51 – Cerro – Hospital Covadonga – Cuatro Caminos – Parque Fraternidad

P15: Alamar to Terminal del Trenes
Route: Av. 3ra – Calle 160 – Vía Blanca – Vía Monumental – Puente Santa Fé – 10 de Octubre – Independencia (Guanabacoa) – (Regla) – Primer Anillo del Puerto – Av. del Puerto – Terminal de Coubre – Egido – Terminal de Trenes

P16: Santiago de las Vegas to Vedado
Route: Parque Santiago – Boyeros – Av. Independencia – Av. Rancho Boyeros – Av. G – Linea

A treacherously potholed four-lane freeway—the **Autopista Circular** (route Calle 100 or *circunvalación*)—encircles southern and eastern Havana, linking the arterial highways and separating the core from suburban Havana. It intersections are dangerous.

Parking

A capital city without parking meters? Imagine. Parking meters were detested during the Batista era, mostly because they were a source of *botellas* (skimming) for corrupt officials. After the triumph of the Revolution, *habaneros* smashed the meters. However, the state increasingly is applying fees to park roadside, with *custodios* (in red vests) on hand to collect fees.

No Parking zones are well marked. Avoid these like the plague, especially if it's an officials-only zone. Havana has an efficient towing system for the recalcitrant.

Never leave your car parked unguarded. In central Vedado, the Hotel Habana Libre Tryp has an underground car park (CUC0.60 for one hour, CUC6 maximum for 24 hours).

Rental Companies

All hotels have car rental booths, and there are scores of outlets citywide.

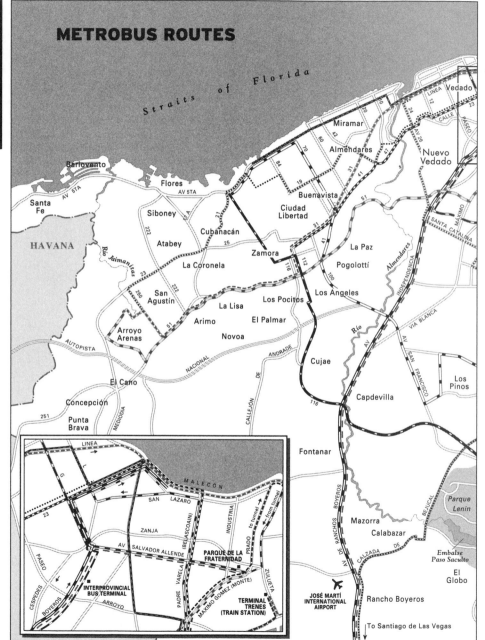

METROBUS ROUTES

CASTILLO DE LOS
TRES REYES DEL MORRO

SEE DETAIL

MALECÓN

SAN LAZARO

ZANJA

ALLENDE

PRADO

MONTE

ARROYO

GÓMEZ

VIA BLANCA

AV CAMILO

CALZADA DE OCTUBRE

CALZADA DE LUYANO

VIA BLANCA

Bahía de la
Habana

Ciudad
Panamericano   27

Loma
Cabaña

Casablanca

Antonio
Guiteras

Regla   10

VIA DE OCTUBRE

Guanabacoa

La
Ceiba

23

32   Cojimar

Río Cojimar

AV COJIMAR

VIA BLANCA

MONUMENTAL

1HA   3

968   1HB   3J   5A

7MA   64   5F   168

Alamar

Jocomino

Mañana

EOYULA

MIGUEL

La
Víbora

AV DE 10

ACOSTA

Lawton

CIENFUEGOS

Río

CALZADA DE GÜINES (DOLORES)

Sevillano

Mirador de
Lawton

Víbora
Park

La Cumbre

AUTOPISTA

Parraga

CALZADA

CALZADA

CALZADA DE SAN AGUSTIN

Diezmero

Hondo

El
Calvario

Embalse
Río Hondo

San Francisco de Paula

NACIONAL

La Guinera

Eléctrico

DE

Santa María
del Rosario

GLOBO

EL

CARRETERA

Embalse
Ejercito
Rebelde

AV

SAN

Cotorro

CARRETERA

FRANCISCO

CENTRAL

MANAGUA

0   1 mi

0   1 km

BUS LINES

▬▬	PC
—	P1
–	P2
....	P3
....	P4
– – –	P5
▬▬	P6
– –	P7
– – –	P8
▬▬	P9
▭▬	P10
▭▬	P11
– –	P12
▬▬	P13
▭▬	P14
– – –	P15
▬▬	P16

© AVALON TRAVEL

Transtur (Calle L #456, e/ 25 y 27, Vedado, tel. 07/835-0000, reservas@transtur.cu, www.transtur.cu) operates the two main car rental agencies, **Cubacar** and **Havanautos** (tel. 07/285-0703, http://havanautos.com). They have a selection of small and mid-range cars, and **Cubacar** (Calle 21, e/ N y O, Vedado, tel. 07/836-4038) even rents BMWS 5-series for CUC185 daily or CUC180 per day for week-long rentals. **Rex** (tel. 07/273-9166 or 683-0303, www.rex-rentacar.com) competes with Audis and has offices at the airport; Malecón y Linea, Vedado (tel. 07/835-6830); plus Hotel Copacabana (tel. 07/202-7684); and 5ta Av. y 92, Miramar (tel. 07/209-2207); Av. 194, e/ 15 y 17, Siboney (tel. 07/273-9166); at the cruise terminal (tel. 07/862-6343); and near the airport at Avenida Rancho Boyeros y Calzada de Bejucal, Plaza de la Revolución (tel. 07/683-0303).

Car Repairs

Your car rental company can arrange repairs. However, if you need emergency treatment, **Oro Negro** (5ta Av., esq. 120, Miramar, tel. 07/208-6149; Calle 2, esq. 7ma, Miramar, tel. 07/204-5760; and Av. 13, esq. 84, Playa, tel. 07/204-1938) has *servicentros* open Monday–Saturday 8 A.M.–7 P.M. Cubalse, which oversees sales of cars in Cuba, has a major automotive repair shop at **Agency Multimarcas** (Av. 222, esq. La Lisa, tel. 07/204-8743).

You can arrange a tow through **Agencia Peugeot** (tel. 07/766-1463 or 879-3854), which charges CUC1 per kilometer outbound and CUC1 per kilometer for the tow.

BY MOTORCYCLE AND SCOOTER

Renta de Motos (3ra Av., esq. Miramar, tel. 07/204-5491; daily 9 A.M.–9 P.M.) rents scooters for CUC12 two hours, CUC15 three hours, or CUC23 per day (CUC21 per day for rentals of 3–10 days). It does not offer insurance.

If you're staying in Cuba any length of time, consider buying a Chinese-made Dayang scooter (CUC1,845) or Suzuki GN125

(CUC2,332) from **Agencia Vedado** (Calle 23 #753, e/ B y C, Vedado, tel. 07/833-3994, ventas23@23c.automotriz.cubalse.cu).

BY BICYCLE

Bicycling offers a chance to explore the city alongside the Cubans themselves, although the roads are a bit dodgy, with bullying trucks and buses pumping out fumes, plus potholes and other obstacles to contend with (an average of two cyclists are killed in traffic accidents in Havana every three days).

The municipal government provides specially converted buses—the **Ciclobus**—to ferry cyclists and their *bicis* through the tunnel beneath Havana harbor (10 centavos). Buses depart from Parque de la Fraternidad and Av. de los Estudiantes.

Alas, the two entities formerly renting bicycles no longer do so, but you can buy bikes from **El Orbe** (Monserrate #304, e/ O'Reilly y San Juan de Díos, Habana Vieja, tel. 07/860-2617; Mon.–Fri. 9 A.M.–6 P.M., Sat. 9 A.M.–5 P.M.).

BY FERRY

Tiny ferries (standing room only—no seats) bob across the harbor between the Havana waterfront and Regla (on the east side of the bay) and Casablanca (on the north side of the bay). The ferries leave on a constant yet irregular basis 24 hours, from a wharf called Muelle Luz on Avenida San Pedro at the foot of Calle Santa Clara in Habana Vieja (tel. 07/797-7473 in Regla); 10 centavos; five minutes.

CITY TOURS

Havanatur (Calle 23, esq. M, Vedado, tel. 07/830-3107 or 07/201-9800; daily 8 A.M.–8 P.M.) offers a city tour, including walking tour, plus excursions to key sights in the suburbs and, of course, further afield.

Agencia de Viajes San Cristóbal (Oficios #110, e/ Lamparilla y Amargura, tel. 07/861-9171, www.viajessancristobal.cu; daily 8:30 A.M.–5 P.M.) offers a wide range of excursions throughout the city, from a walking

Muelle Luz terminal for the ferry to Regla, Avenida San Pedro

tour of Habana Vieja (daily 10 A.M.), to an "Eclecticismo y Modernismo" tour of modern Havana for architecture buffs. This agency can also arrange private guides.

You can book through hotel tour bureaus.

Jiniteros (street hustlers) will offer to be your guide. Although perhaps great for showing you the offbeat scene that most tourists miss, they're usually pretty useless as sightseeing guides.

Getting Away

DEPARTING CUBA
By Air
Airlines serving Havana have flights that usually depart Havana on the same days they arrive.

Cubana (Calle 23 #64, e/ P y Infanta, Vedado, tel. 07/838-1039 or 834-4446, www.cubana.cu; Mon.–Fri. 8:30 A.M.– 4 P.M., Sat. 8 A.M.–1 P.M.) has a fully computerized reservation system. Cubana also has a sales office in Miramar (Calle 110, esq. 5ta, tel. 07/202-9367; Mon.–Fri. 8:30 A.M.–4 P.M.).

José Martí International Airport
The airport (switchboard tel. 07/266-4644, www.airportcuba.com/?Action=Airport_ JM), at Wajay, 25 kilometers southwest of downtown Havana, is accessed by Avenida de la Independencia (Avenida Rancho Boyeros).

Make sure you arrive at the correct terminal for your departure.

U.S.-bound charter flights depart **Terminal Two** (Terminal Nacional, tel. 07/275-1200), on the north side of the runway.

Terminal Three (tel. 07/642-6225, or tel. 07/266-4133 for arrivals and departures), about one kilometer west of Terminal Two, handles all international flights. The departure tax (CUC25) must be paid at a separate counter after you've checked in with the airline. The foreign exchange bank refuses to accept Cuban pesos. There's an Internet café in the departure lounge.

Terminal Five (also called Terminal Caribbean), about three kilometers west of the international terminal, at the northwest corner of the airport, handles small-plane flights (mostly domestic) offered by Aero Caribbean.

GETTING TO THE AIRPORT

No buses serve the international terminals. A tourist taxi to the airport will cost about CUC15–20 from Havana. You may be able to negotiate less with the driver.

A bus marked "Aeropuerto" operates to Terminal One—the domestic terminal—from the east side of Parque Central in Habana Vieja. It's intended for Cubans only. The *cola* (line) begins near the José Martí statue. There are two lines: one for people wishing to be seated (*sentados*) and one for those willing to stand (*de pie*). The journey costs one peso, takes about one hour, and is very unreliable (departures are about every two hours). You can also catch Ómnibus #480 or Metrobus P12 from the west side of Parque de la Fraternidad (you can also get on the P12 near the University of Havana on Avenida Salvador Allende). Both go to Santiago de las Vegas via the domestic terminal (Terminal One), but will let you off about 400 yards east of Terminal Two. Do *not* use this bus for the international terminal.

EXPLORING BEYOND HAVANA

Make your reservations as far ahead as possible.

By Air

Cubana (Calle 23 #64, e/ P y Infanta, Vedado, tel. 07/838-1039 or 834-4446, www.cubana.cu; Mon.–Fri. 8:30 A.M.–4 P.M., Sat. 8 A.M.–1 P.M.) offers service to all major Cuban cities.

Most domestic flights leave from José Martí International Airport's **Terminal One** (Av. Van Troi, off Av. Rancho Boyeros, tel. 07/266-4644 or 275-1200).

AeroGaviota (Av. 47 #2814, e/ 28 y 34, Rpto. Kohly, tel. 07/204-2621 or 203-0668) flights depart from Aeropuerto Baracao, on the Autopista Habana–Mariel, about three kilometers west of Marina Hemingway.

By Bus

Tourist Buses: Modern **Víazul** (Av. 26, esq. Zoológico, Nuevo Vedado, tel. 07/881-1413, fax 07/66-6092, www.viazul.cu; 7 A.M.–9 P.M.) buses serve provincial capitals and major tourist destinations throughout the country. They depart Terminal Víazul, which has a café and free luggage storage. City bus #27 connects the Víazul terminal to Vedado and Centro Habana. Víazul buses make a 10-minute stop at the **Terminal de Ómnibuses Nacionales** (Av. Independencia #101, esq. 19 de Mayo, Víazul, tel. 07/870-3397; daily 6:30 A.M.–9:30 P.M.), two blocks north of Plaza de la Revolución. You can also make reservations and board the buses here. The terminal is served by local bus #47 from the Prado (at Ánimas) in Habana Vieja; by bus #265 from the east side of Parque Central; and by buses #67 and 84 from La Rampa in Vedado. Facilities include a bank, snack bars, and an information booth (tel. 07/870-9401).

Cuban tour agencies such as Havanatur and Veracuba offer transfer seats on tour buses serving key tourist destinations. Check with tour desks in hotel lobbies.

Public Buses: Astro buses to destinations throughout the country leave from the Terminal de Ómnibuses Nacionales (Av. Independencia #101, esq. 19 de Mayo, Víazul, tel. 07/870-3397; daily 6:30 A.M.–9:30 P.M.). However, in 2009 Astro ceased accepting foreigners on its buses except for students with appropriate ID, who can travel like Cubans for pesos. Make your reservation as early as possible, either at the bus terminal or at the **Agencia Reservaciones de Pasaje** (Factor y Tulipán, Nuevo Vedado, tel. 07/881-5931 or 07/55-5537). Your name will be added to the scores of names ahead of you.

If you don't have a reservation or miss your departure, you can try getting on the standby list (*lista de espera*, tel. 07/862-4341) at **Terminal La Coubre** (Av. del Puerto y Egido, tel. 07/872-3726), in southwest Habana Vieja. Interprovincial buses that have unfilled seats call in here after departing the Terminal de Ómnibus Nacionales to pick up folks on the standby list. The *lista de espera* service is at the western end of the terminal.

Buses to towns throughout Havana Province depart from Calle Apodaca, e/ Agramonte y Avenida de Bélgica.

By Train

Estación Central de Ferrocarril: The main station is the Central Railway Station (Egido, esq. Arsenal, Habana Vieja, tel. 07/861-2959 or 862-1920), or Terminal de Trenes. Trains depart here for major cities. Unfortunately, Cuba's Kafaesque Communist system comes into play when you try to buy a ticket, which must be done from the hideously dysfunctional **Terminal La Coubre** (Av. del Puerto, tel. 07/862-1012), 400 meters south of the main railway station at *taquilla* (booth) #3. Tickets can be purchased up to one hour prior to departure, but you must purchase your ticket before 8 P.M. for a nighttime departure. You may be able to buy tickets in pesos in the main station, but you'll usually need to book days, or weeks, in advance.

Estación 19 de Noviembre: Local commuter trains (*ferro-ómnibuses*) operate from this station (Calle Tulipán and Hidalgo, tel. 07/881-4431), also called Estación Tulipán, south of Plaza de la Revolución. Trains depart to San Antonio de los Baños at 10:05 A.M. and 4:25 and 8:30 P.M. (CUC1.50); to Artemisa at 8:30 A.M. and 5:45 P.M. (CUC2.20); and to Batabanó at 5 P.M. (CUC1.80).

Return trains depart from San Antonio at 5:35 A.M. and 1:55 and 6:15 P.M.; from Artemisa at 5:30 A.M.; and from Batabanó at 5:25 A.M.

Estación Casablanca: The "Hershey Train" operates to Matanzas five times daily from Casablanca's harborfront station (tel. 07/862-4888) on the north side of Havana harbor.

By Taxi

Cubataxi (tel. 07/855-5555) and the three car rental companies offer chauffeured excursions by car or minivan within a 150-mile radius of Havana. Typical round-trip prices are: to Varadero CUC180, Bay of Pigs CUC320, and Viñales CUC250. Hourly rates for a chauffeured taxi are on a sliding scale, from CUC15 the first hour (20-km limit) to CUC80 for eight hours (125-km limit), typically with CUC0.80 per kilometer for extra distance.

Freelance Cabs: Penny-pinchers might try finding a *colectivo* taxi near the central railway or main bus station. *Colectivo* drivers are officially banned from taking foreigners, but with luck you might find someone willing to take you.

Organized Tours and Excursions

You can book excursions at tour desks in all tourist hotels.

Belgian-owned **Transnico** (Lonja del Comercio #6D, Habana Vieja, tel. 07/866-9954) specializes in special-interest tours, including bicycle tours, music and dance programs, and train trips.

GREATER HAVANA
AND HAVANA PROVINCE

Encircling Havana's heartland is a freeway, the *circunvalación,* beyond which the suburban residential districts gradually merge into the countryside. Suburban Havana has many sights that lure Cuban families (at least those with cars and the money for gas) for day trips on weekends, although few tourists venture this far afield, and fewer still to the outlying eponymous province, which extends 65 kilometers east and west and 40 kilometers south of Havana's city limits. The most popular site, and a must-see, is the Museo Ernest Hemingway, in the bucolic hilltop community of San Francisco de Paula.

Suburban Havana is ringed with small time-worn colonial towns such as San Antonio de los Baños and Artemisa that seem trapped in a centenary time-warp and give a good foretaste of what much of provincial Cuba still looks like. Think of oxen drawing rumbling carts through dusty streets, some still cobbled, lined with simple dwellings with wooden colonnades and red-tile roofs (or even thatch) and walls of wattle-and-daub and you have the picture. Most of Havana province is agricultural, especially the low-lying southern plain, whose rich red soils feed fruit trees and vegetables. This southern half of the province is the bread basket of the city and visually appears to be the wealthiest region in Cuba, as reflected in the many relatively well-maintained homes of local farmers. The southern shore, however, is a soggy no-man's-land of swamp and mangroves, where lowly fishing villages are among the most deprived and down at the heels in Cuba. No road runs along the southern shore

© CHRISTOPHER P. BAKER

HIGHLIGHTS

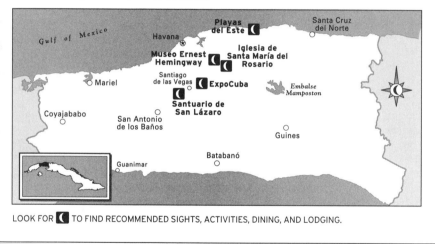

☾ Santuario de San Lázaro: This national shrine and pilgrimage site is best visited on the 17th of each month and especially on December 17th for the Procession of the Miracles, when thousands of pilgrims come to beseech favors of San Lázaro (page 169).

☾ ExpoCuba: This exhibition center provides a tangible expression of Cuba's achievements in the arts, culture, science, and technology (page 173).

☾ Museo Ernest Hemingway: "Papa's" former home is preserved as it was on the day he died. His sportfishing boat, the *Pilar,* stands in the grounds (page 179).

☾ Iglesia de Santa María del Rosario: The sleepy colonial village of Santa María del Rosario boasts this simple historic church with priceless murals and an exquisite gilt baroque altar (page 182).

☾ Playas del Este: Gorgeous palm-shaded beaches and turquoise seas can be found within a 30-minute drive of downtown Havana (page 186).

LOOK FOR ☾ TO FIND RECOMMENDED SIGHTS, ACTIVITIES, DINING, AND LODGING.

and I can think of no reason to send you there, other than to the sole coastal township of Batabanó, from where the ferries depart for Isla de la Juventud.

The northern shore east of Havana is another matter. Within a 40-minute drive of downtown Havana, white beaches unfold beneath the shade of coconut palms. Shelving into turquoise waters, these stunning sands lure *habaneros* in droves on weekend, when the music cranks up, spontaneous games of volleyball break out, and many a new romance is formed. Most foreign visitors who spend time in Havana yet seek some beach time tend to head to well-known Varadero, but the beaches of Havana's Playas del Este are nicer, have most of the water sports and services one could need, and benefit from being accessible to ordinary Cubans. En route from Havana city, you'll pass through the district of La Habana del Este, extending east for some 30 kilometers along the shore as far as the Playas del Este and exclusively comprising dreary high-rise postrevolutionary urban enclaves, most famously the urban blight of Alamar.

Inland much of the northern province is hilly and pocked with reservoirs that supply fresh water to *habaneros*. The Escaleras de Jaruco, southeast of the city inland of Playas del Este, is a woodsy bucolic retreat appealing to hikers and popular as a picnic spot for city-folk with wheels. These hills, and those of the Sierra de Camarones, further east, are quite dramatic, with deep canyons and sheer-faced knolls reminiscent of the *mogotes* of world-renowned Valle del Viñales, in Pinar del Río Province. As yet they are untapped for tourism, despite their unique beauty, and exploring along dusty rural roads that cut through these valleys is one of the pleasures of day excursions through Havana Province.

PLANNING YOUR TIME

Fortunately, most of the sites of interest in this region lie close to the city, with shining stars diminishing in number and brilliance with distance. The main sights can be broken into a two-day excursion, with day one concentrating on the neighboring districts of Boyeros and Arroyo Naranjo to the southwest; and a second combining the district of Cotorro and the beaches, southeast and east of Havana. A third day will suffice for exploring the more distant colonial villages.

Though buses run to most villages, few of the stand-alone sites are served by public transport which, in any event, is fickle and often overcrowded. For exploring, you'll need wheels. Scooters are available for hire at Playas del Este and prove perfect for whizzing around (basically, the five miles of beaches are linked by a single road), but should not be hired to get you to and from the city—the roads are far too congested, fast, and dangerous. Hire a taxi or your own rental car.

West of Havana, the coast is visually of little interest, although scuba divers might head to Playa Baracoa, where scuba diving is offered at the run-down hotel of Villa Cocomar.

To experience old-time village life in the 21st century, follow the Carretera Central westward (take Avenida 51 from Marianao) through a string of yesteryear townships: Bauta, Caimito, Guanajay, and Artemisa, where a side trip to Antiguo Cafetal Angerona may interest anyone wishing to see plantation ruins that clearly recall the epoch of slavery. Before arriving at Bauta, a turn-off to the village of El Cano provides an entrée to a lifestyle that has changed little in recent times; many local inhabitants still make pottery in age-old tradition.

In the district of Boyeros, the timeless hamlet of Rincón is the setting for **Santuario de San Lázaro,** an important pilgrimage site. A visit here can be combined with the nearby Mausoleo Antonio Maceo, where the mulatto hero general of the Wars of Independence is buried, near where he fell outside the village of Santiago de las Vegas. A short distance east (but unimaginably hard to reach directly, due to convoluted roads and poor signage), in the Arroyo Naranjo district, are a quartet of attractions for anyone with a specialist interest. If you have children in tow, plan a visit to Parque

GREATER HAVANA

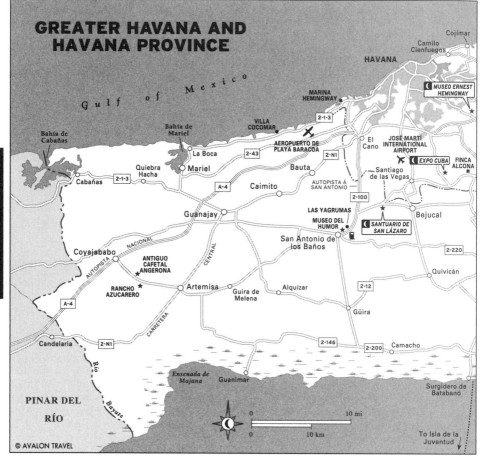

GREATER HAVANA

GREATER HAVANA AND HAVANA PROVINCE

Zoológico, a second-rate zoo but with all the elephants, lions, monkeys, and serpents you and your kids could ever hope to see; and Parque Lenin, a vast park with a small amusement park, horseback rides, boating, and more. A regular excursion for Cuban schoolkids is **ExpoCuba,** a permanent expo touting Cuban achievements in every field. A good two hours or more is required to do it justice. A commuter train from Havana will deliver you there, and enthusiasts of botany can also take it to visit the botanic garden, Jardín Botánico Nacional, across the street

from ExpoCuba. However, the sprawling garden is too vast to explore on foot, and arriving and touring by car is recommended.

A pilgrimage to Ernest Hemingway's former home, Finca Vigía, is an absolute must for anyone spending time in Havana. Now the **Museo Ernest Hemingway,** it is best combined with a visit to the seaside village of Cojímar, with its bust of Hemingway, its tiny fortress, and La Terraza restaurant, once frequented by "Papa" and serving excellent seafood dishes and cocktails. When visiting the museum, however, be sure to journey the

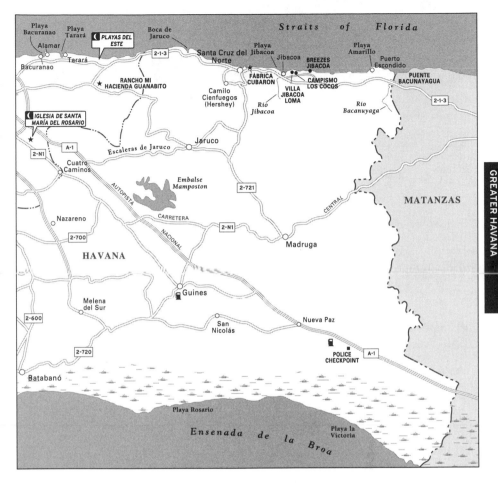

extra five miles to Santa María del Rosario to admire one of the prettiest churches in Cuba, **Iglesia de Santa María del Rosario.**

Beach lovers will want to head east along the coast highway that leads past the eyesore high-rise communities of Alamar and Celimar. Immediately beyond begin the beaches of **Playas del Este.** Unless you want to mingle with a young Cuban crowd, skip the first beach, Bacuranao, in favor of Tarará, which has fantastic sands and good facilities, including restaurants, bars, and water sports. One look at Tarará is enough

to make anyone add an additional day to his or her stay at the beaches of Playas del Este. Eastward, the contiguous beaches of Playa Mégano and Santa María del Mar are lively with Cubans on weekends, though the police presence is significant and Cubans here like to keep to themselves for that reason. Playas del Este has numerous hotels, although they are mostly desultory and I much prefer overnighting in Havana, with day-time forays out to the beach. The last of the Playas del Este is Guanabo, backed by a Cuban village where *casas particulares* are offered.

Beyond Playas del Este, the coast road winds over rugged hills and descends via the industrial port town of Santa Cruz del Norte, with a rum factory (not open to view). Nearby, inland, the small town of Hershey is the decaying setting for a now-closed sugar factory and township founded by the Hershey chocolate company. A short distance beyond, a side road leads off the highway to Playa Jibacoa, a beautiful beach with simple *cabinas* or the option of a relatively ritzy all-inclusive resort. This coastal drive is worth it not least for the fantastic views offered from the Puente Bacunayagua, spanning an eponymous river that is the boundary with Matanzas Province.

The beach resorts have bars and grills serving food, but elsewhere finding food can be a challenge. If you plan on a full day of touring, it pays to plan ahead by stocking up with snacks.

© CHRISTOPHER P. BAKER

The Monumento Ernest Hemingway in Cojímar features a bronze bust made from items donated by local fishermen.

Western Havana Province

HAVANA TO MARIEL

Beyond Marina Hemingway, you leave Havana behind as Avenida 5ta becomes the coast road (route 2-1-3) to Pinar del Río Province. The shore is unremarkable, except for **Playa Baracoa,** about 16 kilometers west of Havana and popular on hot weekends with Cubans. Some five kilometers further west, the rather dull **Playa Salado** is the setting for a go-kart race track and scuba diving center at Villa Cocomar.

About 45 kilometers beyond the marina, you arrive at **Mariel.** This port city (pop. 29,000), founded in 1792 deep inside a flask-shaped bay, is best known as the site of the famous "boatlift" in April 1980, when 120,000 Cubans departed the island and sailed away to Florida. It's a small and sleepy town despite its polluted port status. Mariel is ringed by docks and factories, including a cement factory that casts a pall of dust over everything for kilometers around. The **Museo Histórico** (Calle 132 #6926, tel.

063/92554), opposite the church, tells of the city's development, but isn't worth making a stop in its own right.

The Moorish-inspired building atop the hill on the outskirts north of town is a vision of beau geste (it's a military zone, and off limits).

Beyond Mariel, Route 2-1-3 continues west to **Cabañas,** beyond which you pass into Pinar del Río Province. It's a stunning drive as you pass through quintessentially Cuban landscapes, with distant *centrales* belching out black smoke above sensuously rolling green hills of cane, the Sierra del Rosario off to the south, and glimpses of the sea glowing in kaleidoscopic blues.

Buses depart and drop off at Calle 71 (tel. 063/92104).

Accommodations and Food

The run-down **Villa Cocomar** (Carretera Panamericano, Km 23.5, tel./fax 07/205-88090, fax 07/205-8889; CUC29 s, CUC36 d low season; CUC32 s, CUC42 d high season), at Playa Salado, has 47 air-conditioned *cabinas* and a scuba diving center, but unless you're a serious diver it is best avoided. (Cubanacán.)

THE CARRETERA CENTRAL

The old Carretera Central—route 2-N1—was the main thoroughfare to Pinar del Río before the Autopista was built. To get there, take Avenida 51 from Marianao to La Lisa and follow the signs. Many of the province's most atmospheric colonial towns line the route, good for a day's foray from Havana. The journey will take you through **Bauta;** nearby **Caimito,** with an attractive ocher-colored colonial-era church fronted by an intriguing mural displaying a fierce bald eagle painted in the Stars and Stripes voraciously attacking a noble Cuban Indian and peasant; and **Guanajay,** with the baroque Teatro Vicente Mora on the town square. South of Guanajay, midway to Artemisa, there's a restored remnant of the **Trocha Mariel-Majana,** a 19th-century fortification built by the Spanish to forestall the Army of Liberation during the Wars of Independence.

EL CANO

This small village, two kilometers east of the Carretera Central, on Havana's southwestern outskirts, was founded in 1723 and has retained elements of its historic charm. Immigrants from the Canary Islands and Majorca brought a tradition of pottery making. Their descendants are still known as skilled potters (*alfareros*), who use local red clays shaped on foot-operated wheels and fired in traditional wood-fired kilns.

ARTEMISA

Artemisa (pop. 35,000), 60 kilometers southwest of Havana, dates from the early 19th century and has a wide main street lined by neoclassical houses fronted with verandas supported by Doric and Ionic columns. The cubist **Mausoleo a las Mártires** (Av. 28 de Enero; Tues.–Sat. 8 A.M.–5 P.M., Sun. 8 A.M.–noon; CUC1) honors 28 Artemisa rebels who participated in the attack on the Moncada barracks

in Santiago in 1953; fourteen were killed in the assault or were later tortured to death in captivity and are buried beneath the cube, which features brass bas-reliefs.

Rancho Azucarero

This 2,200-hectare ranch, which serves as Cuba's main horse-breeding and equestrian center, is stocked safari-style with animals—antelopes, wildebeest, zebras, etc.—imported from Africa in the 1970s for the hunting pleasure of Communist bigwigs. Today the facility breeds English purebred horses for international competition. It is slated to become the Havana Polo Club and horse-racing track. Plans call for a golf course, African-style lodge and an equestrian center. Tour agencies in Havana offer excursions for horseback rides.

Antiguo Cafetal Angerona

Cafetal Angerona, five kilometers west of Artemisa, midway to Cayajabos, was founded as a coffee (and, later, sugar) plantation in 1813 by Cornelio Sauchay, who kept almost 500 slaves. It went out of business about 1910 and is now a national monument, albeit in ruins. Novelist James Michener used the site as the setting for his sugar plantation in his novel *The Caribbean.* Following a stream, Michener records in *Six Days in Havana,* how "it was when I climbed out of the cisterns and onto the plateau above that I came upon the salient fact of this great operation: the immense fenced-in area in which the slaves were kept, an area so vast that five or six football fields could have been fitted in. ... The mournful place, called a *barracón,* had only one gate, beside which rose a tall stone tower in which men with guns waited day and night for any sign of incipient rebellion."

The watchtower and huge cisterns are still intact. There's no entrance fee, but you should tip any guide.

Getting There

Bus #215 operates from Havana's main bus terminal and runs to Artemisa's **Terminal de**

Ómnibus (Carretera Central, at Km 58, tel. 063/36-3527). Trains depart Estación Tulipán in Havana at 6 P.M. for Artemisa, where the station is on Avenida Héroes del Moncada, five blocks west of the main plaza (CUC2.20); return trains depart for Havana at 5:30 A.M.

Southwestern Suburbs

SANTIAGO DE LAS VEGAS

This colonial-era rural town in the midst of the country, 20 kilometers south of Havana, is accessed via Avenida de la Independencia, a fast-paced highway that runs south through the industrial area of Rancho Boyeros to the José Martí International Airport, beyond which it becomes Avenida de los Mártires before entering Santiago de las Vegas.

The *circunvalación*—a poorly maintained four-lane freeway—leads east from Avenida de la Independencia, encircles Havana, and connects with the coast road to Playas del Este.

Mausoleo de General Antonio Maceo Grajales

Avenida de los Mártires rises south of Santiago de las Vegas, passes through pine forests, and deposits you at El Cacahual. Here, Antonio Maceo Grajales (1845–96), the black general and hero of the Wars of Independence, slumbers in a mausoleum in a circular park the size of a football field. The mausoleum also contains the tomb of Capitán Ayudante (Captain-Adjutant) Francisco Gómez Toro (1876–96), General Máximo Gómez's son, who gave his life alongside Maceo at the Battle of San Pedro on December 7, 1896. The granite tombs are engraved in the style of Mexican artist Diego Rivera. The park forms a giant traffic circle, on the east side of which stands a monument in bronze to Coronel (Colonel) Juan Delgado, chief of the Santiago de las

The Iglesia de San Lázaro draws pilgrims who come to request a miracle of the patron saint.

Vegas regiment, who recovered Maceo's body.

The tiny main square in Santiago de las Vegas is pinned by the **Monumento a Juan Delgado Gonzáles,** a marble statue of the local hero.

(Santuario de San Lázaro

Cuba's most important pilgrimage site is the Sanctuary of San Lázaro (Carretera de San Antonio de los Baños, tel. 0683/2396; daily 7 A.M.–6 P.M.; free), on the west side of Rincón, a rustic hamlet about four kilometers southwest of Santiago de las Vegas. Every day, the church, **Iglesia de San Lázaro,** is busy with mendicants come to have their children baptized while others fill bottles with holy water from a fountain behind the church. Behind the church is a leprosy and AIDS sanatorium, **Los Cocos,** Cuba's first sanatorium built to house patients infected with HIV.

San Lázaro is the patron saint of the sick, and is an immensely popular figure throughout Cuba (in *santería,* his avatar is Babalú Ayé). His symbol is the crutch. His stooped figure is usually covered in sores, and in effigy he goes about attended by his two dogs. Limbless beggars and other unfortunates crowd at the gates and plead for a charitable donation.

A procession to the sanctuary takes place the 17th of each month. The annual **Procesión de los Milagros** (Procession of the Miracles) takes place December 17, drawing thousands of pilgrims to beseech or give thanks to the saint for miracles they imagine he has the power to grant. The villagers of Rincón do a thriving business selling votive candles and flowers to churchgoers. Penitents crawl on their backs and knees, and others walk in front of them and sweep the road ahead with palm fronds.

Getting There: If driving, follow Carretera al Rincón, which begins at the bus station on the southwest edge of Santiago de las Vegas; bus #476 also runs from here.

A three-car train for San Antonio de los Baños departs Havana's Estación 19 de Noviembre (Tulipán) at 10:05 A.M. and 4:25 and 8:30 P.M., stopping at Rincón (CUC1). Trains run continuously on December 17.

Food

The **Tabernita** (Av. de los Mártires, tel.

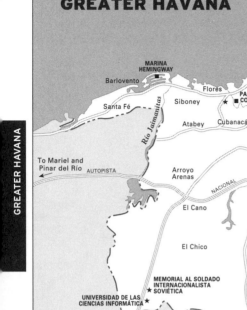

GREATER HAVANA

07/683-2033), a thatched restaurant about one kilometer south of Santiago de las Vegas, serves *criollo* fare and is popular with Cuban families on weekends.

Getting There and Away
Bus M2 runs from Parque de la Fraternidad in Havana to Santiago de las Vegas. Ómnibus #480 also serves Santiago de las Vegas from Havana's main bus terminal (Av. Independencia #101, Plaza de la Revolución, tel. 07/870-3397). The **Terminal de Ómnibus** (Calle al Rincón #43, tel. 07/683-3159) is on the southwest side

of town, on the road to Rincón; you can catch a taxi here to El Cacahual.

ARROYO NARANJO
This *municipio* lies east of Boyeros and due south of Havana.

Parque Zoológico Nacional
Cuba's national zoo, on Avenida Zoo–Lenin (Av. 8, esq. Av. Soto, tel. 07/44-7613, Wed.–Sun. 9:30 A.M.–3:30 P.M.; adults CUC3, children CUC2, vehicles CUC5), southeast of the village of Arroyo Naranjo, about 16

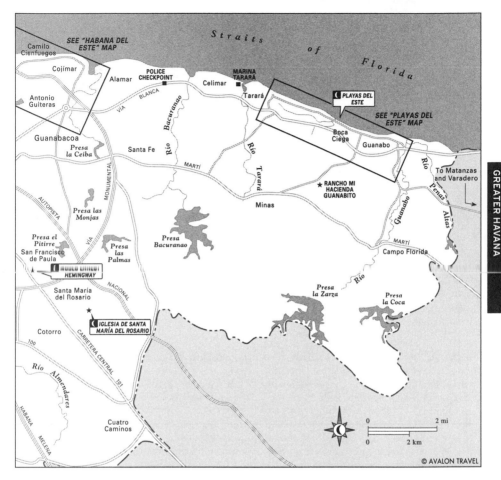

kilometers south of central Havana, covers 340 hectares and contains about 1,000 animals and more than 100 species. You can drive your own car through the park. A walk-through section houses a leopard, tiger, chimps, monkeys, and birds, but the cages are small and bare, many of the animals look woefully neglected, and the conditions are deplorable. The zoo also reproduces more than 30 endangered species and includes a taxidermist's laboratory. A children's area provides pony rides.

Tour buses (40 centavos) depart the parking lot about every 30 minutes and run through the African wildlife park—*pradera africana*—taking you through an expansive area not unlike the savanna of east Africa. Elephants come to the bus and stick their trunks in through the window to glean tidbits. There are rhinos, zebra, wildebeests, ostriches, and hippos, which spend most of their daylight hours wallowing in a deep pool. The bus tours also loops through the *foso de leones*—a deep quarry on the north side of the park. Here you can also sit atop the cliff on a viewing platform and look down upon the lions.

© CHRISTOPHER P. BAKER

a thrilling moment for visitors to the Pradera Africana, in the Parque Zoológico, as elephants put their trunks through the tour bus window

Getting There: To get to the main entrance, take Avenida de la Independencia to Avenida San Francisco (the Parque is signed at the junction) which merges with the *circunvalación.* Take the first exit to the right and follow Calzada de Bejucal south. Turn right onto Avenida Zoo–Lenin (signed). A second entrance is at Carretera de Vento, about one kilometer south from the *circunvalación*—the turnoff from the latter is 200 meters east of Avenida de la Independencia.

Buses #31, 73, and 88 operate between La Víbora and Arroyo Naranjo. A taxi will cost about CUC12 each way.

Parque Lenin

Lenin Park (Calle 100 y Carretera de la Presa, tel. 07/44-2721; Tues.–Sun. 9 A.M.–5 P.M.), east of the zoo, was created from a former hacienda and landscaped mostly by volunteer labor from the city. The vast complex features wide rolling pastures and small lakes surrounded by forests and pockets of bamboo, ficus, and flamboyants. What Lenin Park lacks in grandeur and stateliness, it makes up for in scale. Each September 1, the park is packed for a day of special activities.

The park is laid out west of a dam, Presa Paso Sequito, with a huge reservoir—Ejército Rebelde—to the east. The park is bounded by the *circunvalación* to the north and Calzada de Bejucal to the west; there is an entrance off Calzada de Bejucal. A second road—Calle Cortina de la Presa—enters from the *circunvalación,* runs down the center of the park, and is linked to Calzada de Bejucal by a loop road.

Sights, Galleries, and Museums: The **Galería del Arte Amelia Peláez,** at the south end of Cortina, displays works by the eponymous Cuban ceramist. Behind the gallery is a series of bronze busts inset in rock. A short distance to the west is the **Monumento Lenin,** a huge granite visage of the Communist leader and thinker in Soviet-realist style, carved by Soviet sculpture I. E. Kerbel. Further west, you'll pass an **aquarium** (entrance CUC1) displaying freshwater fish and turtles, including the antediluvian garfish (*manjuari*) and a couple of Cuban crocodiles.

About 400 meters farther west is the **Monumento a Celia Sánchez.** Here, a trail follows a wide apse to a broad amphitheater lined with ferns. At its center is a bronze figure of the national heroine inset in a huge rock. A small museum honors the heroine.

Also worth a visit are the **Taller Cerámica** (ceramic workshop), on the southwest corner of the park; and, on the north side, the Palacio de Pioneros Che Guevara, displaying stainless-steel sculptures of the revolutionary hero.

Horseback Riding: An equestrian center, **Centro Ecuestre** (tel. 07/44-1058; daily 9 A.M.–5 P.M. June–Aug., Wed.–Sun. 9 A.M.–5 P.M. Sept.–July), also called Club Hípico, immediately east of the entrance off Calzada de Bejucal, offers one-hour trips (CUC15) plus riding lessons, and you can rent horses. Horseback riding is also offered at **El Rodeo** (tel. 07/57-8893), the national rodeo arena, in the southeast corner of the park. El Rodeo offers rodeo (entry costs three pesos) every Sunday, with "Rodeo Pionero" (for youth) at noon and competitive adult rodeo at 3 P.M. The "Feria de Rodeo" (National Championships) is held each August 25.

Train Rides: A narrow-gauge railway circles the park, stopping at four stages. The old steam train dates from 1870 and operates daily 10 A.M.–4 P.M. (four pesos), departing Estación Galapagos de Oro and taking 25 minutes to circle the park. Another old steam train dating from 1915 is preserved under a red-tile canopy in front of the disused **Terminal Inglesa.**

Bicycle and Rowboat Rental: You can rent aquatic bicycles and rowboats on the lake at El Rodeo (five pesos for 30 minutes).

For Children: A *parque de diversiones* located in the northwest quarter includes carousels, a miniature "big dipper," and pony rides.

Swimming Pools: There are swimming pools in the **Palacio de Pioneros Che Guevara** and east of the community of Calabazar, on the south side of the park (five pesos).

Getting There: See Parque Zoológico, earlier in this section, for directions on getting there by car. Buses #31, 73, and 88 operate between La Víbora and the park entrance, and bus #113 runs from Marianao. A taxi will cost about CUC15 each way.

Expocuba

ExpoCuba, on the Carretera del Globo (official address Carretera del Rocío, Km 3.5, Arroyo Naranjo, tel. 07/697-4269; Wed.–Sun. 10 A.M.–5 P.M.; closed Sept.–Dec.; CUC1), three kilometers south of Parque Lenin, houses a permanent exhibition of Cuban industry, technology, sports, and culture touting the achievements of socialism. The facility covers 588,000 square meters and is a museum, trade expo, world's fair, and entertainment hall rolled into one. It has 34 pavilions, including booths that display the crafts, products, music, and dance of each of Cuba's provinces. Railroad buffs might check out the vintage rolling stock on the entrance forecourt. There's an information office at the main entrance, plus a currency exchange and bank.

A three-car train runs to ExpoCuba from Estación 19 de Noviembre (Tulipán, Nuevo Vedado, tel. 07/881-4431; CUC1 each way) every Wednesday–Sunday at 9:35 A.M.; it departs ExpoCuba at 5:30 P.M.

Buses #88 and 113 leave for ExpoCuba from the north side of Havana's main railway station weekends at 10 A.M., noon, and 3 P.M., and from Havana's Terminal de Ómnibus at 9 A.M., 11 A.M., and 4 P.M. Bus #80 also serves the park from Lawton.

Jardín Botánico Nacional

This 600-hectare botanical garden (Carretera del Rocío Km 3.5, Arroyo Naranjo, tel. 07/54-9864, www.uh.cu/centros/jbn; daily 9 A.M.–4 P.M.; entrance CUC1, guide CUC2), directly opposite ExpoCuba, doesn't have the fine-trimmed herbaceous borders of Kew or Butchart, but nonetheless is worth the drive for enthusiasts. Thirty-five kilometers of roads lead through the park, which was laid out between 1969 and 1984. You can drive your own vehicle, with a guide.

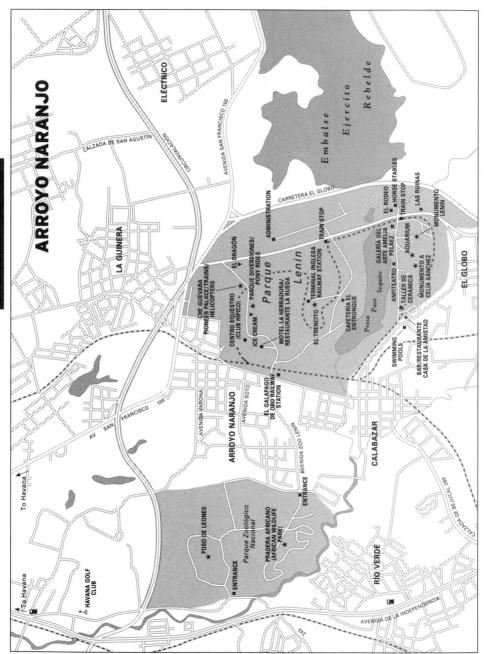

ARROYO NARANJO

ELÉCTRICO

CALZADA DE SAN AGUSTÍN

CIRCUNVALACIÓN

AVENIDA SAN FRANCISCO 100

LA GUINERA

Embalse Ejercito Rebelde

CARRETERA EL GLOBO

ADMINISTRATION

EL DRAGÓN

Parque Lenin

Parque Diversiones/
PONY RIDES

TRAIN STOP

EL RODEO
HORSE STABLES
TRAIN STOP
LAS RUINAS
MONUMENTO
LENIN

CHE GUEVARA
PIONEER PALACE/TRAINS/
HELICOPTERS

TERMINAL INGLESA
RAILWAY STATION

GALERÍA DEL
ARTE AMELIA
PELÁEZ

AQUARIUM
MONUMENTO A
CELIA SÁNCHEZ

CENTRO EQUESTRO
(CLUB HÍPICO)
ICE CREAM

MOTEL LA HERRADURA/
RESTAURANTE LA RUEDA

EL TRENCITO

CAFETERÍA EL
ENTRONQUE

Presa Paso Sequito

ANFITEATRO
TALLER DE
CERÁMICA

EL GLOBO

SWIMMING
POOLS

BAR/RESTAURANTE
CASA DE LA AMISTAD

AVENIDA VARONA

AV SAN FRANCISCO 100

AVENIDA SOTO

EL GALÁPAGO
DE ORO RAILWAY
STATION

ARROYO NARANJO

AVENIDA ZOO LENIN

CALABAZAR

ENTRANCE

To Havana

To Havana

FOSO DE LEONES

Parque Zoológico
Nacional

PRADERA AFRICANO
(AFRICAN WILDLIFE
PARK)

ENTRANCE

RÍO VERDE

CALZADA DE BEJUCAL 289

HAVANA GOLF
CLUB

ENTRANCE

To Havana

AVENIDA DE LA INDEPENDENCIA

243

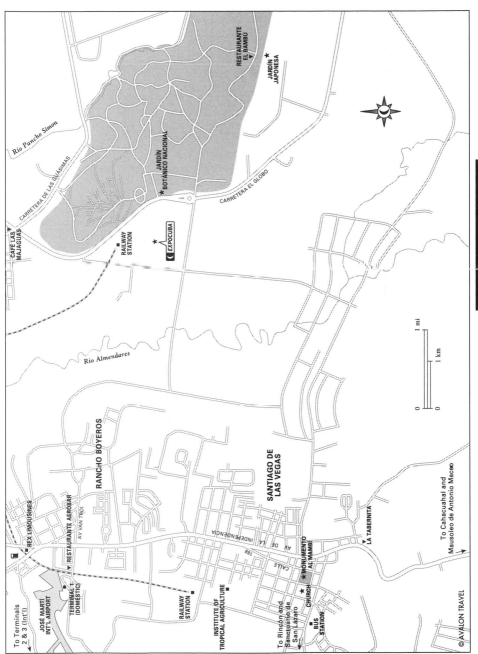

GREATER HAVANA

The garden consists mostly of wide pastures planted with copses divided by Cuban ecosystems and by regions of the tropical world (from coastal thicket to Oriental humid forest). The geographic center contains a fascinating variety of palm trees from around the world. There is even an "archaic forest" containing species such as *Microcyca calocom,* Cuba's cork palm. The highlight is the **Jardín Japonés** (Japanese garden) landscaped with tiered cascades, fountains, and a jade-green lake full of koi. The **Invernáculo Rincón Eckman** is a massive greenhouse named after Erik Leonard Eckman (1883–1931), who documented Cuban flora between 1914 and 1924. It is laid out as a triptych: a cactus house; a room full of epiphytes, bromeliads, ferns, and insectivorous plants; and a room containing tropical mountain plants.

Club de Golf Habana

The Havana Golf Club (Carretera de Vento Km 8, Capdevila, Boyeros, tel. 07/649-8918, ext 111) is hidden east of Avenida de la Independencia in the industrial-residential area called Capdevila, about 20 kilometers south of Havana. The "Diplo Golf Course" was opened as the Rover's Athletic Club in 1948 by the British community and maintained by the British Embassy until given to the Cuban government in 1980. Of four courses in Havana in 1959, this is the only one remaining. The nine-hole course has 18 tees positioned for play to both sides of the fairway. The course, a "woody layout" that is compared to Pinehurst in North Carolina, starts off badly, but the fifth and sixth holes are described as "well-designed holes that could hold their own on almost any course of the world." "Golfito" (as the locals know it) has a minimally stocked pro shop, five tennis courts, a swimming pool, and two restaurants. Membership costs CUC70 plus CUC45 monthly. A round costs nonmembers CUC20 for nine holes (CUC30 for 18). You can rent clubs for CUC10. Caddies cost CUC6.

Food

Cubans travel from Havana to dine at **(Las Ruinas** (Calle 100 y Cortina, tel. 07/57-8286; Tues.–Fri. noon–8 P.M., Sat.–Sun. 10 A.M.–10 P.M.) in Parque Lenin. Looking like something Frank Lloyd Wright might have conceived, it was designed in concrete and encases the ruins of an old sugar mill. It serves continental and *criollo* cuisine (lobster bellevue is a specialty, CUC20) described by readers as both "reminiscent of school dinners" and "the best in Havana." I enjoyed a tasty shrimp enchilada (CUC12).

Parque Lenin has several other basic restaurants and snack bars of mediocre quality, including **El Dragon,** serving quasi-Chinese fare.

The **(Restaurante El Bambú** (tel. 07/54-4106; Tues.–Sun. noon–5 P.M.), overlooking the Japanese garden in the Jardín Botánico Nacional, bills itself as an *eco-restorán* and serves vegetables—beetroot, cassava, pumpkin, spinach, taro, and more—grown right there in the garden. I recommend the *fufo* (mashed boiled banana with garlic), and eggplant cooked in cheese sauce. You're permitted free refills. Locals and foreign students with ID are charged 40 pesos for a meal; other foreigners pay CUC14 for an all-you-can-eat buffet. The restaurant is often booked solid. You can reserve a table by calling ahead.

Southern Havana Province

The landscape of southern Havana Province is intensively farmed. The area is modestly wealthy, with houses that are comfortable by Cuban standards (there are few rustic *bohíos*) and plenty of cars further hint at the regional prosperity. The southern coast is depressingly opposite and melancholic in the extreme.

A network of roads fans out south from Havana, crisscrossed by minor roads that form an unfathomable labyrinth linking small towns of mostly unpretentious appeal. The following are exceptions, worth a day's journey.

SAN ANTONIO DE LOS BAÑOS

This small town (pop. 39,000), founded in 1775 on the banks of the Río Ariguanabo, 30 kilometers southwest of Havana, is appealing, despite its ramshackle state. There is considerable charm to its tiny triangular plaza, ocher church (Calles 66 y 41), and streets lined with colonnaded arcades. The prestigious **Escuela Internacional de Cine y Televisión** (International Cinema and Television School, Carretera Villa Nueva Km 4.5, tel. 0650/38-3152), sponsored by the New Latin American Cinema Foundation, is here, presided over by the great Colombian writer Gabriel García Márquez. The school trains cinema artists from developing nations.

The town boasts a **Museo Municipal** (Calle 66 #4113, e/ 41 y 43, tel. 0650/38-2539, Tues.–Sat. 10 A.M.–6 P.M., Sun. 9 A.M.–noon; free) and a **Casa Bienal del Humor** (aka Museo del Humor, Calle 60 #4116, esq. 45, tel. 0650/38-2817; Tues.–Sat. 10 A.M.–5 P.M., Sun. 9 A.M.–1 P.M.; CUC2) in a beautiful colonial home. The humor museum opened in 1979, when the city hosted the first **Humor Bienal Internacional,** the International Humor Festival, which draws some of the best cartoonists from around the world.

A freeway—the Autopista a San Antonio—links San Antonio with Havana. Midway between the two cities, you'll pass the

Universidad de las Ciencias Informáticas, Cuba's university dedicated to making the country a world power in software technology. On the north side is the gray marble **Memorial al Soldado Internacionalista Soviético,** with an eternal flame dedicated to Soviet military personnel who died in combat.

Accommodations and Food

Hotel Las Yagrumas (Calle 40 y Final Autopista, tel. 0650/38-4460, reservas@yagrumas.isazul.tur.cu; CUC30 s, CUC40 d) overlooks the banks of the Río Ariguanabo one kilometer northeast of town on the Havana road. This colonial-style, red-tile, two-story property has 120 pleasantly decorated air-conditioned rooms with satellite TVs. It has two grills, a café, pool, tennis courts, squash courts, game room, and tour desk. Bicycle and boat rentals, plus boat excursions on the river, are offered. (Islazul.)

The hotel has a good restaurant. Otherwise head to **Tabera del Tío Cabrera** (Calle 56 #3910, e/ 39 y 41; Mon.–Fri. 2–5 P.M., Sat.– Sun. 2 P.M.–1 A.M.), serving *criollo* dishes and hosting an open-air cabaret.

Transportation

Buses serve San Antonio de los Baños from Calle Apodaca, e/ Agramonte y Avenida de Bélgica, Habana Vieja, and arrive or depart San Antonio at the **Terminal de Ómnibus** (Av. 55, tel. 0650/38-2737). Trains serve San Antonio de los Baños from the Estación Tulipán, in Nuevo Vedado, Havana, at 10:05 A.M. and 4:25 and 8:30 P.M. (CUC1.50), returning from San Antonio at 5:35 A.M. and 1:55 and 6:15 P.M.

BATABANÓ

This funky town (pop. 15,000) 51 kilometers due south of Havana was one of the original seven cities, founded in 1515 by Pánfilo de Narváez and named San Cristóbal de la Habana. The settlers lasted only four years before uprooting and establishing a new city

Memorial al Soldado Internacionalista Soviético

on the north coast—today's Havana. Batabanó is surrounded by ugly dormitories for agricultural field hands.

About three kilometers south of Batabanó is **Surgidero de Batabanó,** a rundown place of ramshackle wooden houses, of significance only as the port town from which catamarans depart for Isla de la Juventud. There are no accommodations, so plan your arrival and departure accordingly.

Getting There and Away

A bus to Batabanó's ferry terminal departs Havana's Terminal de Ómnibus (Av. de Rancho Boyeros, esq. 19 de Mayo, Plaza de la Revolución) at 8 A.M. Buy your tickets (CUC2.10) at the kiosk marked "NCC," between gates 9 and 10, open Monday–Friday 8 A.M.–noon and Saturday 8–11 A.M. for advance sales (you pay for the catamaran journey separately in Surgidero, however). You must show your passport when buying the ticket. The journey takes 90 minutes.

A train serves Surgidero de Batabanó from Havana's Estación 19 de Noviembre (Calle Tulipán and Hidalgo, tel. 07/881-4431 or 881-3642) at 5 P.M. (CUC1.80). The return train to Havana departs Surgidero at 5:25 A.M. from the rail station at the end of Calle 68.

There's a Cupet gas station in Batabanó, at the junction of Calle 64 (the main street) and Avenida 73.

Southeastern Suburbs

The Carretera Central (Rt. 2-N1) runs southeast through the Havana suburbs of San Francisco de Paula and Cotorro and, beyond, the rolling hills of the **Alturas de Habana-Matanzas** via the provincial town of Madruga. It's a scenic route to the city of Matanzas.

The Autopista (Rt. A-1) also runs southeast from Havana ruler-straight to the border with Matanzas Province, where it continues as far as Sancti Spíritus. It's wide, fast, and devoid of traffic. However, watch for tractors, ox-carts, and even cattle crossing the freeway, which runs parallel to and north of the old Carretera Central (Rt. 2-N1), skirting the towns and villages that line the old road.

SAN MIGUEL DEL PADRÓN

The *municipio* of San Miguel del Padrón, which extends southeast of Habana Vieja, is mostly residential, with ugly modern factory areas in the lowlands by the harbor and timeworn colonial housing on the hills south of town.

The region is accessed from the Vía Blanca or (parallel to it) Calzada de Luyano via the Carretera Central (Calzada de Güines), which ascends to the quintessential colonial village of San Francisco de Paula, on the city's outskirts, 12.5 kilometers south of Habana Vieja.

En route, you pass through the suburb of Luyano, where Cubans come to throw coins (the money goes to pay for the indigent) into the **Fuente de la Virgen del Camino** (Virgin of the Way), a fountain by acclaimed sculptor Rita Longa at the junction of Calzada de Luyano and Carretera Central. Two blocks east is the **Monumento a Doña Leonor Pérez** (Balear, esq. Leonor Pérez), dedicated to José Martí's mother. The patinated bronze figure sits in a dignified pose atop a marble pedestal. Bas-reliefs depict key moments in Martí's life.

◀ Museo Ernest Hemingway

In 1939, Hemingway's third wife, Martha Gellhorn, saw and was struck by Finca Vigía

(Vigía y Steinhart, tel. 07/91-0809, mushem@ cubart.cult.cu; Wed.–Sun. 9 A.M.–4:30 P.M.; entrance CUC2, rainy days CUC1, guided tours CUC1, cameras CUC5), Lookout Farm, a one-story Spanish-colonial house built in 1887 and boasting a wonderful view of Havana. They rented it for US$100 a month. When Hemingway's first royalty check from *For Whom the Bell Tolls* arrived in 1940, he bought the house for US$18,500. In August 1961, his widow, Mary Welsh, was forced to sign papers handing over the home to the Castro government, along with its contents (see the sidebar *Ernest Hemingway and Cuba*). On July 21, 1994, on the 95th anniversary of Papa's birthday, Finca Vigía reopened its doors as a museum following nearly two years of repairs and remodeling. The house is preserved in suspended animation, just the way the great writer left it.

Bougainvilleas frame the gateway to the 20-acre hilltop estate. Mango trees and sumptuous jacarandas line the driveway leading up to the gleaming white house. No one is allowed inside—reasonably so, since every room can be viewed through the wide-open windows, and the temptation to pilfer priceless trinkets is thus reduced. Through the large windows, you can see trophies, firearms, bottles of spirits, old issues of *The Field, Spectator,* and *Sports Afield* strewn about, and more than 9,000 books and magazines, arranged the way he supposedly liked them, with no concern for authors or subjects. The dining-room table is set with cut crystal, as if guests were expected.

It is eerie being followed by countless eyes—those of the guides (one to each room) and those of the beasts that had found themselves in the crosshairs of Hemingway's hunting scope. "Don't know how a writer could write surrounded by so many dead animals," Graham Greene commented when he visited. There are bulls, too, everywhere bulls, including paintings by Joan Miró and Paul Klee; photographs and posters of bullfighting scenes; and a chalk plate of a bull's head, a gift from Picasso.

ERNEST HEMINGWAY AND CUBA

Ernest Hemingway first set out from Key West to wrestle marlin in the wide streaming currents off the Cuban coast in April 1932. The blue waters of the Gulf Stream, chock-full of billfish, brought him closer and closer until eventually, "succumbing to the other charms of Cuba, different from and more difficult to explain than the big fish in September," he settled on this island of sensual charm. Hemingway loved Cuba and lived there for the better part of 20 years. Once, when Hemingway was away from Cuba, he was asked what he worried about in his sleep. "My house in Cuba," he replied, referring to Finca Vigía, in the suburb of San Francisco de Paula, 12.5 kilometers southeast of Havana.

Walking Havana's streets you can still feel Hemingway's presence. It is easy to imagine the sun-bronzed writer driving in his brand-new Chrysler New Yorker convertible, white mane and beard haloed in tropical light, hoary chest showing beneath khaki shirt, en route for his daily sugarless double daiquiri with his friends.

THE CULT OF HEMINGWAY

Havana's marina is named for the prize-winning novelist. Hemingway's room in the Hotel Ambos Mundos and his former home, Finca Vigía, are preserved as museums. And his likeness adorns T-shirts and billboards. "We admire Hemingway because he understood the Cuban people; he supported us," a friend told me. "His friends were fishermen, jai alai players, bullfighters. He never related to high society," adds Evelio González, one of the guides at Finca Vigía.

Yet the cult of Hemingway is very real. The novelist's works are required reading in Cuban schools. His books are bestsellers. The Cuban understanding of Hemingway's "Cuban novels" is that they support a core tenet of Communist ideology – that humans are only fulfilled acting in a "socialist" context for a moral purpose, not individualistically. (Many of Hemingway's novels appear to condemn economic and political injustices.) "All the works of Hemingway are a defense of human rights," claims Castro, who knows Papa's novels in depth and once claimed that *For Whom the Bell Tolls*, Hemingway's fictional account of the Spanish Civil War, inspired his guerrilla tactics. Castro has said the reason he admires Hemingway so much is that he envies the adventures he had. The two headstrong fellows met only once, during the 10th Annual Ernest Hemingway Billfish Tournament in May 1960. As sponsor and judge of the competition, Hemingway invited Cuba's youthful new leader as his guest of honor. Castro was to present the winner's trophy; instead, he hooked the biggest marlin and won the prize for himself. Hemingway surrendered the trophy to a beaming Fidel. They never met again.

With the Cold War and the United States' break with Cuba, Hemingway had to choose. Not being able to return to Cuba contributed to Hemingway's depression, says his son Patrick: "He really loved Cuba, and I think it was a great shock to him at his age to have to choose

---

Here is where Hemingway wrote *Islands in the Stream, Across the River and into the Trees, A Moveable Feast,* and *The Old Man and the Sea.* The four-story tower next to the house was built at his fourth wife's prompting so that he could write undisturbed. Hemingway disliked the tower and continued writing amid the comings and goings of the house, surrounded by papers, shirtless, in Bermuda shorts, with any of 60 cats at his feet as he stood barefoot on the hide of a kudu.

Hemingway's legendary cabin cruiser, the *Pilar,* is poised beneath a wooden pavilion on the former tennis court, shaded by bamboo and royal palms. Nearby are the swimming pool where Ava Gardner swam naked, and the graves of four of the novelist's favorite dogs.

Alas, the wooden home is falling apart. In 2004, a restoration was initiated, although the Bush administration denied U.S. preservationists a license to travel to Cuba. For more

between his country, which was the United States, and his home, which was Cuba."

PAPA AND THE REVOLUTION

There has been a great deal of speculation about Hemingway's attitude toward the Cuban Revolution. Cuba, of course, attempts to portray him as sympathetic, not least because Hemingway's Cuban novels are full of images of prerevolutionary terror and destitution. "There is an absolutely murderous tyranny that extends over every little village in the country," he wrote in *Islands in the Stream*.

Hemingway's widow, Mary Welsh, told the journalist Luis Báez that "Hemingway was always in favor of the Revolution." Another writer, Lisandro Otero, records Hemingway as saying, "Had I been a few years younger, I would have climbed the Sierra Maestra with Fidel Castro." And Papa was away from Cuba all of 1959, but he returned in 1960, recorded *New York Times* correspondent Herbert Matthews, "to show his sympathy and support for the Castro Revolution." Papa even used his legendary 38-foot sportfishing boat, the *Pilar*, to run arms for the rebel army, claimed Gregorio Fuentes, the weatherbeaten sailor-guardian of the *Pilar* for 23 years. Welsh claims, however, to have been on board when Hemingway dumped his stash of sporting guns and ammunition into the sea so that neither side would get them.

Hemingway's enigmatic farewell comment as he departed the island in 1960 is illuminating: "*Vamos a ganar. Nosotros los cubanos vamos a ganar.* [We are going to win. We Cu-

bans are going to win.] I'm not a Yankee, you know." Before leaving Cuba, however, Hemingway expressed hope that the Revolution would not become Communist, claims writer Claudia Lightfoot. Prophetically, in *Islands in the Stream*, a character says: "The Cubans... double cross each other. They sell each other out. They got what they deserve. The hell with their revolutions."

FINCA VIGÍA'S FATE

After Hemingway's death, Finca Vigía was seized by the Castro government, though the writer had willed the property to his fourth wife, Mary Welsh. The Cuban government allowed her to remove 200 pounds of papers, but insisted that most of their home's contents remain untouched, including 3,000 letters and documents, 3,000 photographs, and 9,000 books... all kept secreted in the humid basement, where they have since been allowed to deteriorate to the point of near ruin. Only in 2002 was this invaluable resource opened to scholars.

In his will, the author left his sportfishing vessel, the *Pilar*, to Gregorio Fuentes (the former skipper couldn't afford its upkeep and it, too, became the property of the government). Meanwhile, Hemingway's sleek black 1955 Chrysler New Yorker escaped and apparently passed into the hands of Augustín Nuñez Gutiérrez, a Cuban policeman, according to writer Joann Biondi. Later, Nuñez hid the car and hopped on a raft for Miami. Popular legend says the car's whereabouts are still a mystery and that the Chrysler still awaits discovery.

information, visit www.hemingwaypreservationfoundation.org.

Getting There: The M7 *camello* metrobus departs from Industria, e/ Dragones y Avenida Simón Bolívar, Parque de la Fraternidad, in Habana Vieja. Bus #404 departs from Avenida de Bélgica (Monserrate) and Dragones. Both travel via San Francisco de Paula.

Paradiso: Promotora de Viajes Culturales (Calle 19 #560, esq. C, Vedado, Havana, tel.

07/832-6928, fax 07/33-3921, paradis@paradiso.artex.com.cu) offers excursions from Havana.

SANTA MARÍA DEL ROSARIO

This charming colonial village surrounded by palm-studded farmland, 20 kilometers south of Parque Central, is in the *municipio* of Cotorro, about five kilometers southeast of San Francisco de Paula, from which it is divided by the *circunvalación*.

The village was founded in 1732 by José

Bayona y Chacón, the Conde (Count) de Casa Bayona, who formed the subject of the movie *La última cena* (*The Last Supper*, 1976), by Tomás Gutiérrez Alea. The town, which was an important spa in colonial days, boasts a number of 18th- and 19th-century buildings centered on **Plaza Mayor,** the main square, fronted by the **Casa del Conde Bayona** (Calle 33 #2404, esq. 24, tel. 07/682-3510; daily noon–10 P.M.), the count's former home, comprising three adjacent structures complete with coach house. Part of the home is now occupied by a bar with snacks.

Curative waters have been tapped at **Balneario de Santa María del Rosario** (Calle 30, esq. Final, tel. 07/682-2734; Mon.–Fri. 8 A.M.–4 P.M.), a near-derelict mineral spa; it's about 400 meters southeast of the church. Behind it rises **Loma La Cruz** (Hill of the Cross), named for the large cross erected by the count to honor those killed in a slave rebellion. There is a fine view of the countryside from the hillcrest.

The **Casa de la Cultura** (Calle 33 #202, esq. 24, tel. 07/682-4259) hosts a *peña* with local musicians each Sunday at 8:30 P.M. Note the intriguing mural by the world-renowned Cuban artist Manuel Mendive, who lives in Luyano.

Getting There: Santa María is served by bus #97 from Guanabacoa, or take the M7 from Parque de la Fraternidad to Cotorro, then catch the #97.

◖ Iglesia de Santa María del Rosario

The main reason to visit the village is to view this baroque church (Calle 24, e/ 31 y 33, tel. 07/682-2183; Tues.–Sat. 8 A.M.–noon, Sun. 3:30–6 P.M.), dominating the plaza. One of the nation's finest, this national monument is colloquially called the Catedral del Campo de Cuba (Cathedral of the Fields of Cuba). The highlight is the spectacular baroque altar of cedar dripping with gold leaf, and the resplendent carved ceiling of indigo, plus four priceless art pieces by José Nicolás de Escalera. Mass is Sunday at 5 P.M.

Finca Alcona

This state-run farm 17 kilometers south of Havana, at the village of Las Guasimas, on the Carretera de Managua outside the village of Managua, raises *gallos* (cockerels) for combat and export (US$150–1,000 apiece), and hosts cockfights in the official *valla*, or ring. A grand **Feria de Gallos de Lidia** (Cockfight Fair) is held in early June. The restaurant features musicians performing popular campesino songs.

The easiest route is to take the Carretera Central to Cuatro Caminos, then turn west on the Carretera a Portugaletes for Managua, 15 kilometers west (midway to Santiago de las Vegas), then turn north and drive five kilometers to Las Guasimas. You can book an excursion through **Ecotur** (Santa Catalina y Boyeros, Havana, tel. 07/54-9855 or 07/57-7647, ecotur@teledata.get.tur.cu).

ESCALERAS DE JARUCO

These rolling hills rising east of the Autopista are popular among *habaneros* escaping the heat for walks and horseback rides. The hills are composed of limestone terraces denuded in places into rugged karst formations laced with caves. Take the turnoff for **Tapaste** from the Autopista, about 15 kilometers east of Havana.

Parque Escaleras de Jaruco (tel. 64/32665) is six kilometers west of Jaruco village and makes a scenic day trip, especially if you return via Playas del Este. It has basic cabins, a simple restaurant, a bar situated in a natural cavern, plus swimming pool and horseback riding and draws Cubans for weekend visits.

Habana del Este and Beyond

Beyond the tunnel under Havana harbor, you pass through a heavily policed toll booth (no toll is charged), beyond which the six-lane Vía Monumental freeway leads east to modern Ciudad Panamericano and, immediately beyond, the time-worn fishing village of Cojímar.

CIUDAD PANAMERICANO AND COJÍMAR

Ciudad Panamericano, three kilometers east of Havana, dates from the 1991 Pan-American Games when a high-rise village was built in hurried, jerry-rigged style to accommodate the athletes, spectators, and press. Several massive sports stadiums rise to each side of the Vía Monumental, most significantly the 55,000-seat **Estadio Panamericano** (Vía Monumental Km 4, Ciudad Panamericano, tel. 07/97-4140).

Cuban tour agencies promote stays at the Hotel Panamericano, but anyone who overnights here will find themselves cut off from Havana in a desultory place with no appeal whatsoever. Fortunately, you can walk to Cojímar, a far more interesting place to stay.

Cojímar

Modern Ciudad Panamericano merges eastward into this forlorn fishing village with a waterfront lined with weather-beaten cottages. Whitecaps are often whipped up in the bay, making the Cuban flag flutter above **Fuerte de Cojímar** (locally called El Torreón), a pocket-size fortress guarding the cove's entrance. It was here in 1762 that the English put ashore and marched on Havana to capture Cuba for King George III. The fortress, built in the 1760s to forestall another fiasco, is still in military hands, and you will be shooed away if you get too close.

Cojímar is best known as the place where Ernest Hemingway berthed his sportfishing boat, the *Pilar*. When Hemingway died, every

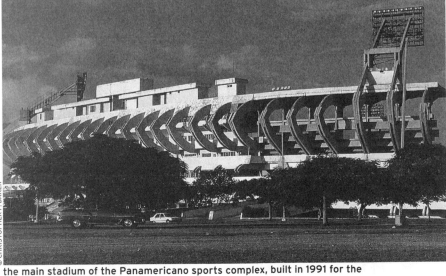

© CHRISTOPHER P. BAKER

the main stadium of the Panamericano sports complex, built in 1991 for the Pan-American Games

GREATER HAVANA

fisherman in the village apparently donated a brass fitting from his boat. The collection was melted down to create the bust of the author—**Monumento Ernest Hemingway**—that has stared out to sea since 1962 from within a columned rotunda at the base of El Torreón. A plaque reads: "Parque Ernest Hemingway. In grateful memory from the population of Cojímar to the immortal author of *Old Man and the Sea,* inaugurated July 21, 1962, on the 63rd anniversary of his birth."

After exploring, appease your hunger with fisherman's soup and paella at Hemingway's favorite restaurant, **La Terraza** (Calle 152 #161, esq. Candelaria, tel. 07/55-9232). The gleaming mahogany bar at the front, accepting dollars only, gets few locals. You sense that Papa could stroll in at any moment. His favorite corner table is still there. He is there, too, patinated in bronze atop a pedestal, and adorning the walls in black and white, sharing a laugh with Fidel.

Cojímar was most famous as the residence of Gregorio Fuentes, Hemingway's former skipper and friend, and the model for "Antonio" in *Islands in the Stream,* and—albeit more contentiously—for Santiago, the fisherman cursed by *salao* (the worst form of bad luck) in *The Old Man and the Sea.* Fuentes, born in 1897, died in 2002 at the grand old age of 104. From 1938 until Hemingway's death, Fuentes was in charge of the writer's sportfishing boat, the *Pilar.* Cojímar's homegrown hero is venerated by Cubans. The old man, who lived at Calle 98 #209, esq. 3D, could often be found regaling travelers in La Terraza, where you can toast to his memory with a turquoise cocktail—Coctel Fuentes.

Accommodations

Hotel Islazul Panamericano (Calle A y Av. Central, tel. 07/95-1001, fax 07/95-1021; CUC35 s, CUC54 d low season; CUC51 s, CUC58 d high season) is popular with budget-tour operators, but despite a refurbishing it offers nothing but regret for tourists. It has a swimming pool (popular with Cubans on

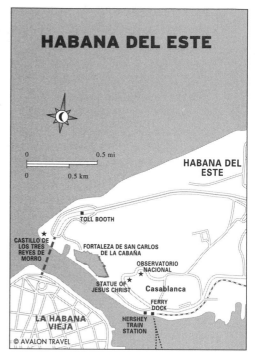

weekends), gym, sauna, car and moped rental, and tourism bureau. **Aparthotel Islazul Costazul** (tel. 07/95-0763, fax 07/95-4104) is part of the hotel complex and offers 475 meagerly furnished two- and three-bedroom apartments. (Islazul.)

In Cojímar, **Casa Hostal Marlins** (Calle Real #128A, e/ Santo Domingo y Chacón, tel. 07/65-3261, cell 891-4899; CUC20-25) has a nice, independent air-conditioned apartment upstairs with kitchenette, TV, an enclosed dining patio, and modern bathroom. A tight spiral staircase leads to a roof terrace for sunning.

Uphill, inland, **Villa Lennon** (Calle Los Pinos #302, e/ 27 y 28, tel. 07/65-0557; CUC20) is a handsome house where hosts Sonia and Joaquín have an independent apartment with a small lounge and kitchen, plus private bath with hot water. You can use the family TV lounge. Cater-corner, **Casa**

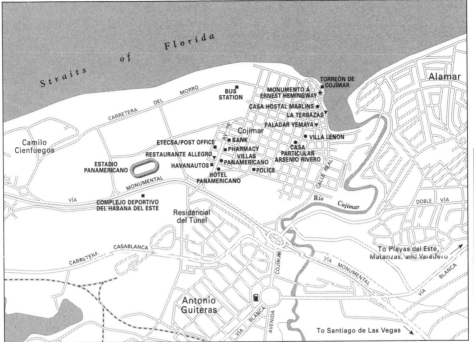

Particular Arsenio Rivas (Calle 27 #98, e/ Maceo y Los Pinos, tel. 07/65-2962; CUC20) has a pleasant, cross-ventilated, air-conditioned upstairs apartment with modern furnishings, a small kitchen, and large modern bathroom with hot water (but no toilet seat) and a terrace shaded by an arbor.

Food

Several uninspired restaurants line Avenida 78 (Paseo Panamericano), the main boulevard in Ciudad Panamericano. The best is **Restaurante Allegro** (Av. 78, e/ 5C y 5D), serving pizzas and Italian dishes.

Far better is 🌙 **La Terraza** (Calle Real #161, esq. Candelaria, tel. 07/93-9232; 10:30 A.M.–11 P.M. daily), Ernest Hemingway's old haunt in Cojímar, where the seafood is good, with a wide-ranging menu that includes paella (CUC6–12), pickled shrimp (CUC6.50), oyster cocktail (CUC2.95), and sautéed calamari (CUC6.15).

Services

Services along Avenida 78 in Ciudad Panamericano include a bank (esq. Calle 5), Cadeca exchange bureau (esq. 5D), post office (e/ 5 y 3), *telecorreo* (esq. 5C), international pharmacy (e/ 7 y 5D), and medical center (esq. 5D).

The **Farmacia Internacional** (tel. 07/95-1157) is at Villa Panamericana.

Getting There and Around

Heading east from Havana on the Vía Monumental, take the first exit marked Cojímar and cross over the freeway to reach Ciudad Panamericano. For Cojímar, take the *second* exit off the freeway.

Metrobus (*camello*) M1 departs the Prado, opposite the Capitolio Nacional, in Habana Vieja, and runs along the Vía Monumental to Ciudad Panamericano. You can also catch it at the corner of Avenida de los Presidentes y

ALAMAR

Immediately east of Cojímar, you'll pass a dormitory city long prized by Fidel Castro as an example of the achievements of socialism. In April 1959, Alamar (pop. 100,000) emerged on the drawing board as the first revolutionary housing scheme in postrevolutionary Cuba. The initial plan for 10,000 people in 4- to 11-story prefabricated concrete apartment blocks was to be fully self-contained in self-sufficient "super-blocks." The sea of concrete high-rise complexes (extending east to the adjacent town of Celimar) was built with shoddy materials by microbrigades of untrained "volunteer" workers borrowed from their normal jobs. Castro was a regular visitor during the early years of construction; Alamar was a matter of pride and joy for him.

Though Cuban planners came to acknowledge its isolating nature and overwhelming deficiencies (the plumbing came from the Soviet Union, the wiring from China, the stoves from North Korea; there were no spare parts budgeted for upkeep), Alamar was vastly expanded beginning in 1976 and today covers four square miles. Today it is a virtual slum. Refuse litters the potholed roads, and the roadside parks are untended. There are no jobs here, either, and few stores, nor proper transportation, and no logic to the maze of streets or to the addresses of buildings, so that finding your way around is a study in maddening frustration.

27 in Vedado. Buses #195 and 265 also run to Ciudad Panamericano.

Bus #58 departs Avenida Rancho Boyeros and Bruzón, Plaza de la Revolución, for Cojímar; you can also catch it at the bottom of the Prado, at the junction with Avenida de los Estudiantes (10 centavos). The return bus departs Cojímar from Calle 99 y 3A.

A free shuttle departs the Hotel Panamericano for Havana four times daily.

Havanautos (tel. 07/95-1093), outside the Hotel Panamericano, rents cars and scooters, as does **Transtur** (tel. 07/95-1235), in Villa Panamericana.

◖ PLAYAS DEL ESTE

Cubans are great beachgoers, and nowhere on the island proves the case more than the Playas del Este. On hot summer weekends all of Havana seems to come down to the beach to meet friends, tan their bodies, play soccer or volleyball, and flirt.

The beaches of Playas del Este stretch unbroken for six kilometers east–west. They are divided by name. A nearly constant tropical breeze is usually strong enough to conjure surf from the warm turquoise seas—a perfect scenario for lazing, with occasional breaks for grilled fish or fried chicken from thatch-roofed *ranchitas*, where you can eat practically with your feet in the water.

Playas del Este is pushed as a hot destination for foreign tourists and, in the mid-1990s, enjoyed some success, bringing tourists (predominantly Italian and male) and Cubans (predominantly young and female) together for rendezvous under *palapas* and palms. Then a police crackdown (to temper the foreigner–Cuban coupling) initiated in early 1999 knocked the wind clear out of Playas del Este's sails. By international standards, it's a nonstarter other than for a day visit.

Care should always be taken when swimming: The waves can be powerful and riptides are common. In winter, the seas are full of jellyfish that locals call *agua mala*. The beaches also get terribly littered. Yuck!

When driving from Havana via the Vía Monumental, it's easy to miss the turn-off, one kilometer east of the second (easternmost) turnoff for Cojímar, where the Vía Monumental splits awkwardly. Take the narrow Vía Blanca exit to the left to reach Playas del Este; the main Vía Monumental swings south (you'll end up circling Havana on the *circunvalación*).

Playa Bacuranao

This small horseshoe cove with a white-sand

beach lies immediately east of Alamar and is popular on weekends with residents of Alamar escaping city life for a day by the sea in the sun. The wreck of an 18th-century galleon lies just off the tiny beach. Coral grows abundantly on both sides of the bay, so if you have snorkeling gear, bring it. Food and beverages are available at Villa Islazul Bacuranao (see *Accommodations*).

Getting There: Buses #62 and 162 pass by Bacuranao, departing from Parque Central in Havana.

Tarará

Beyond Alamar, you'll cross the Río Tarará and pass Tarará, a villa resort hidden at the far western end of Playas del Este, at Vía Blanca Km 19. Before the Special Period, when it was called Campamento de Pioneros José Martí, it was used by Cuban schoolchildren, who combined study with beachside pleasures. Here, too, several thousand young victims of the 1988 Chernobyl nuclear disaster in the Ukraine have been treated free of charge. (It was here also that Castro operated his secret government in the early stage of the Revolution. Che Guevara was convalescing here after his debilitating years of guerrilla warfare in the Sierra Maestra, and the location away from Havana proved perfect for secret meetings to shape Cuba's future while Castro played puppeteer to the official democratic government of President Urrutia.)

Today it is a tourist villa complex, though the beaches are open to Cubans. To the west is a delightful pocket-size beach that forms a spit at the rivermouth; it has a volleyball court and shady *palapas,* plus a restaurant and marina with water sports. (The rivermouth channel is renowned for its coral, large groupers, and schools of snappers—great for snorkeling and scuba diving.) The main beach, **Playa Mégano,** lies further east. It, too, has a sand volleyball court, shade umbrellas, and lounge chairs, and is served by shops and the **Casa Club Cubanacán** complex, with a swimming pool with grill (entrance CUC5, or CUC20 including all

massage on the beach at Playas del Este

you can eat plus six beers) and an elegant restaurant.

Entry is free, but you must show ID—bring your passport in case the occasionally muleminded *custodios* get a case of *burro-cracía.*

Santa María del Mar

Playa Mégano extends east from Tarará and merges into Playa Santa María del Mar, the broadest and most beautiful swathe, with light golden sand shelving into stunning aquamarine and turquoise waters. The beaches are palm-shaded and studded with shade umbrellas. Most of Playas del Este's tourist facilities are here, including bars and water sports, plus a fistful of tourist hotels. In 2005 it was looking more deteriorated than ever, although the beaches are fabulous.

Playa Santa María runs east for about three kilometers to the mouth of the Río Itabo—a popular bathing spot for Cuban families. A large mangrove swamp centered on **Laguna Itabo** extends inland from the mouth of the

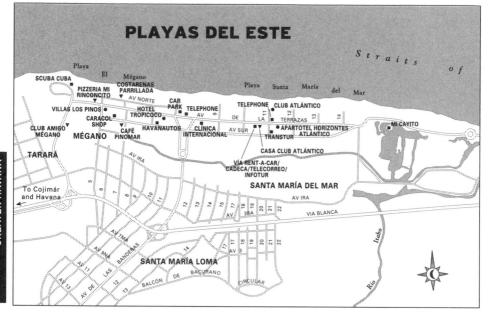

river, where waterfowl can be admired. A coral reef runs offshore at a depth of no more than 20 feet, with lots of brain, elkhorn, and staghorn formations.

Boca Ciega and Guanabo

Beautiful Playa Boca Ciega begins east of the Río Itabo estuary and is popular with Cuban families, many of whom choose to rent simple *cabinas* in the residential and rental complex called Boca Ciega. Playa Boca Ciega merges eastward into Playa Guanabo, the least-attractive beach, but running for several kilometers along the shorefront of Guanabo, a Cuban village with many plantation-style wooden homes. It is the only village at Playas del Este.

For grand views up and down the beaches, head inland of Guanabo to **Mirador de Bellomonte,** where a café and bar (Vía Blanca Km 24.5, tel. 07/96-3431; daily 2 P.M.–2 A.M.) atop the Altura Bellomonte offers fine vistas.

Entertainment

The **Casa Club Cubanacán** (Av. de Terrazas; 10 A.M.–10 P.M. daily) has a pool hall and dance club.

Cabaret Guanimar (3ra Av. y Calle 468; Fri.–Sun. 11 P.M.–3 A.M.; CUC3) has a simple *cabaret espectáculo* followed by a disco. It draws an unsophisticated local crowd.

Recreation

Outlets on the beach rent watercraft (CUC15 for 15 minutes), Hobie-Cats (CUC20 per hour), and beach chairs and lounge chairs (CUC2 per day). **Mi Cayito** rents kayaks and water bikes on the lagoon.

Horses can be rented on the beach in front of Hotel Tropicoco, and are a specialty of **Rancho Mi Hacienda Guanabito** (Calzada de Jústiz, Km 4, Guanabo, tel. 07/96-4711; daily 9 A.M.–8 P.M.), four kilometers inland of Guanabo. This *finca de recreo* (dude ranch) raises animals and features bloodless cockfights (the birds' spurs are covered to prevent them from seriously hurting each other).

Scuba diving is available from the water sports stand on the beach in front of the Hotel Tropicoco, and at **Caribbean Diving Center**

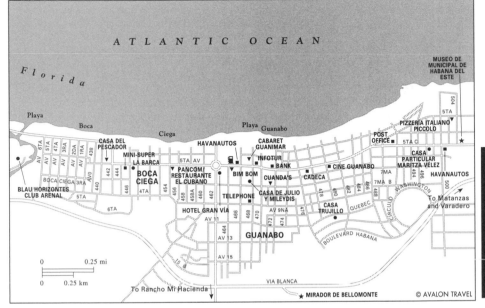

(Casa 4, Tarará, tel. 07/96-0201, fax 07/97-1313, www.caribscuba.com) in Tarará.

Marina Tarará (tel. 07/97-1510 or 07/97-1462, fax 07/97-1499, channel VHF 77 or 108, marina@mit.tur.cu), at the Tarará rivermouth, has 50 berths with water and electricity hook-ups, plus diesel and gas. You can rent yachts, pedal boats are available, and sportfishing charters are offered. Boat excursions include six-hour "seafaris" at 9:30 A.M., featuring fishing, snorkeling, and lunch (CUC55 based on a minimum of four passengers); and a three-hour nocturnal cruise.

Accommodations

Casas Particulares: All the *casas particulares* are located in Guanabo.

One of the best options is ◖ **Casa de Julio y Mileydis** (Calle 468 #512, e/ 5ta y 7ma, Guanabo, tel. 07/96-0100; CUC30–35). Set in a beautiful garden, this air-conditioned apartment is equipped for people with disabilities and has a security box, large lounge with a kitchen, and a small and simply furnished

bedroom. It has a small pool for children. The owners are a delight.

Casa Maritza Vélez (Calle 5D #49610, e/ 496 y 498, Guanabo, tel. 07/96-4389; CUC30–35) is a handsome 1950s house with a beautiful interior in a well-maintained garden. It has two air-conditioned rooms with modern furnishings, old metal-frame beds, soothing pastel colors, and modern tiled bathrooms (but no toilet seats).

Casa Trujillo (Av. Quebec #55, e/ 478 y 482, Guanabo, tel. 07/96-3325, www.cubanasol.com/casatrujillo.htm; CUC30–35) is a two-story family unit with one spacious air-conditioned bedroom, a TV lounge, and a modern kitchen to which guests have access. Miriam Trujillo and Alberto Mendes, your hosts, are fluent in Spanish, French, and English.

Rental Villas: In Boca Ciega, Islazul rents *cabinas,* almost exclusively to Cubans. Few meet international standards.

Hotels: The **Hotel Gran Vía** (Av. 5ta, e/ 502 y 504, tel. 07/96-4300; CUC18 s, CUC21 d low season; CUC22 s, CUC26 d high season) is a simple option catering mostly to Cubans but with three basically furnished rooms for foreigners.

The **Villa Islazul Bacuranao** (Vía Blanca Km 15.5, tel. 07/65-7645, reservas@bacuranao.co.cu; one-bedroom units CUC23 s, CUC25 d low season, CUC26 s, CUC30 d high season; two-bedroom units CUC33 s, CUC38 d low season, CUC38 s, CUC44 d high season) has 52 rooms in air-conditioned, modestly furnished cabanas, each with satellite TV and private bath. Facilities include a restaurant, café, snack bar, swimming pool, and nightly entertainment.

Villas Marina Tarará (Calle 9na, esq. 14, Villa Tarará, tel. 07/97-1462, fax 07/97-1333, comercial@tarara.mit.tur.cu; CUC79 low season, CUC106 high season 2–3 bedrooms; CUC105 low season, CUC132 high season 4–5 bedrooms), run by Cubanacán, offers 94 villas—*casas confort*—with from two to five bedrooms, many with swimming pools. All have satellite TV, radio, telephone, safe, kitchen with fridge, and private parking. No Cuban guests are allowed, and no guests may stay overnight without authority of the management, which even requires a list of guests attending "a social gathering." A grocery, laundry, restaurants, and pharmacy are on-site.

In Santa María, the **Club Amigo Mégano** (Av. de las Terrazas, tel. 07/97-1610, fax 07/97-1624, vmegano@meganohor.tur.cu; CUC32 s, CUC45 d low season, CUC38 s, CUC54 d high season, including breakfast), at the far west end of Playas del Este, is a 10-minute walk from the beach. The 103 air-conditioned cabins are simple yet appealing, with tile floors, bamboo furnishings, tiny satellite TV, small tiled baths with showers, and plate-glass doors opening to verandas. It has a pool. (Cubanacán.)

Hotel Horizontes Tropicoco (Av. de las Terrazas, e/ 5 y 7, tel. 07/97-1371, fax 07/97-1389, recepcion@htropicoco.hor.tur.cu; CUC45 s, CUC75 d low season; CUC55 s, CUC85 d high season) is the most popular place in town. The five-story building was recently renovated and has 188 air-conditioned rooms with simple yet adequate decor and

bamboo furniture, plus telephone, radio, and modern bathrooms. Services include a pleasing restaurant, as well as a bar, tour desk, shops, post office, and car rental. (Cubanacán.)

Managed as an all-inclusive property by a Spanish hotel group, the **Blau Horizontes Club Arenal** (Lago de Boca Ciega, tel. 07/97-1272, fax 07/97-1287, www.bla-hotels.com; CUC70 s, CUC100 d standard low season, CUC 95 s, CUC150 d high season; CUC90 s, CUC120 d suite low season, CUC125 s, CUC190 d high season), in the midst of the lagoon between Playas Santa María del Mar and Boca Ciega, has 166 air-conditioned rooms in three categories. Rooms are spacious and eye-pleasing and have satellite TVs, hairdryers, minibars, and safes. They surround a massive pool with thatched restaurant and bar, and the staff tries hard to keep guests amused with *animaciónes*. But the overall effect is desultory, and the grounds are unkempt. (Cubanacán.)

The **Villas los Pinos** (Av. 4ta, tel. 07/97-1361, fax 07/97-1524, recepcion@pinos.gca.tur.cu; CUC120–220 low season; CUC160–250 high season) offers the most elegant option, with 27 two-, three-, and four-bedroom villas. Some appear a bit fuddy-duddy; others are impressive and up to international standards and have their own private pools. They all have TV, VCR, radio, telephone, and kitchen. Visitors are prohibited. (Gran Caribe.)

Food

Several thatched bars and eateries can be found on the beach. **Mi Casita de Coral,** 100 meters east of the Hotel Tropicoco, serves *criollo* fare 24 hours daily and has some appealing seafoods, including grilled fillet of fish (CUC5) plus spicy lobster enchiladas (CUC8). Likewise, **Casa Club Atlántico** (tel. 971344, ext. 178; 24 hours) is a pleasant airy restaurant offering spaghettis and pizzas, plus a chicken *oferta especial* (lunch special) for CUC2. **Parrillada Costarenas** (Av. Norte, esq. Av. de las Terrazas, tel. 07/97-1361; noon–6 P.M., daily) serves inexpensive grilled fare (CUC5) and offers seaviews from its air-conditioned beachside diner.

Restaurante Mi Cayito (Av. las Terrazas, tel. 07/97-1339; daily 10 A.M.–6 P.M.) is a pleasant thatched restaurant on a small island overhanging the mangroves of Laguna Itabo. It has the usual fare: grilled fish, shrimp, and lobster, but is grossly overpriced (CUC10–26).

In Guanabo, the best place by far is **C Paladar Italiano Piccolo** (5ta Av., e/ 502 y 504, tel. 07/96-4300; noon–midnight daily), a spacious private restaurant with riverstone walls with Greek murals. Run by Greek owners, it offers surprisingly tasty Mediterranean fare, including wood-fired pizzas, served with hearty salads at low prices (CUC5–10).

Giving Piccolo a run for its money is **Casa del Pescador** (5ta Av. #44005, esq. Calle 442, tel. 07/96-3653; noon– 11 P.M. daily), a Spanish-style *bodega* in Boca Ciega, with fishing nets hanging from the ceiling. The menu is huge. Fish dishes average CUC8, including shrimp and lobster. The house specialty is *escabeche* (CUC4).

Pan.Com (5ta Av., esq. 454, tel. 07/94-4061; noon–11 P.M. daily) is a modern, clean eatery in a red-brick building with a choice of airy patio or air-conditioned interior. It serves *criollo* dishes, plus sandwiches, omelettes, burgers, and tortillas.

For ice cream, head to **Bim-Bom,** a clean, modern, well-run operation serving various sundaes and 32 flavors of ice cream along the lines of Baskin-Robbins.

Services

Infotur (Av. Las Terrazas, e/ 11 y 12, tel. 07/97-1261; and 5ta-C Av., e/ 468 y 470, Guanabo, tel. 07/96-3841) tourist information offices offer meager assistance.

In Santa María, the **post office** (Av. de las Terrazas, e/ 10 y 11; 8 A.M.–1 P.M. Mon.–Sat.) is in Edificio Los Corales. In Boca Ciega, the **post office** is at 5ta Avenida and Calle 448; and in Guanabo at 5ta-C Avenida y 492.

The **Clínica Internacional** (Av. de las Terrazas, e/ 8 y 9, tel. 07/97-1032 or 07/96-1810; 24 hours) is 100 yards east of Hotel Tropicoco.

A **Bandec** is at 5ta Avenida, e/ 468 y 470 (tel. 07/96-3320), with a **Cadeca** exchange booth adjacent.

Getting There

Tarará is at Vía Blanca Km 17, 27 kilometers east of Havana. It is signed off the Vía Blanca, as is Playas del Este, with three exits farther east. A taxi will cost about CUC20.

Buses #62, 162, and 262 serve Playas del Este from Parque Central; bus #219 departs from the main bus terminal. Bus #400 serves Guanabo and departs from Parque Taya Piedra, at the junction of Manglar Arroyo and Almanbique, in the Atarés neighborhood.

Warning: If driving, beware the *punto de control* (police control) near Bacuranao. Keep your speed down to 50 kph or you *will* be pulled over and ticketed.

Getting Around

Havanautos has a car and scooter rental office in the parking lot of Hotel Tropicoco, and at 5ta Avenida y Calle 464 (tel. 07/96-3858) and Calle 500-A, e/ 5ta y 7ma (tel. 07/96-3845). **Transautos** (5ta Av., esq. 11), in Santa María, also rents cars. **Vía Rent-a-Car** (5ta Av., e/ 10 y 11, tel. 07/96-1152) is one block west.

SANTA CRUZ DEL NORTE

East of the Playas del Este, the northern shore is hemmed in by low hills. Precious oil lies deep underground, and you'll pass small oil derricks bobbing languidly atop the coral cliff tops. Beyond, Santa Cruz, some 30 kilometers east of Havana, is a ramshackle industrial town steeping in a miasma of photo-chemical fumes and fronted by badly polluted waters. Cuba's largest rum factory, **Fábrica Cubarón,** also known as Ronera Santa Cruz, is here, producing the famous Havana Club (founded in 1878) rums and scenting the air with its own heady aromas. No visits are permitted. The original factory, dating from 1919, stands down by the shore.

About four kilometers south of Santa Cruz and worth the detour is the community of Camilo Cienfuegos, formerly called Hershey

THE MAKING OF RUM

Christopher Columbus introduced sugarcane to Cuba in 1493. *Trapiches* (rudimentary ox-powered mills) squeezed *guarapo* from the cane, which was fermented and mixed with *miel de caña* (molasses), the dark-brown residue left after crystallized sugar has been processed from cane, to produce a crude type of "molasses wine."

The introduction of steam power (and of distilleries in the manufacturing process) in the early 1800s increased sugar production and permitted production of more-refined rum. Havana, Matanzas, Cárdenas, and Santiago de Cuba became major centers for the production of rum. Foremost among the many private companies was Bacardi, founded in Santiago de Cuba in 1868 by Don Facundo Bacardí. (Following the Revolution, the state seized the rum factories and the company today is active in anti-Castroite politics). About one dozen distilleries make about 60 brands of *ron* today.

Production involves fermentation, distillation, aging, and blending. Molasses is first fermented with yeast (which occurs naturally in sugarcane) to transform the sugar into ethanol. The fermented liquid is then heated with compressed vapor and then diluted with distilled water. It is distilled in copper vats to eliminate unpleasant flavors and then aged in oak barrels for one to 15 years. Distilled rums are clear. Darker rums gain their distinct color and flavor from caramels added during the aging process, or naturally from the tannins of the oak barrels. The resulting overproof rum is then diluted and bottled.

and built as a model town by the Hershey chocolate company, which owned the sugar mill now called **Central Camilo Cienfuegos.** Hershey's town had a baseball field, movie theater, an amusement park, the Hershey Hotel, and scores of wooden homes for workers. The facilities still stand, forming a kind of lived-in museum made more intriguing by the quaint trains that serve the town from Casablanca, north of Havana, and Matanzas. The mill closed in 2002 and is now in a derelict state. The Hershey train stops here between Havana and Matanzas. (See the sidebar *A Sugar of a Journey* in the *Matanzas* chapter.)

PLAYA JIBACOA

This beautiful beach, also known as **Playa Amarillo,** about four kilometers east of Santa Cruz, extends east of the Río Jibacoa for several kilometers. A smaller beach—**Playa Arroyo Bermejo**—lies tucked between cliffs at the mouth of the Río Jibacoa, about three kilometers east of Santa Cruz del Norte, bracketed by rocky headlands. Coral reefs lie close to shore, perfect for snorkeling and scuba diving.

Both beaches are popular with Cubans,

who are served by simple *campismos*—holidays camps that may be too basic for most foreign tastes. In time, the master plan for Jibacoa calls for 11 luxury hotels, two 18-hole championship golf courses, health spas, and time-share villas.

Puerto Escondido

About eight kilometers east of the Río Jibacoa, a road leads north to the small coastal village of Puerto Escondido, a "wonderfully cool inlet a few miles down the Cuban coast," wrote Ernest Hemingway, who arrived aboard the *Pilar* to escape the hot summer nights. The spectacular setting—within a wide bend of a deep ravine—is occupied today by **Cubanacán Naútica** (tel. 0692/96-1508, nauhab@cbcan. cyt.cu), offering windsurfing, waterskiing, and excursions by yacht and catamaran, plus diving (CUC25 one dive, CUC35 two dives), snorkeling (CUC10 for two hours), and deep-sea fishing (from CUC75).

Puente Bacunayagua

Camera at the ready? Then take a deep breath for your stop at this bridge, 106 kilometers from Havana and 10 kilometers east of Puerto Escondido (about 2 km after crossing the Havana–Matanzas provincial boundary; it's 14 km from here to Matanzas). The 313-meter-long bridge (the longest and highest—112 meters—in Cuba) spans the gorge of the Río Bacunayagua, which slices through the narrow coastal mountain chain. The Yumurí Valley rolls away to the south, fanning out spectacularly as if contrived for a travel magazine's double-page spread. The views are incredible.

The bridge is a favorite stop for tour buses, and there are facilities, including a bar and restaurant, on the west bank to cater to the hordes. A *mirador* atop the cliff above the bridge offers the best views. Police are usually stationed at either side of the bridge to catch speeding cars.

Accommodations and Food

Basic *campismos* line Playa Jibacoa. Most are restricted to Cubans, but foreigners are catered to at **Campismo Los Cocos** (tel. 0692/29-5231; reservations c/o Cubamar, 3ra Av., e/ 12 y Malecón, Havana, tel. 07/66-2523, fax 07/33-3111, www.cubamarviajes.cu; CUC18 s, CUC28 d low season; CUC19 s, CUC30 d high season), which has 20 small concrete *cabinas* for foreigners amid well-kept lawns. Painted in canary-yellow and deep-blue color schemes, they feature air-conditioning, fans, local TV, simple furnishings, kitchenettes, and modern bathrooms with hot water.

There's a swimming pool, video and games room, plus a restaurant serving mediocre fare. (Cubamar.)

Breezes Jibacoa (Vía Blanca Km 60, tel. 0692/85122, fax 0692/85150, www.superclub-scuba.com; per person CUC80 garden view, CUC94 ocean view, CUC125 suite low season; CUC230/245/265 peak season), run by the Jamaican all-inclusive chain SuperClubs, is a splendid four-star resort with a contemporary take on classical architecture. Its 250 spacious and tastefully decorated rooms and 10 suites center on a vast swimming pool. Facilities include five bars, two restaurants, a café, grill, gym, basketball and volleyball courts, beauty store, a souvenir store, a well-stocked humidor and rum store, plus massage, and a medical center. Reservations are required.

The handsome **Villa Loma Jibacoa** (tel. 0692/85316) was reserved for the exclusive use of Cuban military at last visit.

Getting There

Bus #669 departs Terminal La Coubre, on Desamparados in Habana Vieja, and travels to San Cruz del Norte, where you can catch a taxi or bus #126. Alternately, take a Havana–Matanzas bus and ask the driver to let you off. The Hershey Train departs Casablanca and stops at Jibacoa Pueblo, five kilometers from Jibacoa, and at the Arcos de Canasí station, three kilometers from El Abra, but it's a lonesome walk.

ESSENTIALS

U.S. Law and Travel to Cuba

It is a remarkable anomaly that there are political leaders in this government who believe that they contribute to increasing freedom in Cuba by restraining freedom at home.

– William Rogers, former U.S. Secretary of State

Most *yanquis* harbor the false impression that it's illegal for U.S. citizens to visit Cuba; it's not, it's merely illegal to spend money there (the U.S. Supreme Court has affirmed the constitutional right of unrestricted travel; thus the U.S. government invokes the 1916 Trading with the Enemy Act to prohibit travelers from *trading* with Cuba).

To visit Cuba legally you must either spend no money there, or qualify for a license issued by the U.S. Treasury Department in order to buy goods (such as a meal) or services (an airline ticket or hotel room). Except as specifically licensed by the Office of Foreign Assets Control (OFAC), payments of any kind in connection with travel to Cuba are prohibited, including prepaid tours to companies in third countries.

The regulations change frequently and are open to interpretation by OFAC staff.

© CHRISTOPHER P. BAKER

The Clinton administration eased restrictions. President George W. Bush backtracked with a vengeance, and even restricted Cuban-Americans to one visit every three years. In April 2009, President Barack Obama eased (but did not remove) restrictions for family travel by Cuban Americans (that month bipartisan bills were also introduced to Congress to end restrictions for *all* U.S. citizens and residents).

The regulations apply to U.S. citizens and permanent residents wherever they are located; all people and organizations physically in the United States (including airline passengers in transit); and all branches and subsidiaries of U.S. companies and organizations throughout the world.

To determine if you or your organization qualifies for a **general license** (which does not require prior authorization) or a **specific license** (which does require prior authorization), contact the Licensing Division, **Office of Foreign Asset Control** (U.S. Department of the Treasury, 1500 Pennsylvania Ave. NW, Washington, DC 20200, tel. 202/622-2480, www.treas.gov/offices/enforcement/ofac/programs/cuba/cuba.shtml).

General Licenses

The following categories of travelers are permitted to spend money for Cuban travel without the need to obtain special permission from OFAC, nor are they required to inform OFAC in advance of their visit to Cuba.

Official Government Travelers including representatives of international organizations of which the United States is a member, traveling on official business.

Journalists and supporting broadcasting or technical personnel regularly employed in that capacity by a news reporting organization and traveling for journalistic activities. (Note that the Cuban government requires that you be issued a journalist's visa, not a tourist card.)

Full-time professionals whose travel is directly related to "noncommercial, academic research" in their professional field and whose research will comprise a full work schedule in Cuba and has a likelihood of public dissemi-

nation or whose travel transactions are directly related to attendance at professional meetings or conferences that do not promote tourism or other commercial activity involving Cuba or the production of biotechnological products, so long as such meetings are organized by "qualifying international bodies."

Persons Visiting Family: People with close relatives in Cuba may now visit them once every 12 months for an unlimited period. Such individuals may also apply for specific licenses for additional visits during the 12-month period.

Fully hosted travel, formerly allowed, is no longer permitted.

Specific Licenses

A specific license requires written government approval. Applicants should write a letter to OFAC (https://cubatravel.ofac.treas.gov) stating the date of the planned visit and the length of stay; the specific purpose(s) of the visit; plus the name(s), title(s), and background(s) of the traveler. Allow two or three months.

Special licenses are issued by OFAC on a case-by-case basis authorizing travel transactions by persons in connection with the following travel categories:

Humanitarian Travel and Support for the Cuban People: Persons traveling to Cuba to accompany licensed humanitarian donations or in connection with activities of recognized human rights organizations investigating human rights violations; or travel aimed at promoting "independent activity intended to strengthen civil society in Cuba."

Freelance Journalists: Persons with a suitable record of publication who are traveling to do research for a freelance article. Licenses may be issued for multiple trips.

Professional Research and Meetings: Persons engaging in professional research or attending professional meetings that do not meet the general license requirements.

Educational Research: U.S. universities, colleges, and nongovernmental organizations may apply for one-year travel permits to Cuba that will permit students and academic staff to travel to Cuba. Once such a license is approved, the following categories of travelers affiliated with that academic institution are authorized to engage in travel-related transactions without seeking further approval:

- Undergraduate or graduate students participating in a structured educational program lasting at least 10 weeks in Cuba as part of a course offered at a U.S. undergraduate or graduate institution

- Persons doing noncommercial Cuba-related academic research for the purpose of qualifying academically as a professional (e.g. research toward a graduate degree)

- Students participating in a formal course of study lasting at least 10 weeks at a Cuban academic institution, provided the Cuban study will be accepted for credit toward a degree at the licensed U.S. institution

- Persons regularly employed as teachers at a licensed U.S. undergraduate or graduate institution who plan to teach part or all of an academic program at a Cuban academic institution for at least 10 weeks

- Full-time employees of a licensed institution organizing or preparing for the educational activities described above.

In all cases, students and teachers planning to engage in such transactions must carry a letter from the licensed institution stating the institution's license number and that the individual meets the specific criteria.

Religious Organizations: Specific licenses may be issued by OFAC to religious organizations to authorize individuals affiliated with the organization to engage in travel transactions so long as a full-time program of religious activity is pursued in Cuba under the auspices of the religious organization. Persons wishing to engage in religious activities that are not authorized pursuant to a religious organization's license may also apply for a specific license, including for multiple trips.

Public Performances, Athletic, or Other Competitions and Exhibitions: Persons traveling to participate in such events may apply, so long as the event is open to public attendance and any profits go to a U.S.-based charity of an independent nongovernmental organization in Cuba. Also, amateur or semiprofessional athletes or teams selected for a competition by the relevant U.S. sports federation may travel to participate in athletic competition held under the auspices of an international sports federation, so long as the event is open to the Cuban public.

Private Foundations or Research or Educational Institutions: Persons traveling to Cuba on behalf of such private foundations or research or educational institutes that have an established interest in international relations to collect information for noncommercial purposes.

Export, Import, or Transmission of Informational Materials: Persons traveling to engage in exportation, importation, or transmission of informational materials.

Licensed Exportation: Persons traveling to engage in marketing, sales negotiation, delivery, or servicing of exports of food, agricultural, and medical products.

What You May Spend, Take, and Return Home With

Licensed travelers, including for family visits, are authorized to spend up to the State Department Travel *per diem* allowance, which was US$179 in Havana and US$126 in the rest of Cuba at press time. Journalists may spend more than this allowance (the amount is unspecified) to cover expenses incurred in the reporting of a story, and other licensed travelers may spend additional money "for transactions directly related to the activities for which they received a license."

Money may be spent only for purchases of items directly related to licensed travel such as hotel accommodations, meals, and goods personally used by the traveler in Cuba. Credit cards, including those issued by foreign firms, may *not* be used.

Accompanied baggage is limited to 44 pounds.

Regardless of reason for travel, licensed travelers are not permitted to return to the United States with any Cuban purchases, other than informational material, which may be brought back without limitation (this includes art, CDs, films, etc.). The regulations apply even to foreigners in transit through U.S. airports: since the United States has no transit entry, *all* passengers in transit, say, from Mexico to Europe, must pass through U.S. Immigration and Customs and any Cuban items may be confiscated, whether bought in Cuba or not.

Qualified Travel Service Providers

U.S. law states, "U.S. travel service providers, such as travel agents and tour operators, who handle travel arrangements to, from, or within Cuba must hold special authorizations from the U.S. Treasury Department to engage in such activities."

OFAC licenses companies as authorized Travel Service Providers (TSPs), who are legally entitled to make commercial travel arrangements to Cuba. TSPs can only make reservations for individual travel for licensed travelers. You must obtain approval before proceeding with a reservation. Some TSPs are also CSPs (Carrier Service Providers) licensed to operate their own charters to Cuba.

OFAC also issues TSP licenses to certain companies and organizations permitting them to offer pre-packaged group tours spanning music study to Jewish heritage tours, so long as such programs fall within the above-listed areas for licensed travel. As of March 2003, the Treasury Department began to close what it sees as a "loophole" and no new licenses or renewals of existing ones have been granted.

However, referring to other travel agencies and tour operators (i.e., non-TSPs), "It is possible to provide travel services to U.S. persons legally able to travel to Cuba for family visits, professional research, or news gathering," says Michael Krinsky, a partner in the law firm of Rabinowitz, Boudin, Standard, Krinsky & Lieberman (www.rbskl.com/mk.html), which represents the Cuban government in the United States.

They may also be able to provide services, such as travel arrangements to Jamaica, from where a traveler makes his or her own arrangements for travel to and within Cuba. Treasury Department regulations do not "show a clear penalty against travel agents who book travel this way." Travel agents should double-check the regulations, however, with OFAC or with Krinsky (740 Broadway, New York, NY 10003, tel. 212/254-1111, fax 212/674-4614, mkrinsky@rbskl.com).

Cuban Visas for Licensed Travelers

All licensed U.S. travelers to Cuba must have a visa from the Cuban government prior to reserving their flight. TSPs can assist you in acquiring your visa. TSPs typically charge about US$35 for the visa, and often an additional fee for preparing the documents. Allow at least 30 days for processing.

"Illegal" Travel

Individuals who choose to circumvent U.S. law do so at their own risk, and the author and publisher accept no responsibility for any consequences that may result from such travel.

Every year, thousands (some 20,100 in 2007, according to Cuba, down from 84,500 in 2003) of U.S. citizens slip into Cuba through Canada, Mexico, and other third countries to savor the frisson of the forbidden. Cubans play their part by abstaining from stamping passports (however, many travelers report receiving a small stamp, such as a purple square, page 16 of their passports, familiar to U.S. authorities). In reality, very few people ever have trouble coming back.

Persons subject to U.S. jurisdiction who travel to Cuba without a license bear a "presumption of guilt" and may be required to show documentation that all expenses incurred were paid by a third party not subject to U.S. law.

The U.S. government basically turned a blind eye to illegal travel to Cuba until the

Bush administration, which tightened control of unsanctioned travel. However, as of 2009 things seemed to have eased up. Nonetheless, if Uncle Sam decides to go after perceived offenders, the latter will first receive a questionnaire and, if the Feds believe the law has been broken, a "pre-penalty notice" listing the amount of the proposed fine. (Trading with Cuba illegally is good for up to a US$55,000 fine under provisions of the Helms-Burton Bill, plus up to US$250,000 under the Trading with the Enemy Act, but most demands for fines have been US$7,500.)

Anyone receiving a pre-penalty notice could kill the action dead by requesting a hearing; if issued a penalty notice by OFAC, you have 30 days to appeal. If the case is not settled out of court, the case ostensibly goes before an administrative law judge, who can uphold or dismiss the penalty, but *no* judges are in place to adjudicate! Thus, only *two* people have evern been prosecuted: in January 2005 a judge slapped the first-ever such fine—for US$5,250—on a Michigan couple who had traveled in 2001 on a religious mission; the second penalty was for US$780. If you choose to pay the fine requested in the pre-penalty notice, as many people do, you can negotiate the amount.

How to Defend the Right to Travel: The **National Lawyers Guild** (132 Nassau St., Suite 922, New York, NY 10038, tel. 212/679-5100, fax 212/679-2811, www.nlg.org/cuba/#Travel) has a Cuba subcommittee that can aid in defending against "these restrictions and enforcement actions" and maintains a database of lawyers willing to provide such representation.

The **Center for Constitutional Rights** (666 Broadway, New York, NY 10012, tel. 212/614-6464, fax 212/614-6499, www.ccrjustice.org) is the primary institutional clearinghouse for legal information about the Cuba travel regulations and represents those who have been accused of violating the ban.

Getting There

BY AIR

About 40 airlines service Cuba. The majority of flights arrive at Havana's José Martí International Airport or Varadero's Juan Gualberto Gómez International Airport. Cuba has seven additional international airports: Camagüey (Ignacio Agramonte), Cayo Coco, Cayo Largo del Sur, Cayo Santa María, Holguín (Frank País), Santa Clara (Abel Santamaría), and Santiago de Cuba (Antonio Maceo).

Cuba's national airline is **Cubana de Aviación** (www.cubana.cu), which generally offers lower fares than competing airlines. Cubana has DC-10s and Airbus A-320s that serve Europe and Mexico. However, the workhorses in the stable remain Soviet-made aircraft. The airline is poorly managed, service is charmless, and its safety record is poor.

Fares quoted in this book are based on rates advertised at press time. They are subject to change and should be used only as a guideline.

To get the cheapest fares, make your reservations as early as possible, especially during peak season, as flights often sell out. Low-season and mid-week travel is often cheaper, as are stays of more than 30 days. **STA Travel** (www.statravel.com), with offices worldwide, specializes in low fares.

Most scheduled airlines permit two pieces of checked baggage, although a fee may apply; most charter airlines permit 20 kilos of baggage, and charge extra for overweight bags. Cubana (weight limit 20–40 kg, depending on class) charges extortionate rates for each kilo over your limit. Keep any valuable items, such as laptop computers, in your carry-on luggage. Always reconfirm your reservation and return flight within 72 hours of your departure (reservations are frequently cancelled if not reconfirmed; Cubana is particularly bad in this regard) and arrive at the airport with plenty of time to spare. Reconfirming can be a problem within Cuba for charter ticket holders, as often the local representative is based at a particular resort and may prove elusive. Always keep a photocopy of your ticket separate from your ticket and other documents as a safeguard in the event of loss or theft.

Online Bookings: U.S. websites such as www.orbitz.com and www.travelocity.com are barred from making reservations for Cuba flights. However, many foreign-based websites, including those of airlines such as COPA and Grupo Taca (but not Air Jamaica or Mexicana), offer reservation services for travel to Cuba. Except as specifically licensed by OFAC, it is illegal for any U.S. citizen or resident to make payments in connection with travel to Cuba through such websites.

All international passengers en route to Cuba via the United States, say on a round-the-world ticket, MUST have a separate ticket stock for the Cuba portion and ensure that "Cuba" does not appear on the main ticket stock.

From the United States

Currently, no scheduled commercial flights are permitted between the United States and Cuba.

Licensed Flights: About two dozen companies—called Carrier Service Providers (CSPs)—are authorized to fly direct charters to Cuba from the United States, solely for licensed passengers as permitted by the U.S. Treasury Department. CSPs and licensed TSPs (which can make arrangements for travel to Cuba, but are not licensed to offer their own charter service) may also make reservations for authorized travelers on flights between third countries and Cuba, including Cuban carriers for authorized travelers. Charters use aircraft operated by Continental, Grupo Taca, and United Airlines. Why are prices so high? One, the monopolistic nature of the CSP business; two, because Cuba imposes landing rights of $100–133 per passenger.

The following CSPs are recommended:

- **ABC Charters** (1125 SW 27th Av., Miami, FL 33174, tel. 305/263-6829 or 866/411-1147, fax 305/263-7187, www.abc-charters.com) has flights from Miami to Havana (US$559 round-trip) and Holguín.

- **C&T Charters** (932B Ponce de León Blvd., Coral Gables, FL 33134, tel. 305/445-3337, www.ctcharters.com) has charters to Havana and Camagüey from both Miami ($559 round-trip) and New York ($895 round-trip).

- **Cuba Travel Services** (300 Oceangate, Suite 910, Long Beach, CA 90802, tel. 310/772-2822 or 800/963-2822, www.cubatravelservices.com), with offices in Hialeah and San Juan, offers charter flights from Los Angeles to Havana ($629 round-trip), and from Miami to Havana ($449 round-trip) and Cienfuegos.

- **Marazul Charters** (8324 SW 40th St., Miami, FL 33155, tel. 305/559-7114 or 800/993-9667, www.marazulcharters.com) operates charters from Miami to Havana.

Via Third Countries: The Treasury Department issues the following advisory: Except as specifically licensed by OFAC, "The Regulations prohibit all transactions relating to travel-related tourist transactions in Cuba including prepayment in third countries for Cuba-related expenses" for unlicensed travelers. Nonetheless, thousands of U.S. citizens and residents travel to Cuba through Canada, Mexico, the Caribbean, or Central America aboard foreign airlines using their credit cards.

Under existing U.S. law, citizens showing an airline reservation that includes an onward flight to Cuba will be refused boarding on the flight out of the United States. *Unlicensed travel, therefore, requires completely separate reservations and tickets for your travel to/from a third country and to/from Cuba.* Since you *must* make separate reservations for the two legs, you will need to pick up your bags in your third country destination en route and check in again for the Cuba flight (and vice versa on the way home). Plan accordingly!

U.S. affiliated online search engines such as

www.travelocity.com, www.expedia.com, and www.orbitz.com are barred from displaying Cuba-related flight information.

Travelers should assume a possibility that passenger manifests for flights to Cuba are shared with U.S. authorities. And reservations may be made using the Amadeus reservations system, which the U.S. Department of Homeland Security probably monitors.

From Canada

There are plenty of flights between Canada and Cuba; most fly to Varadero and other beach destinations. Non-licensed U.S. travelers should note that all airlines overflying the United States (e.g. between Canada and Cuba) are required to share their passenger manifests with U.S. Homeland Security.

You might find cheap airfares—about C$400 round-trip—through **Wholesale Travel** (tel. 416/366-0062 or 888/970-3600, www.wholesaletravel.com) and **Travel Cuts** (tel. 866/246-9762, www.travelcuts.com).

A. Nash Travel Inc. (5865 McLaughlin Rd., Unit 2B, Mississauga, Ontario L5R 1B8, tel. 905/755-0647 or 800/818-2004, fax 905/755-0729, www.nashtravel.com) is a recommended Cuba specialist.

Scheduled Flights: Highly regarded **Air Canada** (tel. 800/247-2262, www.aircanada.com) flies from Calgary to Varadero; from Halifax to Holguín; from Montreal to Cayo Coco, Cayo Largo, Havana, Holguín, Santa Clara, and Varadero; from Ottawa to Havana and Santa Clara; from Toronto to Cayo Coco, Havana, Holguín, Santa Clara, and Varadero; and from Vancouver to Havana.

Cuba's **Cubana** (675 King St. West #206, Toronto, tel. 416/967-2822 or 866/428-2262, sales1@cubanaairlines.ca, www.cubana.cu) flies from Montreal to Camagüey, Cayo Largo, Cienfuegos, and Havana; and from Toronto to Camagüey, Cayo Largo, Cienfuegos, Havana, Holguín, Santa Clara, and Santiago de Cuba.

Charter Flights: Most charter flights are designed as beach vacation packages, but charter operators also sell "air-only" tickets.

Air Canada Vacations (tel. 866/529-2079, www.aircanadavacations.com) offers flexible "build-your-own" packages using Air Canada flights.

Air Transat (tel. 866/847-1112, www.airtransat.com) flies from Calgary to Varadero; Edmonton to Varadero; Halifax to Varadero; Montreal to Camagüey, Cayo Coco, Cayo Largo, Holguín, and Varadero; Ottawa to Holguín, Santa Clara, and Varadero; Quebec City to Holguín, Santa Clara, and Varadero; Toronto to Camagüey, Holguín, and Varadero; and Vancouver to Varadero..

Skyservice (tel. 800-701-9448, www.skyserviceairlines.com) flies from Calgary to Varadero; Edmonton to Varadero; Halifax to Cayo Coco and Holguín; Montreal to Holguín;, Ottawa to Varadero; Regina to Varadero; Toronto to Cayo Coco and Varadero; Vancouver to Varadero; and Winnipeg to Holguín and Varadero.

SunWing (tel. 800/761-1711, www.sunwing.ca) has the most extensive service, with flights to eight Cuban destinations from 19 Canadian airports.

Westjet (tel. 888/937-8538, www.westjet.com) flies from Halifax to Cayo Coco and Holguín; Moncton to Varadero; Montreal to Varadero; Ottawa to Santa Clara; Saskatoon to Varadero; and Toronto to Cayo Coco.

From Europe

Direct air service to Cuba is available from most western European countries. You can also fly via Caribbean destinations. Note that if flying aboard a U.S. carrier, you must have your ticket for the Cuban portion issued on a separate ticket stock, and you must make your reservation for the Cuba leg separately.

From France: Havana is served by **Air France** (tel. 0820/320-820, www.airfrance.com), nine times weekly from Paris's Charles de Gaulle airport using Boeing 777s (from about €785 round-trip). **Corsairfly** (tel. 0820/042-042, www.corsairfly.com) flies a Boeing 747 weekly from Paris Orly to Havana. **Cubana** (41 Boulevard du Montparnasse, 75006 Paris, tel. 01/53-63-23-23) flies from

Paris Orly airport to Havana via Santiago de Cuba on Sundays using an Ilyushin L-96 (from €532 round-trip).

Air Europa (tel. 902/401-501 in Spain, www.aireuropa.com) flies between Paris Charles de Gaulle and Havana via Madrid.

Good online resources for discount airfares include www.anyway.fr and www.wasteels.fr.

From Germany: Charter company **Condor** (tel. 0180/5-70-72-02, www.condor.com) flies from Frankfurt and Munich to Holguín and Cayo Coco. **AirBerlin** (0180/5-73-78-00, www.airberlin.com), formerly LTU, flies from Berlin to Varadero on Thursday (from €778 round trip).

A recommended tour operator is **Reisegalerie** (Gruneburgweg 84, 60323 Frankfurt, tel. 069/9720-6000, www.reise-galerie.com), which specializes in Cuba.

From Italy: You can use **Alitalia** (tel. 800/650-055, www.alitalia.it) to connect with Air France, Iberia flights, or Virgin Atlantic flights. Air France and Iberia fly from Milan to Havana via Paris and Madrid, respectively.

Blue Panorama (tel. 06/6021-4737, www.blue-panorama.com) carries the bulk of Italian tourists to Cuba with daily flights from Rome to Cayo Largo, Havana, and Santiago de Cuba (from €635 round-trip), using Boeing wide-body aircraft.

Livingstone (tel. 0331/267-321, www.lauda.it), formerly Lauda Air, flies charters from Milan to Cayo Largo and from Rome and Milan to Havana and Holguín.

From the Netherlands: Havana is served by **Martinair** (tel. 20/60-11-767, www.martinair.com) from Amsterdam (from €619 round-trip).

From Russia: Russian carrier **Aeroflot** (tel. 0495/223-5555 or 8800/333-5555, www.aeroflot.ru/eng/) flies from Moscow to Havana on Monday and Friday (from $1,070 round-trip). **Cubana** (tel. 0495/642-9439, www.cubana.ru) operates a DC-10 once a week from Moscow.

From Spain: Havana is served by **Iberia** (tel. 902/400-500, www.iberia.com), which flies to Havana from Madrid

daily (from €790 round-trip), as does **Air Europa** (tel. 902/401-501, www.air-europa.com). **Cubana** (tel. 091/758-9750, www.cubana.cu) flies from Madrid to Havana and Santiago de Cuba on Monday and Thursday using a DC-10 (from €560 round-trip) using an Ilyushin.

From the United Kingdom: The main carrier is **Virgin Atlantic** (tel. 800/821-5438, www.virgin-atlantic.com), which flies on Wednesday and Sunday from Gatwick to Havana (from £602 round-trip).

Cubana (tel. 020/7536-8177, www.cubanacan.cu) flies from Gatwick to Havana via Holguín on Wednesday (from £457 round-trip).

Air Jamaica (tel. 020/7590-3600, www.air-jamaica.com), which no longer operates from the United Kingdom, has a codeshare agreement with Virgin Atlantic; you can fly the latter to Montego Bay or Kingston and hop over to Havana with Air Jamaica.

Virgin Holidays (tel. 0844/557-5825, www.virginholidays.co.uk) has one- and two-week packages featuring Havana and Varadero.

Good online resources for discount tickets include www.ebookers.com, www.cheap-flights.co.uk, and www.travelsupermarket.com; and for charter flights, **Charter Flight Centre** (tel.0845/045-0153, www.charter-flights.co.uk).

From the Caribbean

From the Bahamas: As of 2008, **Bahamasair** (tel. 242/377-5505, http://up.bahamasair.com) has Nassau–Havana flights on Tuesday, Thursday, and Sunday. at 12:45 P.M. ($329 round-trip). You cannot book via the website.

A **Cubana** charter flight operates daily, except Saturday, to Havana from Nassau at 2:30 P.M. ($329 round-trip, plus US$15 visa and US$7 ticket tax). Check in closes one hour before departure. Neither **Havanatur** (East Bay Shopping Centre, East Bay St., Nassau, tel. 242/393-5281, www.havanaturbahamas.com) nor the other tour agencies in Nassau, such as **Majestic Travel** (tel. 242/328-0908)

PRIVATE AIRCRAFT

Private pilots must contact the **Instituto de Aeronáutica Civil de Cuba** (Calle 23 #64, e/ Infanta y P, Vedado, tel. 07/55-1121, fax 07/834-4571) at least 10 days before arrival in Cuba and at least 48 hours before an overflight.

U.S. owners of private aircraft, including air ambulance services, who intend to land in Cuba must obtain a temporary export permit for the aircraft from the U.S. Department of Commerce before departure.

that book the Cubana flight accept credit card reservations; you'll have to pay a deposit in advance through a Western Union wire transfer or by certified check, which has to be mailed. You can pick up your ticket in Nassau, or have it delivered to the airport for pick-up. Request a written confirmation and receipt of payment. Mid-week, it's often possible to purchase a ticket at the counter two hours before departure time.

Returning from Cuba, you pass through Bahamian immigration (and pay US$15 departure tax), even in transit. Flights to the United States depart from a separate terminal: You pass through U.S. Immigration and Customs here, and officials are wise to the arrival of flights from Havana.

From the Cayman Islands: Havana is served three times weekly by **Cayman Airways** (tel. 345/949-8200, www.caymanairways.com) from Grand Cayman (from US$217 round-trip).

From the Dominican Republic and Haiti: Panama's **Copa** (www.copaair.com) flies between Santo Domingo and Havana via Panama City four times daily (from US$284 round-trip). **Cubana** (Av. Tiradentes y 27 de Febrero, Santo Domingo, tel. 809/227-2040, fax 809/227-2040, cubana.aviacion@codetel.net.do) serves Havana from Santo Domingo on Thursday and Sunday (from US$395 round-trip). Cuba's **Aero Caribbean** (www.aeroca-

ribbean.cu) supposedly flies on Friday and Sunday between Santo Domingo and Santiago de Cuba (US$510 round-trip).

From Jamaica: Troubled **Air Jamaica** (tel. 800/523-5585 in North America, 888/359-2478 in Jamaica, www.airjamaica.com) flies thrice weekly flights from Montego Bay and Kingston to Havana (from US$420 round-trip). U.S. travelers can't book a Cuba leg via Air Jamaica's website: You have to call Jamaica directly, and you have to pay for the Jamaica–Cuba leg upon arrival in Jamaica. The airline has a reputation for losing luggage.

Caribic Vacations (tel. 876/953-9895, www.caribicvacations.com), **Tropical Tours** (tel. 876/953-9100, www.tropicaltours-ja.com), and **Marzouca Marketing & Sales** (tel. 876/971-3859, www.cubaonweb.com) offer charter flights and package excursions from Montego Bay to Havana.

From Central America

Copa (www.copaair.com) and Grupo Taca (www.taca.com) permit you to make reservations and pay by credit card online for flights through Central America.

Taca (tel. 305/870-7500 or 800/400-8222, www.grupotaca.com) has flights twice-daily from El Salvador to Havana (from US$644 round-trip), and daily from Costa Rica (from US$413) with connecting flights from the United States.

COPA (tel. 507/217-2672 or 800/359-2672 in the U.S., www.copaair.com) flies to Havana from Panama City four times daily (from US$548 round-trip).

Cubana (www.cubana.cu) flies to Havana daily from Costa Rica (tel. 506/2221-7625, cubanaju@racsa.co.cr) and from Guatemala (tel. 502/2367-2288) on Saturday.

From Mexico: The national carrier **Mexicana** and its subsidiary **Click** (tel. 59/9848-5998 in Mexico City, 800/801-2010 from elsewhere in Mexico, 800/531-7921 from the United States) has daily flights to Havana from Cancún (from US$297 round-trip), Mexico City (from about US$430 round-trip), and Mérida (from US$402 round-trip). However, you can't book via their website. To make a reservation, you need to call the airline and request a special telephone number (tel. 55/5448-0990) that handles Cuba reservations. You can't pay by credit card (except American Express) but will need to pay in cash at the Mexican gateway airport at least four hours before your departure. (*Note:* Mexicana reportedly has a reputation for delaying luggage on this route.)

Cubana (tel. 52-55/52-506-355 in Mexico City, tel. 52-99/88-877-210 in Cancún, reservaciones@cubanamexico.com) also flies from Mexico City five times weekly (from US$430 round-trip) using a DC-10, and daily from Cancún (from US$306 round-trip) using Soviet planes.

Tourist cards for Mexico are handed out on the flight just before arriving in Mexico. It's a good idea to reconfirm your outbound flight 48 hours before departure.

Cuban-owned **Viajes Divermex** (Av. Cobá #5, Centro Comercial Plaza América, Cancún, Quintana Roo, México CP 77500, tel. 998/884-5005, www.divermex.com) specializes in Cuba packages.

From South America

Lan Chile (tel. 866/435-9526, www.lanchile.com) flies to Havana from Santiago de Chile on Sunday (from US$1,040 round-trip).

Cubana (www.cubana.cu) flies to Havana from Quito, Ecuador; Buenos Aires, Argentina; Sao Paulo, Brazil; Bogota, Colombia; and Caracas, Venezuela.

From Asia

You can fly to Paris, London, Madrid, Mexico City, Canada, or South America and connect with flights to Cuba. If traveling via the United States, flying nonstop to Los Angeles, then to Mexico City or Cancún, is perhaps the easiest route.

STA Travel (www.statravel.com) sells discounted tickets and has a branch in Bangkok (tel. 662/236-0262).

From Australia and New Zealand

The best bet is to fly either to Los Angeles or San Francisco and then to Cuba via Mexico, El Salvador, or Panama; or to Canada and on to Havana. **Air New Zealand** (in Australia tel. 132-476, in New Zealand tel. 0800/737-000, www.airnewzealand.com), **Qantas** (tel. 131-313; in New Zealand tel. 0800/808-767, www.qantas.com.au), and **United Airlines** (tel. 131-777; in New Zealand tel. 0800/747-400) offer direct service between Australia, New Zealand, and North America. A route via Santiago de Chile and then to Havana is also possible.

Specialists in discount fares include **STA Travel** (in Australia tel. 134-782, www.statravel.com.au; in New Zealand tel. 0800/474-400, www.statravel.co.nz).

A good online resource for discount airfares is **Flight Centre** (tel. 133-133, www.flightcentre.com.au).

BY SEA
By Cruise Ship

The U.S. embargo has restricted the cruise industry's access to Cuba. Nonetheless, several foreign cruise ships have featured Cuba on their itineraries. However, none has stood the test of time, not least because in 2005 Castro belittled the cruise industry and said cruise passengers were no longer welcome. Passenger arrivals plummeted from 102,000 in 2005 (generating $15 million) to 11,000 in 2007..

In 2009, Spain's **Visión Crucero** initiated week-long "Treasures of Mexico and Cuba" cruises aboard the 629-passenger *Vision Star.*

England's **Fred Olsen Cruise Lines** (tel. 01473/746-175, www.fredolsencruises.co.uk) features a two-day Havana stopover on its 15-day Caribbean cruises from Bridgetown, Barbados, aboard the *Braemar.*

Germany's **Aida Cruises** (tel. 0381/2027-0707, www.aida.de) occasionally features Havana on its peak-season programs.

In former days, U.S. citizens could partake of these cruises without breaking the law as the in-transit visa used, which allows up to 48 hours in Cuba, means that no port fees apply (this, of course, assumes that you don't spend a dime ashore nor partake of shore excursions arranged by the ship and involving transfer of funds to Cuban entities). However, a prohibition for U.S. citizens regarding "all transactions relating to travel-related tourist transactions in Cuba" now applies.

By Freighter

Hamburg-Süd Reiseagentur GMBH (Ost-West 59, 20457 Hamburg, tel. 040/3705-157, fax 040/370-5242, www .freighter-voyages.com) books passage aboard the *Melfi Iberia* sailing from Italy and Spain to Havana on a 38-day journey (from €3,535).

In the United Kingdom, book through **Strand Voyages** (357 Strand, London WC2R 0HS, tel. 020/7010-9290, www.strandtravel. co.uk). U.S. citizens can book through **Freighter World Cruises** (180 S. Lake Ave., #335, Pasadena, CA 91101, tel. 626/449-3106 or 800/531-7774, www.freighterworld.com).

Germany's **Hapag Lloyd** (www.hapag-lloyd. com) has serviced Cuba in past years.

By Private Vessel

No advance permission is required to arrive by sea. However, it is wise to give at least 72 hours advance warning by faxing complete details of your boat, crew, and passengers to the six official entry ports operated by Cuba's **Marlin Náutica y Marinas** (tel. 07/273-7912, direccion@marlin,tur.cu, www.nauticamarlin.com) and Gaviota (tel. 07/869-5774, www.gaviota-grupo.com). Only a few are up to international par, although most offer fresh water, 110-volt electrical hookups, plus diesel and gasoline.

For cruising, you'll need to register your boat upon arrival and receive a *permiso especial de navegación* (from CUC50, depending on the length of your boat). You'll need an official clearance (a *despacho*) to depart for your next, and each and every, stop. Authorities will usually ask for a planned itinerary, but insist on flexibility to cruise at random toward your final destination. A Permiso de Salida will be issued listing your final destination and possible stops en route.

Two excellent references are Simon Charles's *Cruising Guide to Cuba* and Nigel Calder's *Cuba: A Cruising Guide.*

Uncle Sam requires that U.S. boaters get pre-authorization from the Coast Guard Marine Safety Office (www.uscg.mil/hq/cg5/ cg531/CubaTravel.asp). U.S. boaters are also expressly forbidden to travel to Cuba without an export license from the Commerce Department and a specific license from OFAC. Applications must be made through the Seventh Coast Guard District (tel. 305/415-6920, fax 305/415-6925). All persons subject to U.S. law aboard vessels, including the owner, must be an authorized traveler to engage in travel transactions in Cuba. Vessel owners are prohibited from carrying travelers to Cuba who pay them for passage if the owner does not have a specific license from OFAC authorizing him or her to be a Service Provider to Cuba.

The United States and Cuba do not have a Coast Guard agreement. Craft developing difficulties in Cuban waters cannot expect assistance from the U.S. Coast Guard (however, the U.S. Interests Section *has* arranged such assistance to U.S. yachters), and there are many reports of Cuban authorities being indifferent to yachters in distress, some of whom have had their vessels impounded; in several cases, foreign yachters have lost their vessels to corrupt officials. In case of emergencies requiring financial transactions, such as repair of vessels, travelers should contact OFAC (tel. 202/622-2480) for authorization.

Haut Insurance (80 Chestnut St., Andover, MA 01810, tel. 978/475-0367, www. johngalden.com) handles insurance coverage to yachters cruising in Cuban waters.

Maps and Charts: Yachting charts can be ordered from **Bluewater Books & Charts** (tel. 800/942-2583, www.bluewaterweb.com). In Havana, **Tienda el Navegante** (Calle Mercaderes #115, e/ Obispo y Obrapía, Habana Vieja, tel. 07/861-3625; for boaters, VHF channel 16 CMYP3050; Mon.–Fri. 8 A.M.–5 P.M., Sat. 8 A.M.–1 P.M.) sells nautical charts of Cuban waters.

BY ORGANIZED TOUR

Joining an organized tour offers certain advantages over traveling independently. For example, petty bureaucratic hassles and language problems you may otherwise not wish to face are eliminated, too. However, you'll be almost entirely divorced from the local culture as you are hauled between official tourist sites.

Check the tour inclusions to identify any hidden costs such as airport taxes, tips, service charges, extra meals, etc. Most tours are priced according to quality of accommodations.

Tours from the United States

The following organizations offer trips and/or can arrange trips for licensed academic and cultural organizations:

Art Quest International (801 Idaho Ave., Suite 15, Santa Monica, CA 90403. tel. 310/393-3435, www.artquestintl.com), formerly Cuba Cultural Travel.

Center for Cuban Studies (231 W. 29th St., New York, NY 10001, 212/242-0559, www.cubaupdate.org).

Global Exchange (2017 Mission St. #303, San Francisco, CA 94110, 415/255-7296, www.globalexchange.org). This left-wing organization offers "Reality Trips."

Marazul Tours (8328 SW 40th St., Miami, FL 33155, tel. 305/559-7114 or 800/993-9667, www.marazulcharters.com).

Ya'lla Tours (tel. 800/644-1595, www.yallatours.com).

Volunteer Programs: The Bush administration rescinded the fully hosted travel and person-to-person exchange provisions permitting "solidarity" tours, in which participants perform voluntary work that lets you to contribute to the human community and learn some invaluable life lessons. Nonetheless, the following offer programs:

Pastors for Peace (418 W. 145th St., New York, NY 10031, 212/926-5757, fax 212/926-5842, www.ifconews.org), which operates without a license, delivers humanitarian aid to Cuba through the annual U.S.–Cuba Friendship Caravan, which travels via Canada or Mexico. The **Venceremos Brigade** (P.O. Box 5202, Englewood, NJ 07631-5202, 212/560-4360, www.venceremosbridgade.net) organizes annual solidarity trips and "work-camp" brigades without a license.

Volunteers for Peace (1034 Tiffany Rd., Belmont, VT 05730, 802/259-2759, www.vfp.org) has "International Workcamps" in Cuba for volunteers.

Friendship Force International (34 Peachtree St. NW, Suite 900, Atlanta, GA 3030, 404/522-9490, www.friendshipforce.org) has taken participants to Cuba in past years, as have **People to People Ambassadors** (Dwight D. Eisenhower Bldg., 110 S. Ferrall St., Spokane, WA 99202, 509/568-7000 or 866/794-8309, www.ambassadorprograms.org) and **Witness for Peace** (3628 12th St. NE, Washington, DC 20017, 202/547-6112, www.witnessforpeace.org).

Academic Exchanges and Cultural Programs: Most entities that held licenses to operate academic and cultural-exchange programs no longer do so. Such programs have in past years been offered by the **Cuba Exchange Program** (School of Advanced International Studies at Johns Hopkins University, 1740 Massachusetts Ave. NW, Washington, DC 20036, 202/663-5600, www.sais-jhu.edu); **MacArthur Cuba Scholarly Exchange** (Center for Latin American Studies, University of Chicago, 5848 S. University Ave., Chicago, IL 60637, tel. 773/702-8420, http://clas.uchicago.edu); **Plaza Cuba** (P.O. Box 3083, Berkeley, CA 94703, 510/848-0911, www.plazacuba.com), which specializes in cultural workshops where tour participants learn music and dance; and the **Center for Cross-Cultural Study** (446 Main St., Amherst, MA 01002, tel. 413/256-0011, www.cccs.com), which also oversees the **Cuba Academic Alliance** (www.cccs.com/CubaAcademicAlliance) working to challenge restrictions on academic travel.

Tours from Canada

Cuba Education Tours (2278 East 24th Ave., Vancouver BC, V5N 2V2, tel. 877/687-3817, www.cubafriends.ca) offers "solidarity" and special-interest tours.

Quest Nature Tours (491 King St., Toronto, Ontario M5A 1L9, tel. 416/633-5666 or 800/387-1483, www.questnaturetours.com) offers birding and nature tours.

Real Cuba (Box 2345, Swan River, Manitoba, R0L 1Z0, tel. 306/205-0977, www.realcubaonline.com) offers special theme trips, including bicycling, cultural programs, walking and bird-watching, and art and photography workshops.

WowCuba (430 Queen St., Charlottestown, Prince Edward Island, Canada CIA 4E8, tel. 902/368-2453, www.wowcuba .com) specializes in bicycle tours of Cuba, but has other programs, including scuba diving.

Several companies offer air-hotel beach packages, including **Signature Vacations** (tel. 866/324-2883, www.signaturevacations.com), **Sunquest Vacations** (tel. 877/485-6060, www.sunquest.ca), and **Transat Holidays** (tel. 866/322-6649, www.transatholidays.com).

Tours from the United Kingdom

Captivating Cuba (22 St. Peter's Square, Hammersmith, London W6 9NW, tel. 08444/129-916, www.captivatingcuba.com) offers a wide range of trips.

Journey Latin America (12 Heathfield Terr., London W4 4JE, tel. 020/8747-8315, www.journeylatinamerica.co.uk) offers trips from a "Havana Weekend Break" to self-drive packages.

CubaWelcome (tel. 020/7498-8266, www. cubawelcome.com) offers FIT and group packages, from "Cigars & Golf" to photography and even a "Che Guevara Tour."

Regal Holidays (58 Lancaster Way, Ely, Cambs, CB6 3NW, tel. 01353/659-999, www .regal-diving.co.uk) and **Scuba en Cuba** (7 Maybank Gdns., Pinner, Mddx. HA5 2JW, tel. 01895/624100, www.scuba-en-cuba.com) offer dive packages to Cuba.

San Cristobal UK (2a Eastcheap, London EC3M 1AA, tel. 020/7621-6524, www.scuktravel.com) has sightseeing tours and hotel packages.

Volunteer and Language-Study Programs: The **Cuban Solidarity Campaign** (218 Green Lanes, London N4 2HB, tel.

SPANISH-LANGUAGE COURSES

The **Universidad de la Habana** (Calle J #556 e/ 25 y 27, Vedado, Havana, tel. 07/832-4245 or 870-4667, www.uh.cu/infogral/estudiaruh/postgrado/english.html) offers Spanish-language courses of 20-80 hours (CUC100-300), plus "Spanish and Cuban Culture" courses of 320-480 hours (CUC960-1,392). Courses begin the first Monday of the month, year-round.

The **Centro de Idiomas y Computación José Martí** (José Martí Language and Computer Center, Calle 90 #531, e/ 5ta B y 5ta C, Miramar, Havana, tel. 07/822-9338, fax 07/824-4846, www.ain.cubaweb.cu) also offers Spanish language courses of 20-80 hours (CUC130-330).

Universitur (Calle 30 #768, e/ Kohly y 41, Nuevo Vedado, tel. 07/55-5683, fax 07/55-5978, www.universitur.cu), with regional offices in Canada and Europe, arranges Spanish-language courses at the universities of Havana, Cienfuegos, Ciego de Ávila, Granma, Holguín, and Matanzas, plus Havana's Instituto Superior Politécnico José Antonio Echeverría.

020/8800-0155, www.cuba-solidarity.org) offers "solidarity" work brigades; and **Caledonia Languages Abroad** (72 Newhaven Rd., Edinburgh, EH6 5QG, Scotland, tel. 0131/621-7721, www.caledonialanguages.co.uk) offers volunteer work programs, plus language-study programs. **Cactus Language** (tel. 888/577-8451, www.cactuslanguage .com) has language courses in Cuba.

Tours from Europe

In Germany, contact **Kuba Reisen** (www.reisen-kuba.com) or **Sprachcaffe Cuba Travel** (tel. 069/610-9120, www.sprachcaffe-kuba. com), both with a large range of trips.

In Italy, try **Eden Viaggi** (tel. 039/0721-4421, www.edenviaggi.it), which primarily has hotel packages; or **Lovely Cuba** (tel. 02/4549-8556, www.lovelycuba.com).

STUDYING IN CUBA

Thousands of people every year choose to study in Cuba, be it for a monthlong dance course or six years of medical training. You'll need a solid grasp of Spanish. Bring any supplies you think you'll need; course materials and academic supplies are scant. Be prepared for basic living conditions if signing up for a long-term residential course.

Under existing U.S. regulations, the only U.S. students currently permitted to study in Cuba are undergraduates enrolled in a degree program and who intend to participate in formal study of not less than 10 weeks at a Cuban academic institution; graduate students whose research specifically relates to Cuba; and those students attending universities and colleges that hold specific licenses permitting students and academic staff to travel to Cuba.

Universitur (Calle 30 #768, e/ Kohly y 41, Nuevo Vedado, tel. 07/55-5683, fax 07/55-5978, www.universitur.cu) arranges study at centers of higher learning, plus working holidays.

STUDENT VISAS

You can no longer study in Cuba using a tourist visa, however short the duration of study, unless you travel via Universitur. All others require a student visa (CUC80), which can be requested in advance from the Director of Graduate Degrees of the relevant university 20 days prior to your intended arrival date. Visas can ostensibly be picked up at the Cuban consulate in your country. Visas are good for 30 days but can be extended upon arrival in Cuba for CU25 (you'll need to buy *sellos* at a Bandec).

You can *arrive* in Cuba with a tourist visa, however. You then have 48 hours to register for your university program and request a change of visa status (CUC65). You'll need six passport photos, your passport and tourist card, plus a license certificate for the *casa particular* where you'll be staying.

For study at the **Universidad de la Habana,** contact the Dirección de Posgrado (Calle J #556, e/ 25 y 27, Vedado, tel. 07/832-4245, www.uh.cu).

ARTS, MUSIC, AND DANCE

The **Cátedra de Danza** (5ta #253, e/ D y E, Vedado, tel. 07/832-4625, fax 07/33-3117, www.balletcuba.cu) offers monthlong ballet courses for intermediate- and advanced-level professionals and students (CUC250 monthly), plus courses in modern dance, and a children's vocational workshop.

The **Centro Nacional de Conservación,**

Press Tours (tel. 02/3496-6264, promozione@presstours.it, www.presstours.it) offers special-interest trips, including diving.

Tours from Australia and New Zealand

Caribbean Bound (379 Pitt St., Suite 102, Sydney 2000, NSW, tel. 800/354-104, www.caribbean.com.au) and **Caribbean Destinations** (291 Auburn Rd., Melbourne, VIC 3122, tel. 03/9813-5258, www.caribbeanislands.com.au).

New Zealand's **Innovative Travel** (P.O. Box 21247, Edgeware, Christchurch, New Zealand, tel. 3/365-3910, www.innovative-travel.com) has packages to Cuba.

Volunteer Programs: The **Australia Cuba Friendship Association** (P. O. Box ZK364, Haymarket, NSW 1240, www.sydney-acfs.org) offers "Southern Cross Brigade" work programs.

Restauración y Museología (Calle Cuba #610, e/ Sol y Luz, Habana Vieja, tel. 07/861-2877, fax 07/866-5696, www.cnpc.cult.cu) offers residential courses for urban planners, conservationists, and architects.

The **Instituto Superior de Arte** (Calle 120 #11110, e/ 9na y 13, Cubanacán, tel. 07/208-0288 or 208-8075, fax 07/33-6633, isa@cubarte.cult.cu) offers short-term courses in music, dance, theater, and visual arts. It also accepts foreigners for full-year study beginning in September, for which applicants must take an entrance exam.

The **Unión de Escritores y Artistas de Cuba** (Calle 17 #351, esq. H, Vedado, tel. 07/832-4551, fax 07/33-3158, www.uneac .com) offers courses in the arts and Cuban culture, focusing on music.

The **Taller Experimental de Gráfica** (Callejón del Chorro #6, Plaza de la Catedral, Habana Vieja, tel. 07/862-0979, fax 07/204-0391, tgrafica@cubarte.cult.cu) offers courses in engraving and lithography.

The arts promotion entity **ARTEX** (Av. 5ta #8010, esq. 82, Miramar, tel. 07/833-2710) sponsors courses in the arts and literature. Artex's **Paradiso: Promotora de Viajes Culturales** (Calle 19 #560, esq. C, Vedado, tel.

07/832-6928, fax 07/33-3921, www.soycubano.com/artex/paradiso/index.asp) arranges participation in cultural courses and programs, from children's book publishing to theater criticism, plus festivals such as the International Benny Moré Festival and the International Hemingway Colloquium.

The **Universidad de la Habana** (Calle J #556, e/ 25 y 27, Vedado, Havana, tel. 07/832-4245 or 870-4667, www.uh.cu) has two- to four-week courses in Cuban culture beginning the first Monday of every month.

MEDICAL TRAINING

The Cuban **Ministerio de Salud Pública** (Ministry of Public Health), Calle 23 #201, Vedado, tel. 07/55-5532) offers free scholarships for disadvantaged and minority students from the United States and developing nations to attend the **Escuela Latinoamericana de Medicina** (Latin American School of Medical Sciences, ELACM, Santa Fe, Havana, tel. 07/29-7477, www.elacm.sld.cu). Courses last six years and graduates are full-fledged doctors. Apply through the Cuban Interests Section, 2630 16th St. NW, Washington, DC 20009, 202/797-8518, ext. 109, or at www.afrocubaweb.com/infomed/medscholarships.htm.

Getting Around

BY AIR

Most major Cuban cities have an airport, and virtually every major tourism destination is within a two-hour drive of an airport. Cuba's poorly managed, state-owned airlines have a monopoly. Their safety records do not inspire confidence. Because of hijacking attempts, Cuban authorities restrict the amount of fuel on aircraft on internal flights. I recommend against internal air travel.

Flights are often booked up weeks in advance, especially in the August–December peak season. Tickets are normally nonrefundable. If you reserve before arriving in Cuba, you'll be given a voucher to exchange for a ticket upon arrival in Cuba. Arrive on time for check-in; otherwise your seat will be given away. Delays, cancellations, and schedule changes are common.

Cubana (Calle 23, e/ 0 y P, Havana, tel. 07/834-4449, www.cubana.cu) serves most airports using unreliable Soviet planes. Fares are 25 percent cheaper if booked in conjunction with an international Cubana flight. You can book at tour desks in most hotels.

Aero Caribbean (Calle 23 #64, Vedado, tel. 07/879-7524, fax 07/336-5016, www.aero-caribbean.cu) normally operates charter flights from Havana to Cayo Coco, Holguín, Santiago, Trinidad, and Varadero; between Varadero and Cayo Coco; and between Santiago de Cuba and Baracoa, Holguín, and Varadero. **Aerogaviota** (Av. 47 #2814, e/ 28 y 34, Rpto. Kohly, Havana, tel. 07/203-0668, fax 07/204-2621, www.aerogaviota.com) offers charter flights in 39-passenger Soviet Antonov-26s and 45-passenger French-built ATR-42s, as well as "executive" service in 18-seat helicopters.

BY BUS
Tourist Buses
Víazul (Av. 26, esq. Zoológico, Nuevo Vedado, Havana, tel. 07/881-1413, www.viazul.cu; daily 7 A.M.–9 P.M.) operates bus services for foreigners to key places on the tourist circuit using modern, (overly) air-conditioned buses. Children travel at half price. At press time, a five percent discount was offered for round-trip tickets to Cienfuegos, Trinidad, Pinar del Río, and Viñales. A 10 percent fee applies for cancellations made more than 24 hours before departure; a 25 percent fee applies if you cancel within 24 hours. A 20-kg baggage limit applies; excess baggage is charged one percent of your ticket cost per kilo. Bicycles are charged CUC0.80–4, depending on distance.

Transtur (tel. 07/838-3991, www.transtur. cu) operates tourist bus excursions within Havana and Varadero by open-top double-decker bus, and in Viñales, Matanzas, Trinidad, Holguín, Guardalavaca, and Cayo Coco by minibus.

Public Buses
Virtually the entire population relies on the bus system for travel within and between cities. Between 2005 and 2009, Cuba imported more than 5,000 modern Chinese-made Yutong buses to replace its aging, decrepit fleet of hand-me-downs. There are two classes of buses for long-distance travel: *Especiales* are faster (and often more comfortable) than crowded and slow *regulares,* which in many areas are still old and rickety with butt-numbing seats.

Most towns have *two* bus stations for out-of-town service: a Terminal de Ómnibus Inter-

municipales (for local and municipal service) and a Terminal de Ómnibus Interprovinciales (for service between provinces). Often they're far apart. Terminals are chaotic. Don't rely on published schedules. Beware pickpockets and don't display wads of money when purchasing your ticket.

Interprovincial Services: The state agency **Astro** (Av. Independencia #101, Havana, tel. 07/870-3397) operates all interprovincial services linking cities throughout the island. Most inter-city buses move at night. Demand so exceeds supply that Cubans sometimes have to wait *weeks* for a seat. Foreigners pay in CUC and receive reserved seating (only two seats per bus at last visit). Reservations are essential; do *not* expect to show up at the station and simply board a bus. However, you can buy a ticket as late as one hour before departure. Only one-way tickets are available; book any return or ongoing trip as far in advance as possible. On the day of travel, arrive at the terminal at least one hour ahead of departure, otherwise your seat may be issued to people on the waiting list. If you don't have a reservation or miss your departure, you can try getting on the standby list—*lista de espera*—for Cubans (foreigners, however, are normally shooed away to the CUC-only counter).

A 22-kilogram baggage limit applies, although it seems not to be strictly enforced. Long-distance buses make food and toilet stops, but it's wise to bring snacks and water.

Intermunicipal Services: Usually no reservations are available for the short-distance intermunicipal services (between towns within specific provinces). You'll have to join the queue. At other times, you'll be issued a *tike* (a slip of paper) that records your destination and position in line. You board when your number is called, so don't wander off. Fares are collected on board. Try to board the bus at its originating point.

Camiones: The staple of travel between towns in most areas is a truck, or *camión.* Often these are the only option for public transport, especially in the Oriente. Most travel only to the

VÍAZUL BUS SCHEDULE

Route	Departure Times (Duration)	One-Way Fare
Havana-Santiago Santiago-Havana	9:30 A.M., 3 P.M., and 6:15 P.M. (13 hours) 9 A.M., 3:15 P.M., and 10 P.M. Stops are made at Entronque de Jagüey (CUC12), Santa Clara (CUC18), Sancti Spíritus (CUC23), Ciego de Ávila (CUC27), Camagüey (CUC33), Las Tunas (CUC39), Holguín (CUC44), and Bayamo (CUC44).	CUC51
Havana-Trinidad Trinidad-Havana	8:15 A.M. and 1 P.M. (5 hours, 45 mins) 7:45 A.M. and 3 P.M. Stops are made at Entronque de Jagüey (CUC12), Aguada de Pasajeros (CUC13), Yaguarama (CUC14), Rodas (CUC15), and Cienfuegos (CUC20)	CUC25
Havana-Varadero Varadero-Havana	8 A.M., noon, and 6 P.M. (3 hours) 8 A.M., 4 P.M., and 6 P.M. Stops are made at Matanzas (CUC7) and Aeropuerto de Varadero (by request).	CUC10
Havana-Viñales Viñales-Havana	9 A.M. (3 hours, 15 mins) 2 P.M. A stop is made in Pinar del Río (CUC11).	CUC12
Santiago-Baracoa Baracoa-Santiago	7:30 A.M. (5 hours) 2:15 P.M.	CUC15
Trinidad-Santiago Santiago-Trinidad	8:15 A.M. (12 hours) 7:30 P.M.	CUC33
Varadero-Trinidad Trinidad-Varadero	7:30 a.m. (6 hours) 2:30 p.m.	CUC20

nearest major town, so you'll need to change *camiones* frequently for long-distance travel. Some are open-sided flatbeds featuring basic wooden seats welded to the floor, with a canvas roof. Sometimes it's a truck with a container with makeshift windows cut out of the metal sides, but hot as Hades, with no seats. They depart from designated transportation hubs (often adjacent to bus or railway stations). You pay in pesos as you board: between 1 and 10 pesos, depending on distance. Officially, foreigners are banned, so expect to be turned away by the drivers.

Within Towns: Provincial capitals have intracity bus service, which can mean makeshift *coches* or *camiónes*. Buses—*guaguas,* pronounced WAH-wahs—are often secondhand Yankee school buses or uncomfortable Hungarian or Cuban buses. They are usually overcrowded and cost 10–20 centavos (the standard fare).

Expect a long wait in line. Cuban lines (*colas*) are always fluid but tend to re-form when the bus appears, so you should follow the Cubans' example and identify the last person in line ahead of you by asking for *¿el último?* ("last?"). It's like a game of tag. You're now *el último* until the next person arrives. Thus you don't have to stand in line, but can wander off to find some shade and then simply follow the person ahead of you onto the bus. Many Cubans board through the rear door (although technically this is illegal), in which case, you can pass your fare to the front via other passengers.

Buses sometimes stop only when requested to do so. Bus stops—*paradas*—are usually well marked. To stop the bus, shout *¡pare!* (stop!), or bash the box above the door in Cuban fashion. You'll need to elbow your way to the door well in advance (don't stand near the door, however, as you may literally be popped out onto your face; exiting has been compared to being birthed). Don't dally, as the bus driver is likely to hit the gas when you're only halfway out.

BY TRAIN

The **Ünion de Ferrocarriles de Cuba** operates rail service. One main line spans the country connecting all the major cities, with secondary cities linked by branch lines. Commuter trains called *ferro-ómnibus* provide suburban rail service in and between many provincial towns.

Published schedules change frequently: Check departure and arrival times and plan accordingly, as many trains arrive (and depart) in the wee hours of the morning. The carriages haven't been cleaned in years (windows are usually so dirty you can barely see out of them), and most are derelict in all manner of ways. Few trains run on time, departures are frequently cancelled, and safety is an issue. Three people died when two trains collided near Sibanicu, in Camaguey province, in February 2009; and 28 people were killed when a Manzanillo-bound train from Santiago collided with a bus at a level crossing at Yara, in Granma province, in October 2007. (In 2006, 12 new Chinese diesel trains were shipped to Cuba. In October 2007, it ordered 200 new railway cars from Iran. And in September 2007, Cuba signed a deal with the Venezuelan Economic and Social Development Bank to invest $100 million to improve rail tracks, signals, and communications: Not least, stated Cuban transport minister Jorge Luis Sierra, with a goal of increasing "the [average] speed of our trains from 40 to 100 kilometers per hour.")

Bicycles are allowed in the baggage compartment (*coche de equipaje*). You usually pay (in pesos) at the end of the journey.

Service

Train service has been cut back drastically in the past few years.

The fast *especial* (train #03), also known as the Tren Francés (French train), now operates between Havana and Santiago de Cuba every third day and takes 12.5 hours for the 860-kilometer journey. You can choose *primera especial* (first class), with comfy recliner seats; *primera* (the old second class) has smaller, non-reclining seats. Slower and more basic trains 05 and 07 run every third day when the Tren Francés isn't running (hence, there's service two out of three days). They stop at Santa Clara and Camagüey en route but most of the journey takes place at night. Expect bone-chilling air-conditioning, TVs showing movies (loudly), a poorly stocked *cafetería* car, and *ferromoza* (rail hostess) meal service. Regardless, take snacks and drinks. Relieve yourself before boarding as toilets are grim (and some have no doors); bring toilet paper!

Additional trains operate between Havana and Sancti Spíritus, Camagüey, and Morón.

Slower *regular* trains (colloquially called the *lechero,* or "milkman," because it makes frequent stops) stop at provincial capitals. Some are overcrowded *clase segunda* (second class) with uncushioned wooden seats. *Clase primera* (first class) is marginally better, with padded seats, though still crowded and hardly comfortable. Some routes offer *clase primera especial,* which provides more comfort and, often, basic boxed meals. At local stops, peasants board to sell snacks and coffee.

Reservations

The state agency **FerroCuba** (Av. de Bálgica, Havana, tel. 07/861-9389 or 861-8540, ferrotur@ceniai.cu) handles ticket sales and reservations for all national train service. Foreigners pay in CUC, for which you get a guaranteed first-class seat. In Havana, tickets for foreigners are sold at the dysfunctional Terminal La Coubre (tel. 7/862-1000), 100 meters south of the main railway station (tel. 7/862-1920). Elsewhere you can normally walk up to the FerroCuba office at the station, buy your ticket, and take a seat on board within an hour. Buy your ticket as far in advance as possible. You should also buy your ticket for the next leg of your journey upon arrival in each destination. Reservations can sometimes be made through Infotur offices (in Havana, Varadero, and Cayo Coco; tel. 07/866-3333, www.infotur.cu) and other regional tour agencies. You'll need to show your passport.

Reservations for local commuter services can't be made. You'll have to join the *cola* (queue) and buy your ticket on the day of departure (sometimes the day before; each station usually lists the allotted time for ticket purchase).

© CHRISTOPHER P. BAKER

Most train stations now have a TV to kill the boredom.

Tourist Excursion Trains

Steam-train excursions are offered at several locations, as are multiday tour packages for steam enthusiasts offered by tour companies abroad.

BY TAXI
Tourist Taxis

Most *turistaxis* use modern Japanese or European cars and are radio-dispatched. You can also find them at tourist hotels nationwide. Not all taxi drivers will use their meters: *Taxistas* have their own *trampas* or *estafas* (swindles), such as resetting the meter to record a much lower mileage, then charging you the going rate for the journey. Since his dispatcher records the destination, the taxi driver splits the excess with the dispatcher.

Peso Taxis

Havana and most provincial capitals have peso taxis—deprecatingly called *los incapturables* (the uncatchables)—serving the local population and charging in pesos at ludicrously low

TRAIN SCHEDULES AND FARES

FROM HAVANA

Destination	No.	Origin Station	Depart	Arrive
Bayamo	13	Estación Central	8:25 P.M.	10:30 A.M.
Camagüey	33	Estación Central	2 P.M.	8:50 P.M.
Cienfuegos	19	Terminal La Coubre	7:30 A.M.	6:35 P.M.
Cienfuegos	37	Terminal La Coubre	6:45 P.M.	11:45 P.M.
Guantánamo	25	Combinado	4:38 A.M.	6:50 A.M.
Holguín	15	Estación Central	7 P.M.	8:30 A.M.
Matanzas	905	Terminal La Coubre	12:05 P.M.	4:41 P.M.
Matanzas	907	Terminal La Coubre	4:03 P.M.	7:40 P.M.
Morón	35	Estación Central	4:45 P.M.	11:10 P.M.
Pinar del Río	39	Estación Central	5 P.M.	9:10 A.M.
Pinar del Río	21	Estación Central	10:35 P.M.	4:20 A.M.
Sancti Spíritus	17	Estación Central	9:45 P.M.	6 A.M.
Santiago de Cuba	01	(*Especial*) Estación Central	6:05 P.M.	6:35 A.M.
Santiago de Cuba	11	Estación Central	3:15 P.M.	5:15 A.M.
Santiago de Cuba	31	Estación Central	5:25 P.M.	6:10 A.M.

rates. You'll normally find them at *piqueras* (taxi stands) around the main squares, although they are also assigned to airports, hotels, and other key sites. In 2009, the Cuban government began issuing new licenses for the first time in a decade; the number of private taxis has since doubled.

The workhorses of the taxi system for Cubans are the *colectivos* or *coches* (shared cabs that pick up anyone who flags them down, often until they're packed to the gills), sometimes called *botes* (boats) or simply *máquinas* (machines). They run along fixed routes, much like buses, and charge similar fares. Most are old Yankee jalopies. Some *colectivos* hang around outside railway and bus terminals and provide service between towns. They usually take as many passengers as they can cram in.

TO HAVANA

Origin	No.	Destination Station	Depart	Arrive
Bayamo	14	Estación Central	7:40 P.M.	9:45 A.M.
Camagüey	34	Estación Central	6:35 A.M.	1:35 P.M.
Cienfuegos	38	Terminal La Coubre	2 A.M.	6:50 P.M.
Cienfuegos	20	Terminal La Coubre	7 A.M.	5:50 P.M.
Guantánamo	26	Combinado	6:50 P.M.	9:07 P.M.
Holguín	16	Estación Central	6:15 P.M.	8:50 A.M.
Matanzas	902	Terminal La Coubre	8:30 A.M.	11:31 A.M.
Matanzas	904	Terminal La Coubre	12:30 P.M.	4:05 P.M.
Morón	36	Estación Central	5:40 A.M.	12 P.M.
Pinar del Río	40	Estación Central	5:10 A.M.	9:20 P.M.
Pinar del Río	22	Estación Central	8:45 A.M.	2:30 P.M.
Sancti Spíritus	18	Estación Central	9 P.M.	5:15 A.M.
Santiago	02	(*Especial*) Estación Central	5:05 P.M.	6 A.M.
Santiago	12	Estación Central	8:25 P.M.	10:45 P.M.

FARES (REGULAR) FROM/TO HAVANA
Cacocum (Holguín) CUC26.50; Camagüey CUC19; Ciego de Ávila CUC15.50; Cienfuegos CUC11; Colón CUC6; Florida CUC17.50; Guantánamo CUC32; Holguín CUC26.50; Jatibónico CUC14; Jovellanos CUC5; Las Tunas CUC23; Matanzas CUC3; Morón CUC24; Pinar del Río CUC6.50; Placetas CUC11.50; Sancti Spíritus CUC13.50; Santa Clara CUC10; Santiago de Cuba CUC30 *regular*/CUC62.50 *especial*

Peso-only taxis are not permitted to carry foreigners, but many drivers will run the risk of huge fines.

"Gypsy" Cabs

Illegal "gypsy" cabs driven by freelance chauffeurs are usually beat-up Ladas or American jalopies; they're inherently unsafe and best avoided. Freelance driver-guides hang outside the largest tourist hotels and outside discos late at night. Your fare is negotiable. Educate yourself about *turistaxi* fares to your destination beforehand, as many drivers attempt to gouge you and you may end up paying more than you would in a tourist taxi. Agree on the fare *before* getting in. Make sure you know whether it is one-way or round-trip.

CUBA'S VINTAGE AMERICAN CARS

Automotive sentimentality is reason enough to visit Cuba, the greatest living car museum in the world. American cars flooded into Cuba for 50 years, culminating in the Batista era, when Cuba imported more Cadillacs, Buicks, and DeSotos than any other nation in the world. Then came the Cuban Revolution and the U.S. trade embargo. In terms of American automobiles, time stopped when Castro took power.

Today, Cuba possesses about 450,000 cars, of which perhaps one-sixth are prerevolutionary American autos dating back to the 1920s and '30s. High-finned, big-boned dowagers from Detroit's heyday are everywhere. In certain areas, one rarely sees a vehicle that is *not* a venerable, usually decrepit, classic of yesteryear. Model-T Fords. Chrysler Windsors. Chevy Bel Airs and Impalas. Oldsmobile Golden Rockets. Cadillac Eldorados. Kaisers, Hudsons, and Edsels. They're all there, gleaming in the lyrical Cuban sunlight, inviting foreigners to admire the dashboard or run their fingers along a tail fin.

The mechanical dinosaurs are called *cacharros*. Normally, the word means a broken-down jalopy, but in the case of old Yankee classics, the word is "whispered softly, tenderly, like the name of a lost first love," says Cristina García.

Lacking proper tools and replacement parts, Cubans adeptly cajole one more kilometer out of their battered hulks. Their intestinally reconstituted engines are monuments to ingenuity – decades of improvised repairs have melded parts from Detroit and Moscow (Russian Gaz jeeps are favorite targets for cannibalization, since their engines were cloned from a Detroit engine). One occasionally spots a shining example of museum quality. The majority, though, have long ago been touched up with house paint and decorated with flashy mirrors and metallic stars, as if to celebrate a religious holiday.

Coco-taxis

Toys "R" Us doesn't yet have an outlet in Cuba, but you'd never know it. These bright yellow fiberglass motorized tricycles look like scooped-out Easter eggs on wheels. You'll find them outside major hotels and cruising the tourist zones in major cities. They charge about the same as tourist taxis. However, they have no safety features, and several accidents involving tourists have been reported.

Ciclo-taxis

Ciclo-taxis—the Cuban equivalent of rickshaws—patrol the main streets of most Cuban cities. These tricycles have been cobbled together with welding torches, with car-like seats and shade canopies. They offer a cheap (albeit bumpy) way of sightseeing and getting around if you're in no hurry. Some *ciclo-taxis* are only licensed to take Cubans (who pay pesos). Always negotiate a fare before setting off.

Coches

These horse-drawn cabs are a staple of local transport. In Havana, Varadero, and other beach resorts, elegant antique carriages with leather seats are touted for sightseeing. Elsewhere they're a utility vehicle for the hoi polloi and are often decrepit, with basic bench seats. They operate along fixed routes and usually charge one to three pesos, depending on distance.

BY CAR

Cuba is a great place to drive if you can handle the often perilous conditions. There are no restrictions on where you can go. Cuba has 31,000 kilometers of roads (15,500 kilometers are paved), though even major highways are deteriorated to the point of being dangerous (a major upgrade of roads nationwide was launched in 2008).

The main highway, the Carretera Central (Central Highway), runs along the island's spine for 1,200 kilometers from one end of the country to the other. This two-laner leads through

Some are adorned with multicolored flags to invoke the protection of Changó or another *santería* deity.

Owners of prerevolutionary cars can sell them freely to anyone with money to buy, but the chance of owning a more modern car are slim. Virtually all cars imported since 1959 – Polish Fiats, Soviet UAZs, Jeep-like Romanian AROs, and more recently Mercedes, Nissans, and Citroëns – are owned by the state. New cars are leased out to high-level workers, and others who work for foreign companies, but the cars must be returned if they lose their jobs. Benighted workers such as sports stars and top artists have been gifted or allowed to buy cars, but permission to buy such a car is usually granted in writing from a vice president or even from Fidel Castro himself. The cars can only be resold back to the government, which pays a pittance – in pesos. The government can seize any car sold illegally.

In *Driving Through Cuba*, author Carlo Gébler drives around the island in quest of a '57 Cadillac Eldorado Brougham; a super-deluxe pillarless sedan with a brushed aluminum roof, two front-end protuberances known as "Dagmar" bumpers (which Cadillac unashamedly advertised as "bosoms"), and "a rear end that would've received an X-rating had it been a movie." Alas, the most sumptuous American car ever made proved elusive – not surprisingly, for only 704 Broughams were produced. But you can bet there's at least one to be found on the island. After all, in the 1950s, Havana bought more Cadillacs than any other city in the world. Reason enough to visit!

My own *Cuba Classics: A Celebration of Vintage American Automobiles* (Interlink Books, 2004, www.cuba-automobiles.com) is an illustrated coffee table book that offers a paean to the cars and the owners who keep them running with ingenuity, resourcefulness, and indefatigable good humor.

---

sleepy rural towns. For maximum speed, take the A-1, or Autopista Nacional (National Expressway, sometimes called the *Ocho Vías*—eight-ways), the country's only freeway—eight (unmarked) lanes wide and fast. Construction came to a halt with the Special Period; about 650 kilometers have been completed, from Pinar del Río to a point just east of Santa Clara, and from Santiago de Cuba about 30 kilometers northwestward. *It is extremely dangerous!*

Traffic Regulations

To drive in Cuba, you must be 21 years or older and hold either a valid national driver's license or an International Drivers' License (IDL), obtainable through Automobile Association offices worldwide (www.aaa.com, United States; www.caa.ca, Canada; www.theaa.com, U.K.; www.aaa.asn.au, Australia; or www.aa.co.nz, New Zealand).

Traffic drives on the right, as in the United States. The speed limit is 100 kph (kilometers per hour) on freeways, 90 kph on highways, 60 kph on rural roads, 50 kph on urban roads, and 40 kph in children's zones. Speed limits are vigorously enforced. Seatbelt use is not mandatory, nor are motorcyclists required to wear helmets. Note that it's illegal to 1) enter an intersection unless you can exit, 2) make a right turn on a red light unless indicated by a white arrow or traffic signal (*derecha con luz roja*), or 3) overtake on the right.

Over-zealous traffic police (*tránsitos* or *tráficos*) patrol the highways. Many major highways have *puntos de control*—police control points. Oncoming cars will flash their lights to indicate the presence of police ahead. If you receive a traffic fine, the policeman will note this on your car rental contract, to be deducted from your deposit—there's a space for fines provided on the rental-car papers. The *tráfico* cannot request a fine on the spot, although Cuban police occasionally attempt to extract a subtle bribe. If so, ask for the policeman's name and where you can fight the ticket (this usually results in you being waved on your way).

You must stop at *all* railway crossings before crossing.

Driving Safety

Keep your speed down. Road conditions often deteriorate without warning, and obstacles are numerous: everything from wayward livestock to mammoth potholes. Driving at night is perilous, not least because few roads are lit. Headlights by day are illegal except for emergency vehicles, but you should use yours and be seen). Sticks jutting up in the road usually indicate a dangerous hole.

Accidents and Breakdowns

If your car breaks down, Cubans will offer advice and fix-it skills. If the problem is minor, fine. However, rental car agencies have a clause to protect against damage to the car from unwarranted repairs. For major problems, call the rental agency; it will arrange a tow or send a mechanic.

In the event of an accident, *never* move the vehicles until the police arrive. Get the names, license plate numbers, and *cédulas* (legal identification numbers) of any witnesses. Make a sketch of the accident. Then call the **transit police** (tel. 07/882-0116 in Havana; tel. 116 outside Havana) and rental agency. In case of injury, call for an **ambulance** (tel. 114 nationwide). Do *not* offer statements to anyone other than the police. Do not leave the accident scene; the other party may tamper with your car and the evidence. Don't let honking traffic pressure you into moving the cars. If you suspect the other driver has been drinking, ask the policeman to administer a Breathalyzer test—an *alcolemia*.

Warning: Accidents that result in death or injury are treated like crimes, and the onus is on the driver to prove innocence. Prison sentences can range from one to 10 years. Regardless of the nature of the crime or accident, it can take five months to a year for the case to go to trial. If you are involved in an accident in which someone is injured or killed, you will not be allowed to leave Cuba until the trial has taken place. Contact your embassy for legal assistance.

Gasoline

Gasoline (*petróleo*) and diesel (*gasolina*) are sold at Cupet and Oro Negro stations (*servicentros*) nationwide. Most are open 24 hours. Gas stations are supposed to sell only *especial* (usually about CUC0.83 per liter—about CUC3.15 a gallon) to tourists in rental cars, and you may be refused cheaper *regular,* even if that's all that's available! (Local gas stations, *bombas,* serve *regular* to Cubans only.)

Electricity blackouts often shut the pumps down. If you run out of gas, there's sure to be someone willing to sell from private stock, but it may be watered down.

Insurance

If you have your own vehicle, the state-run organization **ESEN** (Calle 5ta #306, e/ C y D, Vedado, Havana, tel. 07/832-2508) insures automobiles and has special packages for foreigners.

Maps and Directions

Most highways are well signed. However, it's extraordinary how little Cubans know of regions outside their own locale. You may as well ask them directions to the far side of the moon. Rather than asking, "Does this road go to so-and-so?" (which will surely earn you the reply, "*¡Sí, señor!*"), ask "*¿Dónde va esta ruta?*" ("Where does this route go?").

You can buy the *Guía de Carreteras* road atlas at tour desks and souvenir outlets.

Rental

It's not wise to rent a car at the airport upon arrival; relax for a day or two first. Additional drivers are charged CUC15 apiece.

Demand sometimes exceeds supply, particularly the four-wheel-drive vehicles (and a 4WD is recommended only for exploring mountain areas and the extreme south of Isla de la Juventud, especially in rainy season). During Christmas and New Year's season, you'll need reservations, which can only be done within 15 days of your arrival; it's guarantee that your reservation will be honored (ask for a copy of the reservation to be faxed to you and take this with you).

Expect to pay CUC50–185 per day with unlimited mileage, depending on the vehicle; a two-day minimum applies for unlimited mileage rentals. Added charges apply for one-way rentals and for drivers under 25 years of age. Discounts apply for rentals over seven days. The companies accept cash or credit cards (except those issued by U.S. banks). You must pay a deposit of CUC200–500; the agency will run off a credit card authorization that you will receive back once you return the car, assuming it has no damage. You must pay in cash (CUC0.90 a liter) for the first tank of gas before you drive away, although your contract states that you must return the tank empty (an outrageous state-run rip-off). Check the fuel level *before* setting off; if it doesn't look full to the brim, point this out to the rental agent and demand a refund, or that it be topped off (but good luck!). Clarify any late return penalties, and that the time recorded on your contract is that for your *departure with the car,* not the time you entered into negotiations.

Cuba's rental agency cars go unserviced and are often unroadworthy, although in 2009 Transtur (which parents Cubatur, Havanautos, and Rex) purchased 1,500 new vehicles. In-spect your car thoroughly for roadworthiness, and for damage and marks before setting off; otherwise, you may be charged for the slightest dent when you return. Don't forget the inside, plus radio antenna, spare tire, jack, and wrench. Don't assume the car rental agency has taken care of tire pressure or fluids. Note the *Aviso Próximo Mantenimiento* column on the rental contract. This indicates the kilometer reading by which you—the renter!—are required to take the car to an agency office for scheduled servicing; you're granted a 100 kilometers leeway. If you fail to honor the clause, you'll be charged CUC50. This scam is a disgrace, as you may have to drive miles out of your way to an agency and then have to wait hours, or even overnight, for the car to be serviced. I've successfully refused to pay, but clarify this before signing the contract.

Most agencies offer a chauffeur service (CUC40–90 a day).

Rental Companies: Only state-owned car rental agencies operate.

Transtur (Calle L #456, e/ 25 y 27, Vedado, tel. 7/835-0000, fax 07/273-2277, reservas@transtur.cu, www.transtur.cu) operates **Cubacar** (Calle 21, e/ N y O, Vedado, Havana, tel. 07/836-4038); **Havanautos** (tel. 7/204-6547,

MAKING SENSE OF ADDRESSES

In most Cuban cities, addresses are given as locations. Thus, the Havanatur office is at Calle 6, e/ 1ra y 3ra, Miramar, Havana, meaning it is on Calle 6 between (e/ for *entre* – between) First and Third avenues (Avenidas 1ra y 3ra).

Street numbers are occasionally used. Thus, the Hotel Inglaterra is at Prado #416, esq. San Rafael, Habana Vieja; at the corner (esq. for *esquina* – corner) of Prado and Calle San Rafael, in Old Havana (Habana Vieja).

Piso refers to the floor level (thus, an office on *Piso 3ro* is on the third floor). *Altos* refers to "upstairs," and *bajos* refers to "downstairs."

Most cities are laid out on a grid pattern centered at a main square or plaza (usually called Plaza Central, Parque Central, Plaza Mayor, or named for a local revolutionary hero), with parallel streets (*calles*) running perpendicular to avenues (*avenidas*). Some towns, however, have even-numbered *calles* (usually north – south) running perpendicular to odd-numbered *calles* (usually east – west).

Many streets have at least two names: one predating the Revolution (and usually the most commonly used colloquially) and the other a postrevolutionary name. For example, in Havana, the Prado is the old (and preferred) term for the Paseo de Martí. On maps, the modern name takes precedence, with the old name often shown in parentheses.

THE BICYCLE REVOLUTION

In 1991, when the first shipment of Flying Pigeon bicycles arrived from China, there were only an estimated 30,000 bicycles in Havana, a city of two million people. The visitor arriving in Havana today could be forgiven for imagining he or she had arrived in Ho Chi Minh City. Bicycles are everywhere, outnumbering cars, trucks, and buses 20 to 1. The story is the same across Cuba.

Cynics have dubbed Cuba's wholesale switch to bicycles since the collapse of the Soviet bloc as a socialist failing, a symbol of the nation's backwardness. Others acclaim it an astounding achievement, a two-wheel triumph over an overnight loss of gasoline and adversity. *Granma*, the Cuban newspaper, christened it the "bicycle revolution."

GOODBYE TO GAS

American cars had flooded the island for half a century. Then came the U.S. trade embargo. The 1960s saw the arrival of the first sober-looking Lada and Moskovitch sedans, imported in the ensuing decades by the tens of thousands from the Soviet Union, along with Hungarian and Czech buses. Professor Maurice Halperin, who taught at the University of Havana, does not "recall seeing a single adult Cuban on a bicycle in Havana during the entire period of my residence in the city, from 1962 to 1968."

The collapse of the Soviet Union severed the nation's gasoline pipeline. Transportation ground to a halt, along with the rest of the Cuban economy. In November 1990 the Cuban government launched sweeping energy-saving measures that called for a "widespread substitution of oxen for farm machinery and hundreds of thousands of bicycles for gasoline-consuming vehicles," launched as a "militant and defensive campaign" embodied on May 1, 1991, when the armed forces appeared on bicycles in the May Day parade. The government contracted with China to purchase 1.2 million bicycles, and by the end of 1991, 500,000 single-gear Chinese bicycles were in use on the streets of Havana.

BICYCLE CAPITAL OF THE AMERICAS

Overnight, Cuba transformed itself into the bicycle capital of the Americas. "The comprehensiveness and speed of implementation of this program," said a 1994 World Bank report, "is unprecedented in the history of transportation." The report noted that about two million bicycles were in use islandwide. Most were made in Cuba, which established five bicycle factories to supplement the Chinese imports (each factory produces a different model). Cuba imports parts such as small bolts, chains, spindles, and brakes, but makes the frames, forks, and handlebars.

Most *bicis* are cumbersome, hard-to-pump beasts (many with only one gear) weighing as much as an elephant. The bikes are made of poor quality parts and, like more modern Chinese bicycles sold at dollar stores throughout Havana, are basically junk... "after two days, the screws are already falling off," says Linda Nauman, director of **Bicycles Crossing Borders** (tel. 416/364-5329, http://bikestocuba .org), a Canadian cooperative that sends new and used bikes to Cuba.

The bicycles are disbursed through MINCIN (Ministerio de Comercial Interior) to schools, factories, and workers' associations; workers pay 125 pesos – equivalent to about half the average monthly salary – while students pay 65 pesos.

www.havanautos.com), and **Rex** (tel. 7/273-9166, www/rex.cu). There are scores of offices nationwide. There's really no difference between the companies, although rates vary. For example, Havanautos offers 20 types of vehicles, from the tiny Hyundai Atos (CUC411 weekly) to an eight-passenger Hyundai TQ minivan (CUC1,131 weekly), BMW 5-series (CUC1,104 weekly) and Audi A4 convertible (CUC1,729 weekly). Rex Limousine Service has eight models, from the Seat Cordoba (CUC455 weekly) to the Hyundai TQ minivan (CUC980 weekly), BMW 5-series (CUC1,104 weekly) and Audi A4 convertible (CUC1,575 weekly). Rates include 150 kilometers daily; unlimited on rentals of three days or longer.

Gaviota's **Vía Rent-a-Car** (Calle 98 e/ 9ta y 11, Cubanacá, Havana, tel. 07/206-9935, fax 07/207-9502, www.gaviota-grupo.com) rents Hyundais, Peugeots, plus three kinds of Suzuki jeeps.

Gran Car (Calle Marino esq. Santa María, Nuevo Vedado, tel. 07/855-5567, grancardp@transnet.cu) rents 1950s yankee autos with drivers, in Havana and Santiago de Cuba.

Fly-Drive Packages: "Fly & Drive" packages are offered by **WowCuba** (430 Queen St., Charlottestown, Prince Edward Island, Canada CIA 4E8, tel. 902/368-2453 or 800/969-2822, www.wowcuba.com). You simply pick up your vehicle (choose from a Hyundai Atos to an Audi A4 or a minivan) at any of 20 locations throughout Cuba and hit the road armed with vouchers good at any of 60-plus hotels islandwide (from CUC641 single or double for six nights).

Motorhomes: A joint Italian-Cuban venture, Cubamar Campertour, which rented Mercedes and Ford campervans, proved unsuccessful and was disbanded in 2008.

Insurance: It's wise to purchase insurance offered by the rental agency. You have two choices: CDW (Collision Damage Waiver, CUC15–20 daily; with a deductible of CUC200–500) covers accidents, but not theft. Super CDW (CUC20–40) offers fully comprehensive coverage, except for the radio and spare tire. The insurance has to be paid in cash. If you decline insurance, you'll be required to put down a huge cash deposit. If your car is broken into or otherwise damaged, you must get a police statement (a *denuncia*), otherwise you may be charged for the damage.

You can also name any licensed Cuban driver on your rental policy. *However, if you (or anyone else driving your rented vehicle) are deemed at fault in an accident, rental agencies may nullify coverage and seek damages to cover the cost of repairs.* Rental agencies are government controlled and can prevent your departure from the country unless payment is obtained.

Precautions: Theft, including of car

CUBAN TOUR OPERATORS

Agencia San Cristóbal: Oficios #110, e/ Lamparilla y Amargura, Habana Vieja, tel. 07/860-9585, fax 07/860-9586, reservas@sancrist.get.tur.cu. Tours and excursions within Habana Vieja.

Cubamar Viajes: 3ra Av., e/ 12 y Malecón, Havana, tel. 07/832-1116 or 833-2523, www.cubamarviajes.cu. Primarily nature and maritime related programs, including scuba diving; it also offers motorhome rentals.

Cubanacán Viajes: Calle 23 #156, e/ O y P, Vedado, Havana, tel. 07/833-4090, www.cubanacan.cu. A major tour operator with excursions nationwide.

Cubatur: Calle 23, esq. L, Vedado, Havana, tel. 07/833 3569, www.cubatur.cu.

EcoTur, S.A.: Av. Independencia #116, esq. Santa Catalina, Cerro, Havana, tel. 07/41-0306, fax 07/53-9909, ecoturhabana@miramar.co.cu. Focuses on nature and ecotourism.

Gaviota Tours: Av. 49 #3620, Rpto. Kohly, Havana, tel. 07/204-7683, fax 204-9470, www.gaviota-grupo.com.

Havanatur/Tours & Travel: 3ra Av., e/ 33 y 34, Miramar, Havana, tel. 07/66-7027 or 204-0993, fax 07/66-7026 or 204-1760, www.havanatur.cu.

Paradiso: Promotora de Viajes Culturales: Calle 19 #560, esq. C, Vedado, Havana, tel. 07/832-6928, fax 07/33-3921, paradis@paradiso.artex.com.cu. Cuba's premier specialist in cultural programs.

Universitur: Calle 30 #768, e/ Kohly y 41, Nuevo Vedado, tel. 07/55-5683, fax 07/55-5978, www.universitur.cu. Arranges programs and lodgings for foreign students and academics.

parts, is a huge problem. Always park in *parqueos,* designated parking lots with a *custodio* (guard). Alternately, tip the hotel security staff or hire someone to guard your car.

Hitchhikers: Your car rental contract states

DISTANCES IN CUBA
DISTANCE (KM)

	PR	H	M	SC	C	SS
Pinar del Río (PR)	-	176	267	441	419	527
Soroa	89	86	188	362	329	448
Viñales	28	193	295	469	436	555
Havana (H)	176	-	102	276	243	362
Matanzas (M)	267	102	-	197	193	283
Varadero	309	144	42	196	177	282
Santa Clara (SC)	441	276	197	-	74	88
Cienfuegos (C)	419	243	193	74	-	153
Sancti Spíritus (SS)	527	362	283	86	153	-
Trinidad	497	321	271	89	78	67
Ciego de Ávila (CA)	603	438	359	162	229	78
Camagüey (CG)	711	546	467	270	337	184
Santa Lucía	823	658	579	382	446	296
Las Tunas (LT)	835	670	591	394	461	308
Holguín (HG)	913	748	699	472	539	388
Guardalavaca	967	802	723	526	593	440
Bayamo (B)	984	819	740	543	610	457
Santiago de Cuba (S)	1109	944	865	668	735	582
Guantánamo (G)	1191	1026	825	750	817	664
Baracoa	1331	1168	1087	890	957	804

CA	CG	LT	HG	B	S	G
603	711	835	913	984	1109	1191
524	632	756	834	905	1030	1112
631	739	863	941	1012	1137	1219
438	546	670	748	819	944	1028
359	467	591	669	740	865	947
358	466	590	669	739	864	846
162	270	394	472	543	668	750
229	337	481	539	610	735	817
78	184	308	388	457	582	664
143	251	375	453	524	649	731
-	108	232	310	381	506	588
108	-	124	202	273	388	480
220	112	209	287	358	483	565
232	124	-	78	149	274	356
310	202	78	-	71	196	278
364	256	132	54	125	250	332
380	273	149	71	-	125	207
506	398	274	198	125	-	86
588	480	356	278	207	86	-
728	620	496	418	347	226	140

that picking up hitchhikers is not allowed. Many tourists have been robbed, and I do not endorse picking up hitchhikers.

Motorcycles and Scooters
You cannot rent motorcycles in Cuba (except, perhaps, from private individuals). Scooters can be rented in Havana and at resort hotels.

Several North American entities have attempted to organize motorcycle tours, without success, due to U.S. law. **Moto Mundo Bike Tours** (Hoejagervej 8, 8544 Moerke, Denmark, tel. 45/8637-7654, http://moto-mundo. com) offers a 20-day motorcycle tour of Cuba. You must supply your own bike, which will be shipped from Copenhagen!

BY BICYCLE
You'll need to take your own bike, as bike rental was no longer available in Cuba in 2009. A sturdy lock is essential, as bicycle theft is a pandemic.

HITCHHIKING
Despite the recent import of 5,000 Chinese buses, five decades of *fidelismo* have been so catastrophic on transport that the populace relies on anything that moves. Roadways are lined with thousands of hitchers, many of them so desperate after hours in the sun

that they wave peso bills at any passing vehicle—whether it be a tractor, a truck, or a motorcycle. If it moves, in Cuba, it's fair game. The state has even set up *botellas* (hitchhiking posts) where officials of the Inspección Estatal, wearing mustard-colored uniforms (and therefore termed *coges amarillas,* or yellow-jackets) are in charge. They wave down virtually anything that comes along, and all state vehicles must stop to pick up hitchers.

It can be excruciatingly slow going, and there are never any guarantees for your safety. Hence, we don't recommend or endorse hitchhiking. Cubans are officially barred from picking up foreign hitchhikers at the risk of huge fines. If you receive a ride in a private car, politeness dictates that you offer to pay for your ride: *"¿Cuánto le debo?"* after you're safely delivered.

ORGANIZED EXCURSIONS
State-owned companies such as Havanatur offer excursions throughout Cuba. You can book at tour desks in tourist hotels.

Several foreign companies offer tours and have offices in Cuba. I recommend **WowCuba** (Centro de Negocios Kohly, Calle 34 e/ 49 y 49A, Kohly, Havana, tel. 7/272-1777, www. wowcuba.com), with specialist programs.

Getting Away

Cuba charges CUC25 departure tax on international flights.

Cuban check-in staff often scam foreigners by attempting to charge an excess baggage fee where none should apply. Know your legal allowance (which varies between airlines)! Try to use a counter where the scale's screen is visible and check that it is properly zeroed before your bags are put on.

Customs
Cuba prohibits the export of valuable antiques and art without a license.

Returning to the United States: U.S. citizens who have traveled to Cuba are not allowed to bring back any Cuban purchases, regardless of whether or not travel was licensed. The exception is literature and other informational materials. All other Cuban goods will be confiscated, wherever acquired and regardless of value. These restrictions apply to citizens of *any* country arriving from any other country, including in-transit passengers.

Contact the **U.S. Customs Service** (1300 Pennsylvania Ave. NW, Washington, DC

20229, tel. 703/526-4200, www.cbp.gov/xp/cgov/travel).

Returning to Canada: Canadian citizens are allowed an "exemption" of C$750 for goods purchased abroad, plus 1.14 liters of spirits, 200 cigarettes, and 50 cigars. See www.traveldocs.com/ca/customs.htm.

Returning to the United Kingdom: U.K. citizens may import goods worth up to £340, plus 200 cigarettes, 50 cigars, and one liter of spirits. See www.hmrc.gov.uk/customs/arriving.

Returning to Australia and New Zealand: Australian citizens may import A$900 of goods, plus 250 cigarettes or 50 cigars, and 2.5 liters of spirits. See www.customs.gov.au/site/page.cfm?u=4352. New Zealand citizens can import NZ$700 worth of goods, 200 cigarettes, 50 cigars, and three bottles of spirits. See www.customs.govt.nz/travellers.

Immigration and Customs

DOCUMENTS AND REQUIREMENTS
Cuban Tourist Visas

A passport valid for six months from date of entry is required. Every visitor needs a Cuban visa or tourist card (*tarjeta de turista*) valid for a single trip of 30 days (90 days for Canadians); for most visitors, including U.S. citizens, a tourist card will suffice. No tourist card is required for transit passengers continuing their journey to a third country within 72 hours. Tourist cards are issued outside Cuba by tour agencies or the airline or charter company providing travel to Cuba. In some cases, tourist cards are issued at an airport upon arrival within Cuba. They cost US$15 (£15 in the U.K.; flights from Canada include the fee), but commercial agencies sometimes charge US$25 or more. If you're traveling with an organized group, the organization will obtain your visa.

Don't list your occupation as journalist, police, military personnel, or government employer, as the Cuban government is highly suspicious of anyone with these occupations.

Extensions: You can request a single 30-day (90 days for Canadians) tourist visa extension (*prórroga,* CUC25, payable in stamps purchased from branches of the Banco de Comercio y Crédito) at the local immigration office in major cities, or in Havana at **Ministerio de Inmigración** (Calle Factor y Final, off Tulipán, Nuevo Vedado, tel. 07/206-3218).

If you're staying in a *casa particular,* you may need to provide a receipt for the house. Immigration officials don't look kindly on tourists staying in *casas particulares.* To ease your being issued a *prórroga,* consider telling the official that you'll be traveling around the island staying at state hotels; then you won't need to name a lodging in Havana.

There have been reports of visitors who overstay their visa being held in custody until reports are received on their activities in the country. In such an event, you are billed CUC20 daily for the privilege of being jailed! *Do not overextend your stay.* Foreign embassies also report that travelers have been jailed because their passports were torn or damaged.

U.S. Citizens: The Cubans have no restrictions on U.S. tourists. They stamp your tourist card, not your passport. The U.S. government recommends that its citizens arriving in Cuba register at the U.S. Interests Section, in Havana. *All U.S. citizens traveling with a U.S. Treasury Dept. license are now suspect in the eyes of the Cuban government, and there are recent reports of innocent U.S. travelers being investigated and even jailed. Licensed U.S. travelers should assume that they may be under suspicion and should avoid any activities that heighten such suspicion.*

Cuban Émigrés: Cuban-born individuals who permanently left Cuba after December 31, 1970, must have a valid Cuban passport to enter and leave Cuba (you will also need your U.S. passport to depart and enter the United

INTERNATIONAL AIRLINE OFFICES IN HAVANA

The following have offices in the Hotel Habana Libre Tryp, Calle L, e/ 23 y 25, Vedado:

Air Europa   tel. 07/204-6904, ofic.cuba@air-europa.com
Taca   tel. 07/833-3114, fax 07/833-3728

The following have offices at Calle 23 #64, e/ P y Infanta, Vedado:

Aerocaribbean   tel. 07/879-7525, fax 07/836-5016
Aeropostal   tel. 07/55-4000, fax 07/55-4128
Air France   tel. 07/833-2642, www.airfarnce.com/cu
Air Jamaica   tel. 07/833-8011, fax 07/66-2449, havanaventas@airjamaica.com
Cubana   tel. 07/834-4446, 07/834-4447, 07/834-4448, 07/834-4449
LanChile   tel. 07/831-6186, lanchile@enet.cu
Lloyd Aero Boliviano tel. 07/833-1261
LTU   tel. 07/833-3525
Mexicana   tel. 07/833-3532
TAAG   tel. 07/833-3528

The following have offices at the Miramar Trade Center, 5ta Av. y 76, Miramar:

Aero Caribe   tel. 07/873-3621, fax 07/873-3871
Aeroflot   tel. 07/204-5593
COPA   tel. 07/204-1111
Iberia   tel. 07/204-3444
Virgin Atlantic   tel. 07/204-0747, fax 07/204-4094

The following also have offices in Havana:

Air Europe   La Lonja del Comercio, Plaza de San Francisco, Habana Vieja,
                        tel. 07/866-9237
Martinair   Calle 23, esq. E, Vedado, tel. 07/833-3729, fax 07/833-3732,
                        martinair@enet.cu

States). Cuban passports can be obtained from the **Cuban Interests Section** (2639 16th St. NW, Washington, DC 20009, tel. 202/797-8518, htmlcubaseccion@igc.apc.org), or any Cuban embassy or consulate in other countries. Cuban émigrés holding Cuban passports do not need to apply for a visa to travel to Cuba. Cuba does not recognize dual citizenship for Cuban citizens who are also U.S. citizens; Cuban-born citizens are thereby denied representation through the U.S. Interests Section in the event of arrest.

Non-Tourist Visas

Journalists must enter on a journalists' D-6 visa. Ostensibly these should be obtained in advance from Cuban embassies, and in the United States from the **Cuban Interests Section** (2639 16th St. NW, Washington, DC 20009, tel. 202/797-8518, cubaseccion@igc. apc.org). However, processing can take months while your credentials are vetted. If you enter on a tourist visa and intend to exercise your profession, you must register for a D-6 visa at the **Centro de Prensa Internacional** (International Press Center, Calle 23 #152, e/ N y O, Vedado, Havana, tel. 07/832-0526, cpi@cpi. minrex.gov.cu; Mon.–Fri. 8:30 A.M.–5 P.M.). Ask for an Accreditación de Prensa Extranjera (Foreign Journalist's Accreditation). You'll need to supply passport photos. Here, getting a journalist's visa (CUC70) can be done in a day, although you might not get your passport back for a week.

A commercial visa is required for individuals traveling to Cuba for business. These must also be obtained in advance from Cuban embassies, or the Cuban Interests Section in Washington, D.C.

If you enter using a tourist visa and then wish to change your visa status, contact the **Ministerio de Relaciones Exteriores** (Ministry of Foreign Affairs; MINREX, Calle Calzada #360, e/ G y H, Vedado, tel. 07/835-7421 or 832-3279, www.cubaminrex.cu).

Other Documentation Considerations

Visitors need a return ticket and adequate finances for their proposed stay (since 2009, Cuba has no longer required proof of pre-booked accommodations for three nights). The law requires that you carry your passport or tourist card with you at all times. Make photocopies of all your important documents, and keep them separate from the originals, which you can keep in your hotel safe.

Cuban Embassies and Consulates

Cuba has representation in most major nations, including:

Australia: 128 Chalmers St., Surry Hills, NSW 2010, tel. 02/9698-9797, fax 02/8399-1106, asicuba@bigpond.com.au.

Canada: (Embassy and Consulate) 388 Main St., Ottawa K1S 1E3, tel. 613/563-0141, fax 613/540-0068, cuba@embacubacanada.net; (Consulate) 4542 Decarie Blvd., Montreal H4A 3P2, Quebec, tel. 514/843-8897, fax 514/845-1063, seconcgc@bellnet.ca; (Consulate) 5353 Dundas St. W. #401, Toronto ONT M9B 6H8, tel. 416/234-8181, fax 416/234-2754, cubacon1@on.aibn.com.

France: 16 rue de Presles, Paris, tel. 1/45-67-55-35, fax 1/45-67-08-91, conscu@ambacuba.fr.

Germany: (Embassy) Stavangertrasse 20, D-10439 Berlin, tel. 30/9161-1813, fax 30/916-4553, embacuba-berlin@botschaft-kuba.de; (Consulate) Gotlandstr. 15 in 10439 Berlin-Pankow, tel. 030/4473-7023.

Italy: (Consulate) Via Pirelli #30, 20121 Milano, tel. 02/6739-1344, fax 02/6671-2694, concubmi@tiscalinet.it; (Embassy) Via Licinia 7, 00153 Rome, tel. 06/571-7241, fax 06/574-5445, embajada@ecuitalia.it.

Spain: (Embassy) Paseo de La Habana #194, C.P. 28036, Madrid, tel. 34/359-2500, fax 91/359-6145, secreembajada@ecubamad.com; (Consulate) Calle Conde de Peñalver #38, 28006, Madrid, tel. 91/401-0579, fax 91/402-1948, ccubamadrid@telefonica.net.

United Kingdom: 167 High Holborn, London WC1V 6PA, tel. 020/7240-2488, fax 020/7836-2602, http://cuba.embassyhomepage.com.

United States: The **Cuban Interests Section** (2639 16th St. NW, Washington, DC 20009, tel. 202/797-8518, fax 202/986-7283, cubaseccion@igc.apc.org) is under the aegis of the Swiss embassy.

For a complete list of Cuban embassies and consulates, visit http://embacu.cubaminrex.cu.

CUSTOMS

Visitors to Cuba are permitted 20 kilos of personal effects plus "other articles and equipment depending on their profession," all of which must be re-exported. A CUC25 per kilo charge applies over 20 kilos applies. An additional two kilos of gifts are permitted, if packed separately. Visitors are also allowed 10 kilos of medicines, 200 cigarettes, 50 cigars, 250 grams of pipe tobacco, and up to three liters of wine and alcohol. An additional US$200 of "objects and articles for non-commercial use" can be imported, subject to a tax equal to 100 percent of the declared value, but this applies mostly to Cubans and returning foreign residents. Laptops must be declared; you will need to fill out a customs declaration, and the laptop *must* depart Cuba with you. "Obscene and pornographic" literature is banned—the definition includes politically unacceptable tracts. (If you must leave items with customs authorities, obtain a signed receipt to enable you to reclaim the items upon departure.)

For further information, contact the

Aduana (Customs, Calle 6, esq. 39, Plaza de la Revolución, Havana, tel. 07/883-8282, adm@agr.aduana.cu, www.aduana.co.cu).

EMBASSIES AND CONSULATES

The following nations have embassies/consulates in Havana. Those of other countries can be found at the Ministerio de Relaciones Exteriores' website (www.cubaminrex.cu/Directorio Diplomatico/Articulos/Cuba/A.html).

Australia: c/o Canadian Embassy

Canada: Calle 30 #518, esq. 7ma, Miramar, tel. 07/204-2516, fax 07/204-2044.

United Kingdom: Calle 34 #702, e/ 7ma y 17-A, Miramar, tel. 07/204-1771, fax 204-8104.

United States: The **U.S. Interests Section** (Calzada, e/ L y M, Vedado, Havana, tel. 07/833-3551 to 07/833-3559, emergency/after hours tel. 07/833-3026, http://havana.usinterestsection.gov; Mon.–Fri. 8:30 A.M.–5 P.M.) is the equivalent of an embassy but lacks an ambassador. It operates under the protection of the Swiss government. Readers report that it has been helpful to U.S. citizens in distress, and that staff are not overly concerned about policing potential infractions of travel restrictions.

Money

CURRENCY
Convertible Pesos

All prices in this book are quoted in Cuban Convertible Pesos (*pesos convertibles*), denominated by "CUC" (pronounced "say-ooh-say") and often, within Cuba, by "$." As of November 2004, transactions in U.S. dollars (the former currency for all tourist transactions) ceased. Foreigners must now exchange their foreign currency for convertible pesos (at press time one dollar was worth CUC0.89), issued in the following denominations: 1, 3, 5, 10, 20, 50, and 100 peso notes; and 1, 5, 10, 25, and 50 *centavo* plus CUC1 and CUC5 coins. However, Euros are acceptable tender in Varadero, Cayo Coco, and Havana.

Always carry a wad of small bills; change for larger bills is often hard to come by.

Cuban Currency

The Cuban currency (*moneda nacional*), in which state salaries are paid, is the peso, which is worth about four U.S. cents (the exchange rate at press time was about 25 pesos to the dollar). It is also designated "$" and should not be confused with the CUC or U.S. "$" (to make matters worse, the dollar is sometimes called the peso). The peso is divided into 100 *centavos* (also called pesetas).

There is very little that you will need pesos for. Exceptions are if you want to travel on local buses, hang out at boondock bars and restaurants, or buy snacks from street stalls.

In 2008, the government announced that it is planning to do away with a two-currency system.

Exchanging Currency

Foreign currency can be changed for CUC at tourist hotels, banks, and official *burós de cambios* (exchange bureaus) operated by **Cadeca** (Av. 26, esq. 45, Nuevo Vedado, tel. 07/855-5701), which has outlets throughout Cuba. Anyone exchanging U.S. dollars for CUC is charged 10 percent commission; other foreign currencies are not charged. Hence, U.S. visitors should change their dollars into Canadian dollars or Euros *prior* to arriving in Cuba to avoid this surcharge. You can check the current exchange rates at the **Banco Central de Cuba** website (www.bc.gov.cu).

Jiniteros may offer to change foreign currency illegally on the streets. Many tourists are ripped off and muggings have been reported.

CREDIT CARDS

Most hotels, larger restaurants, travel suppliers, and major shops accept credit cards, as long as they are not issued or processed by U.S. banks--the U.S. Treasury Dept. forbids U.S. financial institutions to process transactions involving Cuba (British travelers should check that their cards can be used, as about 20 percent of British-issued cards are outsourced to U.S. companies). Credit card transactions are charged 11 percent commission in Cuba!

You can use your non-U.S. credit card to obtain a cash advance up to CUC5,000 (CUC100 minimum) at branches of Banco Financiero Internacional (BFI) and at some ATMs. U.S. citizens must travel on a cash-only basis as, legally, they are prohibited from using credit cards in Cuba, period, including those issued by foreign banks.

Problem with your card while in Cuba? Contact **Fincimex** (Calle L, e/ 23 y 25, Vedado, Havana, tel. 07/835-6444; Mon.–Thur. 8:15 A.M.–noon and 1–4:30 P.M. and Fri. 8:15 A.M.–noon and 1–3:30 P.M.).

www.moon.com

DESTINATIONS | ACTIVITIES | BLOGS | MAPS | BOOKS

MOON.COM is all new, and ready to help plan your next trip! Filled with fresh trip ideas and strategies, author interviews, informative blogs, a detailed map library, and descriptions of all the Moon guidebooks, Moon.com is all you need to get out and explore the world—or even places in your own backyard. As always, when you travel with Moon, expect an experience that is uncommon and truly unique.

MAP SYMBOLS

▦▦▦	Expressway	**C**	Highlight	✕	Airfield	⚲	Golf Course
▦▦▦	Primary Road	○	City/Town	✈	Airport	**P**	Parking Area
▦▦▦	Secondary Road	◉	State Capital	▲	Mountain	▤	Archaeological Site
======	Unpaved Road	✪	National Capital	✚	Unique Natural Feature	▮	Church
------	Trail	★	Point of Interest			▮	Gas Station
··········	Ferry	•	Accommodation	⚑	Waterfall	◯	Glacier
▰▰▰	Railroad	▼	Restaurant/Bar	▲	Park	▨	Mangrove
▥▥▥	Pedestrian Walkway	■	Other Location	⬤	Trailhead	▨	Reef
▥▥▥	Stairs	Λ	Campground	✗	Skiing Area	▨	Swamp

CONVERSION TABLES

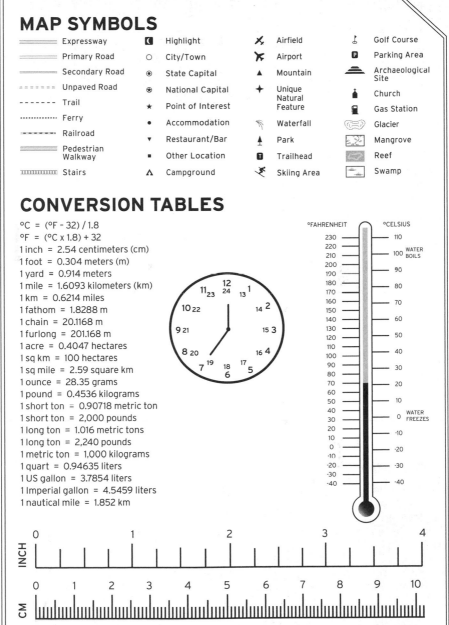

°C = (°F - 32) / 1.8
°F = (°C x 1.8) + 32
1 inch = 2.54 centimeters (cm)
1 foot = 0.304 meters (m)
1 yard = 0.914 meters
1 mile = 1.6093 kilometers (km)
1 km = 0.6214 miles
1 fathom = 1.8288 m
1 chain = 20.1168 m
1 furlong = 201.168 m
1 acre = 0.4047 hectares
1 sq km = 100 hectares
1 sq mile = 2.59 square km
1 ounce = 28.35 grams
1 pound = 0.4536 kilograms
1 short ton = 0.90718 metric ton
1 short ton = 2,000 pounds
1 long ton = 1.016 metric tons
1 long ton = 2,240 pounds
1 metric ton = 1,000 kilograms
1 quart = 0.94635 liters
1 US gallon = 3.7854 liters
1 Imperial gallon = 4.5459 liters
1 nautical mile = 1.852 km

MOON HAVANA
Avalon Travel
A member of the Perseus Books Group
1700 Fourth Street
Berkeley, CA 94710, USA
www.moon.com

Editors: Kathryn Ettinger, Kay Elliott
Series Manager: Kathryn Ettinger
Copy Editor: Amy Scott
Graphics Coordinator: Domini Dragoone
Production Coordinator: Domini Dragoone
Cover Designer: Kathryn Osgood
Map Editor: Kat Smith
Cartographers: Kat Bennett, Suzanne Service
Cartography Director: Mike Morgenfeld
Proofreader: Karen Gaynor Bleske

ISBN: 978-1-59880-540-6

ABOUT THE AUTHOR

Christopher P. Baker

Since 1983, Christopher P. Baker has made his living as a professional travel writer, photographer, lecturer, and tour guide, and is acclaimed for his specialist knowledge of Cuba and Costa Rica, about which he has written 10 books. He has contributed to more than 150 publications worldwide including *Caribbean Travel & Life, Elle, Maxim, National Geographic Traveler, The Robb Report,* and the *Los Angeles Times.* He has been profiled in *USA Today,* and appears frequently on radio and television talk shows and as a guest lecturer aboard cruise ships. Christopher currently escorts cruise-tours to Costa Rica and Panama on behalf of National Geographic Expeditions, and has been privileged to address such organizations as the National Press Club, the World Affairs Council, and the National Geographic Society's *Live... From National Geographic.*

Christopher was born and raised in Yorkshire, England. He received a BA in geography at University College, London, and master's degrees in Latin American studies from Liverpool University and in education from the Institute of Education, London University. He began his writing career in 1978 as Contributing Editor on Latin America for *Land & Liberty,* a London-based political journal. In 1980 he received a Scripps-Howard Foundation Scholarship in Journalism to attend the University of California, Berkeley.

Christopher is the author of more than 20 books, including *Moon Cuba* and *Mi Moto Fidel: Motorcycling Through Castro's Cuba,* winner of two national book awards. In 2008, he was named the prestigious Lowell Thomas Travel Journalist of the Year by the Society of American Travel Writers Foundation. His other awards include the 1995 Benjamin Franklin Best Travel Guide Award (for *Moon Costa Rica*) and the Caribbean Tourism Organization's 2005 Travel Journalist of the Year. You can learn more about Christopher's work on his website, www.christopherbaker.com.